TEACHER'S BOOK B2+
with Digital Pack

W0354044

THiNKiNG SPACE

Brian Hart

CAMBRIDGE
UNIVERSITY PRESS

Contents

CONTENTS

PRONUNCIATION	THINK!	SKILLS
Intonation: showing emotions	**Train to THINK:** Questioning widely accepted theories **Values:** Relationships	**Reading** Article: The power of siblings Website page: Siblings: what's the big deal? **Writing** An email **Listening** Soap opera: *People next door*
Different ways of pronouncing *c* and *g*	**Train to THINK:** The rule of threes	**Reading** Article: Time for a change? Article: The power of dreaming **Writing** A proposal **Listening** Radio programme about staying awake
TOWARDS C1 Advanced practice		
Unstressed words in connected speech	**Train to THINK:** Behaviour based on myths rather than facts **Values:** How do we feel about luck?	**Reading** Article: Blessings in disguise Article: Blog: Serendipity **Writing** A story **Listening** Radio show about luck and lucky charms
Telling jokes: pacing, pausing and punchlines	**Train to THINK:** Divergent thinking	**Reading** Article: You have to laugh, don't you? Article: The world of comedy: Trevor Noah **Writing** A review **Listening** Jokes
TOWARDS C1 Advanced practice		
Connected speech feature: elision	**Train to THINK:** Red herrings	**Reading** Article: Man on a wire Article: Wim Hof: The iceman **Writing** A newspaper article **Listening** Extreme sports
Modal stress and meaning	**Train to THINK:** Making logical conclusions (syllogisms) **Values:** Teamwork	**Reading** Article: To tweet or not to tweet? Article: Fame – a blessing or a curse? **Writing** An essay **Listening** Radio programme about Liverpool F.C.
TOWARDS C1 Advanced practice		
Connected speech feature: assimilation	**Train to THINK:** Understanding irony **Values:** Valuing the beauty around us	**Reading** Article about beauty Blog: What's beautiful for you? **Writing** A formal letter **Listening** Podcast about beauty regimes
Stress in multi-syllable words	**Train to THINK:** Making logical deductions about unknown words **Values:** Learning another language	**Reading** Article: The Rosetta Stone Article: Multilinguals have multiple personalities **Writing** A report from a graph **Listening** The Somerton Man
TOWARDS C1 Advanced practice		
Unstressed syllables and words: the /l/ phoneme	**Train to THINK:** The *ad hominem* fallacy	**Reading** Article: Miscarriages of justice Book review: *The Spirit Level* by Richard Wilkinson and Kate Pickett **Writing** An essay **Listening** Radio programme about disciplining teenagers
Lexical and non-lexical fillers	**Train to THINK:** Doing something for the 'right' reasons	**Reading** Meeting summary: what to drop? Article: Pick up your guitar and (learn to) play **Writing** An essay **Listening** Life after school
TOWARDS C1 Advanced practice		
Intonation: mean what you say	**Train to THINK:** Do as I say, not as I do **Values:** Modern life	**Reading** Article: Internet rage Article: Explaining the modern world: veganism **Writing** A blog post **Listening** Radio phone-in about the stresses of modern life
Shifting word stress	**Train to THINK:** Appropriate sampling	**Reading** Article: Wanted: real-life heroes Article: I just wrote to say … Thank you! **Writing** An article **Listening** Presentation about an inspirational man
TOWARDS C1 Advanced practice		

Pronunciation pages 137–138 **Grammar reference** pages 139–142 **Speaking activities** pages 143–144

Welcome to THINKING SPACE

The course that develops your students' communication and critical thinking skills, values and life competencies so they can successfully meet the challenges ahead. Have you ever asked yourself: "how can I be expected to prepare my students to succeed in a world that's changing so fast?" While it's impossible to predict what specific skills will be in demand by the time our students enter the workforce, there are some things that we as educators can do to ensure our students are as well prepared for their futures as they can be. We know there is an ever-increasing need for individuals to be able to work together effectively with others around the world, and to be able to think creatively and solve problems collaboratively. They also need to be able to analyse and process sources of information more critically, communicate and support their views more effectively, and they need to maintain a positive mindsetin challenging environments.

With **THINKING SPACE** you can be certain you are following the recommendations of new educational law (LOMLOE) and giving your learners the tools they need to build a brighter future for themselves and a better world.

What's exciting and innovative about THINKING SPACE?

We asked teachers what things are important to them.

- High-interest, relevant and thought-provoking topics
- The development of critical thinking, positive values and self-esteem
- A syllabus built upon the Cambridge English Learner Corpus and English Profile
- The inclusion of **Cambridge Exams** practice sections

THINKING SPACE builds and expands on these core strengths:

- The **globally focused content** will appeal to teens' natural curiosities and interests, and feed their growing sense of the world around them.
- The **Life Competencies** strand, supported by entertaining student vlogs and correlated to the Cambridge Life Competencies Framework, will help them develop the vital capabilities they'll need to be successful throughout their lives.
- The authentic, **real-world documentary-style videos** will captivate student interest and provoke meaningful thought and lively classroom discussion.
- Powerful, all-in-one digital tools and support will empower teachers to deliver dynamic and effective lessons.

The story of THINKING SPACE

THINKING SPACE was developed using the latest research into teen cognitive science and best practices and methodologies for the secondary classroom. To learn more, visit **cambridge.es/thinkingspace** or scan this QR code with your smartphone or tablet.

THINKING SPACE and the key competencies

Key competencies are a combination of knowledge, skills and attitudes designed to help young people develop tools which they can use both academically and in a wider social context.

They are an aid to lifelong learning and are an essential part of the compulsory learning curriculum.

The Spanish education system has gradually adapted and adjusted the original descriptors set out by The Council of Europe and the new law, LOMLOE, has defined eight key competencies.

In the case of English language there is an explicit, direct connection with the competence of linguistic communication. However **THINKING SPACE** has been designed to offer numerous opportunities for the development of all eight competences and the specific competencies throughout the course. The treatment of competencies in **THINKING SPACE** is based on the *Cambridge Life Competencies Framework* which clearly defines those found in the new curriculum. Below is a brief description of the new competencies.

LOMLOE Key Competencies

C1 Competence in linguistic communication: The ability to identify, understand, express, create, and interpret concepts, feelings, facts and opinions in both oral and written forms.

C2 Multilingual competence: This competence defines the ability to use different languages appropriately and effectively for communication.

C3 Mathematics, science and technology (STEM) competence: The ability to use different expressions of mathematical thought (numbers, symbols, shapes ...) as well as logic reasoning in order to solve problems in everyday life. It also includes applying knowledge and methodology used to explain nature, as well as using this to transform the environment in responsible and sustainable way.

C4 Digital competence: Digital competence involves the confident, critical and responsible use of, and engagement with, digital technologies for learning, at work, and for participation in society.

C5 Personal, social and learning to learn competence: Personal, social and learning to learn competence is the ability to reflect upon oneself, effectively manage time and information, work with others in a constructive way, remain resilient and manage one's own learning and career.

C6 Citizenship competence: Citizenship competence is the ability to act as responsible citizens and to fully participate in civic and social life, based on understanding of social, economic, legal and political concepts and structures, as well as global developments and sustainability.

C7 Entrepreneurship competence: Entrepreneurship competence refers to the capacity to act upon opportunities and ideas, and to transform them into values for others. It is founded upon creativity, critical thinking and problem solving, taking initiative and perseverance and the ability to work collaboratively.

C8 Competence in cultural awareness and expression: Competence in cultural awareness and expression involves having an understanding of and respect for how ideas and meaning are creatively expressed and communicated in different cultures and through a range of arts and other cultural forms.

Cambridge Life Competencies

A framework to develop skills for life

There have been many initiatives to address the skills and competencies our students need for the 21st century – each relating to different contexts. At Cambridge, we are responding to educators who have asked for a way to understand how all these different approaches to life competencies relate to English language programmes.

The Cambridge Framework sets out to have three dimensions:

BREADTH	DEVELOPMENT	DEPTH
Complete view of transferable skills within one system	How the skills develop across stages of the learning journey	Enough detail to guide teaching and assessment in practical ways

We have grouped the different competencies into six main areas.

- **Creative Thinking**
- **Critical Thinking**
- **Learning to Learn**
- **Communication**
- **Collaboration**
- **Social Responsibilities**

These are supported by three foundation layers that underpin the Framework:

- Emotional Development
- Digital Literacy
- Discipline Knowledge

What Are 'Competencies'?

We call these 'competencies' rather than 'skills', because competencies are more than just skills. The competencies in this Framework are complex and require development in three areas:

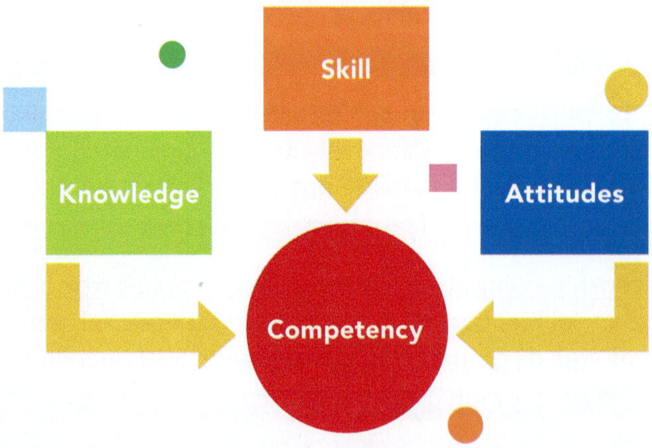

Competencies are defined as a combination of knowledge, skills and attitudes, where:

a) knowledge is composed of the facts and figures, concepts, ideas and theories which are already established and support the understanding of a certain area or subject;

b) skills are defined as the ability and capacity to carry out processes and use the existing knowledge to achieve results;

c) attitudes describe the disposition and mind-sets to act or react to ideas, persons or situations.

Council of the European Union, 2018, p14.

Core Areas: Cambridge Life Competencies and LOMLOE

Creative Thinking

Participating in creative activities	Creating new content from own ideas or other resources	Using newly created content to solve problems and make decisions	C7 Entrepeneurship competence

Critical Thinking

Understanding and analysing links between ideas	Evaluating ideas, arguments and options	Synthesising ideas and information	C7 Entrepeneurship competence

Learning to Learn

Practical skills for participating in learning	Taking control of own learning	Reflecting on and evaluating own learning success	C5 Personal, social and learning to learn

Communication

Using appropriate language and register for context	Managing conversations	Participating with appropriate confidence and clarity	C1 Competence in linguistic communication

Collaboration

Taking personal responsibility for own contribution to a group task	Listening respectfully and responding constructively to others' contributions	Managing the sharing of tasks in a project	Working towards a resolution related to a task	C5 Personal, social and learning to learn C6 Citizenship competence C7 Entrepeneurship competence

Social Responsibilities

Understanding personal responsibilities as part of a group and in society – including citizenship	Taking active roles including leadership	Understanding and describing own and others' cultures	Understanding and discussing global issues – environmental, political, financial and social	C5 Personal, social and learning to learn C6 Citizenship competence C8 Competence in cultural awareness and expression

Foundational layers

Emotional Development	C5 Personal, social and learning to learn
Digital Literacy	C4 Digital competence
Discipline Knowledge	C3 Mathematics, science and technology (STEM)

For a full correlation to the Cambridge Life Competencies Framework, visit **www.cambridge.es/thinkingspace**

cambridge.org/clcf

THiNKiNG SPACE and the Cambridge Life Competencies Framework

Although **THiNKiNG SPACE** focuses on both the *Social Responsibilities* and the *Emotional Development* competencies in the *Cambridge Life Competencies Framework*, all of the six Life Competencies are explored throughout the course.

The table below shows, at a glance, where you can find an activity which concentrates on a particular Core Area. The following table shows which *competencies* are developed in this level.

Competency	Core Area	U1	U2	U3	U4	U5	U6	U7	U8	U9	U10	U11	U12
Social Responsibilities	Understanding personal responsibilities as part of a group / Reflecting on roles	✔	✔										
	Understanding global issues							✔		✔			
	Showing intercultural awareness / Understanding another culture			✔							✔		
Emotional Development	Showing empathy for the feelings of others											✔	✔
	Empathy and relationship skills / Supporting others		✔	✔	✔								
	Identifying and understanding emotions			✔									
Critical Thinking	Evaluating ideas and arguments	✔		✔	✔	✔	✔			✔			✔
	Solving problems and making decisions	✔						✔			✔	✔	✔
	Ranks and scales												✔
Learning to Learn	Practical skills for participating in learning	✔	✔	✔	✔	✔	✔	✔	✔	✔	✔	✔	✔
Communication	Using appropriate language and register for context / Facilitating interactions							✔	✔				
Creative Thinking	Generating ideas				✔			✔					
Collaboration	Listening respectfully and responding constructively to others' contributions	✔	✔	✔	✔	✔	✔	✔	✔	✔	✔	✔	✔
	Taking personal responsibility for own contribution to a group task						✔		✔				
	Agreeing success criteria						✔						
	Comparing communication strategies								✔				
Digital Competency	Responsible use of technology and search engines	✔	✔	✔	✔	✔	✔	✔	✔	✔	✔	✔	✔

Here are a few examples of how activities can help your students develop particular Can Do Statements:

Competency: Creative Thinking

Core Area: Generating ideas

Can Do Statement: Imagines alternatives and possibilities.

*In this Train to **TH!NK** section, students are encouraged to ask questions to come up with their own theories and possibilities.*

You have to laugh, don't you?

A Imagine there was a medicine that improved your physical and mental health at the same time; that had no negative side effects; that was easy to use; that helped you get on better with people; and, best of all, that was totally free. Great, right? Well, there is such a medicine, and it's available to all of us, all of the time – it's called laughter. There's evidence, both scientific and experiential, that laughter is a determining factor in our physical, mental and social wellbeing.

Good for your body

B Whether you just [1]*get the giggles* or you [2]*burst out laughing* when you [3]*find something funny*, laughter does several beneficial things to your body. Firstly, it releases endorphins – chemicals which make us feel good and which can also act as painkillers. Secondly, laughing increases blood flow and relaxes our heart muscles – things that together can help reduce the risk of a heart attack. Thirdly, it relieves physical stress – a person's muscles can be more relaxed for as long as 45 minutes after a good laugh. As if all this wasn't enough, laughing burns calories, too – not many, it's true, but hey, every little helps to keep you slimmer and fitter!

Good for your mind

C Having a good [4]*sense of humour* helps to maintain a positive state of mind, too. When you [5]*get a joke* (it doesn't have to be [6]*hilarious*, just [7]*amusing* or [8]*witty* is good enough) and it makes you laugh or simply smile, you relax a bit. And it's relaxation that helps us deal with difficult emotions like sadness, anxiety or anger. Of course, it doesn't have to be a joke – it can be an amusing comment, a cat video on YouTube, or some slapstick comedy on stage or TV. It doesn't matter – anything that makes you laugh will do. What laughter does is allow us to get a better perspective on our problems, and then we can deal with them better. It's no surprise that many people find that 'laughter therapy' helps with their problems.

Good for your relationships

D You must have watched comedy programmes with a pre-recorded, fake laughter track. Some people find it very annoying, so why do the programme producers add this artificial laughter? Because they know that laughter is contagious – if you hear someone laughing, you're probably going to laugh along. The truth is, laughter does bring people together. A lot of this doesn't come from comedy programmes or jokes, but just from being with people you like and sharing humorous times. And there's evidence that our closest relationships – with parents, siblings and partners – are improved with shared laughter. As the old saying goes: 'The couple that laughs together, stays together.'

It doesn't even need to be real

E Have you ever been in a group of people where someone tells a joke, they get to the [9]*punchline* and everyone laughs, but you don't get it? You'll probably laugh anyway – and that laughter, even if it's fake, will still have a positive effect on you. The endorphins will kick in, your blood flow will increase, any stress that you're feeling will diminish a bit, and the people you're with (and you too) will feel more connected. So, all you have to do is laugh! Find things to laugh about, be with the people who make you laugh, and laugh for no reason at all as often as you can. Laughter definitely is one of the best medicines.

Train to TH!NK

Divergent thinking

Sometimes, we laugh when something weird or unexpected happens: our brains are hard-wired to follow a logical progression of thought, and if something challenges this order, the effect can often lead to some very creative ideas. This is sometimes referred to as divergent thinking, and the effect can be funny.

6 **Look at the question and the three answers.**

What can you do with a one pound coin?

- a buy a bottle of water with it
- b use it to make a decision (heads or tails)
- c put it under the leg of a wobbly chair

1 Which is the most obvious?
2 Which is the funniest?
3 Which is the most creative?

7 SPEAKING **Work in pairs and discuss. How many ideas can you come up with for each one?**

1 What can you do with a pair of ripped jeans?
2 What's your excuse for not handing in your homework?
3 What things can money not buy?

LIFE COMPETENCIES

We all worry sometimes. We worry about what's happening now, or what might happen in the future, or even about things we've done in the past. But it's important not to let worry dominate our lives.

1 ▶ 09 **Watch the vlog. What is Annie's biggest worry?**

2 ▶ 09 **Watch the vlog again. Make notes about what Annie says under the headings.**

My worries
Clothes –
Social media –
The future –

3 SPEAKING **Work in pairs. What advice would you give Annie?**

4 SPEAKING **Read the blog post. Work in pairs or small groups. Discuss which of the quotes in the blog you think:**

- is most useful.
- is least useful.
- is the funniest.
- is the best.

Me and my world

5 **Make a list of five things you tend to worry about. Rank them in order of how important you think they are (1=least important; 5=most important).**

6 SPEAKING **Compare your list with a partner. How could you reduce the amount of time you spend worrying?**

TIPS ON NOT WORRYING TOO MUCH

- **If you are worried about something, share it as soon as possible with someone you trust – a problem shared is a problem halved.**
- **Live as much as you can in the present – the past is over and the future will take care of itself.**
- **Do regular exercise. It's been shown that the more you exercise, the less you tend to worry or lose sleep.**

Don't worry, be happy

Are you a worrier? I am and have been for most of my life, though as I've got older, I've managed to cut down the amount of time I spend worrying about 'what might happen' or 'what someone might think', and so on.

One of the things that's helped me is reading the thoughts of wiser people – here is a small selection of some of my favourite quotes about 'worry'.

A There have been hundreds of terrible events in my life, and most of them never actually happened. *Mark Twain*
B If you ask what is the single most important key to longevity, I would have to say it is avoiding worry, stress and tension. And if you didn't ask me, I'd still have to say it. *George Burns*
C If you want to test your memory, try to recall what you were worrying about one year ago today. *Joseph Cossman*
D Worry never robs tomorrow of its sorrow, it only saps today of its joy. *Leo Buscaglia*
E Worry often gives a small thing a big shadow. *Swedish proverb*
F That the birds of worry and care fly over your head, this you cannot change; but you can prevent them from building nests in your hair. *Chinese proverb*
G If there is no solution to the problem, then don't waste time worrying about it. If there is a solution to the problem, then don't waste time worrying about it. *The Dalai Lama*

Competency: Emotional Development

Core Area: Regulating emotions

Can Do Statement: Manages emotions by using strategies such as re-evaluating.

The following exercises encourage students to show resilience and a sense of perspective.

THINKING SPACE Digital Support

Presenting all your digital tools together in one place!

With **THINKING SPACE**, everything you need is at your fingertips, including Presentation Plus, the powerful front-of-class presentation tool with complete course content, the entire classroom audio and video programs, Teacher's Resource Bank, and Test Generators.

Presentation Plus

- Student's Book and Workbook with interactive exercises
- Embedded links to classroom audio and video
- Additional games and activities
- Accessible online and offline
- Includes link to Kahoot quizzes.

Collaboration Plus

- Students can work together on digital projects online using the Collaboration Plus tools and teachers can set, view, support and grade the work.
- Teachers can share students' project work with the class in the Showcase area.

Teacher's Resource Bank

- Online teacher resource area with support for projects, graded grammar and vocabulary practice worksheets, video worksheets, writing templates, extra speaking activities and more!

Test Generator

- An easy-to-use tool to customize and create end of unit, end of term, and end of year tests, as well as exam practice tests.

Practice Extra

- Mobile-friendly platform and content
- Bite-sized learning activities with audio and video
- Performance tracking.

Test and Train

- Ensure your students are exam-ready with authentic Cambridge Exams practice tests to develop exam strategies and skills
- Test & Train allows you to easily check your students' progress and scores via the teacher view.

For updated information on **THINKING SPACE**'s Digital Tools, visit **cambridge.es/thinkingspace** or scan this QR code.

Warmer

Put students into small groups. Write the prompts below on the board. Explain that the students should speak for one minute about the topic. Ask them to take turns and make sure each student has at least two chances to talk. Once finished, as a whole class, ask students to share something they have learned about a partner.

Do you have any family members living or working abroad? Talk about them.	Is family important to you? Explain why.
Describe the appearance of a member of your family.	Describe the personality of a member of your family.
Who is the oldest member of your family? Talk about him/her.	Are there any rules in your family? What are they? What do you think about them?
Describe the youngest member of your family.	What does your family usually do at the weekend?

▶ 01 Get TH!NKing

Ask the question. Get students to compare their ideas in groups. Play the video and then ask students for feedback.

1 Elicit as much information as possible from the photo. Who are they? Where are they? What do you know about the man? Why is he famous? What about his family? Are there any other members of the family who are famous? What is most striking about the photo? In pairs, ask students to discuss these questions and share their ideas. If necessary, check any information on the internet.

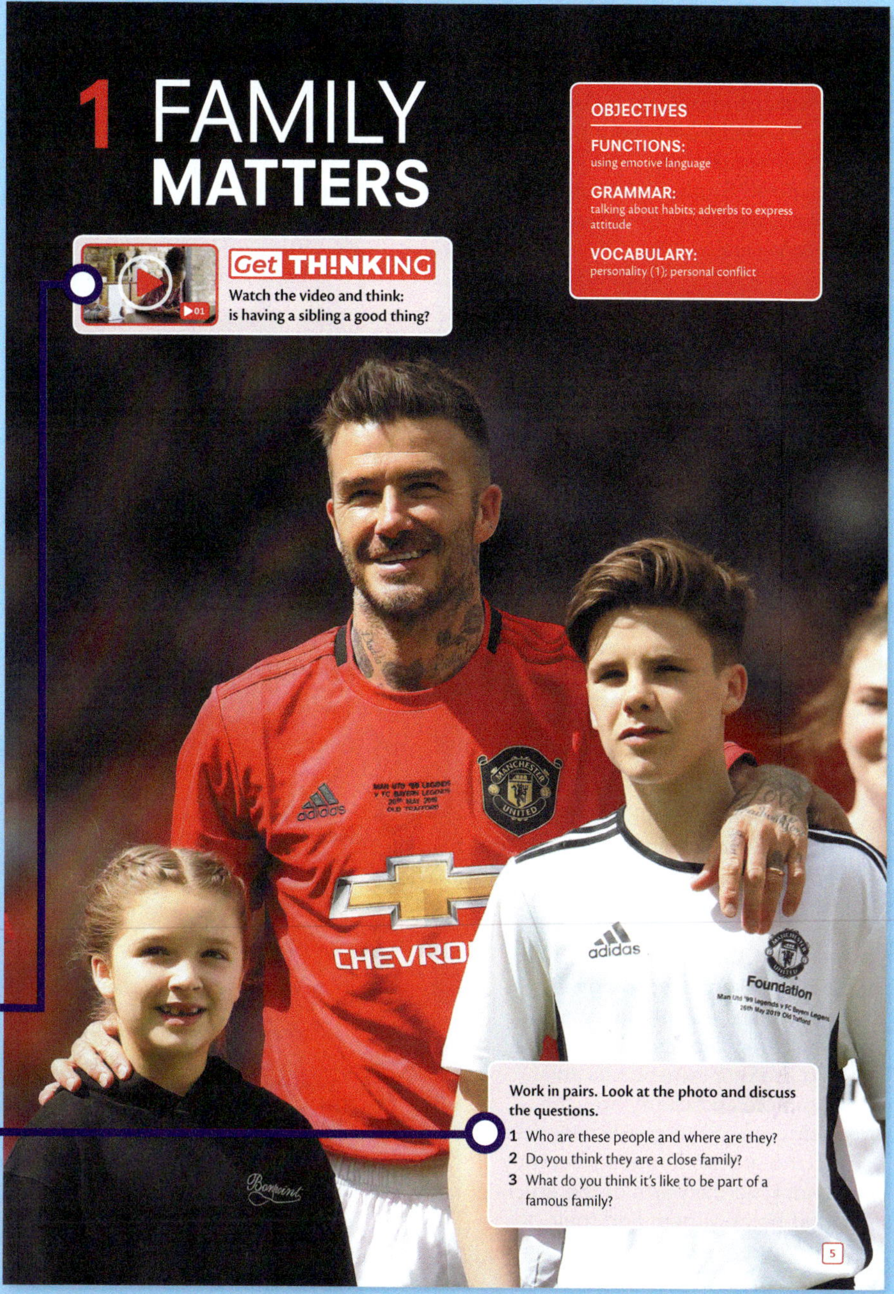

1 FAMILY MATTERS

OBJECTIVES

FUNCTIONS: using emotive language

GRAMMAR: talking about habits; adverbs to express attitude

VOCABULARY: personality (1); personal conflict

Get TH!NKING
Watch the video and think: is having a sibling a good thing?

Work in pairs. Look at the photo and discuss the questions.

1 Who are these people and where are they?
2 Do you think they are a close family?
3 What do you think it's like to be part of a famous family?

5

2 Focus on the question and ask students what *close* means in the context of a family. Ask them to give examples.

3 Ask students to give examples of famous families such as the one shown in the photo. In pairs, ask them to make a list of the pros and cons of being part of a famous family. Share as a whole group.

Objectives

Functions Using emotive language
Grammar Talking about habits; adverbs to express attitude
Vocabulary Personality (1); personal conflict
Values Relationships
Literature *Pride and Prejudice*

Resources for this unit

All available online

Videos
- Get **TH!NK**ing: *Is having a sibling a good thing?*
- Grammar video!: Talking about habits

Tests
- Unit, extension and skills test 1

Worksheets
- Grammar and vocabulary: Basic, Standard and Extension Worksheets
- Project: Family relationships
- Communication: Brothers and sisters
- Literature Worksheets: *Twelfth Night*
- Get **TH!NK**ing and Grammar video! video Worksheets

Warmer

Write on the board: *Who or what has the most important influence on your personality? Is it your parents, your brothers/sisters, your friends, your school?* Students discuss with a partner. Listen to their answers with the whole class.

1 Put a copy of the four pictures up on the board and ask individuals to speculate about the relationship between the people in the photos. Look at the first statement with the whole class as an example.
Students' own answers

2 At the end of the exercise, listen to some of the students' ideas and encourage open-class discussion.

3 **Check/clarify:** *siblings.*
Give students a minute to think about the question, then elicit some answers in open class and write them on the board. Give them just two minutes to scan the article quickly and see how many of their ideas are mentioned.

4 **1.01 Check/clarify:** *categorised, psychology, consensus, IQ, empathy, traits, insecure, clear-cut.*
Do the first question as an example and clarify how the sentence in the gap is connected to the article. Suggest that they underline the parts of the article that helped them find their answers.
A5 B8 C7 D1 E4 F2
(extra sentences: 3, 6)

5 Monitor to help with any difficulties, but do not interrupt as this is a fluency activity.

READING

1 Look at the photos. Who might say each of these things?
1 I love having so many brothers and sisters.
2 The kids all play together so well, and they help each other, too!
3 We tend to argue a lot, but that isn't such a bad thing.
4 It's cool to be an only child.
5 My sister's always teasing me – I'd like a brother as well!
6 Maybe she needs a brother or sister.

2 SPEAKING Work in pairs or small groups. Discuss your answers in Exercise 1.

3 How might having or not having siblings affect our life and personality, do you think? Read the article on page 7 quickly and check your ideas. Discuss in pairs.

4 1.01 Read the article again. Where do these sentences come from? Match with A–F in the article. There are two sentences you won't use. Then listen and check.
1 Having siblings can help you become more skilled socially.
2 No doubt, future research will provide some explanation for this question.
3 This is not to say that an only child will necessarily be unhealthy.
4 In this sense, they have a role model who is more or less their own age, rather than an adult one.
5 After all, people are complex and see themselves in that way.
6 It's one area where arguably the only child has an advantage over people who have siblings.
7 But that's only part of the story.
8 Their findings do not provide us with a very clear-cut answer.

5 SPEAKING Work in pairs. Discuss the following questions.
1 Do you have siblings? If not, who in your family does (e.g. your mother, your father)? Do any of the research findings seem correct about you/them?
2 How important do you think it is whether you're an only child or have siblings? Give reasons.

6

Activity idea Extension

In Exercise 1, ask students to add a sentence to each of the statements to expand on the speaker's viewpoint.

Activity idea Mixed-ability

In Exercise 5, make similar-ability pairings. Allow weaker students time to think about their answers before discussing them. Listen to some of their answers in open class.

Culture note

IQ (Intelligence quotient) is a score that estimates intelligence in humans. It is obtained through a series of standardised tests which give a person's mental age score which is then divided by the person's chronological age. The result is multiplied by 100 to obtain the IQ score. The most common IQ tests are the *Wechlsler Adult Intelligence Scale* and the *Wechlsler Intelligence Scale for Children*. Approximately two-thirds of the population score between IQ 85 and IQ 115 and about 2.5% above 130 and another 2.5% below 70. Because the concept of 'intelligence' is abstract, IQ scores can only be estimates. However, they have been proven to be connected to a variety of factors such as socioeconomic status, nutrition and the foetal environment.

6 Check/clarify: *contradict*. Ask students to work with a partner before checking answers as a class. During feedback, encourage students to vote on whether the statements *contradict* or *don't contradict*.
1 and 3 contradict

7 Give students time to make a note of family and friends and their positions in the family. Ask them to think of adjectives to describe the people and to think about whether they contradict the article.

8 Before students discuss their ideas, elicit one or two examples from the class to get them started. When students have some ideas, regroup students into new groups and encourage them to share information.

THE POWER OF SIBLINGS

Many people dislike any suggestion that human beings can be easily categorised. **[A]** But whether we like it or not, we all fall into one of these two categories: either we are an only child or we have siblings (brothers and sisters). But does it really matter which of these categories each of us is in, and if it does matter, how much and in what way? Many researchers in human psychology have attempted to answer these questions. **[B]** But, overall, the consensus seems to be that it's better to have siblings. Here we take a look at a few advantages. See if you agree!

Siblings can make you smarter

A 2007 study conducted in Norway found that older siblings tend to have a higher IQ than younger ones. This might be due to the fact that first-born children have all their parents' attention, whereas later siblings clearly have that attention divided. **[C]** Interestingly, it also discovered that the higher the test scores of the eldest sibling, the better the scores of the younger brothers and sisters, too. This could be a result of genetics, or because smart older siblings encourage the younger ones to be and act smart, too.

Younger siblings teach the older ones empathy

We used to think that it was younger siblings who learn from the older ones and don't give much back in return. But there's evidence to suggest that younger siblings help their older brother or sister develop empathy and not be as self-centred as an only child. These traits, of course, carry over into adulthood, and it's known that empathy is a determining factor in adult happiness.

Having siblings helps you learn how to manage relationships

[D] Here, it's a case of the more siblings, the better. More brothers and sisters means more time spent in negotiating relationships, arguments, competition, conflict resolution, etc., which leads to learning how to accept the people around you and perhaps be less demanding. A study by The Ohio State University suggests that for each sibling you have, your chance of getting divorced as an adult will fall by as much as two percent.

A good sibling relationship brings mental health benefits

A Harvard University study followed around 300 men and discovered that having a close relationship with a brother or sister when they were young resulted in 93 percent of them feeling positive when they were older. However, the reverse is also true: poor sibling relationships in childhood and adolescence seem to produce adults who are insecure and, in some cases, depressed.

Your siblings can make you physically healthier, too

There's evidence that kids watch their brothers and sisters eating and copy how they eat, more so than they copy their parents. **[E]** Children with siblings also run around a lot, playing games and so on. So general health and weight management in particular can be helped by having siblings. So, if you believe the scientific research out there, it could seem that if you're an only child, you're in danger of missing out! That said, we have to remember that it isn't easy to make definite claims in an area as complex as this. Studies have to be carried out over many years, and there are always many personal, family and cultural aspects that have an effect on whether or not siblings are a good thing. **[F]**

Train to TH!NK

Questioning widely accepted theories

Although we often draw conclusions based on what we've read, heard or observed, it does not mean these conclusions are always 100 percent correct. The article talks about possible advantages/disadvantages of having siblings or not. There will always be plenty of exceptions.

6 Which of these examples contradict claims made in the article?

1 My youngest child Tom is way smarter than his older brother Andy, and he always helps him with homework and things.
2 We've got four children, and Mary, the eldest, is the one who has the fewest friends.
3 Steve didn't have a close relationship with his brothers when he was younger, but he's a great friend to me. He's always upbeat and positive.

7 SPEAKING **Work in pairs. Think of people you know who contradict the claims made in the article.**

8 SPEAKING **Work in pairs. What other theories about families have you heard or read about? Can you think of people you know who contradict these theories?**

7

Homework

Ask students to create a new personality theory. Give them an example of your own to get them started. For example, assign different personality characteristics according to which month people are born in – people born in January tend to be self-centred, etc. As a follow-up in the next lesson, students can try out their theories on different partners. Ask students to make a note of the results to report back to the class.

Activity idea Extension

To introduce the topic of accepting theories, ask: *Do you believe everything you read on the internet? What if it is based on scientific research?* Students discuss the questions in pairs. Listen to some of their answers for feedback.

Critical TH!NKing
Evaluating ideas and arguments
Identifies evidence and its reliability.

Critical TH!NKing
Evaluating ideas and arguments
Gives reasons for an argument's plausibility.

TH!NK more

Worksheets
Project Family relationships
Communication Brothers and sisters
Get **TH!NK**ing *Is having a sibling a good thing?*

Warmer

Ask students to write down three adjectives to describe their own personality. Collect these and read some out to the class (for example, *This person is calm, sociable and intelligent*). The rest of the class guess which student wrote the adjectives.

▶ 02 Grammar video! Talking about habits

1 Students read through sentences 1–4. Ask: *Which words in the sentences refer to habits?* (*will fall by; 's always teasing; used to think; tend to have*). Elicit that in sentence 1, *will* refers to a repeated activity and does not refer to the future.
1 c 2 b 3 a 4 d
RULE: 1 to 2 present continuous 3 will ('ll) 4 tend

2 **Check/clarify:** *grounded*.
If you are short on time, students can do Exercise 2 for homework.
1 to 2 would 3 used 4 to 5 tends 6 will/'ll 7 always 8 not

3 Remind students to check if the sentence requires a positive or negative form. During feedback, check students' pronunciation of *used to* and *tend to*. Draw attention to the elision of the *d* and *t*.
Students' own answers

Workbook p10

Get it Right!
Habits in the present

Student's Book p24

4 Have a reading race for students to find sentences 1–3 in the article.
1 insecure 2 demanding 3 self-centred

GRAMMAR
Talking about habits

Grammar video ▶ 02

1 **Match the example sentences with the descriptions. Then complete the rule.**

1 For each sibling you have, your chance of getting divorced as an adult will fall by as much as two percent.
2 My brother's always teasing me.
3 We used to think that it was younger siblings who learn from the older ones.
4 Older siblings tend to have a higher IQ than younger ones.

a Talks about a habit in the past.
b Expresses irritation about the habit of another person.
c Uses a future construction to talk about what we might expect from someone's behaviour.
d Talks about something that is often (but not always) true.

RULE: There are a number of ways we can talk about habits:
- *used* + [1]... or *would* + infinitive to talk about habits in the past.
- *always* + [2]... tense to refer to behaviour which irritates us.
- [3]... + infinitive to refer to habits in general (not the future).
- [4]... *(not) to* + infinitive to refer to the way a person is likely to behave.

2 **Complete each space in the text with one word.**

My little brother really used [1]... annoy me – and I mean *really annoy* me! Every little thing he did, every little noise he made with his mouth and every little thing he said [2]... drive me crazy. We [3]... to fight all the time and get in big trouble with our parents. It always ended up with both of us being grounded. It was terrible. These days things have improved and we tend [4]... get on a lot better. I'm not sure what changed, but I probably worked out that life would be a lot less stressful if I could try to find him less irritating. It isn't always easy. I mean, he still [5]... to say silly stuff and I find myself getting annoyed, but I [6]... just get up and walk away now. There is one thing that does get me really angry, though: he's [7]... walking into my bedroom without knocking, despite the big 'Keep Out' sign on the door. When he does that, I tell him to 'get lost'. He knows I mean it and tends [8]... to hang about. It's important to make sure that he still knows who's boss!

3 WRITING **Look at the cartoon. What are the dog and the cat thinking? Write three sentences for each. Use the structures for talking about habits from Exercise 1.**

→ workbook page 10

VOCABULARY
Personality (1)

4 **Find the parts in the article on page 7 where these things are said. What word in the article is used instead of the underlined phrase in each sentence?**

1 People who didn't have good sibling relationships when they're younger often feel <u>unsure of themselves</u>.
2 Having siblings means time spent arguing and resolving problems, so you become less <u>likely to put yourself first</u>.
3 The first-born can become not as <u>concerned only with themselves</u> because they've got siblings.

5 **Match the adjectives and the definitions.**

clumsy | competitive | demanding | insecure
outgoing | respectful | self-confident | traditional

1 show admiration and consideration for someone
2 be someone who often has accidents because they don't behave in a careful or controlled way
3 want very much to win or be more successful than other people
4 be calm because you believe in yourself, your ability and knowledge
5 not like change very much
6 be very sociable
7 expect a lot of time and attention from others
8 often feel very unsure of oneself

6 WRITING **Write five sentences about the habits of people you know. Use personality adjectives.**
My sister is really outgoing. She loves talking to people and she knows everyone at school.

7 SPEAKING **Read your sentences to your partner but don't say the personality adjective! Can your partner guess the adjective?**

→ workbook page 12

8

5 During feedback, say the words for students to repeat. Write the words on the board and elicit and mark the stress.
1 res<u>pect</u>ful 2 uncon<u>ven</u>tional 3 self-<u>cen</u>tred 4 re<u>bel</u>lious 5 tra<u>di</u>tional 6 out<u>go</u>ing 7 de<u>mand</u>ing 8 inse<u>cure</u>

6 Tell students that they should use five different personality adjectives and try to include four different ways of talking about habits.
Students' own answers

7 Students could also discuss whether the personality traits of the people they describe fit the theory in the article. Listen to some examples from the class.

Workbook p12

Activity idea Extension

Ask students to find further examples of the structures *will* and *tend to* in the article on page 7.

Activity idea Mixed-ability

In Exercise 5, ask students to cover the eight definitions and read through the words. Students work with a partner to try to define the words.

TH!NK more

Workbook
Grammar p10, Ex.1–5
Vocabulary p12, Ex.1–5
Vocabulary Extra p13, Ex.1–3

Worksheets
Grammar Worksheets 1
Grammar video! Talking about habits
Vocabulary Worksheets 1

8 Monitor and encourage students to speculate and expand on their ideas. Listen to some of their ideas in open class as feedback and write answers on the board to refer to after the audio.

9 🔊 **1.02**
1 They are husband and wife.
2 They are talking about how Emma is always talking on the phone to her brother and sister.
3 Jack is frustrated because they are going to be late to meet their friends for dinner. Emma is annoyed because talking to her family is important to her.

10 🔊 **1.02 Check/clarify:** *exaggerating.*
Encourage students to think about the correct answer to the false statements.
1 F (Emma is talking to her sister Joss.) 2 T 3 T 4 T 5 F (Emma doesn't phone her sister every day. Jack is exaggerating.) 6 T

11 After a few minutes, invite students' reactions in open class prompting them to try to explain their answers.

12 During feedback, pause after each phrase and ask students to repeat it using suitable intonation. Encourage students to sound emotive!
a Jack b Jack c Emma d Jack
e Jack f Jack

13 Ask students to work in pairs to think of further examples of each emotive technique. Listen to some of their ideas as a class.
1 f 2 a, d 3 b 4 d 5 c, e

14 Monitor to help with vocabulary and to make sure students are using emotive language where possible. Then give them time to practise, and ask them to act out their dialogues.

LISTENING

What's on

7.00 – 7.30 pm People Next Door

Things have not been easy between Emma and Jack recently, especially since the accident. Jack's hoping that an evening out with friends will lighten things up. But will it? The country's favourite soap opera moves on.

8 SPEAKING **Look at the photo and read the TV listing. In pairs, discuss the questions and make notes.**
1 How do you think the people in the photo are related?
2 What do you think they're talking about?
3 How are they feeling? Why?

9 🔊 1.02 **Listen to a scene from *People Next Door*. Check your predictions from Exercise 8.**

10 🔊 1.02 **Listen again. Are the statements T (true) or F (false)?**
1 Emma is talking to her mum on the phone.
2 Jack and Emma are fifteen minutes late.
3 Emma's brother is younger than she is.
4 Jack is an only child.
5 Emma phones her sister every day.
6 Jack feels that Emma's family phone her too often.

11 SPEAKING **In pairs, discuss what you think about Jack's attitude and about Emma's attitude in this scene.**

FUNCTIONS
Using emotive language

12 **Look at the sentences from the listening. Who says each one, Emma or Jack?**
a I'm tired of this family. I'm tired of always waiting while you talk to your sister.
b Why do you have to talk to each other all the time?
c I don't understand. I'm sorry we're going to be late but …
d I don't want to go anymore. I really don't.
e Tell me it isn't someone in your family!
f That can wait, can't it?

13 **Match each of the sentences from Exercise 12 with the emotive technique it uses.**
1 question tags
2 repetition of a word (or phrase)
3 rhetorical questions (questions for which you don't expect an answer)
4 emphatic use of the auxiliary verb in statements
5 phrases such as *tell me, I don't understand, you can't be serious* or *you must be joking*

14 WRITING **Work in pairs. Remind yourselves how the scene ended and then write the next eight lines of dialogue. Use emotive language.**

PRONUNCIATION
Intonation: showing emotions Go to page 137.

TH!NK values
Relationships

15 WRITING **Think about your family and your friends. Giving examples to support your choices, write about someone who:**
1 you can tell anything to.
2 you find it difficult to talk to.
3 is really fun to be with.
4 is quite boring to be with.
5 you have the most in common with.
6 you have the least in common with.
7 knows you the best.
8 doesn't know you at all.

16 SPEAKING **Work in pairs. What could you do to improve your relationship with one of the people you wrote about in questions 2, 4, 6 or 8? Take turns to suggest some ideas to your partner. Would you be interested in trying any of these ideas? Why/Why not?**

15 Check/clarify: *most/least in common with.*
Depending on time and the needs of the class, you could ask students either to make notes or to write full sentences.

16 To aid students when giving advice, you might like to quickly elicit some expressions used when making suggestions and write them on the board (for example: *Have you thought about …?; It might be a good idea to …* etc.). Listen to some of their opinions in open class as feedback.

Pronunciation
Intonation: showing emotions
Student's Book p137

Social Responsibilities
Understanding personal responsibilities as part of a group
Identifies positive behaviour in the social groups to which they belong.

Critical TH!NKing
Solving problems and making decisions
Examines possible solutions to a given problem and states how they are effective.

Homework
Ask students to follow up the speaking activity in Exercise 16 by writing six sentences about their family and friends using the prompts 1–8 in Exercise 15 and supporting their choices. As an alternative, they could write five true sentences and one false one. As a follow-up in the next lesson, they could work in pairs and each partner guesses which of the sentences is untrue.

TH!NK more
Workbook
Listening p16, Ex.1–4
Pronunciation p118

Warmer

To revise the topic of siblings, ask: *What are the benefits of having a brother or sister?* Ask students to work with a partner and make a list of at least three benefits and at least three drawbacks of having a brother or sister. In pairs or small groups, students discuss. Encourage students to use some of the personality adjectives from last lesson. Listen to some of their ideas as feedback.

1 Before students read the web page, get them to cover it and just answer the question. Write their ideas on the board.
Students' own answers

2 Set a three-minute time limit to encourage them to skim the web page quickly and not to focus on every word.
Being an only child

3 **1.04 Check/clarify:** *spoiled.* For weaker classes, you could pause the audio after each answer and give students time to answer.
Tell students to underline key information in the web page that helped them to decide whether each sentence is true or false. During feedback, ask students to justify their answers by quoting the text they have underlined. Ask students to correct any false information.
1 F (He thinks it's the opposite.) 2 T 3 T 4 T 5 F (Cathy is off to university so she won't have to put up with her brother anymore.) 6 T 7 T 8 F (He thinks it won't be a bad thing for anyone.)

4 **1.04** Allow students time for pairs to discuss the statements that they agree or disagree with.

READING

1 SPEAKING **Work in pairs. How is life different for someone who is an only child and for someone who has siblings?**

2 **Read the web page quickly. Does the article mostly discuss being an only child or having siblings?**

3 1.04 **Read the web page again and listen. Are the statements T (true) or F (false)?**

1 Greg thinks being an only child is a disadvantage.
2 Robyn is an only child.
3 Robyn believes it's possible for people with siblings to be spoiled.
4 Cathy's parents are not sympathetic to her problem with her brother.
5 Cathy thinks she'll never get away from her brother.
6 Matt thinks the attitude of parents is more important than whether or not you're an only child.
7 Greg thinks the 19th century research is no longer relevant.
8 Greg thinks that the increase in the number of onlies could become a problem.

4 1.04 **Read and listen again. Which statements do you strongly agree or disagree with? Compare with a partner.**

SPEAKING

5 **Work in groups of four. Take turns to talk about a problem you have with a brother or sister. This can be real or imaginary. Give each other advice on how to deal with the problem.**

Think about:
- what exactly it is they do.
- how to describe their behaviour.
- how this makes you feel.
- what you've done to try and improve the situation.
- how they've reacted to this.
- what tactics you might try in the future.

10

SIBLINGS: WHAT'S THE BIG DEAL?

Chatting with my friend Jen the other day, I got quite a surprise – in fact, what she said was really eye-opening for me. She was talking about how her older sister sometimes gets on her nerves and she's always getting into fights with her brothers, but then suddenly she said that even so, she felt sorry for me because I'm an only child. Now I've heard this stuff before, and it always annoys me. I honestly don't understand why people think this way – that somehow not having brothers or sisters is some kind of disadvantage. I've always found it to be quite the opposite! Anyway, I just smiled at Jen and kept quiet. I didn't want to say something I might regret later. But I'm really interested to hear your views about this. Hopefully, I'll hear from some of you who are 'onlies' and also from some who have siblings. **Greg**

Hi, Greg. First of all, we have to acknowledge that all of us can only ever experience either being an only child or having siblings – and since we can't experience both, it's obviously very hard to compare them. Like you, I'm an 'only' and I know lots of other onlies, too. So, I know exactly where you're coming from. I'm really OK with not having brothers or sisters. Lots of people think onlies are spoiled or lonely, but I don't think that's true about me. For sure, some onlies are spoiled, but I'd guess there are people with siblings who are, too. **Robyn**

I've got a sibling and frankly I wish I didn't! A younger brother who makes my life miserable most of the time. He's undoubtedly my parents' favourite, and when I ask them to have a word with him, ask him to behave more considerately, they just tell me to let him be. If I try to talk to him, explain how annoying he can be, it only makes things worse. Still, only a couple of years and I'll be off to university and a long way away, and I won't have to put up with him anymore. **Cathy**

Wow, Cathy. Understandably, you're upset and that's a shame. But I think your post helps us to see that it isn't just a question of whether or not you've got siblings. Let's face it, there are nice siblings and some not-so-nice ones. Some onlies might be lonely not because there aren't any siblings around, but because they aren't much good at making friends. Admittedly, some are spoiled, but there are plenty who aren't – that depends totally on the parents, in my opinion, not on how many kids there are in the family. **Matt**

Spot on, Matt. Not so long ago, I read that some psychologist back in the 19th century (!!) created the idea of the 'only-child syndrome' – that an only child is spoiled, lonely, selfish and what-have-you. But he was looking at kids living on farms, with no other kids around them. That isn't really how things are now, and since these days more and more people are having just one child, inevitably we're going to see more and more onlies – it won't be a bad thing for anyone. **Greg**

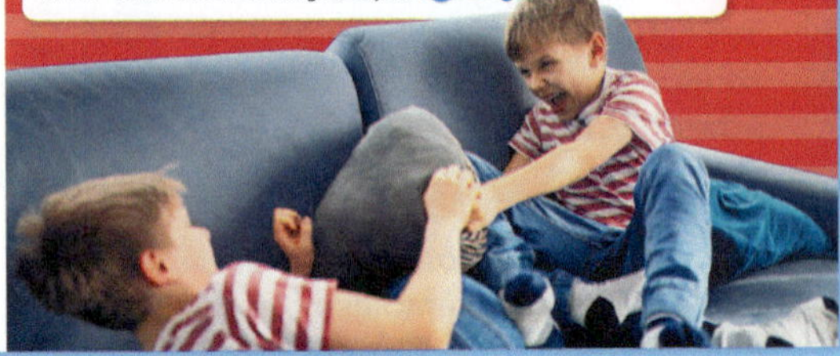

5 Give students time to make notes on their answers before the discussion stage. Monitor and answer any questions about vocabulary, but as this is a fluency practice activity, do not interrupt the conversations unless inaccuracy hinders comprehension.

Activity idea Extension

Divide the class into pairs and ask students to make a list of reasons why the younger siblings on the web page might act as they do. When students have at least three reasons, this could lead into a role play with younger and older siblings discussing the situations. Assigning roles and giving preparation time in this way often leads quieter students to interact more and voice their opinions. Monitor and encourage all students to speak. Develop the conversations into a whole-group discussion.

TH!NK more

Workbook
Reading p14, Ex.1–4

Grammar; Vocabulary

6 Ask students to try to complete the sentences from memory.
1 Hopefully 2 obviously
3 undoubtedly 4 Admittedly

7 RULE: (in any order) honestly, understandably, inevitably, frankly

8 **Check/clarify:** *frank, inevitable.* If you're short on time, you can set this exercise for homework.
Suggested answers
1 Frankly, your haircut looks terrible. / Your haircut looks terrible, frankly!
2 Hopefully, my brother will lend me his jacket. / My brother will hopefully lend me his jacket.
3 Inevitably, I won't pass the test because I didn't study enough.
4 I'm good at languages, but, admittedly, my sister is better than me at Maths.
5 Understandably, you're angry with me for being mean to my sister. / You're understandably angry with me for being mean to my sister.
6 Honestly, I would never hurt my sister. / I would honestly never hurt my sister.
7 Obviously, my brother is jealous of me. / My brother is obviously jealous of me. / My brother is jealous of me, obviously!
8 Undoubtedly, we'll be tired when we arrive. / We'll undoubtedly be tired when we arrive.

Workbook p11

9 Ask students to try to match the phrases from memory before referring back to the web page. During feedback, ask students to explain the meaning of the phrases.
1 g 2 a 3 h 4 b 5 f 6 c
7 d 8 e

10 1 life 2 with 3 say 4 gets
5 up with 6 made 7 be 8 into

11 Give your own example before students do the task. Encourage them to give reasons for their answers and remind the listeners to keep asking questions to get further information.
1 nerves 2 regretted 3 word
4 worse 5 up

Workbook p12

Homework

Ask students to write their answers from their discussions in Exercise 11 and include as many collocations from Exercise 9 as possible.

GRAMMAR
Adverbs to express attitude

6 Complete the sentences with the words in the list. Check your answers in the web page.

admittedly | hopefully
obviously | undoubtedly

1 … , I'll hear from some of you who are 'onlies'.
2 It's … very hard to compare them.
3 He's … my parents' favourite.
4 … , some are spoiled, but there are plenty who aren't.

7 Find four more examples of adverbs to express attitude in the web page and use them to complete the rule.

RULE:
Words like *undoubtedly, hopefully, admittedly, obviously,* [1]… , [2]… , [3]… and [4]… are used to express how we feel about what we're saying.
We usually put them at the start of the clause or immediately after the initial verb.

8 Change the underlined word into an adverb and use it to make one sentence.

1 Your new haircut looks terrible. I'm being frank about this.
2 My brother might lend me his jacket. I live in hope.
3 I will not pass the test because I didn't study enough. This is inevitable.
4 I'm good at languages, but my sister is better than me at Maths. This is something I have to admit.
5 You're angry with me for being mean to my sister. I understand that.
6 I would never hurt my sister. I'm being honest about this.
7 My brother is jealous of me. It's obvious.
8 We'll be tired when we arrive. There's no doubt about this.

→ workbook page 11

VOCABULARY
Personal conflict

9 Match the sentence halves. Use the web page to help you.

1 My little sister really *gets on*
2 Dad said he wants to *have a*
3 Please don't say anything. You'll only *make*
4 I'm really angry, but I don't want to *say something*
5 I really can't *put up*
6 My elder sister *made*
7 Why don't you just *let*
8 He's always *getting into*

a *word* with me. What could it be?!
b *I might regret.*
c *my life miserable* when we were younger.
d *him be* and get on with your own life?
e *fights* with the other kids.
f *with* all that noise anymore!
g *my nerves* when she keeps taking my things.
h *things worse* for me.

10 Choose the correct words to complete the expressions.

1 Mrs Gibson is making my *time / life / days* miserable. She's always picking on me.
2 The teacher had a word *on / to / with* Angela about her attendance and punctuality.
3 Never reply to an angry email immediately in case you *say / reply / tell* something you might regret.
4 I hate the way he drums his fingers on the table. It really *goes / gets / puts* on my nerves.
5 That's the fourth time you've come in without knocking. I won't put *with / up with / up on* it anymore!
6 I was only trying to help, but judging by her reaction, I think I've just *done / made / caused* things worse.
7 If Jason wants to spend all day watching TV, just let him *alone / be / do*. It's his life, not yours.
8 He and his sister are always getting *into / in / with* fights with each other about who sits where at the table.

11 SPEAKING **Complete the questions with the missing words and then discuss them with a partner.**

1 What sort of things really get on your … ?
2 Have you ever said anything you later … ? What was it and what was the consequence?
3 Have you ever had to have a … with someone? Why? What happened next?
4 Can you think of a time when you tried to help someone but only made things … ? What happened?
5 What kind of behaviour do you find difficult to put … with?

→ workbook page 12

Activity idea Extension

Test how well students remember the collocations. Call out either the verb or the noun, and nominate a student to say the whole phrase. For example, you say either *gets on* or *my nerves*, students say the complete phrase: *gets on my nerves*. Alternatively, you could put students in pairs to take turns to test each other in the same way.

TH!NK more

Practice Extra
Unit 1 Practise it!

Workbook
Grammar p11, Ex.6–8
Vocabulary p12, Ex.4–5

Worksheets
Grammar Worksheets 1
Vocabulary Worksheets 1

Warmer

In pairs, give students two minutes to brainstorm a list of films about families or brothers and sisters. Write the titles on the board. For example, *The Sound of Music, What's Eating Gilbert Grape, About a Boy, The Incredibles, The Chronicles of Narnia, Frozen, Little Women, Enola Holmes, Mulan, Onward.* Divide the class into pairs for students to take turns to describe the plot of the films for their partners to guess the title. Listen to some examples in open class and write any repeated themes on the board.

1 Give students a couple of minutes to discuss the question in pairs.

2 **1.05** Encourage students not to focus on every word for now but just to answer the question.

Suggested answers
Jane rarely speaks badly of other people. Elizabeth describes this as her 'goodness' which she (Elizabeth) feels she doesn't possess. When Jane does talk about Bingley's sisters in a slightly less than favourable light, Elizabeth is surprised and delighted to see her sister being assertive. This also shows a closeness between the two sisters, as does Jane's wish that her sister could be as happy as her.

3–4 Encourage students to try to answer the questions before reading again. During feedback, ask students to refer to the parts of the text that support their answers.

Suggested answers
1 being the link between Jane and Mr Bingley, so whenever they were apart, she provided a connection to the other.
2 didn't approve of
3 have a better relationship in time, though she doesn't imagine they'll be as close as they were previously.
4 could have made Jane think badly of Darcy.
5 find someone and be equally as happy as her.
6 extremely lucky since Jane and Bingley got engaged. This contrasts with a few weeks before when there was a lot of gossip and scandal around one of the other sisters, Lydia, running away.

Literature

1 What do you think might be the pleasures and the difficulties of being part of a family with either five sisters or five brothers?

2 1.05 Read and listen to the extract. What do you learn about the relationship between Jane and Elizabeth, and about their individual characters?

Pride and Prejudice

by Jane Austen

Mr and Mrs Bennet, who live in Longbourn, are not very rich. They have five daughters – Jane, Elizabeth, Mary, Lydia and Kitty – and hope to see them all married. Lydia has run away with a soldier but then married him. Elizabeth has a love-hate relationship with the rich and (in her opinion) arrogant Mr Darcy. Mr Darcy's wealthy friend, Mr Bingley, loves Jane but Mr Bingley's sisters do not like her very much. Darcy has just helped Bingley to propose to Jane and she has happily accepted him.

Bingley, from this time, was of course a daily visitor at Longbourn, coming frequently before breakfast, and always remaining till after supper [...].

Elizabeth had now but little time for conversation with her sister; for while he was present, Jane had no attention to bestow on anyone else; but she found herself considerably useful to both of them in those hours of separation that must sometimes occur.

In the absence of Jane, he always attached himself to Elizabeth, for the pleasure of talking of her; and when Bingley was gone, Jane constantly sought the same means of relief.

'He has made me so happy,' said she, one evening, 'by telling me that he was totally ignorant of my being in London last spring! I had not believed it possible.'

'I suspected as much,' replied Elizabeth. 'But how did he account for it?'

'It must have been his sister's doing. They were certainly not very pleased about his acquaintance with me, which I cannot wonder at, since he might have chosen so much more advantageously in many respects. But when they see, as I trust they will, that their brother is happy with me, they will learn to be contented, and we shall be on good terms again; though we can never be what we once were to each other.'

'That is the most unforgiving speech,' said Elizabeth, 'that I ever heard you speak. Good girl! It would upset me, indeed, to see you again being misled by Miss Bingley's pretended good opinion.'

'Would you believe it, Lizzy, that when he went to town last November, he really loved me, and nothing but a persuasion of my being indifferent would have prevented his coming down again!'

'He made a little mistake to be sure; but it is to the credit of his modesty.' [...]

Elizabeth was pleased to find that Bingley had not said anything about the interference of Mr Darcy; for, though Jane had the most generous and forgiving heart in the world, she knew it was a circumstance which would make her think badly of him.

'I am certainly the most fortunate creature that ever existed!' cried Jane. 'Oh! Lizzy, why am I singled out like this from my family, and blessed above them all! If I could only see you as happy! If there were only such another man for you!'

'If you were to give me forty such men, I never could be so happy as you. Till I have your disposition, your goodness, I never can have your happiness. No, no, let me look after myself; and, perhaps, if I have very good luck, I may meet with another Mr Collins in time.'

The situation of affairs in the Longbourn family could not be long a secret. Mrs Bennet was privileged to whisper it to Mrs Phillips, and she took the opportunity, without any permission, to do the same to all her neighbours in Meryton. The Bennets were speedily pronounced to be the luckiest family in the world, though only a few weeks before, when Lydia had first run away, they had been generally believed to be marked out for misfortune.

3 Read the extract again. Complete the sentences with your own ideas.

1 Elizabeth was useful to both her sister and to Mr Bingley by ...
2 Bingley's sister ... his relationship with Jane.
3 Jane hopes that in the future, she and Bingley's sister will ...
4 Elizabeth thinks that Jane's attitude towards Miss Bingley ...
5 Jane really wants Elizabeth to ...
6 Other people start to see the Bennet family as ...

4 SPEAKING Compare your ideas in Exercise 3 with a partner.

12

Activity idea Extension

There have been several film and TV versions of *Pride and Prejudice* that you could watch in class. The most recent was with Keira Knightley as Elizabeth and Matthew Macfadyen as Mr Darcy, released in 2005.

Culture note

Jane Austen was an English novelist born in 1775 in Hampshire, UK. She is known mainly for her six major novels which use irony, realism and humour to critique and comment on the British upper classes and in particular, the need for women at that time to rely on 'a favourable marriage' in order to gain economic security. Her novels form part of the National Curriculum for English in the UK. Austen was the seventh of eight children and began to write as a teenager. Her first book, *Sense and Sensibility*, was published in 1811. *Pride and Prejudice* was her second novel and was written at the age of 21 with the title *First Impressions*, but it was not published until 1813. The first edition sold out quickly and the book was translated into several languages within the first year. Jane Austen's novels were all published anonymously, which was the case for many female authors of the time. Jane Austen died from illness in 1817 at the age of 41.

Writing

5 During feedback, work on pronunciation. Check that they're placing stress on the correct syllable.
1 account for 2 singled out 3 misfortune 4 being misled 5 occur 6 whisper 7 be on good terms 8 was totally ignorant of

6 Encourage students to answer in full sentences. Note any nice expressions or lexical errors to refer to during feedback. At the end, write them on the board to discuss.

5 VOCABULARY **Match the highlighted words or phrases in the extract with the definitions.**

1 explain
2 chose someone (or something) for special attention or privilege
3 bad luck
4 getting information that makes you believe something that's untrue
5 happen
6 not caring about or interested in someone or something
7 get on well; have a good relationship
8 knew absolutely nothing

6 SPEAKING **Work in pairs. Discuss the questions.**

1 Which of the two – Jane or Elizabeth – do you think is older? Why?
2 Imagine you are Elizabeth and someone asks you about Jane's personality. How would you describe her?
3 Now imagine you're Jane. What would you say about Elizabeth?
4 What evidence is there in the extract that Jane and Elizabeth have a very close relationship?

WRITING
An email

1 INPUT **Read the email and answer the questions.**

1 How is the writer related to Sam?
2 How was Sam's relationship with his siblings when he was young? What reason is given for this?
3 How did Sam fall out of favour with his family?
4 What things happened in Sam's life that his parents never knew about?
5 What is the writer now determined to do?

2 ANALYSE **Read the email again. In what order is the following information mentioned?**

- what she plans to do with this information
- what the scandal was
- how she made the discovery about her great-uncle
- the consequence of the scandal
- the little she already knew about her great-uncle
- the evidence she found about his life

3 **Complete with the missing words. Then check in the email. What effect do the missing words and expressions have on the sentences?**

1 She was very old – over a hundred, … … .
2 Anyway, … … … … that he'd done something terrible.
3 My mother had … … known what it was … … .
4 It turns out that, … , he was a conscientious objector.
5 Sadly, … … he never made up with his parents.

4 **Use the words and expressions from Exercise 9 to make these sentences less certain.**

1 He wasn't very well liked by other members of the family.
2 He was a hero in the First World War.
3 He'd spent some years in prison.
4 I never found out if it was true.

Diana
Diana@thinkmail.com

Hi Diana,

I think I told you my great-aunt May died recently. She was very old – over a hundred, I believe. I was helping my mother clear out some of her things when we came across some really interesting papers all about her brother Sam, my great-uncle. I'd heard a few things about him from my grandmother over the years, but on the whole he wasn't talked about much in the family. He was the youngest of five children and generally considered to be the favourite of my great-grandparents. I think the others felt he was quite spoiled.

Anyway, there was a rumour that he'd done something terrible and that's why his name was never mentioned. But my mother had never really known what it was for sure. Well, guess what – we found out everything in a small leather briefcase in my great-aunt's attic. May was the only family member that he'd kept in touch with and he'd written her dozens of letters over the years.

It turns out that, apparently, he was a conscientious objector in World War II and had refused to fight. He was 18 when the war broke out and his parents obviously felt that he'd brought great shame on the family. They sent him away to live with a distant relative in the Scottish Highlands. He eventually became a policeman and made quite a name for himself. In the briefcase, there were loads of newspaper cuttings about things he'd done and even a medal he'd won for bravery.

Sadly, it seems he never made up with his parents and they never got to meet any of the five children he went on to have. I've now made it my mission to try and find some of my missing Scottish relatives.

I'll keep you posted on what I find out! Have you ever made any interesting discoveries about people in your family?

Must run but looking forward to hearing from you soon!

Lots of love, Helen

5 PRODUCE **Write an email.**

You have recently found out about an interesting relative of yours. Write an email to a friend (220–260 words) about the relative. Write about:

- how the person is related to you.
- how they got on with other members of the family.
- what they did that was interesting.

1 Set a two-minute time limit to encourage students to read quickly and focus on the questions.
1 Sam is the writer's great-uncle.
2 His siblings felt he was spoilt because he was their parents' favourite and the youngest.
3 He refused to fight in World War II.
4 He became a policeman, won a medal for bravery and had five children.
5 The writer is determined to find some of her missing Scottish relatives.

2 what she plans to do with this information – 6
what the scandal was – 3
how she made the discovery about her great uncle – 2
the consequence of the scandal – 4
the little she already knew about her great uncle – 1
the evidence she found about his life – 5

3 Discuss the effect of the missing words and expressions as a class.
1 I believe 2 there was a rumour 3 never really; for sure 4 apparently 5 it seems
With the missing words included, the information sounds less definite/certain.

4 Point out that there are various ways to make each sentence less certain. Listen to some of their answers in open class.
1 Apparently,/It seems he wasn't very well liked by other members of the family.
2 Apparently,/I think/I believe he was a hero in the First World War.
3 Apparently,/I think/I believe he'd spent some years in prison.
5 I never found out for sure if it was true. / I never really found out if it was true.

5 This exercise can either be set as homework or done as a collaborative writing activity in class with pairs of students working together. Encourage students to organise their writing as outlined in the exercise and to use narrative tenses.

Homework

In the next lesson, students exchange their emails and make comments and suggestions for their partner.
Tell them not to correct every error, but to look for the following:
What further information would you like?
How could vocabulary be improved?
Are there punctuation and spelling mistakes?

TH!NK more

Practice Extra
Unit 1 Master it!

Workbook
Developing Writing p15

Tests
Unit, extension and skills test 1

Life Competencies

Warmer

Ask students to talk about how much time they spend with friends and family in a typical week, and what they enjoy about it.

▶ 03 Life Lessons: Balancing family and friends

1 ▶ **03** Ask students to compare their ideas.

2 ▶ **03** Invite students to share their answers. Which *differences* and *experiences* have the most impact on how we feel about family and friends?
1 Will says that family is more complicated and can be hard work. With friends it's much easier because you don't have the same responsibility towards them.
2 being the eldest and having to be a referee between his brother and sister; not having the same things in common with a friend and therefore not making an effort

3 **Clarify/check:** *give away, treat, wonder, sensitive.*
She's part of a successful team, and they are all great friends. Also, the team captain and coach rely on her.

4 Encourage students to put themselves in Sam's position and imagine how her sister might feel.
1 whether or not to talk to the coach and whether or not to get her friends' opinions first
2 and 3 Students' own answers
Listen to some of the students' ideas and encourage class discussion.

5 The students should talk about the questions in groups, and then make new groups and compare ideas.

6 Give students about five minutes to make notes on their ideas.

7 Students discuss their ideas and experiences in pairs. Note down useful language to share with the whole class later.

LIFE COMPETENCIES

As we grow older, the balance between family and friends changes. This is normal because our need for independence and support from family changes over time, but it's important to try to find the right balance.

1 ▶ 03 **Watch the vlog. Who do you think Will enjoys being with most – family or friends?**

2 ▶ 03 SPEAKING **Watch the vlog again. Work in pairs. Discuss these questions.**
1 What is Will suggesting about the difference between family and friends?
2 Which particular experiences probably influenced how he feels about family and friends?

3 **Read the text about Sam, who plays for her school football team. As you read, think about what motivates Sam to play for her team.**

4 SPEAKING **Work in pairs and discuss these questions.**
1 What different options does Sam consider when thinking about her problem, and what are the pros and cons of each one?
2 Which option do you think is the best? Could Sam try to solve her problem in other ways?
3 Who do you think will be most affected by the decision Sam takes?

5 SPEAKING **Work in groups. What options are possible in the following situations?**
- Your sister is appearing in a school play the same evening you've been invited to meet friends to watch an important football match.
- A cousin you don't know very well is visiting for the weekend. Your parents want you to spend Saturday showing him around. But you had promised a friend you would help her study for a very important school exam.

I've played in the school girls soccer team since I was about eight. For two years, my aunt – the physical education teacher – was the coach. We had a really successful year when I was 14. We won the league and the cup, and since then we've been great friends. I was a defender and I think I'm pretty good. But sometimes you make a mistake or give away a penalty. And some people would say things like, 'she's only in the team because of her aunt'. That was so unfair. I worked hard and she didn't treat me differently – she maybe even pushed me harder than the others.

Now my situation is reversed: I'm the team captain. Our current coach relies on me for team selection and I always give her my opinion. My sister's now trying to get into the team. She's a good team player and very enthusiastic, but I don't think she has the skills, technically, at the moment. But now I wonder whether I should tell the coach what I think or say nothing and let her make the decision. If my sister isn't chosen because of what I say, I'll feel really bad. She seems really confident, but she's very sensitive to criticism. What's more, I usually talk to my sister when I have a problem, not my friends. I could ask them what they think for a change. I really don't know what the best thing to do is.

Me and my world

6 **Make notes with your ideas about the following questions.**
1 Think of a time when you helped a friend in some way. How did you feel? How did your friend feel?
2 Think of a time when you really enjoyed a family event. Why was it enjoyable? How did you feel?
3 Think of a time when you had to deal with a problem with friends or family. What did you do?

7 SPEAKING **Work in pairs. Compare your ideas with a partner. What advice can you give each other about helping friends or family?**

TIPS ON BALANCING FAMILY AND FRIENDS

- **Good friends respect each other even when they disagree or their opinions differ.**
- **Relationships with friends and family members change over time. It's important to talk with others if you feel you want different things.**
- **Family members can be good friends and good friends can feel part of the family.**

14

Homework

Ask students to write a dialogue between either Sam and her coach, or Sam and her sister. Students can perform their dialogues in a later class.

Activity idea Mixed-ability

Drama activities help weaker students participate equally as reading a script removes some of the anxiety around producing language. Stronger students can be more involved in the writing and directing roles.

Warmer

Put students into small groups and tell them they have three minutes to make a list of all the things people should do to get a good night's sleep. Give them an example (stick to the same sleeping schedule, don't eat a lot before going to bed, don't play videogames in bed, read a book …). Once the time is over, ask student to share their ideas as a whole group. Ask them to decide which the three best ones are and why.

Then ask students to work with another partner and take turns to explain the last four things they do before going to bed. You can give your own examples!

▶ 04 Get TH!NKing

Ask the question. Get students to compare their ideas in groups. Play the video and then ask students for feedback.

1. Elicit as much information as possible from the photo. What animal can they see? Does it seem comfortable? What is it doing? What do they know about koalas? What is most striking about the photo?
2. Ask how many people in the class have a pet. Does the pet sleep a lot? Where do they sleep? Do they move or do funny things when they are asleep? Do they appear to dream?
3. Ask students if they remember their dreams. Put students into pairs and ask them to take turns to tell each other about a dream they have had. Ask them to choose a dream that was memorable or different.

2 SWEET DREAMS

OBJECTIVES

FUNCTIONS: giving advice

GRAMMAR: past tense with hypothetical meaning; adverbs for modifying comparatives

VOCABULARY: sleep; idioms with *sleep* and *dream*

Get TH!NKING ▶04
Watch the video and think: do you get enough sleep?

Work in pairs. Look at the photo and discuss the questions.
1 What's this animal doing, and where is it?
2 Do you think animals dream? If so, what do they dream about?
3 Do you dream every night? What is your most memorable dream?

15

Objectives

Functions Giving advice
Grammar Past tense with hypothetical meaning; adverbs for modifying comparatives
Vocabulary Sleep; idioms with *sleep* and *dream*
Culture Sleep in different cultures

Resources for this unit

All available online

Videos

- Get **TH!NK**ing: *Do you get enough sleep?*
- Grammar video!: Adverbs for modifying comparatives
- Culture: Different ways of sleeping

Tests

- Unit, extension and skills test 2

Worksheets

- Grammar and vocabulary: Basic, Standard and Extension Worksheets
- Project: Our dreams
- Communication: Sleep on it
- Get **TH!NK**ing and Grammar video! video Worksheets

Warmer

Ask: *Which magazines or websites do you read? Have you ever seen a multiple-choice quiz in a magazine or on the internet? What was it about? What are the best and worst features of this type of quiz?* Ask students to discuss the questions before listening to some of their answers as a class.

1 Students do the quiz individually.

2 Encourage students to give reasons for their choices. Ask: *How similar were your answers?*

3 🔊 **2.01 Check/clarify:** *a motion, petition, melatonin, knock-on effect, nodding off.*
Ask students to underline the parts of the text that support their answers. Clarify that even though the information in some sentences may be true, they should put *doesn't say* if the information does not appear in the article. During feedback, encourage students to think about the correct answer to the false statements.
1 T 2 F (Hannah believes that teenagers are getting too tired as a result of having to wake up for school starts as early as 8.30 am.) 3 DS 4 T 5 F (A long-term study at a British state school found that by allowing students to start school an hour and a half later at 10 am …) 6 T 7 T 8 DS

4 If space allows, encourage students to walk around the classroom to find someone who has similar answers. Ask students to report their findings back to the class and encourage them to use the phrase 'So does he/she/ [student's name]'.
Students' own answers

READING

1 **Look at the photos. Can you relate to any of these situations? Read the quiz below and choose your answers.**

2 SPEAKING **Work in pairs. Compare your answers and decide who's the best sleeper.**

3 🔊 2.01 **Read and listen to the article on page 17. Are these sentences T (true), F (false) or DS (doesn't say)?**

1. Hannah Kidner would like to see schools starting later.
2. She believes that a lack of sleep is responsible for students not doing as well.
3. Hannah has the support of several of her teachers.
4. Teenagers have different sleep rhythms to those of adults.
5. The school in the study used to start at 8 am.
6. Some people feel teenagers are responsible for their own lack of sleep.
7. Headmasters can choose when their schools start and finish.
8. Hannah has been successful with her petition.

4 SPEAKING **Work in pairs and discuss the following questions.**

1. How many hours' sleep do you usually get? Do you feel it's too little, too much or just right?
2. How regular are your sleep patterns?
3. What time does your school day start? Would you be in favour of a later/earlier starting time? Why/Why not?

ARE YOU A HEALTHY SLEEPER?

1 You wake up half an hour late for school. You think …
a) I should go to bed earlier.
b) It's time I bought a new alarm clock.
c) That's unusual. I don't usually oversleep.

2 It's 7 am and your dad is yelling at you to get out of bed. You think …
a) I wish I could have another hour in bed.
b) OK, OK! I'm getting up.
c) Why's he shouting? I'm already up.

3 You turned off your light half an hour ago. You think …
a) If only my mind wasn't on that computer game. I want to go to sleep.
b) I'd prefer it if you didn't ask me silly quiz questions. I'm quite a light sleeper and I'm about to fall asleep.
c) Nothing. You're fast asleep and snoring loudly.

4 It's 11 pm and your mum suggests it's time you went to bed. You think …
a) No way. I'm snapchatting Rachel.
b) OK, I'll read for half an hour before I turn my light off.
c) I'm on my way right now.

16

Culture note

Hannah Kidner was 16 when her politics teacher set an assignment to start an online petition on a subject she cared about. Earlier that year, she had written an essay about the importance of sleep. She found several scientific studies which suggested that adolescents had a late-running biological rhythm, and that starting lessons at 10 am could be beneficial. The debate was taken to Parliament by the Labour MP Daniel Zeichner. The UK government responded *"The Department [of Education] has no plans to require secondary schools to start later. The decision on when to start the school day lies with individual schools."*

5 1 a teenager 2 a doctor, a researcher 3 a parent

6 If students disagree, encourage them to come to agreement on the most likely response. After discussing in pairs, put students into small groups to report on their discussions.

Pronunciation

Different ways of pronouncing *c* and *g*

Student's Book p137

Homework

Ask students to write a short text as if they are starting an online petition on a subject they care about. The text should have a heading, a brief outline and cite some research to support their argument. Students present this petition in the next lesson. After each presentation, encourage the class to ask questions. Hold a vote to decide which was the most interesting and well-informed petition.

Activity idea Extension

During the parliamentary debate of Hannah's petition, different perspectives were put forward. Use the transcript or the video footage of the debate and ask students to identify the different perspectives. The transcript and video can be found by searching for *UK parliamentary archived petitions 229178* online.

Emotional Development
Empathy and relationship skills
Shows understanding of other people's perspectives and feelings.

TIME FOR A CHANGE?

In February 2019, the UK government debated a motion calling for the starting time of secondary schools in the UK to be moved back to 10 am. The debate was a direct result of an online petition with nearly 188,000 signatures set up by teenager Hannah Kidner.

Hannah believes that teenagers are getting too tired as a result of having to wake up for school starts as early as 8.30 am. She also claims that if schools were to allow teenagers a later starting time, they would see greater productivity among the pupils and ultimately better exam results. But it isn't just about improving academic performance; many are worried that a lack of sleep is also causing a growing number of health problems in young people, especially when it comes to mental health issues such as exhaustion and depression.

But a later school starting time isn't just the wish of a teen who would like to lie in under the covers for longer every morning. The arguments behind the motion are backed up by extensive scientific research.

It has long been recognised that teenager sleep patterns are different to those of adults and younger children. There is a proven biological reason behind the stereotypical image of the teenager who goes to bed late and doesn't want to wake in the morning, and it's all down to a hormone called melatonin. The release of melatonin is the body's way of letting us know we are falling asleep and should be taking ourselves to bed.

In teenagers, the release of melatonin happens, on average, two hours after it does in an adult, meaning that teens feel tired later than adults do. Since teenagers need between eight and ten hours of sleep per night, the knock-on effect is that they won't want to rise so early the following morning; however, because of early school starts, they need to. The result is a generation of over-tired school children nodding off and taking naps in classrooms all over the country.

A long-term study at a British state school found that by allowing students to start school an hour and a half later at 10 am, there was more than a 50 percent reduction in the number of students who were getting ill. Not only did the later starting time produce healthier pupils, but it also led to better academic results, too.

While the call for the government to recommend an earlier start time in schools was welcomed by many – school children and scientists included – there were those who believed there are plenty of other reasons to explain a generation of over-tired teens. Many took to Twitter to join in the debate, claiming reasons such as soft-parenting and a late-night addiction to gaming as the real causes for teenage tiredness.

The final outcome of the parliamentary debate, however, was somewhat of a disappointment for Hannah, as politicians could see no real reason to officially change the school starting time. They voted to stick with the current policy, which allows all schools to decide when they open and close. This means that Hannah still has the option to try to convince the headteacher of her school to set a 10 am start, but without any official political instruction to back her up, it would seem unlikely that a change will be made.

Train to TH!NK

The rule of threes

The rule of threes states that ideas should be considered from three different perspectives.

The more perspectives you can view a problem from, the better your overall understanding.

For example, imagine an aeroplane is flying through heavy turbulence.

- *An experienced pilot would see it as a normal occurrence and put on the seatbelt sign.*
- *A nervous flyer might convince themselves the plane is about to crash.*
- *A fan of rollercoasters might enjoy the thrill of it.*

5 A teenager is still asleep at 11 am on a Saturday. Who might have the following opinions of the situation?

1 What's the problem? I'm tired.
2 We need to understand that teenage sleep patterns are different to those of adults.
3 He's so lazy these days.

6 SPEAKING **Make notes on how each of the following people might respond to the statement 'Schools should start at 10 am'. Then compare with a partner.**

a teenager a parent a teacher an economist a doctor

PRONUNCIATION
Different ways of pronouncing *c* and *g*
Go to page 137.

TH!NK more

Worksheets
Project Our dreams
Communication Sleep on it
Get TH!NKing *Do you get enough sleep?*

Grammar; Vocabulary

Warmer

Brainstorm ways of getting to sleep when you are worried about something. Write any interesting vocabulary on the board to refer to later.

1 Ask students to try to answer the questions from memory before referring back to page 16 to check.
1 bought 2 could 3 wasn't
4 didn't ask
RULE: 1 past 2 present

2 If you're short on time, you can set this exercise for homework but you could do number 1 in open class to check that students fully understand the task.
1 got up 2 was 3 didn't have
4 respected 5 didn't talk
6 went on 7 showed

3 You may like to give an example of your own to get students started on this. Encourage them to be creative.
Students' own answers

Workbook p18

Get it Right!
would rather

Student's Book p24

4 The final stage could be done as a class competition. Students race to be the first group to find all eight expressions in the quiz and article.
1 c 2 d/f 3 h 4 g 5 f/d 6 b
7 a 8 e

5 If students are struggling with this, encourage them to use English–English dictionaries to complete the exercise as there may not be a direct translation in their own language. During feedback, say the expressions for students to repeat. Point out/elicit that the particle takes the main stress in the phrasal verbs.

GRAMMAR
Past tenses with hypothetical meaning

1 Complete the sentences from the quiz on page 16 with the verbs in brackets. Then complete the rule with *past* and *present*.

1 It's time I ... a new alarm clock. (buy)
2 I wish I ... have another hour in bed. (can)
3 If only my mind ... on that computer game. I want to go to sleep. (not be)
4 I'd prefer it if you ... me silly quiz questions. (not ask)

> RULE: With certain expressions, like *It's time*, *I'd prefer it if*, *I wish* and *If only*, we use the [1]... simple tense to talk about how we would like [2]... situations to be different.
> With *I'd rather* and *I'd prefer*, we use the infinitive when the subject of the second verb is the same as the subject of *I'd rather* and *I'd prefer*. Also, with *I'd rather*, *I'd prefer* and *It's time*, we use the infinitive when there is no second subject.
> *It's time to go.* *I'd prefer to eat now.*
> *It's time we left.* *I'd prefer it if we ate now.*

2 Complete the dialogue with the correct forms of the verbs in the list.

be | get up | go on | not have | not talk | respect | show

Dad Come on, Ella. It's time you [1]... .
Ella ZzzzzzzzZzzzzzzz.
Dad Did you hear me, Ella? You've got fifteen minutes until the school bus arrives.
Ella What?! No! If only it [2]... the weekend. If only I [3]... school today. If only ...
Dad Ella!
Ella Dad, I'd prefer it if you [4]... my melatonin levels.
Dad And I'd prefer it if you [5]... such nonsense.
Ella It isn't nonsense. It's science. Melatonin. It's why I need so much sleep.
Dad I've never heard of it.
Ella Then maybe it's time you [6]... the internet and read about it.
Dad And maybe it's time you [7]... your dad a bit of respect. Now get out of bed!

3 SPEAKING Think about your own sleeping habits and complete the sentences so that they are true for you. Compare with a partner.

1 I wish I could ...
2 If only school ...
3 I'd rather ... today.
4 I wish the teachers ...

→ workbook page 18

VOCABULARY
Sleep

4 Match the words on the left with those on the right to make sleep-related collocations and phrasal verbs. Then check in the quiz and article on pages 16 and 17.

1 nod	a the covers
2 fall	b loudly
3 lie	c off
4 a light	d asleep
5 fast	e a nap
6 snore	f asleep
7 under	g sleeper
8 take	h in

5 SPEAKING Work in pairs and discuss the meaning of each of the collocations and phrasal verbs in Exercise 4, using the context provided by the quiz and article to help you.

6 Which noun collocates with all of these: *a lack of, over, skip, get enough, get seven hours'*?

7 SPEAKING Complete the questions with collocations and phrasal verbs from Exercises 4 and 6, in the correct form. Then ask and answer in pairs.

1 Do you ever ... in the afternoon or do you prefer to just sleep at night?
2 Have you ever ... during a lesson at school? Did anyone notice? What happened? How did you feel?
3 Do you like to ... at the weekend? Or do you get up early? What does it take to get you out from ... ?
4 Do you know anyone who ... when they sleep? What's the best way to prevent this?
5 Are you a ... or is it difficult for you to wake up when you're ... ? Is noise or light more likely to wake you up?
6 Have you ever ... and been late for something really important? What happened?

→ workbook page 20

18

6 Ask students to discuss the meaning of the five expressions and to think of sentences using them all.
sleep

7 Encourage students to justify their answers.
1 take a nap 2 fallen asleep / nodded off 3 lie in; under the covers 4 snores loudly
5 light sleeper; fast asleep 6 overslept

Workbook p20

TH!NK more

Workbook
Grammar p18, Ex.1–4
Vocabulary p20, Ex.1–4
Vocabulary Extra p21, Ex.1–2

Worksheets
Grammar Worksheets 2
Vocabulary Worksheets 2

Listening; Functions

8 The first question can be done as a mingle activity.
Students' own answers

9 🔊 **2.03** Tell students not to worry about understanding every word for now, but to focus on listening for the answer.
✓ hallucinations
✓ a decrease in physical abilities
✓ memory loss
He also experienced difficulty recognising objects by feeling them, trouble with tongue-twisters and an increase in his sense of smell.

10 🔊 **2.03** Give students time to read through the questions. Students may like to work in pairs and try to answer the questions from memory before listening to the audio again.
1 c (or a) 2 c 3 a 4 a 5 b 6 a 7 b 8 c

11 🔊 **2.03** Allow students to compare answers with a partner before feedback. Refer them to the things you wrote on the board at the beginning of the lesson. Were any of them mentioned?
Bake a cake

12 🔊 **2.03** Before playing the audio, give students a minute to try to remember the advice given for each problem.
1 baking; cake 2 trying; beat 3 doing; easier 4 get; lost

13 Encourage students to give reasons for their answers.

Homework

Ask students to keep a journal for two or three days with a record of how much sleep they had, what time they went to bed / woke up and how tired they felt the next day.

LISTENING

8 SPEAKING **Work in pairs and discuss.**

1 What's the longest you've ever gone without sleep?
2 Which of these problems do you think people experience when they don't get enough sleep over an extended period of time?
- hallucinations
- headaches
- a decrease in physical abilities
- problems sleeping
- memory loss
- slow reactions
- impatience

9 🔊 2.03 **Listen to a radio programme about a teenager called Randy Gardner who set a world record for staying awake. Which of the problems in the list above did he experience? Did he have any other problems?**

10 🔊 2.03 **Listen again and choose the correct answers.**

1 Why is it not a good idea to try to beat Randy's record?
a It's much too dangerous.
b Scientists have said it would be impossible to beat.
c The Guinness World Records won't accept it.

2 How many people would you need to set a new world record for the biggest sleepover?
a 2,003
b 2,004
c 2,005

3 How many of Randy's friends took part in the experiment?
a 2
b 3
c 4

4 How did Dr Dement find out about the experiment?
a The story was on the national news.
b He lived locally.
c Randy wrote to him to ask for his help.

5 How long was it before Randy started having problems with his speech?
a after one day
b after two days
c after three days

6 What happened to Randy after five days?
a He had trouble with his short-term memory.
b His basketball skills got worse.
c He didn't want to eat.

7 How long did Randy sleep for at the end of the experiment?
a 11 hours
b 14 hours
c 25 hours

8 What effect did the experiment have on Randy?
a He had strange dreams for many years after.
b He found it difficult to stay awake.
c He suffered from insomnia.

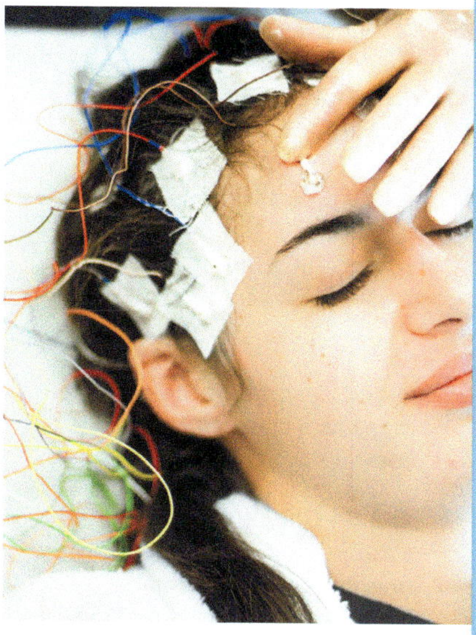

FUNCTIONS
Giving advice

11 🔊 2.03 **Listen to the radio programme again. What does the presenter do when he can't get to sleep?**

12 🔊 2.03 **Complete the advice with the missing words. Then listen again and check.**

1 I find that b… a c… seems to work.
2 I wouldn't recommend t… to b… that particular record.
3 You might want to consider d… something e… .
4 Try not to g… l… in it!

13 SPEAKING **Work in pairs. Think of two pieces of advice for each of these people.**

1 Dan finds it hard to get to sleep at night.
2 Anna keeps falling asleep in lessons
3 Ben's dad snores so loudly Ben can hear him in his bedroom.

I find that …
I'd recommend/I wouldn't recommend …
You might want to consider …
Try not to …

Activity idea Extension

If you want to give students extended speaking practice, ask them to repeat Exercise 8 with a different partner. They will then have an opportunity to improve their answers from the first attempt and should be motivated by clearer, more fluent answers.

Activity idea Mixed-ability

In Exercise 13, weaker students can think of one piece of advice for each of the problems.

TH!NK more

Workbook
Listening p24, Ex.1–3

Warmer

Divide the class into groups of three for students to test each other on the collocations from page 18. Students take it in turns to say the first part of the collocation. The other two compete to be first to complete it and win one point if they do so correctly. You could give a bonus point if students can use the expression in a sentence.

1 Listen to some of the students' ideas as a class, but do not comment at this stage.

2 **2.04 Check/clarify:** *subconscious, paralysis, phenomenon, nightmare*. Set a three-minute time limit to encourage students to read quickly and focus on finding the answers rather than on trying to understand every word.
1a 2b 3c 4b 5b 6a

3 Encourage students to refer to the article when answering and to give reasons why they find that information interesting.

4 To extend discussion, ask students to give any examples of the effect dreams have had on their friends and extended family. Listen to some examples in open class as feedback and encourage further discussion.

READING

1 SPEAKING Work in pairs. Answer the questions in the quiz.

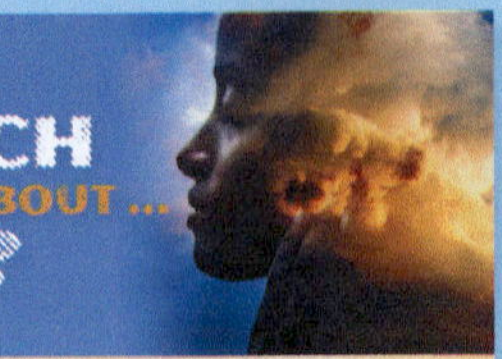

HOW MUCH DO YOU KNOW ABOUT ... DREAMS?

1 What percentage of people remember their dreams when they wake up?
a) 40%
b) 50%
c) 60%

2 How long does the average person spend dreaming every night?
a) less than one hour
b) between one and two hours
c) more than two hours

3 How much time does the average person spend dreaming in their lifetime?
a) one year
b) three years
c) six years

4 How many dreams does the average person have a night?
a) fewer than four
b) between four and seven
c) more than seven

5 What percentage of dreams are negative?
a) 25%
b) 50%
c) 75%

6 What percentage of people dream in colour?
a) 88%
b) 94%
c) 99%

2 2.04 Read and listen to the article to check your answers.

THE POWER OF DREAMING

Everyone dreams – that's a fact! So don't believe those people who say they don't. They are probably among the 60% who forget their dreams as soon as they wake up. Are you one of these people? Do you remember your dreams?

Most sleep specialists agree that dreaming is essential. Research shows that dreaming is a way of allowing our brains to process memories and organise all of the information we pick up around us in our everyday life and discard anything that is irrelevant. It is also widely believed that dreams allow us to deal with emotions and work out problems that might seem to be far more difficult to solve when we are awake. In other words, dreams offer a sort of subconscious nightly therapy session. Most of us will spend an average of about an hour and a half dreaming every night. Over a lifetime, that works out at around six full years of just dreaming! Imagine that! Each night we will have between four and seven different dreams, although it is unusual we will remember more than the last one when we wake up.

Dreams have always been a source of fascination. Most people say they like dreaming and we often awake feeling good about where we've been and what we've seen. More often than not, we will want to share our dreams with family or friends, only to see the dreams frustratingly disintegrate from our memories as we try to recall them. Dreams can also be a source of inspiration, and many artists and poets have woken up with a vision for their new work in their head. Interestingly, several inventions are said to have also been the result of a dream; Larry Page says his idea for Google came in a dream. Likewise, Dmitri Mendeleyev thought up the periodic table while taking a nap.

But some dreams are not nearly as helpful as others. In fact, it's been estimated that about half of our dreams are not very pleasant at all and we will often find ourselves in awkward or compromising situations in them. Often the levels of frustration are increased when we try to change the course of a dream but find we have little power to do anything. Sleep paralysis is a particularly nasty phenomenon that affects some people. It's a condition in which you feel 100% awake but are absolutely unable to move your body. Although the paralysis may only last seconds, it gives the sensation of lasting for a lot longer. Those who experience it say sleep paralysis is considerably more frightening than the worst nightmare. And then there are those dreams that seem to predict the future and leave us feeling uneasy about the day to come. There are several famous examples of people who really did dream about what was going to happen. For example, Abraham Lincoln foresaw his own assassination and several people reported having dreams that predicted the tragedies of the sinking of the *Titanic* and the 9/11 attacks.

There are many odd and fascinating facts about dreams that scientists are still investigating. Why is it, for example, that 12% of people say they only dream in black and white? And what is it that makes some people act out their dreams by sleepwalking? One thing is for sure: for as much we understand dreams, there is still a whole lot more to be discovered. So, dream on!

SPEAKING

3 Which information in the article do you find most interesting and/or surprising? Why?

4 Do you believe our dreams are trying to tell us something? Give examples to support your opinion.

20

Culture notes

Dmitri Mendeleyev (also written as Dmitry Mendeleev) was a Russian chemist and inventor who developed the periodic classification of the elements. He found that when all the known chemical elements were arranged in order of increasing atomic weight, the resulting table displayed a recurring pattern (or *periodicity*). He created a grid-like diagram and following this system, he could even predict the qualities of still-unknown elements. In 1869, he published the very first periodic table of elements and so became known as the founder of the periodic law. He died in St Petersburg, Russia in 1907.

The Periodic Table has changed slightly since Mendeleyev first published it. In the modern version of the periodic table, elements are in order of atomic number in periods and groups. The elements are arranged into rows, called periods, in order of increasing atomic number. The vertical columns, called groups, contain the elements that have similar properties. The metal elements are found on the left-hand side of the periodic table, and the non-metal elements are found on the right.

TH!NK more

Workbook
Reading p22, Ex.1–4

Grammar; Vocabulary

▶ 05 Grammar video! Adverbs for modifying comparatives

5 During feedback, point out how the adverb emphasises the comparative.
1 … is considerably more frightening ….
2 … seem to be far more difficult ….
3 … are not nearly as helpful ….
RULE: 1 formal 2 informal

6 Before students complete the gaps, ask them to quickly read the paragraph to get a general understanding and ask: *Did he have a nice dream? Why (not)?* (No. It was creepy and scary.).
1 nearly 2 considerably 3 way
4 like 5 notably 6 significantly
7 far 8 nowhere

7 1 nowhere near as tired
2 is way more comfortable than
3 not nearly as exciting as
4 is nothing like as warm

8–9 Monitor to help with vocabulary and to check students are using modifying comparatives correctly.

Workbook p19

10 During feedback, say the idioms for students to repeat and check pronunciation.
1 sleep 2 sleep 3 dreams
4 dream 5 dream 6 dream
7 sleep 8 dreams

11 1 beyond my wildest dreams
2 in your dreams
3 a dream come true
4 let me sleep on it
5 get your beauty sleep
6 lose sleep over
7 I'd never dream of doing
8 dream job

12 When students have completed the exercise, you may like to regroup students and ask them to repeat the exercise with new partners.

Workbook p20

Homework

Ask students to write five sentences comparing themselves to a member of their family using modifying adverbs.

GRAMMAR
Adverbs for modifying comparatives

Grammar video ▶ 05

5 **Put the words in brackets back into the example sentences. Then read and complete the rule.**

1 Sleep paralysis is more frightening than the worst nightmare. (considerably)
2 Dreams allow us to deal with emotions and work out problems that seem to be more difficult to solve when we are awake. (far)
3 But some dreams are not as helpful as others. (nearly)

> **RULE:** As well as using *a lot* and *much* to emphasise a comparison, we can use other adverbs, such as *considerably, far, significantly, extensively, notably, way* and *drastically*. By using these words, we achieve a greater level of variety in our speaking and writing.
> - *Notably* and *Significantly* are used in more [1]*formal / informal* spoken contexts and in writing.
> - *Way* is used in more [2]*formal / informal* spoken contexts.
> - To emphasise a(n) *(not) as … as* construction, we can use *not nearly, nothing like* and *nowhere near.*

6 **Complete with the missing words.**

Why are other people's dreams not [1]n… as interesting as mine? My dreams are [2]c… more exciting than most other people's, but no one seems interested in hearing about them. It's strange. Anyway, the other day I had a really weird dream. It was [3]w… more weird than my usual dreams. I was on a bus to school. It wasn't my normal bus though. In fact, it was nothing [4]l… my normal bus at all. It was [5]n… slower for a start and it was [6]s… older, too, but it was definitely the school bus and all my friends were on it. Suddenly, I heard a really horrible noise. It was like a bee buzzing, only it was [7]f… louder. It was really creepy, but it was [8]n… near as scary as what happened next. What did happen next? I can't remember. It was frightening though. It really was.

7 **Complete the second sentence so that it has a similar meaning to the first. You must use between three and six words including the word given.**

1 I feel a lot less tired than I did five minutes ago. **NOWHERE**
I feel … now as I did five minutes ago.
2 My bed is nothing like as comfortable as yours. **WAY**
Your bed … mine.
3 My dreams were far more exciting when I was a child. **NEARLY**
My dreams these days are … when I was a child.
4 I hope tonight is much less warm than last night. **NOTHING**
I hope tonight … as it was last night.

8 WRITING **Write a short text about a dream you can remember (or make one up). Include modifying comparatives.**

9 SPEAKING **Tell your dream to a partner. Whose dream was the strangest?**

→ workbook page 19

VOCABULARY
Idioms with *sleep* and *dream*

10 **Complete the sentences with either *sleep* or *dream(s)*.**

1 It's a difficult decision. *Let me … on it* and I'll let you know tomorrow.
2 It isn't such a big problem – certainly nothing to *lose … over*.
3 I can't believe I'm getting the chance to study in Italy! That's *beyond my wildest …* .
4 You really think I'd do that?! *I'd never … of doing* something so mean. He's my brother.
5 I'd love to be a teacher. It's my *… job*.
6 I can't believe I've been signed by Liverpool. It's *a … come true*.
7 We've got an early start in the morning and you need to *get your beauty …* .
8 Do you imagine I'd buy you a sports car? *In your …* !

11 **Which expressions in italics in Exercise 10 could be replaced with these words?**

1 more or better than I could ever hope for
2 no way
3 the realisation of my ultimate ambition
4 give me some time to think about it
5 sleep well so that you're fresh and at your best the next day
6 worry too much about
7 It's just not in my character to do
8 perfect profession

12 SPEAKING **Work in pairs and discuss the questions.**

1 What's your dream job?
2 What would be a dream come true for you?
3 What would you never dream of doing?
4 Which of the idioms in Exercise 10 can you translate directly into your language? How would you translate the other ones?

→ workbook page 20

Activity idea Extension

Write on the board: *How often do you remember your dreams? Do you write them down to help you remember them? Tell your partner about recent dreams you have had.* Students discuss in pairs. Listen to some of their ideas as a class and make a note of any recurring dream themes on the board.

Activity idea Extension

Give students three minutes to write five key words from one of their dreams. Student A shows student B the five words for him/her to guess what happens in the dream. Student A then recounts the original dream. You could make the exercise competitive by giving students one point each time they use an adverb to modify a comparative.

TH!NK more

Practice Extra
Unit 2 Practise it!

Workbook
Grammar p19, Ex.5–7
Vocabulary p20, Ex.5–6
Vocabulary Extra p21, Ex.3

Worksheets
Grammar Worksheets 2
Vocabulary Worksheets 2
Grammar video! Adverbs for modifying comparatives

Warmer

Ask students: *What time do you usually go to bed? How many hours' sleep do you usually get each night? Are you a light or deep sleeper? Do you sleep well or badly?* Elicit reasons for feeling tired or sleeping badly. In pairs, students discuss how well they sleep, what causes them to sleep badly and what helps them to sleep well. Bring the discussion to a close with a group discussion.

▶ 06 TH!NK
Different ways of sleeping

1 Set a two-minute time limit to encourage students to read quickly and focus on the task. Tell them not to worry about difficult vocabulary at this stage as this will come up later.

1 the widespread availability of artificial light 2 7.5 hours a night

2 🔊 **2.05** Tell students to underline information in the text that helped them answer each question.

1 We sleep at least an hour less each night than a century ago, and several hours less than before industrialisation and electricity.
2 Monophasic sleep is sleep in one concentrated period, whereas polyphasic sleep is sleep broken up into several chunks.
3 Japan
4 Mediterranean countries, Africa and China
5 because life is more busy
6 to increase productivity
7 It (probably) degraded the quality of night-time sleep.

TH!NK
Different ways of sleeping

Culture

1 Scan the article for the answers to the following questions.

1 What caused a change in sleeping patterns across a number of countries?
2 How long, on average, do people sleep for?

Sleep in different cultures

It is quite apparent that there are significant differences in sleep patterns in different parts of the world, and that sleep patterns have also changed over time. Traditions, cultural values and local conditions and environments all have a bearing on sleep practices and attitudes.

One major source of these differences is the widespread availability of artificial light, which, since its introduction in the mid-nineteenth century, has led to dramatic changes in sleep patterns in the industrialised world. It is thought that today we sleep at least an hour less each night than was the custom just a century ago, and probably several hours less than before industrialisation and electricity. According to some studies, artificial lighting has encouraged people to go to bed later and to sleep in a single concentrated burst throughout the night (monophasic sleep), rather than the more segmented and broken-up sleep patterns (polyphasic or biphasic sleep) that were previously the norm.

During the long nights of the winter months, our prehistoric ancestors – and, according to some researchers, more recent ancestors up until about two hundred years ago – may have broken sleep up into two or more chunks, separated by an hour or two of quiet restfulness. In nomadic societies, even today, it is more common for people to have this kind of biphasic sleep, or sometimes even more flexible and fragmented polyphasic sleep periods, sleeping on and off throughout the day or night, depending on what is happening.

Even within the developed world, there are significant differences in sleep patterns. A study carried out in ten countries in 2005 revealed some of these regional variations. For instance, while the average time the study participants slept was about 7.5 hours a night, the results from individual countries varied from 6 hours 53 minutes in Japan to 8 hours 24 minutes in Portugal. Over 42% of Brazilians took regular afternoon naps, compared to only 12% of Japanese people. Over 32% of Belgians complained of insomnia and other sleep problems, while only 10% of Austrians claimed not to sleep well.

In the past, particularly in many Mediterranean countries, people used to take frequent naps during the day, or 'siestas', although, in the hustle and bustle of the modern world, it is less ubiquitous than it once was. Naps are also common in parts of Africa and China.

The experience of Japan is a clear example of the way a change in culture can affect sleep patterns. In the post-war years, Japan was keen to rebuild and reassert itself and, as one expression of patriotism, Japanese workers were encouraged to start work early (and often finish late as well). The *inemuri* (a nap taken at work in order to increase productivity) was encouraged as a way for an employee to demonstrate their commitment, even though it probably degraded the quality of night-time sleep even more.

Today, sleep is perhaps more undervalued in Japan than anywhere else, and sleep deprivation is endemic.

It is clear, then, that there are cultural and historical differences in the amount of sleep we get and the way we get it. Yet one thing is for sure: the need for sufficient sleep, however we may define this, is universal and unchanging.

2 🔊 2.05 **Read and listen to the article again. Then answer the questions.**

1 How has the number of hours we sleep changed over the centuries?
2 What's the difference between monophasic and polyphasic sleep?
3 Which country was found to sleep the least?
4 In which countries is it usual to have a short sleep in the afternoon?
5 Why are naps becoming less common?
6 Why was the *inemuri* introduced in Japan?
7 What effect did it have?

22

Culture note

In 2016, a study in the journal *Science Advances* reported the sleep trends that were being seen worldwide via an app. According to the data, people in the Netherlands are getting the most rest per night, while those in Singapore and Japan are getting the least. In general, it was found that geographically close countries with similar cultures also had similar night-time habits. A similar study in *Sleep Medicine* showed that children in Hong Kong go to bed on average 3 hours later than children in New Zealand.

Netherlands	8h 5m
New Zealand	8h 4m
France	8h 3m
Australia	8h 1m
Belgium	8h 1m
Canada	7h 58m
United Kingdom	7h 54m
United States	7h 52m
Japan	7h 30m
Singapore	7h 24m

3 Make a note of any nice expressions in English that students use during the activity. At the end write them on the board for the class to copy, and praise the student who used them.

4 Ask students to cover the definitions. Give them two minutes to find the highlighted words in the article and discuss their meanings with a partner. Students uncover the definitions to check their ideas and complete the exercise.
1 common 2 undervalued 3 burst 4 fragmented 5 insomnia 6 have a bearing on 7 commitment 8 ubiquitous

1 Before doing the task, ask students: *What is a proposal?* (A written plan or suggestion based on evidence.) *Who might write a proposal?* (They are often written in business and in academia.) Ask students to discuss the questions with a partner. Listen to some of their ideas in open class.
1 lack of sleep and its effect on behaviour and performance
2 introducing a quiet room where employees can catch up on sleep

2 *Students' own answers*

3 Give students time to read through the key things to mention and check understanding.
a specific problem – A
a summary of the problem and the proposed solution to it – D
an idea for a solution – B
justification of why it's a good solution – C

4 Give students time to make notes in preparation for writing a proposal. Monitor to help with any questions. Encourage them to use some of the sleep-related vocabulary from the unit. If you're short on time, set this exercise for homework.

SWEET DREAMS UNIT 2

3 SPEAKING **Work in pairs and discuss the questions.**
1 What sleeping habits are typical in your country?
2 Which of the habits mentioned in the article would be unusual in your culture?
3 In what way do you think sleeping habits have changed over the last few decades?

4 VOCABULARY **Match the highlighted words or phrases in the article to the definitions.**
1 to do something to show that you still have power
2 not given enough importance
3 in one time rather than separated out into several short chunks
4 consisting of several separate parts
5 difficulty sleeping
6 to have an influence or effect on
7 loyalty
8 found everywhere

WRITING
A proposal

1 INPUT **Read the proposal and answer the questions.**
1 What problem is the proposal trying to tackle?
2 What recommendation does it make?

2 ANALYSE **Read again and answer the questions.**
1 How well does the proposal answer the question?
2 How varied is the language?
3 How well organised is it?

3 PLAN **When writing a proposal, the key things to mention are:**
- a specific problem
- a summary of the problem and the proposed solution to it
- an idea for a solution
- justification of why it's a good solution

Match each of these areas to the paragraphs A–D in the proposal.

4 PRODUCE **Write a proposal supporting the idea that the school day should start two hours later. Use the stages outlined in Exercise 3 to help you organise your ideas.**

Write a proposal supporting the idea that your place of work should introduce a nap room for employees.

A A recent study has shown that less than half of all Americans are getting enough sleep each night and that an overtired workforce is costing the economy millions of dollars in lost productivity each year. Clearly, anything that is losing big business so much money warrants investigation.

B Among several ideas that have been put forward, one of the most popular has been the introduction of nap rooms in many businesses across the US. As the name suggests, a nap room is a place where employees can have a short rest during the working day in order to recharge their batteries. A nap room can be anything from a designated dark room with several beds to specially designed sleep pods.

C The idea is that rather than falling asleep at their desk, tired workers can take time out in the nap room if they need to do so. Those companies that have installed one are already reporting rises in the effectiveness of their workforce.

D Lack of sleep is clearly a widespread problem among the population and the introduction of a nap room in our offices would greatly benefit the well-being of the staff. If we could be offered a quiet room where we could catch up on sleep during breaks, we would see an overall improvement in our performance and efficiency, which in turn would increase the company's productivity.

23

Homework
If you are short on time, students can do Writing Exercise 4 for homework. If you have done this in the class, ask students to exchange their proposals with another student for them to read and give feedback on content and structure. Students could check if the proposal uses the same structure as the template. They should also decide which is the most/least interesting part of the proposal.

Activity idea Extension
On completion of Writing Exercise 4, ask students to exchange their proposals with another student. If students have access to the internet in the classroom, this could be done electronically. Ask them to read and evaluate on the basis of **content** (were all points included? How interesting were the ideas?); **organisation** (did each paragraph include a clear and distinct idea like the model answer?); **communicative purpose** (were you convinced by it?); and language.

TH!NK more
Practice Extra
Unit 2 Master it!
Workbook
Developing Writing p23
Tests
Unit, extension and skills test 2

1 Explain that there are different ways to talk about present habits. For example: *The teacher gives us homework every day. / The teacher is always giving us homework.*

Students at this level often use *use(d) to* when talking about present habits. Write on the board *The teacher uses to give us homework every day.* Elicit why this is incorrect and how the sentence could be corrected.

1 People tend to / will often form close relationships with friends they have most in common with.
2 My older brother is always teasing me. It's so annoying!
3 My sister often gets on my nerves as she will borrow / tends to borrow / is always borrowing my clothes without asking.
4 Jenny says that her biology teacher is always picking on her. It makes her quite upset.
5 Annoyingly, my best friend tends to act rather self-centredly, so we sometimes fall out.
6 Elderly people will often have / tend to have traditional values.

2 Focus students on the example sentences, and elicit why the second sentence for each example is incorrect. Point out that would *rather (not)* is followed by the base form of the verb.

1 Would you rather have a siesta now or go to bed early tonight?
2 A study has found that teenagers need more sleep ~~rather~~ than adults.
3 I'd rather I wasn't such a light sleeper. I tend to wake up several times during the night.
4 Tom would rather not ~~staying~~ stay up late tonight because he has an exam tomorrow.
5 Some dreams have more meaning ~~rather~~ than others.
6 Kate would rather ~~taking~~ take a nap in the morning than in the afternoon.

GET IT RIGHT!

UNITS 1 & 2

Habits in the present

Learners often incorrectly use *use(d) to* when talking about present habits.

✓ *At school, classmates **tend to** discuss the TV programmes which they watched the night before.*
✓ *At school, classmates **will** discuss the TV programmes which they watched the night before.*
✗ *At school, classmates ~~use to~~ discuss the TV programmes which they watched the night before.*
✓ *Kate **is always taking** my pen and not giving it me back!*
✗ *Kate ~~use to take~~ my pen and not giving it me back!*

1 In all of the sentences, *use(d) to* is incorrectly used in order to talk about present habits. Rewrite the sentences using an appropriate form for talking about the present. Try to use a variety of different forms in your answers.

0 Teenagers use to behave quite rebelliously.
Teenagers tend to behave quite rebelliously.
1 People use to form close relationships with friends they have most in common with.
2 My older brother always used to tease me. It's so annoying!
3 My sister often gets on my nerves as she uses to borrow my clothes without asking.
4 Jenny says that her biology teacher always uses to pick on her. It makes her quite upset.
5 Annoyingly, my best friend uses to act rather self-centredly so we sometimes fall out.
6 Elderly people often use to have traditional values.

would rather

Learners often make mistakes with *rather*, failing to use *would*/*'d* when talking about preferences, and using it unnecessarily in other structures.

✓ *They **would rather** watch videos than play football.*
✗ *They ~~rather~~ watch videos than play football.*
✓ *Many boys dream of becoming politicians, whereas girls **would rather** become journalists.*
✗ *Many boys dream of becoming politicians, whereas girls would rather ~~prefer to~~ become journalists.*
✓ *Do you know where I can have a coffee, or **perhaps** a beer?*
✗ *Do you know where I can have a coffee, or perhaps ~~rather~~ a beer?*

2 All of the sentences contain errors with *rather*. Rewrite the sentences correctly.

0 Can we meet a bit later? I rather have a lie-in tomorrow morning if you don't mind.
Can we meet a bit later? I'd rather have a lie-in tomorrow morning if you don't mind.
1 Would you have a siesta now or go to bed early tonight?
2 A study has found that teenagers need more sleep rather than adults.
3 I rather I wasn't such a light sleeper. I tend to wake up several times during the night.
4 Tom would rather not staying up late tonight because he has an exam tomorrow.
5 Some dreams have more meaning rather than others.
6 Kate would rather taking a nap in the morning than in the afternoon.

24

1 In C1 Advanced Reading and Use of English Part 1, candidates have to read a short text with eight numbered spaces, then decide which of the four words provided belongs in each gap. This part of the exam tests understanding of words within a context.

Encourage your students to do the following when they approach this task:

- Skim the text to find out the topic and general meaning.
- Work through the eight questions, reading the whole sentence to choose the correct word to complete each gap.
- After choosing an answer, check the other three options and decide why they are wrong.
- Read the completed text again to make sure it makes sense.

1C 2A 3C 4D 5D 6B 7C 8A

Workbook p25

2 In C1 Advanced Reading and Use of English Part 4, candidates have to read six questions. Each question contains three parts: a lead-in sentence, a key word and a second sentence of which only the beginning and the end are given. Candidates have to fill the gap in the second sentence so that the completed sentence has a similar meaning to the lead-in sentence, using the key word in the form given. This part of the exam tests lexical and grammatical structures and the ability to paraphrase.

TOWARDS C1 Advanced

READING AND USE OF ENGLISH
Part 1: Multiple-choice cloze

→ workbook page 25

1 **For questions 1–8, read the text below and decide which answer (A, B, C or D) best fits each gap. There is an example at the beginning (0).**

0 A over B in C across D into

Anyone who googles the word 'dreams' will come ⁰C thousands of sites that offer to interpret your dreams. However, there is no system of dream interpretation that is ¹... up by scientific research. Consequently, many of these sites offer nothing more than guesswork, and, indeed, the interpretations do not ²... much from those that were around thousands of years ago. So, for example, if you dream that you are being chased, you are supposedly fleeing from uncomfortable ³... . Many people dream that an authority ⁴... asks them for personal identification but they are unable to ⁵... it – this, it is suggested, indicates that you are struggling to ⁶... a feeling of social inadequacy. There is as yet no scientific data to ⁷... these ideas. However, some scientists are gathering reports from dreamers that, in the future, will ⁸... a correlation to be made between dreams and actual waking experiences.

	A	B	C	D
1	held	pushed	backed	grown
2	differ	change	resemble	offer
3	remembrances	remembers	memories	recalls
4	individual	character	officer	figure
5	manufacture	discover	search	produce
6	overdo	overcome	overreact	oversee
7	suppose	discover	support	report
8	allow	make	research	provide

READING AND USE OF ENGLISH
Part 4: Key word transformation

→ workbook page 71

2 **Complete the second sentence so that it has a similar meaning to the first sentence, using the word given. Do not change the word given. You must use between two and five words, including the word given. Here is an example (0).**

0 Thieves broke into our school last night.
BROKEN
Our school *was broken into by* thieves last night.

1 I really think my mother should buy a new car.
TIME
It's ... a new car.

2 My sister sings very well and could become a star.
SUCH
My sister is ... she could become a star.

3 'Have you taken your medicine?' my mother asked me.
IF
My mother asked me ... my medicine.

4 Before, I wanted to go to the museum, but now I don't want to go anymore.
MIND
I have ... going to the museum.

5 Everyone knows that she is considering an attempt at the world record.
KNOWN
She ... considering an attempt at the world record.

6 Please do not stop the work you are doing.
CARRY
Please ... work.

25

Encourage your students to do the following when they approach this task:

- Read the first sentence to understand the meaning.
- Pay attention to any verb in the second sentence as it will often indicate whether to use a singular or plural noun.
- Write only the words that fill the gap.
- Check that the gap has between two and six words, including the key word.
- Check that the key word has been used in the same form as it was given.
- Read the completed sentence again to make sure it makes similar sense to the first one.

1 (about/high) time my mother bought
2 such a good singer
3 if I had taken
4 changed my mind about
5 is (commonly/widely) known to be
6 carry on with your

Workbook p71

1 1 unconventional 2 dream 3 lie-in 4 sleep 5 insecure 6 rebellious 7 nod off 8 nerves 9 oversleep 10 miserable

2 1 got rid of 2 to have 3 Regrettably 4 nowhere near 5 Understandably 6 considerably

3 1 Manchester United are nowhere ~~nearly~~ near as good as Barcelona.
2 My younger brother is always taking my things without asking.
3 I'd prefer it if we ~~leave~~ left half an hour earlier.
4 Sadly, not many of the birds ~~sadly~~ were able to survive.
5 I wish I ~~don't~~ didn't have so much homework.
6 Being the oldest in the family, my brother ~~will~~ tends to be the most traditional / my brother ~~will~~ is the most traditional.

4 1 find; Tell
2 to worry; what
3 consider; do
4 putting; understand

TEST YOURSELF UNITS 1 & 2

VOCABULARY

1 Complete the sentences with the words/phrases in the list. There are four extra words/phrases.

asleep | dream | insecure | lie-in | miserable | nerves | nod off | oversleep | rebellious | sad | sleep | take a nap | traditional | unconventional

1 My aunt's very … . She got married in a bright red dress and with dyed silver hair.
2 I'd love to be someone who designs beds. It would be my … job.
3 I've got nothing to do tomorrow morning, so I'm going to have a … .
4 Don't worry about it. It's nothing to lose … over.
5 He might seem very confident, but underneath he's quite … and worries a lot.
6 My younger sister is quite … and doesn't like being told what to do.
7 I often … when I'm watching TV. It's so annoying as I miss the end of the programme.
8 I wish he'd stop asking so many annoying questions. He's really getting on my … .
9 I'm going to set my alarm for 7 am because I don't want to … .
10 My older brother was really mean when we were younger and he made my life … .

GRAMMAR

2 Complete the sentences with the words/phrases in the list. There are two extra words/phrases.

considerably | get rid of | got rid of | hopefully | nowhere near | regrettably | to have | understandably

1 It's time we … this old TV.
2 Boys tend … more friends than girls when they're younger.
3 … , we had to come home three days early from our holiday.
4 It's … as hot as it was yesterday.
5 … , no one is very happy about the fare increase on the buses.
6 It's … hotter today than it was yesterday.

3 Find and correct the mistake in each sentence.

1 Manchester United are nowhere nearly as good as Barcelona.
2 My younger brother always is taking my things without asking.
3 I'd prefer it if we leave half an hour earlier.
4 Not many of the birds sadly were able to survive.
5 I wish I don't have so much homework.
6 Being the oldest in the family, my brother will be the most traditional.

FUNCTIONAL LANGUAGE

4 Choose the correct options.

1 A I *find / discover* that adding eggs helps make a lighter cake.
B *Inform / Tell* me you haven't done that! I'm allergic to eggs.
2 A Try not *worrying / to worry* too much. It's only a bike.
B But *what / how* about work tomorrow morning? How am I going to get there?
3 A You might want to *think / consider* inviting Dan to your party.
B I plan to invite him. I really *do / plan*. I just haven't seen him in a while.
4 A I'd recommend *to put / putting* your books away. Why don't you watch a bit of TV instead?
B I don't *get / understand*. Are you telling me not to study?

MY SCORE
22–30 | 10–21 | 0–9

26

The Cambridge Life Competencies Framework

Social Responsibilities
Reflecting on roles
Watch this video for a tip on understanding social responsibilities.
Scan the QR code here.

Unit Opener

Warmer

Write on the board three numbers (e.g: your birthday, the year someone important was born, the number of siblings you have…). Explain to students that there is no connection between the numbers. Tell them they have to guess why those numbers are important by asking *yes/no* questions. Once they have guessed, give them a minute to think of their three numbers and play as a whole class with volunteers that want to come out to the board. Alternatively, put them in groups of four to play together. Monitor while they ask questions.

▶ 06 Get TH!NKing

Ask the question. Get students to compare their ideas in groups. Play the video, then ask students for feedback.

1 Elicit as much information as possible from the photo. What does it show? Where would you see these numbers? Does it seem attractive? Ask students what strikes them the most about the photo, and what the photo and the word *lucky* imply? In pairs, ask students to discuss these questions. Share their ideas.

2 Focus on the photo and the title of the unit. Ask students, in pairs or threes, to make a list of situations in which numbers and luck are connected (e.g. lottery, bingo, numerology, lucky number). Write all the possible options on the board.

3 LUCKY FOR SOME?

Get TH!NKING
Watch the video and think: how lucky are you?

OBJECTIVES

FUNCTIONS: giving encouragement to someone who's feeling nervous

GRAMMAR: mixed conditionals (review); alternatives to *if*

VOCABULARY: phrasal verbs; expressions with *luck*

Work in pairs. Look at the photo and discuss the questions.

1 Where would you see these numbers?
2 How can numbers be (un)lucky?
3 Is winning a lot of money always lucky? Why/Why not?

27

3 Ask students to give examples of situations in which a lot of money can be won (e.g. winning the lottery, betting, competitions on TV). Then ask them whether it's always lucky to win money and elicit any problems that could emerge from winning money (e.g. relatives and friends asking you for money, feeling insecure about what to do with the money, making bad choices with the money and consequently losing it).

Objectives

Functions Giving encouragement to someone who's feeling nervous
Grammar Mixed conditionals (review); alternatives to *if*
Vocabulary Phrasal verbs; expressions with *luck*;
WordWise: Expressions with *over*
Values How do we feel about luck?
Life Competencies Not worrying too much

Resources for this unit

All available online

Videos
- Get **TH!NK**ing: *How lucky are you?*
- Grammar video!: Alternatives to *if*
- Vlog: Not worrying too much

Tests
- Unit, extension and skills test 3
- End of term test 1

Worksheets
- Grammar and vocabulary: Basic, Standard and Extension Worksheets
- Project: As luck would have it
- Communication: Lucky breaks
- Grammar presentation: Mixed conditionals
- Literature Worksheets: *Twelfth Night*
- Get **TH!NK**ing, Grammar video! and Life Lessons video Worksheets

Warmer

Ask students: *Are you a lucky person? Do you know anybody who is lucky? What is the luckiest thing that has ever happened to you?* Students discuss the questions in small groups and decide who the luckiest person in their group is. Listen to some of their answers in open class as feedback.

1 Give a couple of your own suggestions before students do the exercise.

2 Tell students not to worry about unknown words, but to focus on getting an overall understanding of the article and on completing the exercise.
1 A 2 C 3 B
2 Molly thinks she was lucky that no one answered the phone when she tried to cancel her job interview, as if they had, she would not be working at the smaller school now.
Suzanne thinks she was lucky that she broke her ankle while rock climbing as she believes that if she had not fallen over, she would not have met her husband.
Edwin thinks he was lucky that he was outside in the storm, as being struck by lightning helped him to regain his sight and hearing.

3 🔊 **3.01** Complete question 1 as a class. Encourage students to think about the correct answer to the false statements.
1 T 2 F (The interview there went well and the next day they phoned to offer me a job.) 3 F (The interview there went well …) 4 F (The sun was shining and it was a beautiful day.) 5 T 6 T 7 F (When it began to rain heavily, he sheltered under a tree.) 8 T

4 Monitor and help with any difficulties, but as this is a fluency activity, do not interrupt to correct errors unless they impede communication.
1–3 Students' own answers
4 'Miracles do happen' is a true story.

A

B

C

READING

1 SPEAKING **Look at the photos. For each one:**
1 describe what you think is happening/has happened.
2 say what might happen next.
3 say how each person could possibly be unlucky.
4 say how each person could possibly be lucky.

2 **Read the magazine article quickly.**
1 Match the stories (1–3) to the photos.
2 How does each person think they were lucky?

3 🔊 3.01 **Read the text again and listen. Are the statements T (true) or F (false)?**
1 The large school was Molly's first choice.
2 Molly's interview at the large school was unsuccessful.
3 Molly was not very good at the interview as she was too nervous.
4 It was dark, and Suzanne fell over and hurt her ankle.
5 Suzanne would not have met her husband if she had not broken her ankle.
6 Edwin had lost his sight in a bad accident a few years earlier.
7 Edwin went to stand under the tree to avoid being hit by lightning.
8 After Edwin had had a rest in bed, he could see again.

4 SPEAKING **Work in pairs and discuss the questions.**
1 In your opinion, who was the luckiest person: Molly, Suzanne or Edwin? Who was the least lucky?
2 Which story do you like the most/least? Why? Compare with a partner.
3 Can you think of any other blessings in disguise that you or people you know have experienced?
4 One of these stories is a true story. Which one do you think it is?

28

5 Before students do the task, get them to cover the dictionary definition and ask: *Who do you think is better at driving: women or men?* Listen to some of their answers as a class.
1 It doesn't say; it just says that women are not worse drivers than men.
2 Students' own answers

6 If students have access to the internet, ask them to search for the origin of these widely held beliefs and make notes on their findings.
1 personal 2 widely held
3 widely held 4 widely held
5 personal 6 personal

7 At the end of the exercise, listen to some of the students' ideas and encourage open-class discussion.

Homework

Ask students to write a short text about a lucky moment that has happened to them or to someone they know. If they haven't had any, or the subject is too personal, they can interview members of their family or friends or invent some ideas. As a follow-up, students can present their story to the class in the next lesson. After each presentation, encourage the rest of the class to ask questions and finally hold a class vote to decide which was the luckiest.

Culture notes

Malham Cove in the Yorkshire Dales, UK, is an 80-metre-high curving cliff of white limestone created as glaciers moved over the landscape over the last one and a half million years. The glacial water originally ran over the top as a massive waterfall but today, the water flows underground, leaving a sheer rock face which is popular with climbers.

Edwin Robinson, a truck driver from Falmouth, Maine in the US, was blinded by a car accident in 1971. In 1980, he claimed that his sight was restored after he was struck by lightning.

Social Responsibilities
Showing intercultural awareness
Appreciates their own culture and its value.

Critical TH!NKing
Evaluating ideas and arguments
Gives reasons for an arguments plausibility.

Blessings in disguise

1 Just a phone call away

During my last year at college, just over two years ago, I started to apply for teaching jobs. Two schools in my home town offered me an interview. The first was a large school with 1,200 pupils and the second was a smaller one with 500 pupils. I really wanted to work at the large school because I thought it was a better place overall. The interview there went well and the next day they phoned to offer me a job. Of course, I accepted their job offer immediately. I quickly phoned the other school to turn down the interview but no one answered the phone. The next morning, I got a phone call from the headteacher of the large school. She said that there was no longer a vacancy there as the teacher had decided to stay on and didn't want to leave after all. I went to the job interview at the small school and I got the job. I still work there and I love it, so it all worked out in the end. If somebody had picked up the phone that afternoon, I would not have got this wonderful job. ***Molly***

2 Every cloud has a silver lining

It was my 21st birthday. I wanted to do something different – something that I would remember for the rest of my life, so I arranged to go rock climbing with some friends. We went to Malham Cove in the Yorkshire Dales. The sun was shining and it was a beautiful day. When we set off, we were all laughing and chatting. Then suddenly, I fell over. I landed badly on my ankle and I couldn't walk. I needed to go to hospital, but my friends and I didn't have a car. Another climber at the cove, James, had a car. 'I'll give you a lift to the hospital,' he said, and so my friends helped me to the car and we set off for the hospital. This was not how I wanted to spend my birthday! At the hospital, we learned that my ankle was broken. That evening, we had my birthday party as planned and James stayed for that, too. In the end it was a very special day because it was the day that James and I met. If I had not fallen over, I would not have met James. A year later we got married. ***Suzanne***

3 Miracles do happen

I read an amazing story about an elderly man who was blind and deaf. His name was Edwin Robinson, and he had lost his sight in a very serious accident. Then, one fateful night, nine years after his accident, there was a terrible thunderstorm. He was wandering around outside in the field near his house looking for his hen, and swinging his white metal stick as he walked along. When it began to rain heavily, he sheltered under a tree. Seconds later, he was struck by lightning and fell to the ground. For twenty minutes, he lay there unconscious. When he came to, he stumbled back to the house. Understandably, he felt very tired, so he went to bed for a nap. When he woke up that evening, he discovered that he could see and hear again. It was unbelievable! When his wife came into the room, he said, 'I can see you! I can see the house. I can read. If the hen didn't run away all the time, I wouldn't have been out in that storm!' It was incredible. ***Scott***

Train to TH!NK

Behaviour based on myths rather than facts

Sometimes we change our behaviour or make a decision because of a myth or false belief. These myths can range from culturally shared false beliefs, such as 'breaking a mirror means bad luck' to more personal ones, such as 'I wear my lucky T-shirt to every football match that my team plays in'.

Most of us are aware that such behaviour has no actual influence on the outcome of an event, but despite this, we still act as if the false belief we have is fact.

5 SPEAKING **Work in pairs. Read this dictionary definition of a myth and answer the questions.**

myth *noun* (FALSE IDEA)
a commonly believed but false idea:
Statistics disprove the myth that women are worse drivers than men.

1 According to the dictionary entry, who are worse at driving: women or men?
2 If someone believes women are worse drivers than men, how might this affect their behaviour?

6 **Which of these myths do you feel are personal beliefs and which are widely held ones?**
1 I always put my left leg into the bath first.
2 If I spill salt accidentally, I throw it over my shoulder and make a wish.
3 I never walk under a ladder. It brings bad luck.
4 I never travel on Friday 13th. It's an unlucky day.
5 I tap my phone three times before I turn it on.
6 I always use the same pen to do my exams.

7 SPEAKING **Discuss in pairs. Which myths do you or people you know have? How do these myths affect your/their behaviour?**

Activity idea Extension

Write the following vocabulary on the board:

black car three-legged dog last piece of chocolate money on the floor blind man on Sunday red rose ten pigeons

Ask students to work individually to invent three myths using the vocabulary. For example, *if you see a three-legged dog, say 'woof' three times and you will be rich.*

When students have completed their myths, divide the class into small groups for students to share their myths and decide which two sound the most believable.

TH!NK more

Worksheets
Project As luck would have it
Communication Lucky breaks
Get TH!NKing *How lucky are you?*

Warmer

To revise past participles, give students a verb in the infinitive and ask students to say the past tense to get a point and the past participle to get another point. Repeat with two or three different verbs and then get students to play 'past forms tennis'. In pairs, one student says an infinitive verb and the other replies with the correct past form and past participle as quickly as possible.

1 Ask students to try to match the sentence halves before checking on page 29.
1 b 2 a 3 c
RULE: 1 present 2 past

Pronunciation
Unstressed words in connected speech

Student's Book p137

2 1 hadn't lived; wouldn't speak
2 wouldn't be; hadn't learned
3 hadn't eaten; I'd be
4 wasn't always; wouldn't have got
5 would still be; hadn't said
6 was; would have been chosen

3 Encourage students to answer in full sentences. If you're short on time, set this exercise for homework.
1 I wouldn't know how to play the game if my friend hadn't explained it to me yesterday.
2 If I had some money, I would have bought a present for my mum.
3 If my sister hadn't had an accident, she wouldn't be in hospital.
4 If he wasn't a very talented tennis player, he wouldn't have won four tournaments last year.
5 If I hadn't missed the train, I'd (already) be in Manchester now.

4 Give an example of your own to get students started.

Workbook p28

TH!NK more

Workbook
Grammar p28, Ex.1–4
Vocabulary p30, Ex.1–2
Vocabulary Extra p31, Ex.1–2
Pronunciation p118

Worksheets
Grammar presentation Mixed conditionals
Grammar Worksheets 3
Vocabulary Worksheets 3

GRAMMAR
Mixed conditionals (review)

1 Match the beginnings and endings of these sentences from the article. Then complete the rule with *present* and *past*.

1 If somebody had picked up the phone that afternoon,
2 If I had not fallen over,
3 If the hen didn't run away all the time,

a I would not have met James.
b I would not have got this wonderful job.
c I wouldn't have been out in that storm.

RULE:
Mixed conditionals are used:
- to connect an imaginary past (*had* + past participle) with a ¹... result (*would* + infinitive) as in sentences 1 and 2.
- to connect a hypothetical present (past simple) with a ²... result (*would have* + past participle) as in sentence 3.

PRONUNCIATION
Unstressed words in connected speech
Go to page 137.

2 Choose the correct options.

1 My cousin lived in Chicago for five years as a child. If she *didn't live / hadn't lived* there, she *wouldn't speak / wouldn't have spoken* English as well as she does.
2 Yo-Yo Ma plays the cello exceptionally well. He *wouldn't be / wouldn't have been* as famous as he is if he *didn't learn / hadn't learned* from such a young age.
3 I don't feel very well. If I *hadn't eaten / didn't eat* two bars of chocolate, *I'd be / I'd have been* OK now.
4 I'm never on time. If I *wasn't always / hadn't always been* late, I *wouldn't get / wouldn't have got* in trouble with the teacher yesterday.
5 She was really rude to me. We *would still be / would still have been* friends now if she *didn't say / hadn't said* those things.
6 I'm not very good at football. If I *was / had been* a better player, I'm sure I *would have been chosen / would be chosen* for the school team last week!

3 Rewrite the sentences using a mixed conditional structure.

0 I'm tired today because I didn't sleep well last night.
If I'd slept well last night, I wouldn't be tired today.
1 I know how to play the game. My friend explained it to me yesterday.
2 I haven't got any money. I didn't buy a present for my mum.
3 My sister had an accident. She's in hospital.
4 He's a very talented tennis player. He won four tournaments last year.
5 I missed the train. I'm not in Manchester yet.

4 WRITING **Write two mixed conditional sentences about yourself or someone you know.**

1 If … , I wouldn't be here now.
2 … if I'd had a bit more luck.

→ workbook page 28

VOCABULARY
Phrasal verbs

5 Replace the words in bold with phrasal verbs from the list in the correct form.

come to | fall over | pick up
run away | set off | stay on
turn back | turn down | work out

1 Everything **went well** in the end and I was happy.
2 I couldn't go on. It was too cold and dark so I **went back home**.
3 The dog **escaped** and I found him two days later.
4 I **continued** at university for another year.
5 I fainted, and when I **became conscious again**, the horse had gone.
6 I didn't want the job so I **didn't accept** their offer.
7 I **slipped** and broke my arm.
8 We **left** at six o'clock in the morning. It was still dark.
9 If only she had **answered** the phone this morning, we wouldn't have missed each other.

6 SPEAKING **Work in pairs and answer the questions.**

1 Have you ever set off for a trip and forgotten something?
2 Have you ever fallen over and broken an arm or a leg? How did it happen?
3 Have you ever turned down an invitation to a party and regretted it later? What happened?

7 WRITING **Use phrasal verbs from Exercise 5 to write two more questions for your partner.**

8 SPEAKING **Work in pairs. Ask and answer your questions.**

→ workbook page 30

Get it Right!
Conditionals

Student's Book p46

5 Do the first question with the class as an example.
1 worked out 2 turned back
3 ran away 4 stayed on 5 came to
6 turned down 7 fell over
8 set off 9 picked up

6 Monitor to encourage students to use the phrasal verbs in their answers and to check they are being used correctly.

7 If you want to stretch students, ask them to use the verbs they are least comfortable with, or tell them which verbs you would like them to write questions with.

8 To maximise interaction, you could set this up as a mingle activity with students asking their questions to a number of different students.

Workbook p30

Activity idea Fast finishers

Ask students to write alternative *would* clauses for sentences 1–5 in Exercise 3.

Activity idea Mixed-ability

In Exercise 6, stronger students can work individually to write their answers. They could also be asked to expand on their answers.

9 Put a copy of the six pictures up on the board and do the exercise as a class before students open their books. Nominate individuals to name the three people (Charles Dickens, Roald Dahl, Richard Gasquet). Write a few of their ideas on the board, but do not comment at this stage.

10 3.03
Charles Dickens used a compass so that he could always face north while he slept and wrote.
Roald Dahl was a pilot during the Second World War.
Richard Gasquet asks to use the same tennis ball for the next game if he wins a point.

11 3.03
1 Charles Dickens 2 Richard Gasquet 3 Roald Dahl

12 3.03
1 compass 2 slept 3 pilot 4 in the newspaper 5 the same ball

13 Encourage students to guess meaning from context if they are not sure. If they are still unclear, allow them to use a dictionary for clarification.
Students' own answers

Workbook p30

14 Monitor and answer any questions about vocabulary, but as this is a fluency practice activity, do not interrupt the conversations unless inaccuracy hinders comprehension.

15 Allow students six to eight minutes to make notes. Encourage them to use a variety of adjectives.

16 Encourage students to give reasons for their choices and to use conditional sentences in their discussions if possible.

Homework

Ask students to research someone from around the world who has had some good luck. As a follow-up, students can present this person to the class in the next lesson.

Emotional Development
Identifying and understanding emotions
Discusses what makes them feel different emotions.

LISTENING

9 Can you name the people in the photos above? What's the connection between the famous people and the objects?

10 3.03 Listen and check your ideas from Exercise 9.

11 3.03 Listen again to Holly, Nick and Antony and answer the questions.
1 Who carried a compass with him everywhere?
2 Who likes to use a winning ball?
3 Whose plane crash resulted in him finding a new career?

12 3.03 Listen again. Complete each sentence with between one and three words.
1 When Charles Dickens travelled anywhere, he took a ... with him.
2 Charles Dickens always ... facing north.
3 Roald Dahl was a ... when his plane crashed.
4 The famous writer C.S. Forester published Roald Dahl's story ... .
5 If Richard Gasquet wins a point, he wants to use ... again.

VOCABULARY
Expressions with *luck*

13 SPEAKING **Read the sentences. What do the underlined phrases mean? Discuss in pairs.**
1 A Your pen must have broken. You've got ink all over your shirt.
B Oh no! I've got an interview this afternoon! It's <u>just my luck</u>.
2 He always wears those shoes when he plays. He thinks they <u>bring him luck</u>.
3 A Does the number 21 bus stop here?
B Yes – and <u>you're in luck</u>. Look, there's one coming now.
4 A I missed the last train by 15 seconds!
B Oh, <u>bad luck</u>. What did you do – walk home?
5 A I failed my driving test.
B Oh, sorry to hear that. <u>Better luck next time</u>.
6 A Did you get wet on your walk?
B No! <u>As luck would have it</u>, we got home just before the rain started.
7 A It was my first ever go at one of those competitions, and I won!
B Huh! <u>Beginner's luck</u>.
8 A Dad's agreed to drive me to football practice. I think I'll ask him if he can pick me up, too. I don't feel like walking home.
B That might be <u>pushing your luck</u>. He'll be watching TV later.

→ workbook page 30

SPEAKING

14 Work in pairs and answer the questions.
1 Have you ever had bad luck that turned into good luck? When/How?
2 Do you or does anyone you know have any things that they do to bring them good luck?
3 Give an example of a time when you've pushed your luck.

TH!NK values
How do we feel about luck?

15 Make notes on how you'd feel in each of these situations.
1 You know someone who, in the past, said things about you that you didn't like. You hear that they had some bad luck – they slipped and broke their right arm just before an important exam.
2 You hear that someone you like very much has just won a competition and the prize is a week's holiday in a wonderful place.
3 You take a multiple-choice test. You don't know many of the answers at all but you guess them. You discover that you got a score of 17 out of 20.

16 SPEAKING **Work in pairs. Compare your answers to Exercise 15 and then discuss these questions.**
1 What would be the best response to each situation?
2 Is this a true reflection of how you really feel?
3 What, if anything, would be an inappropriate response?

Culture notes

Charles Dickens was a moralist, satirist and social reformer and is probably the best-known English novelist of the Victorian era. His novels criticise the injustices of the time, especially the brutal treatment of the poor.

Roald Dahl was a spy, fighter pilot, medical inventor and author from Wales. He is best known for his world-famous children's books.

Richard Gasquet is a French professional tennis player who reached the 2007 and 2015 semi-finals of the Wimbledon Championships and the semi-finals of the 2013 US Open.

Emotional Development
Empathy and relationship skills
Shows understanding of other people's perspectives and feelings.

TH!NK more

Workbook
Listening p34, Ex.1–2
Vocabulary p30, Ex.3–4

Worksheets
Vocabulary Worksheets 3

Reading

Warmer

Write on the board: *gobbledygook*; *berserk*; *flabbergasted*. Ask: *What do you think the words mean? What part of speech are they?* In pairs, students discuss, then feed back as a class. Give definitions and ask students to match to the words. (*gobbledygook* – language with no meaning, perhaps because it is too technical (n); *berserk* (adj) – out of control with anger or excitement; *flabbergasted* (adj) – very surprised). Do students know any other strange English words?

1 Before students read the blog, write *serendipity* on the board and ask students to discuss what they think it means. Write their ideas on the board but do not comment.

2 Set a two-minute time limit to encourage students to read quickly and to focus on gist rather than specific information.
the fact of finding something interesting, pleasant or valuable by chance.

3 **3.04 Check/clarify:** *fortuitous, eradicate.*
Encourage students to underline key text that supports their answers.
1 He was hoping to take a photograph of a heron.
2 It also had a rare woodpecker in it.
3 They feel that it is very difficult to define and translate.
4 The blog mentions the discovery that laughing gas could be used as an anaesthetic.
5 The blog cites the example of William Perkin discovering the colour purple when he was looking for a cure for malaria.
6 The writer gives the example of her friend's discovery of a story that she could write an article about when visiting a café.

4 At the end of the exercise, listen to some of the students' ideas and encourage open-class discussion.
1 ✗ 2 ✓ 3 ✓

READING

1 **Look at the title of the blog. Have you ever seen this word before? What do you think it means?**

2 **Read the blog quickly to check your ideas from Exercise 1.**

3 3.04 **Read and listen to the blog again and answer the questions.**
1 What was the wildlife photographer hoping to do?
2 What was lucky about the photo he took?
3 How do translators feel about the word 'serendipity'?
4 What example is mentioned of serendipity in science?
5 What example is given of serendipity in history?
6 What example of serendipity does the writer give from her own experience?

4 **Are these things examples of serendipity or not? Why/Why not? Compare your answers with a partner.**
1 You've lost a ring at home. You look everywhere for it. Then a family member comes in and says: 'Look! I found your ring in the car.'
2 A footballer tries to kick the ball to score a goal. He kicks it very badly, but accidentally passes it to another player in his team, who scores.
3 You're looking for a book in your room. You look on a shelf and see a DVD that you thought you'd lost.

5 SPEAKING **Work in pairs. Discuss your answers to the questions.**
1 How would you translate the word 'serendipity' into your language?
2 Do you know of any examples of serendipity from a film/book/TV show?
3 Have you experienced serendipity in your own life (or has someone you know)?

32

Janet's 'odd word' blog

This week: 'serendipity'

Serendipity

A wildlife photographer was waiting, hoping to get a shot of a relatively rare bird, a particular kind of heron. He'd waited several frustrating hours with no luck at all. He needed a photo soon, otherwise it would be too dark and he would have to come back the next day and start all over again. Suddenly, to his delight, a heron settled on a branch right in front of him. He raised his camera, focused in and took the shot just before the heron flew away. Feeling particularly pleased with himself, the photographer looked at the image. To his astonishment, he saw that behind the heron, his photograph had also captured a very, very rare woodpecker flying past. He hadn't seen it, but without even trying, he'd photographed an even rarer bird than the one he was aiming for.

This is an example of serendipity – a word which, according to some translators, is among the ten most difficult English words to define and translate. It means something like 'the fact of finding interesting or valuable things by chance'. The key thing is that if you come across something fortuitous by chance, it's serendipity, provided that you weren't consciously trying to find that thing at the time.

Cases of serendipity can be found in numerous fields, such as science. Back in the 1800s, a man called Horace Wells was at a demonstration of laughing gas (ether and nitrous oxide). After being given the gas, the patient started laughing, as expected. But then he suddenly fell over and cut his leg rather badly. To everyone's surprise, the man reported that he couldn't feel any pain. Wells hadn't been looking for it, but he'd made a medical discovery – certain gases reduce and can even almost eradicate pain. Had Wells not been there that night, anaesthesia might have taken longer to be discovered.

History offers further examples. In 1856, 18-year-old William Perkin wanted to make a drug form of quinine to cure malaria. Instead, he discovered the colour purple. He failed to make quinine and instead got a thick brown liquid in the bottom of the beaker. However, when he washed the beaker with alcohol, the brown liquid turned into a beautiful bright purple. William forgot about malaria and made a lot of money from his new purple dye instead. He was looking for one thing and found another.

Most of us can probably think of at least one example of serendipity in our own lives. A friend of mine was trying to come up with an idea for an online article but got completely stuck. Frustrated, she decided to go out to a local café. She sat there and as she was sipping her coffee, she heard two people talking behind her. A man was telling a story that sounded so unbelievable that she knew it had to be true. She asked the people if she could interview them for the article – unless she got their permission, she wouldn't be able to use their story. They agreed and her article turned out to be one of the top trending articles of the week.

5 Give students time to reflect and make notes on their answers before speaking.

Culture notes

Horace Wells, born 1815, was an American dentist who pioneered the use of nitrous oxide as surgical anaesthesia. He is widely recognised as the discoverer of anaesthetic gases.

William Perkin, born 1838, was a British chemist from London. At the age of 15 he enrolled at the Royal College of Chemistry, publishing his first research paper a year later. Prior to his discovery of purple dye, Tyrian purple was used to produce purple clothes. It was made from the glandular mucus of a species of carnivorous sea snail and tens of thousands of snails were needed to make a useful amount of dye. As a result, purple clothing was linked with emperors, monarchs and great prestige, and for most people, purple was unaffordable. Perkin's discovery made it much more accessible.

TH!NK more

Workbook
Reading p32, Ex.1–4

Grammar; WordWise; Writing

▶ 08 Grammar video! Alternatives to *if*

6 Ask students to try to answer the questions from memory before checking on page 32.
1 otherwise 2 provided 3 Unless

7 Point out that *imagine* and *suppose* are used to introduce questions.
1 as long as 2 Suppose 3 Imagine
RULE: 1 as long as 2 otherwise 3 unless 4 suppose

8 During feedback, check understanding by asking students to rephrase the sentences using *if*.
1 as long as 2 Imagine 3 unless 4 otherwise

9 If you're short on time, set this exercise for homework.
1 I always enjoy eating out in restaurants as long as the food's good.
2 I never work at the weekend unless I have to.
3 Everyone deserves some good luck. Otherwise, it isn't fair.
4 I don't mind working hard provided that I get good exam results.

Workbook p29

10 Ask students to work with a partner and complete the exercise.
1 fell over 2 Just over 3 all over 4 overall 5 all over again

11 During whole-class feedback, work on pronunciation and intonation of the sentences.
1 overall 2 all over again 3 fell over 4 just over 5 all over

Workbook p30

12–13 The notes for this exercise can be done in class and the writing set for homework. Give students time to make some notes and then ask them to tell their stories to a partner. Ask students to give each other feedback. They should say how it could be made more interesting and point out any important elements that should be included. Give students time to revise their notes accordingly so that they are prepared for the main writing as homework.

Activity idea Fast finishers

Ask students to rewrite sentences 1–4 in Exercise 8 using different alternatives to *if*.

GRAMMAR
Alternatives to *if*

Grammar video ▶08

6 **Complete the sentences from the blog on page 32.**

1 He needed a photo soon, … it would be too dark.
2 If you come across something fortuitous by chance, it's serendipity, … that you weren't consciously trying to find that thing at the time.
3 … she got their permission, she wouldn't be able to use their story.

7 **Read these sentences. Which word(s) could be replaced with *if*? Then complete the rule with *unless, otherwise, as long as* and *suppose*.**

1 You can borrow it as long as you're careful with it.
2 Suppose you were on holiday – what would you be doing now?
3 Imagine you could live anywhere in the world – where would you live?

> **RULE:** There are many alternatives to *if*, including *provided that, as long as, unless, otherwise, suppose* and *imagine*.
> - We use *provided that* and [1]… in the same way as *if*, but they make the main clause even more dependent on the condition.
> - The word [2]… is used after an order or suggestion to indicate what the result will be if the order or suggestion isn't followed.
> - When we use the word [3]… instead of *if*, it gives the verb that follows a negative meaning.
> - *Imagine* and [4]… are often followed by a second or third conditional clause.

8 **Choose the correct options.**

1 Everything will be fine *as long as / suppose / unless* you're very careful.
2 *Imagine / Provided that / Unless* you could meet someone famous – who would you choose?
3 We'll arrive before eleven o'clock *provided that / unless / otherwise* the traffic is bad.
4 Go to bed early, *unless / as long as / otherwise* you'll be tired tomorrow.

9 **Rewrite the sentences using the word in brackets.**

1 I always enjoy eating out in restaurants if the food's good. (as long as)
2 I never work at the weekend if I don't have to. (unless)
3 Everyone deserves some good luck. If not, it isn't fair. (otherwise)
4 I don't mind working hard if I get good exam results. (provided that)

→ workbook page 29

WordWise
Expressions with *over*

10 **Complete these sentences from the unit with words and phrases from the list.**

all over | all over again | fell over | just over | overall

1 But then he suddenly … and cut his leg rather badly.
2 … two years ago, I started to apply for teaching jobs.
3 Your pen must have broken. You've got ink … your shirt.
4 I really wanted to work at the large school because I thought it was a better place … .
5 He would have to come back the next day and start … .

11 **Choose the correct options.**

1 It rained a bit, but we had a good weekend *overall / all over.*
2 We weren't listening, so the teacher had to tell us *overall / all over again.*
3 It was really windy last night and a lot of trees *all over / fell over.*
4 It took us *just over / all over* five hours to drive home.
5 Look at this mess! There are books and clothes *all over / just over* the floor.

→ workbook page 30

WRITING
A story

12 PLAN **You are going to write a story. It must begin or end with this sentence:**

It was the luckiest day of my life.

1 Decide whether to base this on a true story or an invented one. Make sure there's luck involved.
2 Think about and make notes on the following:
- the background (where you were, what was happening, etc). Use narrative tenses.
- how the event proved to be lucky and changed things in your life. Try to use conditionals and some of the 'luck' vocabulary in the unit.

13 PRODUCE **Write your story (250–300 words).**

Language note

Point out to students that we use *provided that* and *as long as* when the result of the sentence is positive.

Provided that/As long as it is sunny, we will go to the beach.

Provided that/As long as you study hard, you will pass the exam.

We cannot follow *provided/as long as* with a negative outcome.

~~*Provided that/As long as it rains, we won't go to the beach.*~~

Homework

You could set the writing task for homework. As a follow-up in the next lesson, ask students to exchange their stories with another student for them to read and make comments and suggestions.

TH!NK more

Practice Extra
Unit 3 Practise it!

Workbook
Grammar p29, Ex.5–7
Vocabulary Extra p31, Ex.1–3
WordWise p30, Ex.5

Worksheets
Grammar Worksheets 3
Vocabulary Worksheets 3
Grammar video! Alternatives to *if*

Developing Speaking; Phrases for fluency; Functions

Warmer

Divide the board into two columns. Write the following lucky charms on one side and the country or region from which they come on the other, but mixed up. In pairs, give students four minutes to match the lucky charms with the country:

Dala horse (Sweden), *cornicello* (Italy), *dreamcatcher* (US), *gris-gris* (Ghana), *Hamsa* (North Africa/ Middle East), *Jin Chan: golden toad* (China), *maneki-neko: waving cat* (Japan), *nazar boncuğu: to protect against the evil eye* (Turkey), *worry dolls* (Guatemala), *acorns* (England), *shamrock* (Ireland).

Can students think of any others?

1 **3.05** Tell students to cover the dialogue and discuss the questions in pairs before listening.
Jo is learning to drive a car and her dad is helping her.
The shamrock is a lucky charm.

2 **3.05** To encourage speed-reading, do this as a race and ask students to find the expressions as quickly as possible.
1 Jo's test is on Saturday. It's important for her because she wants the freedom of driving a car while she's at university.
2 Her father drove 35 miles an hour in a 30-mile-an-hour zone for two minutes.
3 The charm may keep her calm and she has nothing to lose.

3 At the end of the exercise, encourage open-class discussion.
Dad says them all.
Students' own answers

4 During feedback, point out the use of question marks and exclamation marks and say the expressions for students to repeat. Check pronunciation and intonation.
1 now and again
2 What have you got to lose; assuming
3 After all
4 we'll sort something out
5 that is

DEVELOPING SPEAKING

1 3.05 **Look at the photos. What do you think the girl and the man are doing? What do you know about the shamrock? Read, listen and check your ideas.**

Jo: Dad, what am I going to do? I've got my driving test on Saturday and I'm still making mistakes. I so want to get my licence and I'm going to fail, I know I am!
Dad: Calm down, Jo! I'm sure you'll be fine. After all, everyone makes mistakes now and again.
Jo: But Dad, I can't afford to fail. If I go off to university without a driving licence, then I won't have as much freedom as I hoped!
Dad: Oh, we'll sort something out. And like I said, you'll be fine ... assuming the examiner isn't concentrating at the time.
Jo: What?
Dad: I'm joking, Jo. Try not to worry so much! You can pass even if you make a mistake.
Jo: Oh? So how do you know that?
Dad: Experience. When I did my test, I did 35 miles an hour in a 30-mile-an-hour zone for about two minutes. Luckily, the examiner didn't notice! I think it was my lucky shamrock that did it.
Jo: Your lucky shamrock? I didn't know you had something like that, Dad.
Dad: Well, kind of, you know. You can take it on Saturday. If you want to borrow it, that is.
Jo: I don't think a lucky charm is going to make a difference. Either I drive well enough to pass or I don't.
Dad: But Jo, what have you got to lose? I think having the shamrock will help you keep calm. It certainly won't do you any harm.
Jo: Maybe you're right. OK, I'll take it along. Now, can we do another ten minutes' practice, please?

2 3.05 **Read and listen to the dialogue again and answer the questions.**
1 When is Jo's test and why is it important for her?
2 What mistake did her father make in his test?
3 Why does Jo agree to take the charm with her?

Phrases for fluency

3 **Find these expressions in the dialogue. Who says them? How do you say them in your language?**
1 After all
2 now and again
3 we'll sort something out
4 assuming ...
5 ..., that is
6 What have you got to lose?

4 **Use the expressions in Exercise 3 to complete the dialogues.**
1 A Do you go there very often?
B No, only ... .
2 A You should ask Sarah to go to the cinema with you. ... ?
B Well, nothing I guess, ... I ask her and she says yes!
3 A Your Spanish is amazing!
B Not really. ... , my mum is from Peru.
4 A You've invited 50 people to the party? We can't provide food for 50 people!
B Oh, don't worry – ... !
5 A Do you want to watch that film on TV?
B Yes – if it's OK with you, ...

FUNCTIONS
Giving encouragement to someone who's feeling nervous

5 **Complete what Jo's father says when Jo tells him she thinks she'll fail her test.**
Dad: '... , Jo! I'm sure you'll ... .'

6 **Which of these expressions could also be used to give someone encouragement when they're feeling nervous?**
- You've got this!
- What a nightmare!
- Take a deep breath.
- I've got my fingers crossed for you.

7 ROLE PLAY **Work in pairs.**
Student A: Tell student B something that you feel nervous about.
Student B: Give encouragement to student A using and expanding on the expressions in Exercises 5 and 6.
Then switch roles. Who did the best job of encouraging their partner?
Possible topics:
- you're about to sing in front of the whole school
- you're about to take a university entrance exam
- you're about to play in a crucial football or basketball match.

34

5 Calm down; be fine

6 During feedback, drill the phrases, exaggerating slightly, and encourage students to use wide-ranging intonation.
You've got this!; Take a deep breath.; I've got my fingers crossed for you.

7 Allow students six to eight minutes to prepare their role plays. Monitor to make sure students sound sympathetic and encourage them to develop the conversations. This activity can work as a mingle with students swapping partners after each exchange.

Activity idea Extension

Disappearing sentences: write the dialogues from Exercise 4 on the board or project them on the IWB. Make A/B pairs. Students practise the dialogues in their pairs. Cover a small section of the dialogue, beginning from the right-hand side of the screen or board. Students repeat the dialogues trying to remember the whole thing, including the parts they can no longer see. Cover more and more of the dialogue, with students practising at each stage, until eventually nothing is left on the board. Ask for volunteers to perform for the class or have all As and all Bs perform in unison.

TH!NK more

Workbook
Phrases for fluency p34

Life Competencies

Warmer

Write *worried* on the board and ask students to think of synonyms *(anxious, stressed, apprehensive, angst-ridden, troubled, unsettled, fretful)*. Ask students to give themselves a mark for their general level of worry between 0 and 10. Does their ability to remain unworried change depending on the situation?

▶ 09 Life Lessons: Not worrying too much

1 ▶ **09** Ask students to compare their ideas with a partner.
Mr Harrison and her maths exam

2 ▶ **09** Ask students to try to answer the questions from memory before watching the video again to check.
Clothes – What clothes to wear to school, what clothes to wear to the party, what clothes to wear for the vlog, what clothes to wear to go to town.
Social media – should I really post that? Why on earth did I post that? Why are none of my friends responding to me? Why did I ever even start this silly social media account?
The future – What am I going to do with my life? What do I want to be in this world? Will there even be a world for me to do anything in?

3 After a few minutes, invite students' reactions in open class prompting them to try to explain their answers.

4 As a follow-up, students can discuss the statements as a class and come up with a definitive list.

5 Give students three or four minutes to think about their answers. Encourage them to make notes.

6 Monitor and prompt students to keep talking, but as this is a fluency activity, do not interrupt to correct mistakes. While monitoring, note down any common errors to review together at the end.

LIFE COMPETENCIES

We all worry sometimes. We worry about what's happening now, or what might happen in the future, or even about things we've done in the past. But it's important not to let worry dominate our lives.

1 ▶ 09 Watch the vlog. What is Annie's biggest worry?

2 ▶ 09 Watch the vlog again. Make notes about what Annie says under the headings.

My worries
Clothes –
Social media –
The future –

3 SPEAKING Work in pairs. What advice would you give Annie?

4 SPEAKING Read the blog post. Work in pairs or small groups. Discuss which of the quotes in the blog you think:

- is most useful.
- is least useful.
- is the funniest.
- is the best.

Me and my world

5 Make a list of five things you tend to worry about. Rank them in order of how important you think they are (1=least important; 5=most important).

6 SPEAKING Compare your list with a partner. How could you reduce the amount of time you spend worrying?

TIPS ON NOT WORRYING TOO MUCH

- If you are worried about something, share it as soon as possible with someone you trust – a problem shared is a problem halved.
- Live as much as you can in the present – the past is over and the future will take care of itself.
- Do regular exercise. It's been shown that the more you exercise, the less you tend to worry or lose sleep.

Don't worry, be happy

Are you a worrier? I am and have been for most of my life, though as I've got older, I've managed to cut down the amount of time I spend worrying about 'what might happen' or 'what someone might think', and so on.

One of the things that's helped me is reading the thoughts of wiser people – here is a small selection of some of my favourite quotes about 'worry'.

A There have been hundreds of terrible events in my life, and most of them never actually happened. *Mark Twain*

B If you ask what is the single most important key to longevity, I would have to say it is avoiding worry, stress and tension. And if you didn't ask me, I'd still have to say it. *George Burns*

C If you want to test your memory, try to recall what you were worrying about one year ago today. *Joseph Cossman*

D Worry never robs tomorrow of its sorrow, it only saps today of its joy. *Leo Buscaglia*

E Worry often gives a small thing a big shadow. *Swedish proverb*

F That the birds of worry and care fly over your head, this you cannot change; but you can prevent them from building nests in your hair. *Chinese proverb*

G If there is no solution to the problem, then don't waste time worrying about it. If there is a solution to the problem, then don't waste time worrying about it. *The Dalai Lama*

Homework

Ask students to write a short text describing a time when they found themselves worrying about something. Did they apply any of the tips on page 35? If not, how could they have done? They can use the notes they made in Exercise 5.

TH!NK more

Practice Extra
Unit 3 Master it!

Worksheets
Life Lessons: Not worrying too much

Tests
Unit, extension and skills test 3
End of term test 1

Warmer

Go through the background notes and clarify the setting of the story. Ask students if they have heard of Emily Brontë or any of the Brontë sisters.

Culture note

Emily Brontë (1818-1848) is one of the three Brontë sisters (the other two being Charlotte and Anne Brontë), who were all authors. Charlotte Brontë is best known for having written *Jane Eyre*.

1. 3.06 We can assume that Nelly seems to be happy working for the Earnshaw family as she is treated as part of the family, almost in the same way as Mr Earnshaw treats his children. There are also references to Mr Earnshaw's personality: 'he didn't forget me for he had a kind heart.'
2. We learn they were hard and long distances had to be covered walking (60 miles in three days) and they could be dangerous: 'he was nearly killed – he would not have such another walk only to be frightened to death!'. People who stayed behind never knew when travellers would come back.
3. Students' own answers. Possible answer: the little black-haired boy Mr Earnshaw came with.
4. Students' own answers. Possible answer: the arrival is possibly a good thing as they seem like an open family.
5. Students' own answers.
6. Encourage students to think of a) changes in life between living in an isolated place in the past and now; b) changes in how people travel and how far people walk. Write them in two columns on board and discuss as an open group.

Literature
WUTHERING HEIGHTS
BY EMILY BRONTË

In 1801, a man named Lockwood rents a house in an isolated part of northern England. The owner of the house lives a few miles away in an old manor called Wuthering Heights. Lockwood wants to know more about the people from Wuthering Heights, so he asks his housekeeper Nelly to tell him about them.

1 3.06 **Read and listen to the text and think about the following questions: Do you think Nelly was happy working for the Earnshaw family? Why/Why not?**

Nelly drew up her seat, obviously pleased to find me so companionable. Before I came to live here, she began – waiting no further invitation to her story – I was almost always at Wuthering Heights; because my mother had looked after Mr. Hindley Earnshaw when he was sick, that was Hareton's father, and I got used to playing with the children: I did small jobs too, and helped to make hay, and waited around the farm ready for anything that anybody would ask me to do. One fine summer morning – it was the beginning of harvest, I remember – Mr. Earnshaw, the old master, came downstairs, dressed for a journey; and, after he had told Joseph what was to be done during the day, he turned to Hindley, and Cathy, and me – for I sat eating my porridge with them – and he said, speaking to his son, 'Now, my little man, I'm going to Liverpool today, what shall I bring you? You may choose what you like: only let it be little, for I shall walk there and back: sixty miles each way, that is a long distance!' Hindley named a <u>fiddle</u>, and then he asked Miss Cathy; she was hardly six years old, but she could ride any horse in the <u>stable</u>, and she chose a <u>whip</u>. He did not forget me; for he had a kind heart, though he was rather severe sometimes. He promised to bring me a pocketful of apples and pears, and then he kissed his children, said good-bye, and set off.

It seemed a long while to us all – the three days of his absence – and little Cathy often asked when he would be home. Mrs. Earnshaw expected him by supper-time on the third evening, and she put the meal off hour after hour; there were no signs of his coming, however, and at last the children got tired of running down to the gate to look. Then it grew dark; she would have sent them to bed, but they begged sadly to be allowed to stay up; and, just about eleven o'clock, the door opened and in stepped the master. He threw himself into a chair, laughing and <u>groaning</u>, and told them he was nearly killed – he would not have such another walk only to be frightened to death! Then, opening his great-coat, he said 'See here, wife!' We crowded round, and over Miss Cathy's head I saw a dirty, black-haired child; big enough both to walk and talk: indeed, its face looked older than Catherine's; yet when it was set on its feet, it only stared round, and repeated over and over again some <u>gibberish</u> that nobody could understand.

Glossary

fiddle – violin
stable – a building where horses are kept
whip – a piece of leather or rope that is fastened to a stick and is used for hitting animals
groaning – making a deep, long sound showing great pain or unhappiness
gibberish – spoken words that have no meaning

2 **What do we learn about the way people made journeys at this time?**

3 **Why do you think Nelly remembers this story so clearly?**

4 **Do you think the arrival of the child will be a good or bad thing for the family? Why?**

5 **Which of the characters in the extract would you like to know more about? Why?**

6 SPEAKING **Work with a partner and discuss these questions.**
1. How do you think living in a very isolated place is different today than it was at this time?
2. What is the longest distance you have ever walked? Describe it to your partner or the whole class.

Warmer

Draw/project a happy and a sad emoji on the board. Put students in pairs. Tell them they have two minutes to come up with as many happy and sad situations as they can. The winning pair will have more situations than the rest. Once the time is over, ask students to share their ideas as a whole group and write on the board if necessary.

▶ 10 Get TH!NKing

Ask the question. Get students to compare their ideas in groups. Play the video, then ask students for feedback.

1 Elicit what the students think is happening in the photo. Ask: *What does it show? Where are they and why? Why are they happy? What type of relationship do they have? What can we say from what they are wearing? What time of the year is it?* Ask students to think what about the main focus is. Have a class vote on what the main focus is.

2 Elicit what students think the people in the photo have been doing before the photo was taken and write them on the board. Monitor to make sure they use the present perfect continuous correctly. Ask them to justify their answers by giving examples of how they look or what they are wearing. Ask students if they would feel the same way in the situations students came up with.

3 Encourage students to think of situations that make them laugh and the reason why. Ask them to share their ideas with a partner. As an extended activity, put all the situations together and as a whole group decide which is the funnier.

Objectives

Functions Responding to jokes
Grammar Emphatic structures; boosting
Vocabulary Laughter; idioms with *laugh* and *joke*
Literature *Three Men in a Boat*

Resources for this unit

All available online

Videos

- Get **TH!NK**ing: *What sorts of things make you laugh?*
- Grammar video!: Emphatic structures

Tests

- Unit, extension and skills test 4

Worksheets

- Grammar and vocabulary: Basic, Standard and Extension Worksheets
- Project: Jokes
- Communication: Laughter is the best medicine
- Grammar presentation: Emphatic structures
- Get **TH!NK**ing and Grammar video! video Worksheets

Reading

Warmer

Ask: *What type of things do people tell jokes about?* Give students some examples to get them started, for example, animals in strange situations, funny things small children say. Give students three minutes to work in pairs and make a list of typical topics. Listen to their ideas in open class.

1 Encourage students to give reasons for their choices and to attempt to agree on the best ranking.

2 After a few minutes, invite students' reactions in open class prompting them to try to explain their answers.

3 **4.01** Tell students not to worry about unknown vocabulary.
A 2 B 3 C 1 D 4

4 **Check/clarify:** *endorphins, heart attack, calories, slapstick comedy, contagious.*
Ask students to read points 1–8 and check understanding before attempting the exercise. Ask them to underline the parts of the text that support their answer.
1 D, E 2 A, B 3 D, E 4 A 5 D 6 A, B 7 B, E 8 A, B, C, E

5 Make sure all students are speaking and encourage quieter students to give their opinion.

A

C

B

D

READING

1 SPEAKING **Rank these situations from most (1) to least (6) enjoyable for you. Compare your ideas with a partner.**

- your best friend telling a funny story at break time in school
- your little brother or sister getting scared by a fake spider
- your dad telling you the same joke for the tenth time
- watching your favourite comedy series
- being asked to tell a joke to a crowd of people
- standing with a group of friends who are all laughing at a joke that you don't get

2 SPEAKING **Work in pairs. Look at the photos on this page. Why do you think the people are laughing in each one?**

3 4.01 **Read and listen to the article on page 39. Say the order in which the situations in the photos are referred to in the article.**

4 **Read the article again. In which paragraph (A–E) are the following points made? Some paragraphs include more than one point.**

1 We have a strong tendency to laugh together with other people.
2 Laughing can be a way of reducing physical pain.
3 Artificial laughter can be as useful as real laughter.
4 Laughter brings benefits in several different areas of our lives.
5 A marriage can benefit from laughter.
6 Laughter is known to have positive effects on our future health.
7 Laughter can help to reduce our stress levels.
8 Laughing about anything at all is good for us.

5 SPEAKING **Work in pairs and discuss the following questions.**

1 How many times do you think you laugh in a day?
2 What are the things that most often make you laugh?
3 Which of the three benefits mentioned in the article can you relate to? Give examples.
4 Can you think of a time when you found yourself laughing at something that wasn't really funny?

38

6 At the end of the exercise, listen to some of the students' ideas and encourage open-class discussion.

7 Before students discuss their answers, elicit one or two examples in open class to get them started. Monitor to help with vocabulary and to ensure quieter students have an opportunity to speak. Avoid error correction unless the error really hinders comprehension. The focus of this task is on fluency, not on practice of structures or lexis. When students have some ideas, regroup them into new pairs and encourage them to share information. Listen to some of the best comments in open class as feedback.

Homework

Ask students to keep a journal for two or three days and make a note of the things that made them laugh, who/what it was and why it was funny.

Activity idea Extension

Take an object (a sieve or a pair of scissors are good examples) into the classroom and show it to students without saying anything. In open class, ask students to consider possible uses for the object, encouraging them to be as creative as possible by praising those who come up with the most imaginative ideas.

HAVING A LAUGH UNIT 4

You have to laugh, don't you?

A **Imagine there was a medicine that improved your physical and mental health at the same time; that had no negative side effects; that was easy to use; that helped you get on better with people; and, best of all, that was totally free. Great, right? Well, there is such a medicine, and it's available to all of us, all of the time – it's called laughter. There's evidence, both scientific and experiential, that laughter is a determining factor in our physical, mental and social wellbeing.**

Good for your body

B Whether you just [1]*get the giggles* or you [2]*burst out laughing* when you [3]*find something funny*, laughter does several beneficial things to your body. Firstly, it releases endorphins – chemicals which make us feel good and which can also act as painkillers. Secondly, laughing increases blood flow and relaxes our heart muscles – things that together can help reduce the risk of a heart attack. Thirdly, it relieves physical stress – a person's muscles can be more relaxed for as long as 45 minutes after a good laugh. As if all this wasn't enough, laughing burns calories, too – not many, it's true, but hey, every little helps to keep you slimmer and fitter!

Good for your mind

C Having a good [4]*sense of humour* helps to maintain a positive state of mind, too. When you [5]*get a joke* (it doesn't have to be [6]*hilarious*, just [7]*amusing* or [8]*witty* is good enough) and it makes you laugh or simply smile, you relax a bit. And it's relaxation that helps us deal with difficult emotions like sadness, anxiety or anger. Of course, it doesn't have to be a joke – it can be an amusing comment, a cat video on YouTube, or some slapstick comedy on stage or TV. It doesn't matter – anything that makes you laugh will do. What laughter does is allow us to get a better perspective on our problems, and then we can deal with them better. It's no surprise that many people find that 'laughter therapy' helps with their problems.

Good for your relationships

D You must have watched comedy programmes with a pre-recorded, fake laughter track. Some people find it very annoying, so why do the programme producers add this artificial laughter? Because they know that laughter is contagious – if you hear someone laughing, you're probably going to laugh along. The truth is, laughter does bring people together. A lot of this doesn't come from comedy programmes or jokes, but just from being with people you like and sharing humorous times. And there's evidence that our closest relationships – with parents, siblings and partners – are improved with shared laughter. As the old saying goes: 'The couple that laughs together, stays together.'

It doesn't even need to be real

E Have you ever been in a group of people where someone tells a joke, they get to the [9]*punchline* and everyone laughs, but you don't get it? You'll probably laugh anyway – and that laughter, even if it's fake, will still have a positive effect on you. The endorphins will kick in, your blood flow will increase, any stress that you're feeling will diminish a bit, and the people you're with (and you too) will feel more connected. So, all you have to do is laugh! Find things to laugh about, be with the people who make you laugh, and laugh for no reason at all as often as you can. Laughter definitely is one of the best medicines.

Train to TH!NK

Divergent thinking

Sometimes, we laugh when something weird or unexpected happens: our brains are hard-wired to follow a logical progression of thought, and if something challenges this order, the effect can often lead to some very creative ideas. This is sometimes referred to as divergent thinking, and the effect can be funny.

6 **Look at the question and the three answers.**

What can you do with a one pound coin?

a buy a bottle of water with it
b use it to make a decision (heads or tails)
c put it under the leg of a wobbly chair

1 Which is the most obvious?
2 Which is the funniest?
3 Which is the most creative?

7 SPEAKING **Work in pairs and discuss. How many ideas can you come up with for each one?**

1 What can you do with a pair of ripped jeans?
2 What's your excuse for not handing in your homework?
3 What things can money not buy?

39

Activity idea Extension

Write the following questions on the board:

1 *In which jobs do you have to be creative? Would you like to do one of those jobs? Why (not)?*
2 *Do teachers need to be imaginative? Why (not)?*
3 *How do you feel when you are asked to be imaginative and come up with new ideas?*
4 *What helps you think in a divergent way?*

Ask students to write a short text answering the questions. As a follow-up, ask students to discuss some of their ideas in open class in the next lesson.

Creative TH!NKing
Generating ideas
Generating multiple ideas.

Creative TH!NKing
Generating ideas
Builds on others' ideas.

TH!NK more

Worksheets
Project Jokes
Communication Laughter is the best medicine
Get TH!NKing *What sorts of things make you laugh?*

Warmer

Ask: *What is your favourite joke? Can you tell it in English? Does it work in English or is there a translation barrier?* Give the students a few moments to discuss in pairs and ask some of them to tell their (clean!) jokes to the class.

▶ 11 Grammar video! Emphatic structures

1 During feedback, refer to the rules and read through the *Look* box and check understanding.
1 What; is 2 it; that 3 all; is
RULE: 1 what 2 it 3 all

2 Do the first item with the whole class as an example.
1 What adults forget is how it feels to be a child.
2 It's the way (that) he always interrupts me when I'm telling a joke that I don't like.
3 All I watch on TV is comedy shows.
4 What you have to remember is that many people don't find those kinds of jokes very funny.
5 It's you that he's laughing at, Dad, not your joke.
6 All you need to do is say sorry and she'll forgive you. / All you need to say is sorry and she'll forgive you.

3 If you're short on time, set this exercise for homework.

Workbook p36

Get it Right!
Cleft sentences

Student's Book p46

4 To practise students' scanning skills, tell students to find the phrases in the article as quickly as possible. When students have found the verbs, ask them to try to work out the meanings.
a 2 b 6 c 7 d 5 e 3 f 9 g 4 h 8 i 1

TH!NK more

Workbook
Grammar p36, Ex.1–3
Vocabulary p38, Ex.1–2

Worksheets
Grammar presentation Emphatic structures
Grammar Worksheets 4
Grammar video! Emphatic structures
Vocabulary Worksheets 4

GRAMMAR
Grammar video ▶ 11
Emphatic structures

1 Complete the sentences from the article on page 39 with the missing words. Then complete the rule with *it's*, *what* and *all*.

1 … laughter does … allow us to get a better perspective on our problems.
2 And …'s relaxation … helps us deal with difficult emotions.
3 So, … you have to do … laugh!

RULE: To make our language more emphatic we can use cleft sentences:
Cleft sentences with 1… shift the focus of attention to the end of the sentence.
Cleft sentences with 2… shift the focus of the attention to the beginning of the sentence.
Cleft sentences with 3… have the meaning of *the only thing*.

Look
Another way we can add emphasis is by adding *do* or *does* to a positive statement, for example *Laughter does bring people together.*

2 Rewrite the sentences using the words in brackets.

1 Adults forget how it feels to be a child. (What …)
2 I don't like the way he always interrupts me when I'm telling a joke . (It's … that …)
3 I only watch comedy shows on TV. (All …)
4 You have to remember that many people don't find those kinds of jokes very funny. (What …)
5 Dad, he's laughing at you, not your joke. (It's … that …)
6 You only need to say sorry and she'll forgive you. (All …)

3 SPEAKING Complete the sentences so that they are true for you. Then discuss with a partner.

1 What really makes me laugh …
2 It's … that makes me cross.
3 All I want for my birthday this year …
4 It's … that causes most of the problems in the world.

→ workbook page 36

VOCABULARY
Laughter

4 Look back at the words and phrases in italics in the article on page 39 and match the correct number (1–9) with the definitions.

a to suddenly laugh very hard
b very, very funny
c funny, in a way to make you smile
d understand [a joke]
e to see the funny side of something
f the last line of a joke
g the ability to see the funny side of things
h funny in a clever way
i start to laugh again and again, in a quiet but uncontrolled way

5 Complete each space with one word, using your answers to Exercise 4 to help you.

My dad is terrible at telling jokes. His jokes are never very funny; at best, they're just 1… . The problem is no one ever really 2… his jokes. The fact that he often forgets the 3… clearly doesn't help. When he gets to the end of the joke, he 4… laughing because he thinks his jokes are always completely 5… . Of course, we all start getting the 6… , which makes him think that we 7… his joke funny. He doesn't realise it's him we're laughing at, not his joke. Luckily, our very clever mum is usually around to say something 8… – unfortunately, Dad doesn't always understand!

6 Answer the questions. Make notes.

1 What sort of things give you the giggles? What do you do to try to stop them?
2 What kind of jokes do you find funny?
3 Which things do you think we shouldn't laugh at?
4 Do you prefer to tell jokes or to listen to them?
5 What do you do if you don't get a joke that someone tells you?

7 SPEAKING Compare your answers with other students. Can you find anyone who shares your sense of humour?

→ workbook page 38

SPEAKING

8 Think about funny things that happened this week. Make notes on:

1 two things you did that made other people smile.
2 two funny things that you shared or saw online.
3 two things that made you smile.
4 two things that you found hilarious.

9 SPEAKING Work in pairs and compare your answers. Who has the funniest anecdote?

40

---

5 Before students do the exercise, ask them to read through the paragraph quickly to get an overall understanding and answer the question: *Who's better at telling jokes, Mum or Dad?* (Mum)
1 amusing 2 gets 3 punchline 4 bursts out 5 hilarious 6 giggles 7 find/found 8 witty

6 Encourage students to note down reasons for their answers and help with vocabulary as necessary.

7 If space allows, this activity would also work well as a mingle with students standing up and comparing answers with other students. When students have compared with several others, divide the class into pairs for students to report back on their findings.

Workbook p38

8 Tell students to think about exactly why the things were funny and which words they might use to describe the things to a partner. Monitor and help with vocabulary as required.

9 **Check/clarify:** *anecdote*.
At the end of the exercise, listen to some of the funniest anecdotes in open class.

10 🔊 **4.02** If there is an interactive whiteboard in the classroom, this activity would best be done as a heads-up activity with the whole class.
1 A 2 D 3 B

11 🔊 **4.02** Give students some time to discuss what they remember from the first listening. Play the audio again while students listen and make notes. You could give students the audio script to check their ideas.

12–13 🔊 **4.02** Hold a quick class vote to decide which was the funniest joke.

14 🔊 **4.03** Elicit/explain that there are different ways to respond to jokes. Ask students how they might have responded to the jokes in the listening (*laugh*, *groan*, *sound confused*). Write any correct answers on the board.
1 😊
2 😊
3 😊
4 🤨

15 🔊 **4.03** Pause after each phrase and ask students to repeat the phrase using suitable intonation. Encourage students to sound enthusiastic in the positive responses!
1 good one 2 Very funny 3 must remember 4 don't get

16 To extend discussion, regroup students to compare their ideas.

17 You could move on to pronunciation at this stage prior to doing the speaking task. You may like to tell students a joke of your own to get them started. Tell them to practise telling it to each other several times.

18 Listen to some of the jokes in open class and discuss which is the funniest.

Pronunciation
Telling jokes: pacing, pausing and punchlines
Student's Book p137

LISTENING

10 🔊 4.02 **Listen to three jokes and match each one with a picture. There is one extra picture.**

A

B

C

D

11 🔊 4.02 **Listen again and make notes on the following for each joke.**
1 Who are the main characters?
2 What happens?
3 What's the punchline?
4 Why is it funny?

12 🔊 4.02 **Listen again and rate each of the jokes from 5 (hilarious) to 0 (I didn't get it).**

13 SPEAKING **Work in groups of three. Choose one of the jokes and tell it to the others.**

FUNCTIONS
Responding to jokes

14 🔊 4.03 **Read and listen to four jokes. What do the people think of them? Choose 😊 or 😣 or 🤨.**

1
Why is 6 afraid of 7?
Because 7 8 9.

2
What do you call a deer with no eye?
No idea.

3
I phoned the local hospital. I said, 'Is that the local hospital?' The woman said, 'Well, it depends where you're phoning from.'

4
Knock, knock!
Who's there?
Tank.
Tank who?
You're welcome.

15 🔊 4.03 **Complete the phrases in order to make the responses. Listen again and check.**
1 That's a g… o… .
2 Ha ha. V… f… .
3 I m… r… that one.
4 I d… g… it.

16 SPEAKING **Work in pairs. Discuss these questions. Think about the jokes you heard in Exercises 10 and 14.**
1 Which of the jokes, if any, did you find funny? Did you dislike any of them? Why?
2 Some people have said that the joke about the elderly couple could be considered to be in bad taste. What do you think?
3 Which of these jokes work in your language?
4 Are there any jokes that you know that wouldn't work in English?

17 SPEAKING **Work in pairs. Think of a joke and practise telling it in English.**

18 SPEAKING **Tell your joke to another pair. Respond appropriately to each other's jokes. Whose joke was the funniest?**

PRONUNCIATION
Telling jokes: pacing, pausing and punchlines
Go to page 137.

Homework
Ask students to write a short text answering the question: *Who is the funniest person in your family / out of your friends and why?* Encourage them to use some of the expressions from Exercise 4. As a follow-up, students can present this person to the class in the next lesson. After each presentation, encourage the rest of the class to ask questions and finally hold a class vote to decide which was the most interesting presentation.

Activity idea Extension
Ask students to work in pairs to rewrite the following sentences using emphatic structures:
I don't like it when my brother laughs at me.
My sister only eats vegetables.
They stole my skateboard, not my bicycle.
You only need to call me and I will come straight round.

Activity idea Fast finishers
Students can write sentences including different emphatic structures from the rule on page 40. Listen to some of their examples in open class.

Creative TH!NKing
Generating ideas
Imagining alternatives and possibilities.

TH!NK more
Workbook
Listening p42, Ex.1–3
Pronunciation p119

Warmer

To revise the vocabulary from last lesson, call out part of a phrase from Exercise 4 on page 40, and elicit the whole phrase. For example, say: *giggle*; students say: *(get) the giggles*. Pairs take turns to test each other in the same way.

1 Put these questions up on the board in order to avoid students getting distracted by the text.

2 Set a time limit to encourage students to read quickly.
1 He is the son of a black Xhosa woman and a white Swiss man; he can speak several languages; when he started as a comedian, a lot of his comedy referred to the racial situation in his home country and his international outlook.
2 He has written a book, appeared in a South African soap opera, taken part in a reality dancing show, and he runs his own talk show.
3 His book was a bestseller, he has had a lot of appearances on TV shows, he has attracted attention from people outside of his native country and was listed in *Time* magazine's 100 most influential people.

3 🔊 **4.05 Check/clarify:** *regime, recognition.*
Encourage students to underline the parts of the text that support their answers.
1 a black Xhosa woman and a white Swiss man
2 Relationships between people of different skin colours were banned under apartheid.
3 Because his parents have different backgrounds.
4 his early life in South Africa as the apartheid regime came to an end and the new freedoms that came after, a time when his family was very poor
5 Because his friends dared him to.
6 In 2010 he was offered the opportunity to run his own talk show, *Tonight with Trevor Noah*.
7 Although viewing figures dropped a little at first, the show still had an excellent audience and Noah was offered a five-year renewal.

READING

1 SPEAKING **Work in pairs. Ask and answer the questions.**
1 Which comedy shows do you enjoy watching? Why?
2 Who are the most famous comedians in your country? Are there many international comedians?
3 Are there daily comedy shows in your country? How popular are they?

2 **Read the article quickly and answer the questions.**
1 In what ways is Trevor Noah unusual?
2 Apart from hosting a comedy show, what other things has he done?
3 What examples are given of how he's been successful?

3 🔊 4.05 **Read the article again and listen. Answer the questions.**
1 Who were Trevor Noah's parents?
2 Why did his parents keep their relationship secret?
3 Why does he speak so many languages?
4 What was his book *Born a Crime* about?
5 Why did he first go on stage as a stand-up comedian?
6 How did he start to learn how to be a talk-show host?
7 What happened when he took over *The Daily Show*?

SPEAKING

4 **Work in pairs. Make a list of the three most popular comedians from your country. What makes them so entertaining?**

5 **Work in groups. Agree together on the best comedian from your country.**

THE WORLD OF COMEDY: TREVOR NOAH

Since 2015, Trevor Noah has been hosting *The Daily Show*, a well-known comedy programme on US TV. He took over from the very successful Jon Stewart, and since then, the show has definitely gone from strength to strength. So who is Trevor Noah?

Trevor Noah is South African. He was born in Soweto, a township near Johannesburg, in 1984. He's the son of a black Xhosa woman and a white Swiss man. In South Africa in those days, under apartheid, relationships between people of different skin colours was banned, and his parents had to keep their relationship secret. This fact of his birth certainly accounts for many things about him: for example, the fact that he speaks several languages, including English, Zulu, Xhosa, Sotho, Tsonga, Tswana, Afrikaans and Swiss German; the fact that when he started as a comedian, a lot of his comedy referred to the racial situation in his home country; and his international outlook (he says of himself: 'I've always wanted to be a comedian in the world. I don't want to be labelled a South African comedian.').

In 2016, he published a highly successful book entitled *Born a Crime: Stories from a South African Childhood*, and it became an immediate bestseller in New York and beyond, containing stories of his early life in South Africa as the apartheid regime came to an end and the new freedoms that followed; stories like eating caterpillars at a time when his family was extremely poor, or being thrown out of a car driven by gangsters.

In his late teens, Noah appeared in a South African soap opera, and later, when his friends dared him to, he went on stage as a stand-up comedian for the first time. This led to numerous appearances on all kinds of TV shows in South Africa – for example, he took part in a reality dancing show in 2008 – and his career began to take off. In 2010, he was offered the opportunity to run his own talk show, *Tonight with Trevor Noah*, which gave him the chance to acquire the skills of being a talk-show host.

Noah's reputation grew and soon he attracted the attention of people outside his native country. In 2012, he appeared on a famous US show, *The Tonight Show With Jay Leno* – the first African comedian to do so. The following year he got his own TV show in the US, and then, crucially, in 2014 he was invited to appear on Comedy Central's *The Daily Show* with Stewart.

Then, in 2015, Noah took over after Stewart's retirement. Although viewing figures dropped a little at first (not surprising, given how popular Stewart had been), the show still had an excellent audience and Noah was offered a five-year renewal in 2017. His story is unquestionably one of success and recognition (in 2018, he was listed in *Time* magazine's 100 most influential people). Who knows where he will go next.

42

4 Think of examples in open class and write them on the board. Make sure all students know all of the comedians.

5 Allow students time for groups to discuss and rank the comedians in order of how funny they are. Hold a class vote to decide who they feel is the funniest.

Culture notes

Jay Leno is an American comedian, writer and from 1992 to 2014 was host of *The Tonight Show with Jay Leno* – a late-night weekday talk show which regularly had over 7 million viewers and was shown on various channels all over the world.

Jon Stewart is an American comedian, writer and political commentator and from 1999 to 2015 was the host of *The Daily Show* – a late-night weekday talk and satirical news show drawing almost 2.5 million viewers nightly.

TH!NK more

Workbook
Reading p40, Ex.1–4

Activity idea Extension

Ask: *Would you like to be a professional comedian? Why (not)? What do you think a professional comedian's life is like?* Give students three minutes to discuss the questions in small groups.

6 Elicit that the words in brackets are all adverbs.
1 The show has definitely gone from strength to strength.
2 This fact of his birth certainly accounts for many things about him.
3 Then, crucially, in 2014 he was invited to appear on Comedy Central's *The Daily Show*.
4 His story is unquestionably one of success and recognition.
RULE: 1 after 2 before 3 between

7 1 She is undeniably one of the funniest actors in the world.
2 *I Feel Pretty* is undoubtedly her best film.
3 It is literally the funniest film I've ever seen.
4 She clearly loves playing ordinary people.
5 Her performance in *Thank You for Your Service* was utterly convincing.
6 She will definitely win an Oscar one day.

8 Read through the sentences about Amy Schumer in Exercise 7 as an example. Ask students to write similar information about a comedian or actor of their choice using at least four boosting adverbs. Monitor and help students with ideas and vocabulary as necessary.

Workbook p37

9 Ask students to try to match the sentence halves.
1 g 2 h 3 d 4 a 5 f 6 b 7 c 8 e

10 If you're short on time, set this exercise for homework.
1 head off 2 joke 3 have; last laugh 4 laughing stock
5 joking aside 6 other side; face
7 laughing matter 8 burst out

11 Divide the class in pairs for students to write their replies.

Workbook p38

GRAMMAR
Boosting

6 **Rewrite the sentences from the article to include the word in brackets. Then complete the rule with *before*, *after* and *between*.**

1 The show has gone from strength to strength. (definitely)
2 This fact of his birth accounts for many things about him. (certainly)
3 Then, in 2014 he was invited to appear on Comedy Central's *The Daily Show*. (crucially)
4 His story is one of success and recognition. (unquestionably)

RULE: When we want to make a statement stronger, we can use an adverb such as *unquestionably, definitely, crucially* or *certainly*.
These adverbs come:
[1]... the verb *to be*
[2]... other verbs
[3]... auxiliary and main verbs
Other common adverbs include *undoubtedly, undeniably, clearly, absolutely, utterly, entirely, essentially, exactly, literally* and *totally*.

7 **Put the words in order to make sentences.**

My favourite comedian is Amy Schumer.
1 the / undeniably / she / world / of / funniest / is / actors / one / the / in / .
2 is / film / undoubtedly / best / *I Feel Pretty* / her / .
3 I've / is / seen / funniest / it / literally / the / film / ever / .
4 playing / she / ordinary people / loves / clearly / .
5 convincing / her / was / *Thank You for Your Service* / performance / in / utterly / .
6 day / an / win / she / definitely / one / Oscar / will / .

8 WRITING **Write four sentences about a comedian or actor that you really like, using adverbs to make your statements stronger. Keep their name a secret!**
Read your sentences to your partner. Can he/she guess who you're describing?

→ workbook page 37

VOCABULARY
Idioms with *laugh* and *joke*

9 **Match the sentence halves.**

1 The team really are *a laughing*
2 Your exam result *is no*
3 I love this programme. I *laugh my*
4 When we saw we were wearing the same dress, we *burst out*
5 It was very funny to hide my shoes, but *joking*
6 He might think it's funny now, but he'll be *laughing*
7 I can't believe United paid £30 million for him. *It's a*
8 They call you a nerd because you study hard, but you'll *have*

a *laughing*. What else could we do? It was too late for either of us to change.
b *on the other side of his face* when his parents read his school report.
c *joke*. He's rubbish – not even remotely worth that amount.
d *head off* every time I watch it.
e *the last laugh* when you get into the best university in the country and they all fail their exams.
f *aside*, I need to leave. Where are they?
g *stock*. They haven't won a game for more than a year.
h *laughing matter*. 30 percent is just not good enough.

10 **Complete with the missing words from the idioms in Exercise 9.**

1 Have you heard Sarah's new joke? I laughed my ... when she told me.
2 I got a one percent pay rise. One percent! It's a ... !
3 I know you think I've got no talent for acting, but I'll ... the ... when I'm rich and famous.
4 You can't wear that Wonderwoman costume to the end-of-year ball. You'll be the ... of the party.
5 Yes, I know it's funny to laugh at me in a suit, but ... , do you think it's appropriate for a job interview?
6 You'll be laughing on the ... of your ... when I'm your boss one day.
7 These new tax rules are no ... . Many families will find themselves a lot poorer.
8 When she slipped on the banana skin, I ... laughing. I couldn't help myself.

11 WRITING **Write a reply to each of the sentences. Use one of the idioms in each one.**

1 He thinks it's funny to drive his Porsche around town at 100 km per hour.
2 Did you think the film was funny?
3 Milo's parents aren't going to be happy when they see what he's done to their car. I can't believe he isn't more worried. He still seems to think it's funny.

→ workbook page 38

Homework

Certain adverbs are only used to emphasise extreme adjectives. Ask students to decide which of the adverbs can be used with all types of adjective and which can only be used with extreme adjectives.

All adjectives: *unquestionably, definitely, undoubtedly, certainly, undeniably, clearly, essentially, literally*

Extreme adjectives: *absolutely, utterly, entirely, totally*

Ask students to write five sentences including adverbs they would not normally use.

Activity idea Fast finishers

Ask students to write sentences about their friends using some of the boosting adverbs.

TH!NK more

Practice Extra
Unit 4 Practise it!

Workbook
Grammar p37, Ex.4–7
Vocabulary p38, Ex.3–4
Vocabulary Extra p39, Ex.1–3

Worksheets
Grammar Worksheets 4
Vocabulary Worksheets 4

Warmer

Ask students to think of a list of films and books involving water and write the titles on the board. Divide the class into pairs for students to take turns describing a film or book for their partners to guess the title. Listen to some examples in open class and write any repeated themes on the board.

1 Get students to cover the text. Give them a minute to discuss the question in pairs.

2 **4.06** Encourage students not to focus on every word for now but just to find the answer to the question.
cold beef, potatoes, cabbage, peas, half a tin of salmon, two eggs

3 **Check/clarify:** *light-heartedness, scraped, smothered, remnants, evinced, earnest.*
Tell students not to worry about other difficult vocabulary at this stage as this will come up later. Encourage them to think about the correct answer to the false statements.
1T 2T 3DS 4T 5T 6F
([George] said he had never heard of water rats in Irish stew, and he would rather be on the safe side, and not try experiments)

Culture note

Jerome Klapka Jerome was a comic writer from Walsall, England. Born in 1859, he came from a fairly well-off family but, due to his father's bad investments, grew up in poverty. At the age of 15 he was orphaned and forced to leave his education to support his family. He worked in journalism, teaching and acting but was not particularly successful in any of these. He is best known for his humorous travelogue *Three Men in a Boat*, which was published in 1889 and inspired by his honeymoon trip along the Thames. It was an instant success, but although he wrote several novels and story collections over the next few decades, none of his follow-up work achieved the same level of success. Jerome K. Jerome died in Northampton in 1927 after suffering a series of strokes.

Literature

1 How good do you think three middle-aged English men (in the 19th century) might be at cooking? How often do you imagine they cook for themselves? Under what circumstances might you expect them to cook?

2 4.06 Read and listen to the extract and make a list of the things they put into the Irish stew.

Three Men in a Boat
(to say nothing of the dog)

by Jerome K. Jerome

In this famous, late-nineteenth century novel, a man called J and his two friends Harris and George decide to take a holiday to improve their health. They travel along the River Thames in a small boat (and they take their dog, Montmorency, with them). They are not very good sailors, or cooks, and the novel tells of their many odd adventures.

It was still early when we got settled, and George said that, as we had plenty of time, it would be a splendid opportunity to try a good, slap-up supper. He said he would show us what could be done up the river in the way of cooking, and suggested that, with the vegetables and the remains of the cold beef and general odds and ends, we should make an Irish stew.

It seemed a fascinating idea. George gathered wood and made a fire, and Harris and I started to peel the potatoes. I should never have thought that peeling potatoes was such an undertaking. The job turned out to be the biggest thing of its kind that I had ever been in. We began cheerfully, [...], but our light-heartedness was gone by the time the first potato was finished. The more we peeled, the more peel there seemed to be left on; by the time we had got all the peel off and all the eyes out, there was no potato left – at least, none worth speaking of. George came and had a look at it – it was about the size of a peanut.

He said:

'Oh, that won't do! You're wasting them. You must scrape them.'

So we scraped them, and that was harder work than peeling. [...] We worked steadily for twenty-five minutes, and did four potatoes. [...] I never saw such a thing as potato-scraping for making a fellow in a mess. It seemed difficult to believe that the potato-scrapings in which Harris and I stood, half smothered, could have come off four potatoes. [...]

George said it was absurd to have only four potatoes in an Irish stew, so we washed half-a-dozen or so more, and put them in without peeling. We also put in a cabbage and a few peas. George stirred it all up, and then he said that there seemed to be a lot of room to spare, so we looked through both the baskets, and picked out all the odds and ends and the remnants, and added them to the stew. [...]

Then George found half a tin of salmon, and he emptied that into the pot.

He said that was the advantage of Irish stew: you got rid of such a lot of things. I fished out a couple of eggs that had got cracked, and put those in. [...]

I forget the other ingredients, but I know nothing was wasted; and I remember that, towards the end, Montmorency, who had evinced great interest in the proceedings throughout, strolled away with an earnest and thoughtful air, reappearing, a few minutes afterwards, with a dead water rat in his mouth, which he evidently wished to present as his contribution to the dinner; [...].

We had a discussion as to whether the rat should go in or not. Harris said that he thought it would be all right, mixed up with the other things, and that every little helped; but George stood up for precedent. He said he had never heard of water rats in Irish stew, and he would rather be on the safe side, and not try experiments.

3 **Read the extract again. Are the statements T (true), F (false) or DS (doesn't say)?**

1 George said they should make Irish stew using just some beef and vegetables.
2 After the men peeled the potatoes, they were very small.
3 Scraping the potatoes was the most difficult work they'd ever done.
4 George wanted to look for other things to put in the stew because he thought it was too small.
5 Montmorency killed a rat.
6 The men didn't put the rat in the stew because there was no room for it.

44

4 Before students do the exercise, write the highlighted words on the board. Tell students to find the words in the extract as quickly as possible. Then ask them to try to work out the meaning of the phrases. Compare their meanings with the definitions in the book.
1 to spare 2 scrape 3 peel 4 be on the safe side 5 steadily 6 odds and ends 7 every little helped 8 fished out

5 Encourage students to speak at length and to use vocabulary from the extract. Listen to some of the students' ideas and encourage open-class discussion.

1 Let students compare their answers in pairs before feedback.
entertaining ✓ hilarious ✓

2 If students are unsure about cleft sentences and boosting adverbs, refer them to examples earlier in the unit.
Cleft sentences:
What I like most about it is the perfect mixture of travel guide … and comedy …
But it's exactly this lazy boat ride of a journey that makes it so good.
Boosting adverbs: utterly, clearly, exactly, undeniably

3 *1 What the three of them decide is that they are over-worked and in need of a holiday.*
2 It's when you suddenly burst out laughing that you get the strangest looks.
3 What some of my friends said was that it was too old-fashioned and that the plot moved far too slowly.

4 During feedback, ask students to refer to the text to explain their choices.
[B] a description of what the writer likes / doesn't like – advice 3
[A] a brief synopsis of the story – advice 1
[C] a recommendation – advice 2

5 If you're short on time, students can do the preparation in class and complete the writing at home. Alternatively, this could be done as a collaborative writing activity in class with pairs of students of a similar level working together.

4 VOCABULARY **Match the highlighted words or phrases in the extract with the definitions.**

1 left over; more of something than you need or want
2 to take off a layer of something by rubbing with a hard or sharp object
3 remove the skin (of a vegetable or fruit)
4 not take any risks
5 in a smooth and regular way, without hurrying
6 various small things of different kinds
7 everything, no matter how small, was useful
8 got something out (usually with fingers)

5 SPEAKING **Work in pairs. Discuss the questions.**

1 Do you think the men enjoyed their meal when they finally ate supper? Why/Why not?
2 What was the worst meal you have ever eaten or cooked? Why was it so bad? Tell your partner about it.

WRITING
A review

1 INPUT **Read the review. Which of these adjectives would the reviewer agree describe the book?**

boring | depressing | entertaining
exciting | hilarious | old-fashioned

2 ANALYSE **Read the review again and find:**

- two examples of cleft sentences.
- four examples of boosting adverbs.

3 **Rewrite these sentences from the review using a cleft sentence to add emphasis.**

1 The three of them decide that they are over-worked and in need of a holiday.
What the three of them decide …
2 You get the strangest looks when you suddenly burst out laughing.
It's when you …
3 Some of my friends […] said it was too old-fashioned and that the plot moved far too slowly.
What some of my friends said was …

Note: It's good to use boosting and cleft sentences in your review to give it more impact. But be careful not to use too many. This could result in your writing sounding artificial.

4 PLAN **Match each paragraph with its function. Then match the functions with advice for writing a review.**

- a description of what the writer likes/doesn't like
- a brief synopsis of the story
- a recommendation

1 Don't give too much away.
2 Say who it might appeal to.
3 Don't forget to give reasons for your opinions.

5 PRODUCE **Write a review of a book or film (220–260 words).**

- Give a short summary.
- Say how you feel about it.
- Say whether you'd recommend it and, if so, to whom.

[A] Jerome K. Jerome is sitting in the living room of his house, describing an ever-growing list of illnesses from which he fears he is suffering to his sympathetic friends Harris and George. The three of them decide that they are over-worked and in need of a holiday. After deciding that a vacation in the countryside would be too dull and a voyage at sea too dangerous, they decide that a boating trip up the River Thames from London to Oxford would be perfect. So, the next Saturday, accompanied by Jerome's dog Montmorency, they set off for a fortnight of amusing storytelling and mild misadventure, all set in the background of the idyllic English countryside.

[B] Originally published in 1889, *Three Men in a Boat* was recently voted number 33 on the *Guardian*'s list of the 100 greatest novels of all time and there's one simple reason for this: it's utterly brilliant. What I like most about it is the perfect mixture of travel guide, which is what it was originally intended to be, and comedy – two of my favourite genres. The book is laugh-out-loud funny, which can be quite embarrassing if you're reading it on a crowded underground train on your way to college! You get the strangest looks when you suddenly burst out laughing.

[C] Clearly, though, it isn't for everyone. Some of my friends didn't find it so humorous and said it was too old-fashioned and that the plot moved far too slowly. But it's exactly this lazy boat ride of a journey that makes it so good. If you're looking for a highly enjoyable cruise into the eccentricities of the English, with a cast of undeniably colourful characters, then this might just be the book for you.

Homework

If you are short on time, students can do Exercise 5 for homework. If you have done this in class, ask students to exchange their reviews with another student for them to read at home and give feedback on content and structure. Students could check if the review uses the same structure as the template. They should also decide which the most/least interesting part of the review is.

Activity idea
Peer correction

On completion of the writing task, ask students to exchange their reviews and read and evaluate on the basis of **content**, **organisation**, **communicative purpose** and **language**. They should avoid focusing solely on accuracy.

TH!NK more

Practice Extra
Unit 4 Master it!

Workbook
Developing Writing p41

Tests
Unit, extension and skills test 4

Emotional Development
Supporting others
Works at maintaining healthy relationships.

1 Write *If I would have the money, I'd buy a new phone* and *If I had the money, I'd buy a new phone* on the board. Elicit which one of the sentences is correct and why.

1 … if you ~~would~~ had had …
2 If my brother ~~isn't~~ wasn't / weren't so lazy … / If my brother ~~isn't~~ hadn't been so lazy …
3 … if we ~~would~~ had won …
4 … if he ~~would have~~ had asked Sam …
5 If I ~~wouldn't have~~ hadn't argued with my friends …
6 If there ~~wouldn't have been~~ wasn't / weren't so much traffic … / If there ~~wouldn't have been~~ hadn't been so much traffic …

2 Remind students there are various alternatives to *if* in conditional sentences.

1 You can go out to play football provided you finish your homework first.
2 I won't go to the party unless you promise not to wear that old jacket.
3 You have to work hard, otherwise you won't achieve your goals.
4 Provided we leave now, we'll be in plenty of time for the train.
5 The doctor won't see you tomorrow unless it's urgent.
6 She should / must train every day, otherwise she won't get into the team.
7 Professional footballers can play until they are 40 as long as they don't get injured.

3 1 What often makes us laugh is the misfortune of others.
2 It's the actions of just two members of the team that have made us all a laughing stock.
3 What made Ollie laugh his head off was seeing his teacher playing air guitar to a rock song.
4 What they don't understand is that we will have the last laugh.
5 All Simon said was that the show was hilarious.
6 It's no secret / It's not a secret that many people enjoy watching funny videos on YouTube.

CAMBRIDGE ENGLISH CORPUS · CAMBRIDGE QUALITY GUARANTEE

GET IT RIGHT!

UNITS 3 & 4

Conditionals

Learners often use *would* in the *if*-clause when it's more accurate to use the past simple or past perfect.
✓ *If **I'd known**, I wouldn't have said anything.*
✗ *If I ~~would've known~~, I wouldn't have said anything.*

1 Rewrite the sentences so they are correct.

0 We would be there by now if we would have caught the bus.
We would be there by now if we had caught the bus.
1 The car wouldn't have broken down if you would have had it serviced.
2 If my brother isn't so lazy, he would have passed the exam.
3 We would be rich now if we would have won the lottery.
4 John would have been pushing his luck if he would have asked Sam to help him.
5 If I wouldn't have argued with my friends, we would have been talking to each other now.
6 If there wouldn't have been so much traffic, I would be at home already.

Alternatives to *if* in conditional sentences are rarely used by Spanish speakers.
✓ *You can borrow it **provided** you look after it.*
✓ *You can't borrow it **unless** you look after it.*
✓ *Look after it, **otherwise** you won't borrow anything of mine again!*

2 Rewrite the sentences using the words provided.

0 You can borrow it if you look after it. (as long as)
You can borrow it as long as you look after it.
1 You can go out to play football if you finish your homework first. (provided)
2 I'll go to the party if you promise not to wear that old jacket. (unless)
3 You have to work hard or you won't achieve your goals. (otherwise)
4 If we leave now, we'll be in plenty of time for the train. (provided)
5 The doctor will see you tomorrow but only if it's urgent. (unless)
6 She won't get into the team if she doesn't train every day. (otherwise)
7 Professional footballers can play until they are 40 if they don't get injured. (as long as)

Cleft sentences

Learners at this level often avoid using emphatic structures such as cleft sentences.
The unexpected often makes us laugh. =
✓ *It's often the unexpected that makes us laugh.*
✓ *What makes us laugh is often the unexpected.*
The only thing I want to do is have some fun. =
✓ *All I want to do is have some fun.*

3 Rewrite the sentences using *It's … that …*, *What …*, or *All …* to add emphasis.

0 A sense of humour is simply the ability to see the funny side of things.
All *a sense of humour is, is the ability to see the funny side of things.*
1 The misfortune of others often makes us laugh.
What …
2 The actions of just two members of the team have made us all a laughing stock.
It's …
3 Ollie laughed his head off when he saw his teacher playing air guitar to a rock song.
What …
4 They don't understand that we will have the last laugh.
What …
5 Simon only said that the show was hilarious.
All …
6 Many people enjoy watching funny videos on YouTube and it isn't a secret.
It's …

46

1 🔊 **4.07** In C1 Advanced Listening Part 3, candidates have to listen to a longer interview and answer six four-option multiple-choice questions. This part of the exam tests understanding of the detailed meaning of the text, attitudes and opinions.

Encourage your students to do the following when they approach this task:

- Read and listen to the instructions carefully.
- Read all the questions and options and think about the context.
- On the first listening, try to understand the gist and choose the best option.
- On the second listening, check that the answers are correct and focus on detailed understanding of the attitudes or opinions.

1B 2C 3A 4B 5D 6D

Workbook p43

TOWARDS C1 Advanced

LISTENING
Part 3: Multiple choice

→ workbook page 43

1 🔊 4.07 **You will hear part of a podcast interview in which the actor Daniela Merchant is talking about a book she's read that discusses the role of luck in people's lives. For questions 1–6, choose the answer (A, B, C or D) which fits best according to what you hear.**

1 Daniela's main criticism of the beginning of the book she's read is that the writer
- A tries to blame other people's actions for his own misfortunes.
- B fails to explain the exact circumstances behind an incident.
- C seems unable to come to terms with a past disappointment.
- D assumes that the reader is familiar with his previous books.

2 In terms of the difference between luck and fate, Daniela feels that the book
- A could make it clearer what the two terms mean.
- B should have considered a wider range of situations.
- C makes an interesting point about people's attitudes.
- D relies too heavily on the writer's personal experiences.

3 Daniela agrees with the interviewer's point that
- A natural ability is still regarded as necessary for success.
- B it's becoming more acceptable to make mistakes these days.
- C most people think success or failure is largely a matter of chance.
- D society is becoming less tolerant of those who use bad luck as an excuse.

4 Daniela explains that the second half of the book highlights
- A how family values can inform our decisions.
- B how some factors of our birth influence our lives.
- C how each generation tends to view things differently.
- D how inherited features are more important than upbringing.

5 Daniela believes that her acting career has been successful because
- A she adopted an exceptional actor as her role model.
- B she did her training at a particularly prestigious college.
- C she was able to appreciate and learn from the work of others.
- D she benefited from an unplanned change in her training course.

6 Daniela's overall assessment of the book she's read is that
- A it's more likely to appeal to a younger readership.
- B some parts of it are more clearly written than others.
- C it's entertaining, but shouldn't be taken too seriously.
- D the writer argues too strongly for the main idea behind it.

WRITING
Part 2: A proposal

2 **Write an answer to the following task.**

A local school has a piece of land that it wants to build on. In preparation for a meeting to discuss the plans for the project, the school has asked students to write a proposal. Imagine you're a student at this school. In your proposal, explain what type of building you think it should be and why, how to make sure all students in the school benefit from it, and suggest ways in which the building could be used by the local community outside school hours.

Write your proposal (220–260 words).

2 In C1 Advanced Writing Part 2, candidates are given a choice of three tasks, one of which is to write a proposal of about 240 words. For the proposal, students are given information about the context, topic purpose and readership and must make suggestions, supported by factual information and evaluation. This part of the exam tests the candidates' ability to write well-organised texts with functional language for evaluating and making suggestions and a good range of persuasive language.

Encourage your students to do the following when they approach this task:

- Candidates should read all the tasks and consider the topic and the language that is needed in each before choosing the task that best suits them.
- For the chosen task, identify what is required and who it is for, and what kind of information is needed.
- Make a plan, referring closely to the question.
- Look for opportunities to develop ideas and show a range of language.
- Write a rough draft before writing the final answer. Make sure that it is well organised and has a range of tenses, expressions and vocabulary.
- Read the work again to check that it makes sense and that all the content points have been included. Check the spelling.

1 1 in 2 off 3 stock 4 turn
5 beginner's 6 away 7 to
8 punchline 9 matter 10 giggles

2 1 speak 2 It 3 didn't speak
4 What 5 could speak
6 hadn't spoken

3 1 I'll ~~do certainly~~ certainly do all I can to help you.
2 Unless we ~~don't~~ leave now, we'll miss the train.
3 If I hadn't eaten so much, I wouldn't ~~have felt~~ feel so ill now.
4 It was the journey ~~what~~ that was most fun.
5 He's ~~made clearly~~ clearly made a lot of enemies.
6 ~~Provided that~~ Imagine you could go anywhere in the world, where would you go?

4 1 remember 2 good
3 get 4 funny 5 Never 6 bad
7 beginner's 8 Just

TEST YOURSELF UNITS 3 & 4

VOCABULARY

1 Complete the sentences with the words in the list. There are four extra words.

away | beginner's | giggles | in | matter | off | on | over | punchline | stock | through | to | trick | turn

1 You need to go to the supermarket? Well, you're … luck. I'm just about to drive to town.
2 I loved that film. It was so funny that I laughed my head … .
3 Don't wear that shirt. You'll be the laughing … of the party.
4 He wanted to offer me the job, but I decided to … it down.
5 I can't believe I won. I've never played cards before. It must be … luck.
6 Oh no! Where's my bag? That boy has run … with it.
7 When the patient came … , the nurse asked him if he could remember his name.
8 I'm terrible at telling jokes. I always forget the … .
9 You've broken the window. I don't think this is a laughing … .
10 I always get the … when Mr Harrison tells me off. I just can't help laughing.

GRAMMAR

2 Complete the sentences with the words/phrases in the list. There are two extra words/phrases.

all | could speak | didn't speak | don't speak | hadn't spoken | it | speak | what

1 Unless you … to the headmaster first, you won't be able to use the hall for the party.
2 … was Dave who suggested the idea.
3 If I … Spanish fluently, they wouldn't have offered me the job. I can't wait to start!
4 … annoyed me most was the wait.
5 Imagine you … another language, which language would you choose?
6 If you … to her so rudely yesterday, you might still be friends.

3 Find and correct the mistake in each sentence.

1 I'll do certainly all I can to help you.
2 Unless we don't leave now, we'll miss the train.
3 If I hadn't eaten so much, I wouldn't have felt so ill now.
4 It was the journey what was most fun.
5 He's made clearly a lot of enemies.
6 Provided that you could go anywhere in the world, where would you go?

FUNCTIONAL LANGUAGE

4 Choose the correct options.

1 That's a great joke. I must *learn / remember* that one. Thanks.
2 Ha, ha! That's a *fun / good* one.
3 Thanks for explaining the joke. I just didn't *catch / get* it at first.
4 Ha ha – very *funny / hysterical*.
5 A I can't believe I didn't win the poetry competition.
B *Never / Don't* mind. You can always try again.
6 A Can you believe we lost the match in the last minute?
B That really is *bad / worse* luck.
7 He'd never played football before and scored three goals. Talk about *starter's / beginner's* luck.
8 I've missed the bus by a minute. *Only / Just* my luck!

MY SCORE
22–30 | 10–21 | 0–9

48

The Cambridge Life Competencies Framework

Critical THINKing
Evaluating ideas and arguments
Watch this video for a tip on developing your students' critical thinking skills. Scan the QR code here.

Unit Opener

Warmer

Ask students to give examples of extreme sports. Write them on the board and add these extra ones if they haven't already been mentioned: *caving, hang-gliding, skydiving, skysurfing, mountaineering, bull running, rafting, wakeboarding, bouldering, parachuting, bobsleighing*. You could show pictures or videos from the internet to clarify the meaning if necessary.

Once finished, clean the board and ask students to make a list in pairs of the ones they remember. Tell them to be careful with the spelling. Ask a volunteer to come up to the board and ask the other students to take turns spelling the sport for the volunteer to write on the board.

▶ 12 Get TH!NKing

Ask the question. Make sure students understand the word *stunts* (an exciting or dangerous action, often in a film, usually performed by a trained stuntman/stuntwoman). Get students to compare their ideas in groups. Play the video and then ask students for feedback.

1 Elicit what the students can see in the photo. What does it show? Where was it taken? Does it seem attractive? Would they like to be there? Why/Why not? In pairs, ask students to discuss these questions. Ask them to share their experiences of a similar situation.

2 Ask students to think of adjectives that define how they feel in a situation like the one shown in the photo. Provide support with vocabulary if needed. Then ask them how they feel about theme parks and scary rides.

3 Ask students to give examples of situations in which people enjoy being scared (going on a scary ride, watching a horror film, visiting a haunted house …). Ask them to match the situation with one of the adjectives they thought of. Then ask them if they enjoy these types of situations. Why/ Why not?

Objectives

Functions Giving and reacting to an opinion
Grammar Participle clauses; verbs of perception with infinitive or gerund
Vocabulary Thrill seeking; idioms with *hot* and *cold*
Culture Extreme sports

Resources for this unit

All available online

Videos

- Get **TH!NK**ing: *Which stunts do you enjoy watching?*
- Grammar video!: Participle clauses
- Culture: Extreme sports

Tests

- Unit, extension and skills test 5

Worksheets

- Grammar and vocabulary: Basic, Standard and Extension Worksheets
- Project: Thrills of a lifetime
- Communication: Thrill seekers
- Literature Worksheets: *Around the World in Eighty Days*
- Get **TH!NK**ing and Grammar video! video Worksheets

Warmer

Ask: *Do you like thrills? What is the most dangerous thing you have ever done?* Students discuss the questions in pairs.

1 Before students open their books, put a copy of the pictures up on the board and elicit the names of the activities (bungee jumping, skydiving, wingsuiting, kayaking) and some adjectives to describe them.

2–3 Monitor and help with vocabulary and ideas. After students have discussed in pairs, re-group them. Ask each group to compile a longer list of reasons and think of as many different reasons as possible for wanting or not wanting to do the activities. Encourage open-class discussion.

4 Give students a three-minute time limit to encourage them to read the article quickly to get a general understanding and answer the question.
Philippe Petit describes himself as a performing artist.

5 **5.01 Check/clarify:** *dash, stunt, death-defying, audacious, diligently, pylons.*
Ask students to try to put the events in order from memory before referring back to the text to check.
4, 10, 2, 8, 9, 1, 7, 3, 5, 6

6 Allow time to discuss and put the walks in order in question 3. Have a quick show of hands to find out which activities are the most dangerous, etc.

Pronunciation
Connected speech feature: elision
Student's Book p137

READING

1 Look at the photos. Which of the adjectives and phrases would you use to describe these activities?

awe-inspiring | awesome
boring | challenging
dangerous | exciting | not for me
rewarding | terrifying | unsafe

2 SPEAKING Work in pairs. Think of three reasons why people might want to do these activities and three reasons why they might not.

3 Compare your ideas with others in the class.

4 Read the article quickly. How does Philippe Petit describe himself?

5 5.01 Read the article again and listen. Put these events in the order that they happened.

- Petit takes his high-wire act to Australia.
- Petit's mental state is assessed.
- Petit learns his skill from Rudy Omankowsky Jr.
- Petit lies down on the wire.
- Petit is arrested.
- Petit practises his skill at his parents' home. (*1*)
- Petit starts his walk between the Twin Towers.
- Petit walks across the towers of the Notre-Dame cathedral.
- Petit and his team fly over the Twin Towers in a helicopter.
- The team fire an arrow between the Twin Towers.

6 SPEAKING Work in pairs and discuss the questions.

1 Would you like to do something like this? Why/Why not?
2 On the day Petit walked between the Twin Towers, how do you think he felt
 a as he stepped onto the wire?
 b half way into his walk?
 c at the end of his walk?
3 Make a list of three other high-wire walks Petit could do. How exciting, dangerous, challenging and terrifying would they be? Rank them from 1 (least) to 5 (most) for each adjective in turn.

PRONUNCIATION
Connected speech feature: elision Go to page 137.

Culture notes

The original World Trade Center was a group of seven buildings in New York City, USA. It opened in 1973 and at the time of their completion, the Twin Towers (1 and 2 World Trade Center) were the tallest buildings in the world. Both were destroyed in 2001 during the September 11 attacks.

Philippe Petit /pəti/ is a French high-wire artist who became famous for his unauthorised walks between the towers of the Notre Dame Cathedral in Paris on a wire in 1971. He also crossed Sydney Harbour Bridge, Australia, on a wire in 1973 before wire walking between the Twin Towers of the World Trade Center in New York in 1974.

7 Check/clarify: *daredevils, exploits.*
Elicit that *red herrings* are often used in crime stories where a clue is used to distract readers from the true story.
B

8–9 Encourage students to use the question in Exercise 7 as an example.

Homework

Ask students to research someone from around the world who has done / does extreme sport or an extreme challenge. As a follow-up, students can present this person to the class in the next lesson. After each presentation, encourage the rest of the class to ask questions and finally hold a class vote to decide which was the most interesting presentation.

Activity idea Extension

Ask students to work in pairs and discuss the following questions.

1 *Have you ever tried an extreme sport? What was it like? How did you feel? Would you do it again?*
2 *Which extreme sport, if any, would you most like to try? Why?*
3 *Are you able to identify with the thrill-seeker described in the text? If so, in what ways?*

Critical TH!NKing
Evaluating ideas and arguments
Identifies evidence and its reliability.

In the early morning rush hour on 7th August 1974, commuters in New York City stopped their mad dash to work to look up in the sky. Way up above them there seemed to be someone walking between the recently constructed Twin Towers of the World Trade Center. As the crowds grew larger, the person stopped walking and lay down as if he were floating in thin air.

Four hundred metres above, French-born Philippe Petit looked down on the people below. They were his audience and looked like ants to him. Petit had started his stunt at 7 am, when he first walked out onto the thin wire that passed between the towers. For the next three quarters of an hour, he entertained the New Yorkers below him by walking between the towers, often stopping to sit or lie down on the wire. Eventually, having made eight crossings, Petit took a bow and walked back inside. Arriving safely back on solid ground, Petit handed himself over to the police who were waiting for him.

Since the authorities thought anyone attempting such a death-defying feat must be crazy, he was first taken to a mental-health hospital to determine whether or not he was mad. When they decided he wasn't, he was charged with public disorder offences, but all charges were dropped soon after and Petit was a free man, able to enjoy all the publicity and fame that his tight-rope walk had earned him.

Petit's audacious act had been many months in the planning. With a small group of friends, he had made many plans, assessing and minimising the risks of the challenge he had set himself, including hiring a helicopter, from which they took photos of the towers from above. When he was completely sure that everything was in place, Petit and his team set about preparing for the main event. One member of his team had an office inside one of the towers and the night before, he was able to sneak the team and their heavy equipment up to the top floors of the tower, which were still under construction. Knowing they had a lot to do, the team worked quickly throughout the night. First, they shot an arrow (to which a line was attached) across to a contact on the roof of the other tower. Then, they used this line to pull across a heavy wire. Finally, this wire was secured tightly between the two towers. Petit was ready to step out and introduce himself to the world. Had they not prepared so diligently, the walk might well have ended in disaster.

But the walk between the Twin Towers was not the Frenchman's first daredevil act. Petit had always been a risk-taker, ever since he had first tied a rope between two trees in his parents' garden and practised walking between them. As a young man living in Paris, he met a Czech tight-rope walker called Rudy Omankowsky Jr., who showed him how to prepare ropes for large-scale walks. His first big appearance came in June 1971 when he walked between the two towers at the front of the Notre-Dame cathedral in Paris. Two years later, he was in Sydney to walk along the pylons of the famous harbour bridge. Like the Twin Towers, neither of these walks had permission from the authorities, but Petit has always refused to accept that he is just a stuntman willing to take risks to make himself famous – he insists that he is a performing artist.

Train to TH!NK

Red herrings

A red herring is often introduced to deliberately cause a distraction from the main issue by appearing to have some actual importance when, in fact, it has none. By thinking critically, we can train ourselves to identify red herrings quickly and not be misled by them. This ultimately places us in a better position to make decisions based only on the facts that are truly important to the issue.

7 Read the text in the box and answer the question. Which sentence does not show how Petit has inspired modern daredevils?

A He has shown that with good preparation, anything is possible.
B He has also had two films made about him.
C He showed how doing such stunts would not get you into trouble with the law.

> Philippe Petit is an inspiration to many of today's daredevils. His careful planning showed how it was possible to achieve the most audacious of stunts without putting any other person's life in danger. He has also been the subject of at least two films. His exploits have often caused the authorities many headaches. Although, in theory, such actions might be illegal, it would make the authorities very unpopular if they charged these daredevils with a crime.

8 WRITING **Work in pairs. Write a multiple-choice question for the article. Include a red herring.**

9 SPEAKING **Work with another pair. Identify each other's red herring.**

TH!NK more

Worksheets
Project Thrills of a lifetime
Communication Thrill seekers
Get **TH!NK**ing *Which stunts do you enjoy watching?*

Warmer

Write on the board: *1 A man saw a gorilla running through the jungle; 2 Running through the jungle, a man saw a gorilla.* Ask: *Do these sentences have the same meaning? (No), What's the difference? (In the first sentence, the gorilla is running; in the second sentence, the man is running).* Ask students to come up with similar pairs of sentences. Write any correct pairs on the board to refer to later.

▶ 12 Grammar video! Participle clauses

1 b, d, a, c
RULE: 1 time 2 reasons 3 conditions 4 results 5 the same 6 present 7 past

2 Point out that students can look at the rule to check their answers if necessary.
1 After climbing/they climb into a glass cage, the thrilled and terrified tourists are lowered into the water with the crocodiles.
2 If it is carried out correctly, the dive is completely safe.
3 After you've returned to the safety of the beach, you can look at the amazing pictures taken by our professional photographer.
4 If you share these photos with your friends, you will be the talk of the town.

GRAMMAR
Participle clauses

Grammar video ▶ 13

1 Look at the sentences from the article. What meanings do the participle clauses (in bold) express? Decide if they mean *at the same time, after, because* or *if*. Then complete the rule with *reasons, time, the same, results, conditions, present* and *past*.

Having made eight crossings, Petit took a bow and walked back inside.
Had they not prepared so diligently, the walk might well have ended in disaster.
Arriving safely back on solid ground, Petit handed himself over to the police.
Knowing they had a lot to do, the team worked quickly throughout the night.

> **RULE:** We form participle clauses with the present or past participle.
> Participle clauses are used to:
> - talk about [1]... relationships (things happening at the same time, or one after the other).
>   *He was looking down at the crowds, **feeling** very excited.* (While he looked down at the crowds, he felt ...)
> - give [2]... to explain an action or event.
>   ***Learning** how to prepare ropes properly, Petit decided to try more ambitious walks.* (Because he learned ...)
> - talk about [3]... .
>   ***Done** correctly, high-wire walking is not as dangerous as it looks.* (If you do it correctly, high-wire walking ...)
> - talk about [4]... .
>   *Petit made the rope higher for each walk, gradually **allowing** him to **get used to** the heights.* (... as a consequence, this gradually allowed him to get used to the heights.)
>
> We can introduce participle clauses with *before, after, while, by, since* and *on*.
> We can only use a participle clause if the subject of the two clauses is [5]... .
> *While white-water rafting, **Jenny** broke her leg.*
> We use [6]... participles for active clauses and we use [7]... participles for passive clauses.
> ***Jumping** out of the plane, Emma felt exhilarated.*
> ***Carried** by the wind, she parachuted safely down to the ground.*

2 Read these sentences taken from a leaflet about the Saltwater Croc Dive in Darwin, Australia. Transform the participle clauses to make longer sentences with *after* or *if*.

A sure way to become A DAREDEVIL ...
Saltwater crocodile watching

[0]Having opened its doors last year, Saltwater Croc Dive has become the best place to get a close look at the world's most dangerous reptiles. (After)
[1]Having climbed into a glass cage, the thrilled and terrified tourists are lowered into the water with the crocodiles. (After)
[2]Carried out correctly, the dive is completely safe. (If)
[3]Having returned to the safety of the beach, you can look at the amazing pictures taken by our professional photographer. (After)
[4]Sharing these photos with your friends, you will be the talk of the town. (If)

After opening its doors last year, Saltwater Croc Dive has become the best place to get a close look at the world's most dangerous reptiles.

3 Use a participle clause to shorten each of the following sentence constructions.

0 Because she'd noticed there was something wrong with her parachute, she didn't jump out of the helicopter.
Having noticed that something was wrong with her parachute, she didn't jump out of the helicopter.
1 If you do these exercises regularly, they'll help you to become extremely fit.
2 After they'd watched the stunt, most people were speechless.
3 While we were watching the people in their canoes, we decided to try it, too.
4 She's always been aware of the risks, and because of this, she's never had any serious accidents.
5 He learned how to climb from his father. He became passionate about climbing.

→ workbook page 46

52

3 If you're short on time, set this exercise for homework. Go through the first item to make sure students are clear on what to do.
1 Done regularly, these exercises will help you to become extremely fit.
2 Having watched/After watching the stunt, most people were speechless.
3 (While) watching the people in their canoes, we decided to try it too.
4 Having always been aware of the risks, she's never had any serious accidents.
5 Having learned/After learning how to climb from his father, he became passionate about it. / Having learned from his father, he became passionate about climbing.

Workbook p46

Get it Right!
Participles and gerunds

Student's Book p68

TH!NK more

Workbook
Grammar p46, Ex.1–6

Worksheets
Grammar Worksheets 5
Grammar video! Participle clauses

4 During feedback, say the phrases for students to repeat. Pay attention to the linking of sounds between words such as *risk-taker* (the *k* is almost silent), *kick out of* and *death-defying*. Also point out that *assess* is stressed on the second syllable.
1 g 2 a 3 e 4 f 5 h 6 c 7 d 8 b

5 1 daredevil 2 risk-taker 3 (real) kick out of 4 minimises/minimised the risk 5 audacious 6 stunts 7 assess the risk 8 death-defying

Workbook p48

6 Allow students six to eight minutes to prepare their discussions. If students have access to a recording facility (using their mobile phones, for example), they could record their conversation and play it back to check their own pronunciation and intonation. They can then repeat the exercise and listen for improvements.

7–8 5.03 Elicit *theme park*. After students have discussed the questions about the photo, elicit some answers and create a list on the board to refer to after the listening, but do not comment. Students then listen and compare.

9 5.03 **Check/clarify:** *and the like, adrenalin rush, simulates.* Give students time to read through sentences 1–6 before playing the audio. Ask students to work with a partner to try to answer the questions from memory.
1 extreme sports 2 simulates 3 risking 4 thrill seekers 5 brains 6 (daily) problems / worries

10 Remind students to think about what is risky for people in general, not just for themselves, and to think of reasons for their choices.
Students' own answers

11–12 Check understanding of *feel alive* with an example. Hold a class vote to decide on the best order to rank the six items.

VOCABULARY
Thrill seeking

4 Match the sentence halves.

1 The skydiver completed an epic *stunt* when
2 Jumping from a plane without
3 As Jenny walked on the narrow edge of the building, 75 metres above ground,
4 She's a real *daredevil*. Have you ever seen
5 We need to *assess the risk* of doing this climb
6 This documentary explains why some people *get a real*
7 She'd never do anything extreme
8 Did you see the video of his *death-defying*

a a parachute is extremely *audacious*.
b leap from the Statue of Liberty?
c *kick out of* doing extreme sports.
d without *minimising the risk* beforehand.
e she said she wasn't scared. She was a *risk-taker* by nature.
f videos of her insane extreme mountain skiing?
g she somersaulted from one glider to another at 180 km per hour.
h before making the decision to go.

5 Complete the sentences with the correct form of the words and expressions in italics in Exercise 4.

1 Jumping over ten buses on his motorbike, the … performed another terrifying feat for the crowds.
2 She often climbs without a harness. She's a … .
3 My sister gets a … extreme mountain climbing. She loves it.
4 She … of injury by wearing a helmet.
5 It was an … thing to do. It showed the young hang-glider's skill, strength and lack of fear.
6 He's performed … in many different films, but his most famous was in *Everest*.
7 You need to … before you decide whether or not to climb the building.
8 He performed his … jump from the top of the Eiffel Tower without a parachute.

→ workbook page 48

SPEAKING

6 ROLE PLAY **Work in pairs. Student A: Go to page 143. Student B: Go to page 144.**

LISTENING

7 SPEAKING **Work in pairs and look at the photo. In what way is this activity different from extreme sports, such as bungee jumping or base jumping? In what way is it similar?**

8 5.03 **Listen and compare your answers to what the expert says.**

9 5.03 **Listen again and complete these sentences with one or two words.**

1 According to the psychologist, risk-takers need the adrenalin rush they get from doing … .
2 Going on a roller coaster isn't really dangerous, but it … real danger.
3 Some people don't seek an adrenalin rush. They have no interest in … their lives.
4 People who love taking risks are commonly described as … .
5 Some people do dangerous activities to feel adrenalin levels rise in their … .
6 Another theory is that they can forget their … by doing dangerous activities.

SPEAKING

10 Rank the activities from 1 to 6 according to how risky they are (1 = not very risky; 6 = very risky).

riding a motorcycle without a helmet
base jumping
playing tennis
walking in the countryside
playing ice hockey
swimming in the sea

11 Now rank the activities from 1 to 6 according to how much they make people 'feel alive' (1 = not very alive; 6 = fully alive).

12 SPEAKING **Work in pairs. Compare your results with your partner.**

Homework

Ask students to keep a journal for two or three days and make a note of the activities they do, or if they don't do any, what activities their family have done, and how risky they were on a scale of 1 (not at all risky) to 6 (very risky).

Activity idea Extension

Write the following on the board:

1 *Do people take risks in order to feel alive?*
2 *How often do you take a risk?*
3 *What type of risks do you take?*
4 *What would you recommend as the best way to feel alive?*

Ask students to discuss the questions in pairs or small groups. Listen to some of their ideas in open class.

TH!NK more

Workbook
Vocabulary p48, Ex.1–4
Vocabulary Extra p49, Ex.1–3
Listening p52, Ex.1–3

Worksheets
Vocabulary Worksheets 5

Warmer

Ask students: *Where is the coldest place you've been? How cold was it? How did it feel?* Divide the class into pairs for students to discuss these questions. After a few minutes, discuss as a class to see who has been to the coldest place.

1–2 Give your own experience as an example to get students started on this exercise.

3 Give students a three-minute time limit to encourage them to read quickly. Tell students not to try to understand every word, but to focus on answering the question and getting a general understanding of the text.
Staying in direct contact with ice for the longest time; running the fastest half marathon in bare feet; climbing Mount Kilimanjaro in only shorts; swimming for the greatest distance under ice.

4 **5.04** Ask students to underline the language in the text that helped them answer.
1 The freezing water is enough to send the human body into panic, causing a fatal heart attack.
2 He is in the water for 15 minutes.
3 He created his ability using breathing techniques that allow him to get into a mindset where he is able to convince his body that it is not bothered by the freezing temperatures.
4 Because he claims that his method brings about an improved immune system.
5 When his wife died.
6 Hof tours the world giving inspirational talks and offering courses on which students can learn the Wim Hof method. He has also made many appearances on TV in many countries to promote his ideas and talk about the successes he has enjoyed.

5 After students have discussed in pairs, re-group them into small groups for students to report back on their discussions and share opinions.

READING

1 **Read the statements. Which ones do you agree with?**
- I never sleep with the air conditioning on.
- I prefer a cold winter to a hot summer.
- I often take cold showers.
- I often wear T-shirts and shorts when others are in long trousers and jumpers.

2 SPEAKING **Compare with a partner and discuss.**

3 **Read the article below quickly. Find three of the world records that Wim Hof holds.**

4 5.04 **Read the article again and listen. Answer the questions.**
1 Why is the first minute in freezing water the most dangerous?
2 How long does Hof stay in the water?
3 How did Hof create his ability to survive freezing temperatures?
4 Why are scientists interested in Hof?
5 What event changed Hof's life?
6 What does Hof do these days?

5 SPEAKING **Work in pairs and discuss the questions.**
1 Do you think anyone could learn the Wim Hof method? Why/Why not?
2 Would you be interested in learning the method? Why/Why not?

WIM HOF: THE ICEMAN

A man sits cross-legged on top of a small mound of ice in Glacier View, Alaska. The temperature is -3°C. He is surrounded by nothing but ice and water. He feels the cold air blowing across his body. He is wearing only shorts and a headband to keep his long hair away from his face. He seems to be meditating. He gets up and walks towards the water's edge. At 2°C, it is just above freezing point. The man bends down and with cupped hands, he pours the water over his face. He feels the ice-cold water run down his face and then he slowly walks into the water and starts swimming. The first minute is the most dangerous – the freezing water is enough to send the human body into panic, causing a fatal heart attack. But a minute is nothing for this extraordinary man. He is in the water for 15 minutes. This would be more than long enough to kill most ordinary people, but one thing is for certain: Wim Hof is no ordinary person.

Wim Hof is a 60-year-old Dutchman who has the ability to endure extreme cold. He developed this ability through using particular breathing techniques. These techniques allow him to get into a mindset where he is able to convince his body that it is not bothered by the freezing temperatures. He has been studied by scientists to see exactly what it is that makes him so remarkable, although Hof himself claims there is no physiological difference. He believes that his techniques can be learned by anyone. Furthermore, he claims that his method brings about an improved immune system – something that the scientists are keen to explore further.

Hof's remarkable journey started with heartache when his wife died, leaving him with four young children to raise on his own. At first, he was unsure how he would cope and he looked for alternative ideas to help him overcome the grief. This led him to the discovery that through his relationship with coldness, he was able to control his breathing and begin to deal with the intense physical pain that he felt. This led him to more and more extreme adventures, which tested his body to its limits and allowed him to explore hidden depths within his mind. It was the start of a long healing process. These days, Hof tours the world, giving inspirational talks and offering courses. On these courses, students can learn the Wim Hof method to help them tune into the inner power of their body to help them cope with the everyday stresses of modern life. He has also made many appearances on TV in several countries to promote his ideas and talk about the successes he has enjoyed.

Unsurprisingly, Hof also holds several world records when it comes to enduring extreme cold; in fact, he holds 26. To break the record for staying in direct contact with ice for the longest time, he stood in a glass box which was filled up with ice cubes while officials watched. After 1 hour and 53 seconds, and to a huge cheer from the audience, the record was his. Other records he holds include running the fastest half marathon in bare feet, climbing Mount Kilimanjaro in only shorts, and swimming for the greatest distance under ice.

54

Culture note

Wim Hof is a Dutch extreme athlete. He is the holder of 21 Guinness World Records and got his nickname 'The Iceman' by breaking a number of records related to cold exposure including: climbing Mount Kilimanjaro in shorts and running a half marathon above the Arctic Circle barefoot. A scientific study in 2018 showed that Wim Hof's method of controlling his breathing, heart rate and blood circulation activated areas of the brain responsible for pain suppression, giving hope to the idea that the technique could be used as an endogenous painkiller.

TH!NK more

Workbook
Reading p50, Ex.1–4

Grammar; Vocabulary; Functions

6 sentence 2
RULE: 1 part of an action
2 an entire action

7 Go through the first sentence as an example, making sure students are clear on why that particular form is used.
1 scream 2 banging; blowing
3 standing 4 run 5 crawling
6 dripping

Workbook p47

8 Encourage students to guess answers if they are not sure. Ask them to discuss the meaning of each idiom in pairs.
1 hot 2 cold 3 hot 4 cold
5 cold 6 hot

9 If you are short on time, you could set this for homework.
1 hot and bothered
2 the cold shoulder; poured cold water; hot under the collar
3 hot water; out in the cold

Workbook p48

10 5.05 Give your own example to get students started.
1 Dialogue 1: The man thinks the person was too old to climb; the woman thinks it's dangerous for young as well as old people.
Dialogue 2: The woman thinks driving fast cars is exciting; the man thinks it's OK to be a thrill seeker, but that fast cars are dangerous, polluting, a waste of money and not something he would do for excitement.
2 Students' own answers

11 5.05 During feedback, say the phrases for students to repeat and check pronunciation. Point out the strong stress on *my* in *To my mind*; *I* in *the way I see it* and *I* in *That's not how I see things*, to emphasise the speaker's opinion.
To my mind, that's … – 1
Yes, I suppose you're right. – 2
I don't accept that … – 3
The way I see it is … – 1
I hadn't thought of that. – 4
That's not how I see things. – 3
True. – 2
I'd go along with that. – 2
OK. Point taken. – 4

12 Allow students six to eight minutes to prepare their discussions. Encourage them to use the key language.

GRAMMAR
Verbs of perception with infinitive or gerund

6 **Read the sentences from the article. In which sentence is the sensation felt from when it starts to when it ends? Choose the correct options in the rule.**

1 He feels the cold air **blowing** across his body.
2 He feels the ice-cold water **run** down his face .

RULE: We use a verb of perception (*see, hear, feel*) plus a gerund to say we have experienced [1]*an entire action / part of an action.*
I ***saw*** *a man* ***painting*** *a house.*
I ***felt*** *my heart* ***beating*** *fast.*
I ***heard*** *someone* ***playing*** *the piano.*
We use a verb of perception plus an infinitive to say we have experienced [2]*an entire action / part of an action.*
I ***saw*** *a man* ***paint*** *a picture.*
I ***felt*** *her hand* ***touch*** *my shoulder.*
I ***heard*** *someone* ***close*** *the door.*

7 **Complete the sentences with the correct form of the verb in brackets.**

1 We heard somebody … and then it was silent. (scream)
2 The noise was terrible and it went on for hours. We heard people … drums and … whistles loudly. (bang, blow)
3 When he woke up after the operation, he saw lots of people … around his bed. (stand)
4 When we were driving home, I suddenly saw a deer … across the road before it disappeared. (run)
5 I was lying in bed when I became aware of an insect … on my face. I switched on the light, but couldn't see anything. (crawl)
6 The rain was beating down on the roof of the car, and I suddenly felt water … down onto the back of my neck. (drip)

→ workbook page 47

VOCABULARY
Idioms with *hot* and *cold*

8 **Read the sentences. Complete the idioms with *hot* (x3) or *cold* (x3).**

1 It was only a joke. There's no need to *get so … under the collar* about it.
2 I tried to talk to Ann, but she completely ignored me and *gave me the … shoulder*.
3 When your dad finds out you've scratched his car, you'll *be in … water*.
4 I don't mean to *pour … water on* your idea but it really isn't very practical.
5 No one's told me anything. I've been completely *left out in the …* .
6 Her interview is today and she's getting very *… and bothered* about it. She just needs to relax.

9 **Use the idioms in Exercise 8 to complete the dialogues.**

1 A This is so annoying! I can't log in to my computer, but I'm sure this password is correct.
B OK. There's no point getting all … about it. Try a different one.
2 A I saw Steve today and he completely gave me … .
B Well, I'm not surprised after you … on his ideas for his new website.
A Well, they were really silly. I don't know why he got so … about what I said.
3 A Be careful when you see Sally. You're really in … with her.
B Why? What did I do?
A I think she feels you left her … when you booked the holiday without asking her. She isn't at all happy with you.

→ workbook page 48

FUNCTIONS
Giving and reacting to an opinion

10 5.05 **Listen to the dialogues and answer the questions.**

1 What opinions are expressed in dialogue 1? And in dialogue 2?
2 In each case, who do you agree with?

11 5.05 **Listen to the dialogues again and match the phrases with functions 1–4 below.**

1 giving an opinion
2 agreeing
3 disagreeing
4 conceding a point

- To my mind, that's …
- Yes, I suppose you're right.
- I don't accept that …
- The way I see it is …
- I hadn't thought of that.
- That's not how I see things.
- True.
- I'd go along with that.
- OK. Point taken.

12 ROLE PLAY **Work in pairs. You're going to discuss extreme sports and try to convince your partner of your opinion. Student A: Go to page 143. Student B: Go to page 144. Use the phrases from Exercise 11 in your discussions.**

55

Homework
Ask students to research an extreme sportswoman. They can find a picture and write a description of the person and what they do. If students do not have access to the internet, they can create their own ideas. As a follow-up, students can bring the picture to the next lesson and present their person to the class. If students are struggling to think of someone, you could give them the following people to research: *Tanya Streeter* (world champion free diver), *Brooke Raboutou* (free climber), *Kristin Boese* (kite surfer), *Malia Manuel* (surfer), *Catie Munnings* (rally driver).

Activity idea Fast finishers
Ask students to write two example sentences describing entire actions that they have heard or seen today and two sentences describing parts of actions that they have heard or seen. Listen to some of their examples in open class after feedback.

TH!NK more
Practice Extra
Unit 5 Practise it!
Workbook
Grammar p47, Ex.7 Vocabulary p48, Ex.5–6
Worksheets
Grammar Worksheets 5
Vocabulary Worksheets 5

Warmer

In pairs, give students two minutes to write down as many extreme sports as possible. Go through the alphabet, asking students to offer an extreme sport beginning with each letter (*abseiling, base/bungee jumping, cave diving, downhill skateboarding …*) Students vote on which sport they think is the most extreme.

▶ 14 TH!NK

Extreme sports

1 Ask students to read the article very quickly to answer the questions.
1 Cerro Negro, Nicaragua; Piazza Santa Croce, Florence, Italy; La Quebrada, Acapulco, Mexico.
2 Possible answers: They are all extreme.
Calcio storico is a team game. The general public are not allowed to do cliff diving. Volcano boarding involves a volcano.

TH!NK
Extreme sports

Culture

GOING TO THE EXTREME

1 **Look at the photos and read the article quickly. Then answer the questions.**
1 Where are these places?
2 What do the activities have in common? What differences are there between them?

We all have different interests, that's for sure, and extreme sports are certainly not for the faint-hearted. They're for those people who live on adrenalin and whose idea of hell is sitting at home watching TV. If you're looking for that ultimate thrill, no matter how brief, there are places you can go to get the most exhilarating experiences. Here are a few of them.

VOLCANO BOARDING

Fancy a plunge down the sides of an active volcano on a thin piece of board at speeds of up to 95 kilometres per hour? Yes? Well, then volcano boarding might just be the sport for you. The most popular location for this sport is the volcano of Cerro Negro in Nicaragua, where more than 20,000 people have already enjoyed the experience, which some might describe as madness, since the dangers include falling off and getting really badly cut or even being hit by scorching molten lava. You could even get histoplasmosis, a particularly nasty disease of the lungs caused by breathing in toxic gases.

CALCIO STORICO

If you ever find yourself going for a wander through the Piazza Santa Croce in the beautiful Italian city of Florence in late June, you may well come across an extraordinary sight: dozens of men dressed in historical costumes, chasing a ball and stopping at nothing to get to it. Calcio storico is a game you won't find anywhere else in the world. It's probably best described as a mixture of football and rugby with a lot of wrestling thrown in. Four teams of 27 players, representing each of the four districts of Florence, compete in semi-finals and a final to find that year's champion. The general idea is to score as many 'cacce' as you can by throwing the ball over marked-out goals around the pitch. Of course, you also need to stop your opponents doing the same thing and can use tactics such as punching, elbowing and head-butting to help you, although these days kicks to the head are no longer allowed.

CLIFF DIVING

La Quebrada, Acapulco, is the site of the famous cliff divers' performance. Since 1934, this has been one of Mexico's top attractions. The divers leap from cliffs 41 metres above the Pacific, landing in water just over three metres deep. There are five performances daily, including four evening shows, performed by divers carrying torches – an unforgettable display.

Anyone who's watched Acapulco's cliff divers plunge into the rough sea may wonder how daring and tricky an act this is. Ramirez Vasquez, who comes from a family of cliff divers, says that timing is key. He explains that in order to hit the water when it's at its deepest and ultimately, safest, cliff divers have a five-second window during which the wave is high. It takes three seconds to reach the water, giving them a two-second margin of error.

In preparation for his twice-daily dive, Vasquez works out from 8 am to 10 am, five times a week. Meditation is also part of his routine. He still gets nervous before each and every dive, despite his vast experience. An average diver who starts their career at 17 and ends it at 45 will do 15,560 dives into the Quebrada. Many cliff divers have been involved in accidents, most caused by the impact of the water. Remarkably, no deaths have been recorded to date.

56

Culture notes

Volcano boarding (also known as volcano surfing or lava boarding) is an extreme sport performed sliding down volcano slopes. The first known instance of the sport was filmed by Zoltan Istvan of the National Geographic Channel in 1995, however there has been a similar sport called *he'e holua* in Hawaii since ancient times.

Calcio storico (also known as *Calcio Fiorentino*) is an early form of football that originated in Italy during the Middle Ages. However, a similar game called *harpastum* (or *harpustum*) was played during the time of the Roman Empire. The game was revived in 1930s Italy and was widely played by amateurs in the streets.

Cliff jumping (also known as tombstoning when upright without equipment or BASE jumping if with a parachute) can be traced back to the islands of Hawaii nearly 250 years ago. The legend goes that Kahekili II, the king of Maui, would force his warriors to leap off a cliff to land in the water below as a way of showing how fearless and loyal they were. It later evolved into a competition and spread to other parts of the world. In 2015, Laso Schaller dived more than 58 metres setting a new world record (Olympic divers jump a maximum of 10m!). From that height, divers can be travelling over 112 km/h when they hit the water.

2 🔊 **5.06 Check/clarify:** *molten lava, histoplasmosis, wrestling, tactics, punching, elbowing, head-butting.*
Tell students to just focus on answering the question. Tell them to underline the information in the text that helped them answer each question.
1 Piazza Santa Croce, Florence
2 Cerro Negro, Nicaragua
3 La Quebrada, Acapulco
4 Piazza Santa Croce, Florence
5 Piazza Santa Croce, Florence
6 La Quebrada, Acapulco
7 Cerro Negro, Nicaragua
8 Piazza Santa Croce, Florence

3 1 wander 2 opponents 3 plunge 4 window 5 faint-hearted 6 thrill 7 impact 8 scorching

4 Encourage students to express themselves in English and to use any vocabulary they have learned from the article. Hold a class vote to decide which is the most popular (if any!).

1 Allow students to compare answers in pairs before feedback.
The key part of the bungee jump – according to the writer's editor – is the free-fall and precisely the part that the writer fails to remember. It lasted eight and a half seconds.

2 how high the jump was – 1
where the bungee jump was – 3
how long the jump lasted – 7
what the writer thought about the jump – 8
when the writer did the jump – 2
the journey to do the jump – 6
where the writer stayed – 4
when the writer realised how scary the jump might be – 5

3 This could be done as a quick reading race.
Thirty-six hours later, having checked into my simple but charming hotel in the heart of the city, I spent the evening talking with locals about my imminent jump.

4 Divide the class into small groups so that they can share ideas before writing individually. Students make notes as preparation for writing. Students should organise their stages in the same way as the example in Exercise 1. They should use words and phrases from the unit.

2 🔊 5.06 **Read the article again and listen. At which of the three places …**
1 could you see people dressed in clothes from the past?
2 could you be burned by hot rock?
3 are even experienced participants always scared before the activity?
4 can you see a sport that doesn't take place anywhere else?
5 will you see people wrestling in a public square?
6 will you see people leap from a 41-metre cliff into the sea below?
7 could you see a dangerous eruption?
8 could you see several people competing in a game?

3 VOCABULARY **Match the highlighted words in the article with the definitions.**
1 a casual walk
2 the people you play against in a sporting contest
3 fall or move down very quickly or with force
4 a length of time when it's possible to do something
5 not brave
6 a strong feeling of excitement, joy
7 force or action (created by one object hitting another)
8 very, very hot

4 SPEAKING **Work in pairs and discuss the questions.**
1 Which of these sports would you most like to try? Put them in order of preference.
2 Which of these sports would you most like to watch? Put them in order of preference.
3 What's your view on these and other extreme sports?

WRITING
A newspaper article

1 INPUT **Read the newspaper article. Why did the writer choose this title?**

Eight and a half seconds I'll never remember

Had anyone asked me a year ago if I'd ever be standing in a small cabin, looking out over a 134-metre drop, preparing to launch myself towards the ground below, I'd have told them they were mad. But that's exactly where I found myself yesterday morning.

I've never been much of a daredevil. I've ridden a few of the smaller roller coasters at Alton Towers, but that's about it. So why was I now about to risk life and limb for the sake of a newspaper story?

The idea to 'do' the world's highest bungee jump came from my editor. When he requested a travel article on New Zealand, naturally I leapt at the chance. It was only while I was travelling to the airport that a text came from him suggesting I check out the Nevis bungee in Queensland. OK, I thought, there's no harm in that.

Thirty-six hours later, having checked into my simple but charming hotel in the heart of the city, I spent the evening talking with locals about my imminent jump. That's when I started to wonder if I'd completely taken leave of my senses. 'It's the highest in the world,' they told me. Had any of them done it? 'No.'

The beautiful drive out to the privately owned jump is worth an article of its own, but that isn't what my editor wants. He wants to know about the longest eight and a half seconds of my life as I free-fell through the air, with only a thin wire to save me from certain death. Well, I'm pretty sure it was the most frightening experience of my life – the only problem is, I don't really remember a single thing about it.

2 ANALYSE **Read the article again and put the information below in the order in which it is mentioned.**
- how high the jump was
- where the bungee jump was
- how long the jump lasted
- what the writer thought about the jump
- when the writer did the jump
- the journey to do the jump
- where the writer stayed
- when the writer realised how scary the jump might be

3 **Find an example of a participle clause in the article.**

4 PRODUCE **Write a newspaper article (200–250 words) about one of the other extreme sports you've read about in this unit.**
- Either imagine you did it or you saw someone else doing it.
- Think carefully about how to introduce the details of the experience. It doesn't need to be in chronological order.
- Present the facts throughout the article to maintain interest.
- Try and include at least two participle clauses.

Activity idea Mixed-ability

In Culture Exercise 3, stronger students could look at the eight words in the article and try to deduce meaning from context before referring back to the definitions and completing the exercise. With weaker classes, you could even give students the first letter of each word to guide them.

Homework

If you are short on time, students can do Exercise 4 for homework. If you have done this in the class, ask students to exchange their newspaper articles with another student for them to read at home and give feedback on content and structure. Students could check if the article uses the same structure as the example. They should also decide which the most/least interesting part of the article is.

TH!NK more

Practice Extra
Unit 5 Master it!

Workbook
Developing Writing p51

Tests
Unit, extension and skills test 5

Warmer

Read through the information. Ask students if they've read the book. If they haven't, ask them to scan the text and explain whether they would like to or not.

Culture note

Jack London (1876–1916) was an American journalist and writer whose work provides a realistic depiction of people and places. His most famous works include the novels *The Call of the Wild* and *White Fang*, and a collection of short stories, *To Build a Fire and Other Stories*.

1 5.07 The senses mentioned in the text are sight, touch, taste and smell.

2 His mother is a source of tenderness, food and warmth. She also protects her pups from danger by not allowing them out of the cave.

3 'It was dark' (line 14); 'His world was very small. Its limits were the walls' (line 15); 'he had early discovered that one wall of his world was different from the rest. This was the mouth of the cave and the source of light' (lines 17 and 18); 'Never, in that period, did any of them crawl toward the dark corners of the back wall' (lines 25 and 26). The description of the cave helps us understand how White Fang feels limited in both space and light.

4 The writer compares the pups to plants because they are both living beings, searching for light.

5 Encourage students to think of examples and to talk about them. You could suggest novels such as *Animal Farm*, *Charlotte's Web* and *Life of Pi*. Encourage a discussion as a group on whether domesticated animals are still connected to their wild origins. Establish who agrees and who disagrees. Then divide the class and have a debate.

Literature

WHITE FANG
BY JACK LONDON

White Fang is a wild wolfdog whose father was a wolf called One Eye. This extract describes him as a pup. Jack London's novel follows White Fang's life and adventures in the Klondike Gold Rush in the 1890s in Canada.

1 5.07 **Read and listen to the text and answer the following question: which of the senses do you think are most important for the pups?**

He was different from his brothers and sisters. Their hair already betrayed the reddish colour like their mother, the she-wolf; while he alone, in this particular detail, took after his father. He was the one little grey one of the litter. He had bred true to his wolf origins – in fact, he had bred true, physically, to old One Eye himself, with but a single exception, and that was that he had two eyes to his father's one. The grey cub's eyes had not been open long, yet already he could see with steady clearness. And while his eyes were still closed, he had felt, tasted, and smelled.

He knew his two brothers and his two sisters very well. He had begun to play with them in a feeble, awkward way, and even to argue. And long before his eyes had opened, he had learned by touch, taste, and smell to know his mother – a source of warmth and liquid food and tenderness. Most of the first month of his life had been passed sleeping; but now he could see quite well, and he stayed awake for longer periods of time, and he was coming to learn his world quite well. His world was gloomy; but he did not know that, for he knew no other world. It was dark; but his eyes had never had to adjust themselves to any other light. His world was very small. Its limits were the walls; but as he had no knowledge of the wide world outside, it did not feel small.

But he had early discovered that one wall of his world was different from the rest. This was the mouth of the cave and the source of light. He had discovered that it was different from the other walls long before he had any thoughts of his own. It had been an irresistible attraction before even his eyes opened and looked upon it. The life of his body, the life that was the very substance of his body, had urged his body toward the light in the same way that the chemistry of a plant urges it toward the sun.

Always, in the beginning, before his conscious life dawned, he had crawled toward the mouth of the cave. And in this his brothers and sisters were one with him. Never, in that period, did any of them crawl toward the dark corners of the back wall. The light drew them as if they were plants; the chemistry of the life that composed them demanded the light as a necessity of being; and their little bodies crawled blindly and chemically, like the leaves of a vine toward the sun. Later on, when each developed individuality and became personally conscious of feelings and desires, the attraction of the light increased. They were always crawling toward it, and being pushed back from it by their mother.

Glossary

litter – a family of animals such as dogs, cats or pigs, born at the same time

feeble – weak

tenderness – the quality of being gentle, loving or kind

gloomy – dark in a way that is unpleasant and makes it difficult to see

urged – strongly advised someone to do a particular thing

2 **What do we learn about White Fang's mother?**

3 **Find phrases in the text describing where the pups live. How do these help us to imagine the setting of the story?**

4 **Why do you think the writer compares the pups to plants?**

5 SPEAKING **Work with a partner and discuss these questions.**

1. Can you think of any other stories in which the main character is an animal?
2. Do you think domesticated animals (for example, dogs and cats) are still connected to their wild origins?

Warmer

Ask students to think of famous people whom they admire and the reasons why they admire them. Show them some photos of very famous people (a football player, an actor, a writer, a singer …) and elicit why they are famous. Ask them to each think of a famous person. In small groups, they should ask yes/no questions of a member of the group to find out who the famous person is. The student who guesses correctly takes the next turn.

Alternatively, prepare some photos of celebrities that the students all know of and stick one to each student's back. They should mingle and take turns asking their partners questions to guess who they are.

▶ 15 Get **TH!NK**ing

Ask the question. Get students to compare their ideas in groups. Play the video and then ask students for feedback.

1. Ask students what they think of the photo. Who does it show? (Cate Blanchett.) Who is she? Why is she there? Why is it a special occasion? What does the photo imply? What is most striking about it? In pairs, ask students to discuss these questions. Then ask them to share their ideas and feelings as a group.
2. Ask them to think of the pros and cons of being a celebrity. Would they want to be famous? Why/ Why not?
3. Write *Should famous people be good role models?* on the board. Divide the class into two. Half the class think of why they agree, the other half think of why they disagree. Ask students to discuss their ideas in the two groups and then hold a debate.

6 FAMOUS LIVES

OBJECTIVES

FUNCTIONS: complaining

GRAMMAR: modals (1) *may, might, can, could, will, won't*; modals (2) *should, shouldn't, must, mustn't, can't*

VOCABULARY: admiration; fame

Get TH!NKING
Watch the video and think: would you like a life of fame and fortune?

Work in pairs. Look at the photo and discuss the questions.
1 What has just happened?
2 What are some advantages and disadvantages of being really famous?
3 Should famous people be good role models? Why/Why not?

59

Objectives

Functions Complaining
Grammar Modals 1: *may, might, can, could, will, won't*; modals 2: *should, shouldn't, must, mustn't, can't*
Vocabulary Admiration, fame
Values Teamwork
Life Competencies Having a wide range of interests

Resources for this unit

All available online

Videos
- Get **TH!NK**ing: *Would you like a life of fame and fortune?*
- Grammar video!: Modals 1: *may, might, can, could, will, won't*
- Vlog: Having a wide range of interests

Tests
- Unit, extension and skills test 6
- End of term test 2

Worksheets
- Grammar and vocabulary: Basic, Standard and Extension Worksheets
- Project: Rich and famous
- Communication: Followers
- Literature Worksheets: *Around the World in Eighty Days; Ozymandias, The New Colossus*
- Get **TH!NK**ing, Grammar video! and Life lessons video Worksheets

Reading

Warmer

Describe a well-known celebrity without naming him/her and elicit guesses from the class. Divide students into pairs and ask them to take turns to describe a celebrity for their partner to guess. Listen to some examples in open class as feedback.

1 Find out which celebrities are most talked about by eliciting their names and having a quick hands-up to see how many groups mentioned him/her in their discussions.

2 With books closed, put a copy of the pictures up on the board. Ask students to try to name the actors in B, D and E (B: Hugh Jackman, D: Brad Pitt, E: Timothée Chalamet).
1 B/C/E 2 B/C/E 3 A 4 E 5 D

3 *Students' own answers*

4 Give students two minutes to scan the article quickly to find the answer to the question.
Their private lives should remain exactly that – private.

5 **6.01 Check/clarify:** *intrusive, contemplated, privacy, amiable, sincere, invade his privacy, take my word for it, go viral, foolhardy, disagreeable shown in a negative light, affable.*
Read through the sentences and check students understand them. During feedback, ask individuals to refer to the parts of the text that support their answers.
4, 5, 1, 3, 1, 3, 2, 1

6 To extend discussion on question 4, ask students to make a list of the advantages and disadvantages of being famous. Listen to some of their ideas in open class as feedback and encourage further discussion.

READING

1 SPEAKING **Work in pairs and discuss.**
1 Which celebrities are currently in the news or have been recently? Why are they in the news?
2 Do you think celebrities are in the news too much? Why?

2 **Look at the people in the photos (A–E). Match each one to the thoughts below.**
1 I can't believe I'm this close to him/her!
2 Can't wait to post this on Instagram!
3 Look this way! Smile for the camera.
4 'You really look like that famous actor.' 'I get that a lot.'
5 This is my downtime. I'm not at work now.

3 SPEAKING **Compare with a partner. What other thoughts might the celebrities and their followers be having?**

4 **Read the magazine article quickly. How does the author feel about a celebrity's right to privacy?**

5 6.01 **Read the article again and listen. In which paragraph are each of these points made? Which words and phrases in the article helped you choose your answers?**
- It was the right decision not to tweet about the YouTuber.
- A celebrity's private life is his or her business and no one else's.
- Many celebrities are not keen to have a fan take a selfie with them.
- We think too much about the lives of celebrities.
- A celebrity's fame relies on followers commenting about them on social media.
- If you are going to tweet about a celebrity, tweet something positive.
- The author feels it would be uncomfortable to be the focus of attention on social media.
- People wrongly think of celebrities as friends because they recognise them.

6 SPEAKING **Work in pairs and discuss the questions.**
1 Name the three most popular celebrities among people of your age. Why are they popular? Do you like them? Why/Why not?
2 Which famous people, if any, do you follow on Twitter or in the media?
3 Why do you think that some people find the lives of celebrities so interesting?
4 Would you like to be famous? Why/Why not?

60

Culture notes

Hugh Jackman is an Australian actor and producer, best known for playing Wolverine in the *X-Men* film franchise and P. T. Barnum in *The Greatest Showman*. In addition to his Hollywood film career, Jackman is known for his theatre work, particularly musicals on Broadway and in Melbourne.

Brad Pitt is an American actor best known for his unconventional characters. He first came to prominence in the 1991 film *Thelma & Louise* but it was his role in the crime thriller *Seven* that gave him his breakthrough. Along with his former wife Angelina Jolie, Pitt often uses his celebrity status as a platform for speaking out on a number of humanitarian causes.

Timothée Chalamet, born 1995, is an American actor whose breakthrough was in 2017 with the lead role of Elio Perlman in *Call Me by Your Name*, for which he earned an Academy Award nomination. Chalamet is fluent in both English and French.

To tweet or not to tweet?

1 When you buy your plane ticket, you never know who you will be sitting next to on the plane, and on this particular flight, I was sitting next to a famous YouTube star – an [1]*idol* of mine, in fact. Of course, my first thought was to ask him for a selfie, but then I asked myself: would that be intrusive? This was a private moment in his life and celebrities can become very upset when fans ask for selfies. Then I thought: he makes his living from being famous, so does he have a right to a private life? If people didn't tweet about him, he wouldn't be so famous, would he? I contemplated the issue of celebrity and privacy for a few moments more. His face was so familiar, I felt as though I knew him. In reality, he was a stranger and you wouldn't ask a complete stranger for a selfie, would you?

2 Of course, you don't know who I'm talking about, do you? Here are some clues: he posts *Minecraft* videos on his YouTube channel and has 25 million subscribers who [2]*worship* him. He's got a vlog that I'm [3]*addicted* to. No? You still don't know who he is? I may just have to tweet about this. But then it could go viral. I could get a million likes, who knows. But would I be happy being [4]*the centre of attention*? I don't think so.

3 It's then that I remember reading Alankrutha Giridhar's tweets. She was the 25-year-old who shared her story about sitting next to the Academy Award-nominated actor, Timothée Chalamet, on a three-hour flight. Just about the only thing she didn't share was where she flew to on that flight because she didn't want people to know Chalamet's location. That was sensible of her. She tweeted everything else in 21 social media posts. Was that a foolhardy thing to do? It might have been if she had said disagreeable things about him and he was shown in a negative light, but she only commented on how affable he was. It was great publicity for him, really. And as there was no harm done, you might forgive her. After all, he did give her permission to tweet after the flight had landed. Still, I won't tweet about the celebrity sitting next to me. It wouldn't be fair. This is his private life and despite everyone's [5]*fascination* with him, they don't need to know that he's just ordered a chocolate bar and a hot chocolate. Besides, he may be annoyed if I tweet about him and I don't want that. Our [6]*obsession* with finding out every little detail about the lives of celebrities is wrong.

4 And so I don't tweet. I slip my phone into my bag, and I decide to talk to him instead. I tell him that I follow him on YouTube and that I'm a [7]*huge fan* of his vlog. He's interested to know what I think of it and I tell him. We chat and he's actually very amiable and sincere. We have a lot of similar interests and we have a fascinating conversation. I think about that, and I'm content that I chose not to invade his privacy. I will remember this flight for the rest of my life, but take my word for it, just a few friends and I will be the only ones who know who I sat next to that day.

5 We are [8]*fixated* on finding out about the private lives of celebrities but I've come to the conclusion that their private lives should remain exactly that – private.

Train to TH!NK

Making logical conclusions (syllogisms)

A syllogism is a system of logic where a conclusion is drawn from two propositions that are assumed to be true. It is often attributed to the Greek philosopher Aristotle, who used the following example:

All men are mortal. (proposition 1)

Socrates is a man. (proposition 2)

Therefore, Socrates is mortal. (conclusion)

Syllogisms can only work if both propositions are true, so before we accept any conclusion, we should consider whether each of the propositions on which it is based is indeed true.

7 **Look carefully at these two syllogisms. Find the flaws in the logic of each conclusion.**

1 A lot of famous people love attention.
Timothée Chalamet is famous.
Therefore, he loves being tweeted about.

2 Celebrities enjoy being the centre of attention.
Chalamet is a celebrity.
Therefore, Chalamet enjoys being the centre of attention.

8 WRITING **Work in pairs. Write a valid conclusion and an invalid conclusion for this syllogism.**

Scorpion is an album by Drake.
Lucy has all of Drake's albums.
Therefore, …

7 Check/clarify: *attributed, mortal.* Encourage students to give reasons for their answers.

1 The first proposition doesn't claim that all famous people love attention or that those who do, love being tweeted about.

2 The first proposition doesn't claim that all celebrities enjoy being the centre of attention.

8 Listen to some examples with the class as feedback.

Homework

Ask students to write three syllogisms of their own with two propositions and a conclusion. They can decide to include a valid or invalid conclusion. As a follow-up in the next lesson, in pairs, students can take turns to read their syllogisms. Their partners have to decide if the conclusion is valid or invalid.

Activity idea Mixed-ability

In Exercise 7, divide the class into pairs roughly according to level. Allow weaker students some time to think about their answers before discussing them. Monitor, helping with vocabulary as required and encouraging students to use English in their answers. Listen to some of their answers with the whole class.

TH!NK more

Worksheets
Project Rich and famous
Communication Followers
Get TH!NKing *Would you like a life of fame and fortune?*

Critical TH!NKing
Evaluating ideas and arguments
Gives reasons for an argument's plausibility.

Grammar; Pronunciation; Vocabulary

Warmer

In pairs, ask students to describe their favourite actor/YouTuber, etc. to their partner.

▶ 16 Grammar video! Modals 1: *may, might, can, could, will, won't*

1 Give further examples if necessary.
1 will 2 could 3 might 4 could 5 can 6 won't 7 may 8 will
RULE: a 4 and 7 b 2 c 5 d 6 e 3 f 8 g 1

2 Monitor to help with any difficulties and to make a note of any repeated problems to refer to during feedback.
1 a is hypothesising or talking about possibility while b is using *may* for concession.
2 a is an example of *might* to make a prediction about the future while *might* in b is used to speculate about the present.
3 a uses *can* for theoretical possibility while *can* in b describes ability.
4 *could* in a describes possibility while *could* in b describes past ability.
5 *will* in a is used to talk about a future possibility (relating to the *if*-clause) while *will* in b describes habitual behaviour.
6 *won't* in a functions as a refusal and *won't* in b functions as a prediction about a future event.

Workbook p54

GRAMMAR
Modals (1) *may, might, can, could, will, won't*

Grammar video ▶16

1 Find the modal verbs in these sentences from the article on page 61 and then match each modal with the meanings they give to the sentences in the rule box.

1 When you buy your plane ticket, you never know who you will be sitting next to on the plane.
2 But then it could go viral.
3 And as there was no harm done, you might forgive her.
4 I could get a million likes, who knows.
5 Celebrities can become very upset when fans ask for selfies.
6 Still, I won't tweet about the celebrity sitting next to me.
7 Besides, he may be annoyed if I tweet about him and I don't want that.
8 I will remember this flight for the rest of my life.

RULE:
a hypothesising: example … and …
b talking about possibility: example …
c talking about typical behaviour: example …
d refusing: example …
e making a concession: example …
f a belief about the future: example …
g theoretical possibility: example …

2 SPEAKING Work in pairs. Discuss the difference in meaning of the modal verb in a and b in each pair of sentences. Pay attention to any time references.

1 a I may watch the film tonight – I'll see how I feel.
b He may be rich and famous, but has his work taken over his life?
2 a It might rain later. I think I heard that on the weather forecast this morning.
b They might be French. I think they said something about her parents living in Paris.
3 a Learning a new language can be difficult.
b He can speak three languages.
4 a We could have a problem.
b My grandfather could solve most problems.
5 a We'll be a bit late if we don't hurry.
b Children will get restless if they've got nothing to do.
6 a He won't tell me. It's so annoying. I really want to know!
b I really don't want to go to the party. I won't know anyone there.

→ workbook page 54

PRONUNCIATION
Modal stress and meaning Go to page 137.

VOCABULARY
Admiration

3 Match the words in italics (1–8) in the article on page 61 with the meanings.

a someone or something that everyone is focused on
b having very strong habits that are hard to break
c extreme interest in
d something that you think about all the time
e someone admired or adored by lots of people
f a very big admirer
g not take your eyes off something
h to adore

4 Complete the text with words and phrases from the list.

addicted | centre of attention | fascination | fixated | huge fan | idols | obsession | worshipped

When I was growing up, the TV was very much the [1]… in our house. Mum, Dad, me, my baby sister – we were all [2]… on that little box in the living room. It caused a lot of arguments, too.

Take Saturday mornings, for example. Lola wanted to watch her pop [3]… performing on children's TV. Dad wanted to watch the football preview programme to get the latest news on his football team. He [4]… Chelsea! Mum and I were [5]… to the cookery programmes. We couldn't get enough of them. Mum was a [6]… of one chef and she even wrote him a letter once.

The problem is these programmes were all on at the same time and we only had one TV. These days, people's [7]… with the TV seems to be much less pronounced. There's a new [8]… in most people's lives: their smartphone or social media.

→ workbook page 56

62

Pronunciation
Modal stress and meaning

Student's Book p137

3 Before students do the exercise, write the italicised words on the board. Tell students to find the words in the article as quickly as possible. When they have seen them being used in context, ask them to try to work out the meaning of the phrases. Compare their meanings with the definitions in the book.
a 4 b 3 c 5 d 6 e 1 f 7 g 8 h 2

4 1 centre of attention 2 fixated 3 idols 4 worshipped 5 addicted 6 huge fan 7 fascination 8 obsession

Workbook p56

TH!NK more

Workbook
Grammar p54, Ex.1–4
Vocabulary p56, Ex.1
Pronunciation p119

Worksheets
Grammar Worksheets 6
Vocabulary Worksheets 6
Grammar video! Modals 1: *may, might, can, could, will, won't*

Get it Right!
Modals

Student's Book p68

Activity idea Extension

Ask students to scan the article on page 61 and underline all the modal verbs. Who can find the most?

5 Monitor and help with vocabulary as necessary. Listen to some of their answers in open class and note them on the board to refer to during feedback on Exercise 6.

6 6.03 Tell students they do not need to understand every word and that they should focus on listening for which of the reasons are mentioned before listening again to find any extra ones.
The rise of social media, marketing campaigns that are special to events or holidays held in different countries around the world and merchandise.

7 6.03 Ask students to try to answer the questions from memory before listening again to check.
1 Doesn't correspond
2 Presenter
3 Doesn't correspond
4 Steve
5 Steve
6 David
7 Steve
8 Steve
9 David
10 David
11 Doesn't correspond
12 David

8 Before starting the discussion, give students some time to work individually and think about their answers to the questions.

9–10 Ask students to work individually.

11 Encourage students to give reasons for their choices and to debate with their classmates.

12 At the end of the exercise, listen to some of the students' ideas and encourage open-class discussion.

LISTENING

5 **Work in pairs. Make a list of the ways a sports team can become successful globally.**

6 6.03 **Listen to a radio programme about Liverpool F.C. and how the team is marketed around the world. Which of the ways you listed in Exercise 5 did you hear? Which other ways were mentioned?**

7 6.03 **Listen again and match the speaker (Steve, David or the presenter) with the sentences which paraphrase the ideas expressed. There are three sentences that don't correspond to any of the speakers.**

1 In my heart, I know it's wrong to support them.
2 Millions of supporters follow their football team online.
3 My family supports Liverpool and so do I.
4 Social media has played a large part in making the team popular around the world.
5 Campaigns don't all take place at the same time of year.
6 In Colombia, Liverpool fans meet up to watch a live broadcast of a match.
7 If a team loses a match, their merchandise still sells.
8 The weather can affect merchandise sales.
9 He probably won't go to watch a football match in the UK.
10 They can buy the Liverpool shorts and shirt in Colombia.
11 You will always be alone.
12 You will always have the support of other fans.

SPEAKING

8 **Discuss in small groups.**

1 What sports teams do you follow?
2 How do you feel when they lose?
3 How do you feel when they win?
4 What do these teams mean to you?
5 Are there any famous players from your country who play in overseas teams?
6 How do people in your country feel about this?

TH!NK *values*

Teamwork

9 **Rank the following qualities in order of how important they are to be a good team player (1 = least important; 5 = most important).**

- being a good listener
- possessing strong leadership skills
- having a small ego
- liking your teammates
- respecting your teammates

10 **Think of and note down other important qualities and decide on your final top five.**

11 SPEAKING **Work in groups of four. Compare your ranking and agree on a new list of five.**

12 SPEAKING **Discuss in pairs.**

1 How easy was it to come up with a group list?
2 Did your group work well as a team? Why/Why not?
3 What sports teams can you think of that are an example of
a good teamwork?
b bad teamwork?
4 What makes them good/bad?

63

Homework

Ask students to write sentences about their family and friends using some of the vocabulary from Exercise 3. Encourage students to be positive in their tone.

Activity idea Extension

Divide the class into groups. Ask students to discuss why their group would make a good team, using the qualities from Exercise 9 in their descriptions. To encourage creativity, allow them to add two famous people to their team and decide why they would improve teamwork. Monitor and help with vocabulary and ideas as necessary. When students have discussed at length, regroup students into new groups of four for students to describe why they would make a good team and debate which of the teams would be best. Nominate individuals to report back on their discussions in open class as feedback.

Collaboration
Taking personal responsibility for own contribution to a group task
Makes relevant suggestions.

Collaboration
Working towards task completion
Encourages other students to agree on a solution after a negotiation.

Collaboration
Working towards task completion
Identifies issues and challenges.

TH!NK more

Workbook
Listening p60, Ex.1–2

Warmer

Show some paparazzi pictures of current celebrities and write their names on the board. Ask: *How often do you see photos of these celebrities? What are the celebrities doing in the photos? Do you think the celebrities want to be photographed?* Divide the class into pairs or small groups for students to discuss the questions. Listen to some of their ideas in open class.

1 Listen to some of the students' ideas as feedback and write answers on the board to refer to after the reading.

2 Set a two-minute time limit for this to encourage students to read quickly and to focus on gist rather than specific information.

3 🔊 **6.04 Check/clarify:** *a blessing, a curse, up-and-coming, limelight, recognition, charm, a crush, the face of, paparazzi, keep a low profile, stalkers, envy, jealousy, gossip, part and parcel, unflattering, derogatory comments, fame and fortune.*
1 You must wear them and you must be photographed in them.
2 the constant recognition
3 promoting brands and starting up your own business
4 being judged on everything they wear and do, and reading nasty comments

4 Before students do the exercise, write *take* on the board and ask them to give different examples of its use. Write any correct examples on the board.
1 taken over his life 2 taking an interest in 3 take my word for it 4 take it (that) 5 take; personally

5 1 personally 2 an interest 3 my word for it 4 take it

Workbook p56

READING

1 SPEAKING Work in pairs. Imagine you are a celebrity. What would be the advantages and disadvantages of your celebrity status?

2 Read the article quickly. Which of your ideas are mentioned?

3 🔊 6.04 Read the article again and listen. Answer the questions.
1 What do you need to do in return for being given expensive clothes?
2 What do celebrities soon become tired of?
3 What kind of opportunities does fame bring?
4 What can celebrities find very hurtful?

WordWise
Expressions with *take*

→ workbook page 56

4 Look at these sentences from the unit so far. Complete them with the phrases from the list.

take [...] personally | take it (that) | take my word for it | taken over his life | taking an interest in

1 He may be rich and famous, but has his work … ?
2 Are people … you because they like you or because you are famous?
3 But … , just a few friends and I will be the only ones who know who I sat next to that day.
4 David, I … you've never seen them play at Anfield.
5 It's almost impossible not to … the comments … .

5 Choose the correct options.
1 I told her I wasn't meaning to criticise. Why does she always take everything so *over / personally*?
2 It's always nice when someone else takes *my word / an interest* in you and your life.
3 You don't believe me? Well, don't take *my word for it / it personally*. Ask Mr Jones.
4 What a big smile! I *take it / take your word for it* you've had some good news!

FAME
– A BLESSING OR A CURSE?

Being a celebrity has advantages and disadvantages. Read this article and decide for yourself whether the life of a celebrity is a blessing or a curse.

THE ADVANTAGES

Getting special treatment Luxurious homes and cars, luxury holidays and expensive clothes can all be yours; in fact, you shouldn't ever need to buy clothes again, as global brands will give them to you in return for you wearing their clothes and being photographed in them. Restaurants will seat you at their best table and give you star treatment. What's not to like?

Being recognised For up-and-coming celebrities, being recognised can be a giant ego-boost and they never grow tired of being in the limelight. Adoring fans wanting a selfie with you can be very flattering. However, for others the constant recognition can quickly become tiresome, so celebrities should perhaps be prepared for the initial charm to wear off.

Adoring fans Adoring fans can often develop a celebrity crush on their favourite actor or pop star. The fan mail that celebrities receive can be both inspiring and motivating, as well as very humbling. After all, who wouldn't like to have their own fans and followers?

Business opportunities Fame brings with it other opportunities for the popular celebrity. For example, Michael Jordan didn't only make a living from playing basketball; he was also the face of Nike and he promoted many other brands. Being famous can open other doors in life and celebrities often start up other businesses. For instance, female stars such as Kylie and Beyoncé have their own fashion labels and beauty brands.

THE DISADVANTAGES

No privacy As an A-list celebrity, you can't lead a normal life. You can't have a quiet meal with friends in a restaurant; you can't just go to a beach and swim; you can't go shopping or do any of the things you like to do without the constant intrusion of fans and paparazzi.

Some celebrities have strategies to combat this invasion of their privacy. They will go to enormous lengths to keep a low profile and avoid appearing in newspapers and magazines. For five or six months, Daniel Radcliffe always ventured out wearing the same clothes. The paparazzi following him couldn't sell any photos of him because it looked like they were all taken on the same day.

Attracting fake friends and stalkers Are people taking an interest in you because they like you or because you are famous? You must constantly be on your guard and your celebrity status will attract envy, jealousy and gossip. There is also the danger of being harassed by stalkers. These are people who become obsessed by their idol and their obsession can potentially turn into threats and violence.

Being judged Celebrities should always watch what they wear and what they do, because the media is constantly judging them. Reading nasty and insulting comments and lies about yourself is a part and parcel of a celebrity's daily routine. It's almost impossible not to take the comments personally. How would you like to see unflattering photos of yourself and read derogatory comments about anything from your weight to your choice of clothes? Is fame and the fortune it brings really worth it? What do you think?

64

Culture notes

Michael Jordan is a former American basketball player who led the Chicago Bulls to six NBA championships. He dominated the sport from the mid-1980s to the late 1990s and is considered one of the best basketball players of all time.

Kylie Minogue is an Australian singer and actress. Originally a child actor, she rose to fame in Australia and the UK on the popular soap opera *Neighbours.* In 1988 she mostly left her acting career behind and made her debut album *Kylie*. In 2020, she became the first female artist to reach the number 1 in the British album charts in five consecutive decades.

Beyoncé Knowles is an American singer-songwriter who rose to fame in the late 1990s as the lead singer of *Destiny's Child.* In 2003 she released her first solo album *Dangerously in Love* which won her five Grammy Awards. In 2021, with her 28th Grammy award she set the record for the most Grammys won by a female artist.

Daniel Radcliffe is a British actor who starred as Harry Potter in the series of films based on the books by J.K. Rowling. Radcliffe made his acting debut in the 1999 TV movie *David Copperfield,* playing the title role. Continuing to release films, Radcliffe has also starred in several theatre productions both on Broadway and in the West End.

TH!NK more

Workbook
Reading p58, Ex.1–4
WordWise p56, Ex.5

Grammar; Vocabulary; Writing

6 Ask students to try to complete the sentences from memory before checking on page 64.
1 should 2 can't 3 must
4 should
RULE: a 1 (should) b 3 (must)
c 2 (can't) d 4 (should)

7–8 Tell students that there is more than one possibility for each answer. During feedback, give further examples for clarification if necessary.

9 Assign different sentences to different groups. Give students time to prepare and practise their dialogue. Challenge them to remember it without consulting their notes.

Workbook p55

10 1 h 2 a 3 f 4 g 5 c 6 d 7 e 8 b

11 Encourage students to develop their answers and to use the expressions and any vocabulary they have learned from the article.
1 a low profile 2 list 3 limelight
4 stalker 5 celebrity crush

Workbook p56

12 Point out that students need to read the titles, not discuss them.

13 Point out that in a well-structured piece of writing, each paragraph should have its own purpose, which is why it is written as a separate paragraph. Elicit examples of further information that could be added to the essay.

14 If you're short on time, students can do the preparation in class and complete the writing at home. This can be done as a collaborative writing activity in class with pairs of students of a similar level working together to complete the exercise.

Homework

If you are short on time, students can do Exercise 14 for homework. If you have done this in class, ask students to exchange their essays with another student for them to read at home and give feedback on content and structure. Students could check if the essay uses the template. They should also decide which the most/least interesting part of the essay is.

GRAMMAR
Modals (2) *should, shouldn't, must, mustn't, can't*

6 **Complete the example sentences and check them in the article. Then match each modal with its function.**

1 Celebrities … perhaps be prepared for the initial charm to wear off.
2 As an A-list celebrity, you … lead a normal life.
3 You … constantly be on your guard.
4 Celebrities … always watch what they wear and what they do, because the media is constantly judging them.

RULE:
a what you'd expect (under normal circumstances): example …
b strong advice: example …
c it's reasonable: example …
d advice: example …

7 **Read the sentences. In each one, who do you think is talking to whom? What do you think they are talking about?**

1 a You should think carefully about the offer.
b You should arrive on time if you leave now.
2 a You shouldn't stay up too late.
b You shouldn't be surprised if she says 'no'.
3 a They must be really happy about the news.
b You must watch this film.
4 a You mustn't tell anyone.
b You mustn't be too hopeful.
5 a You can't go to the party.
b She can't be very popular.

8 SPEAKING **Work in pairs. Look at the sentences in Exercise 7 and discuss the difference in meaning of the modal verb in a and b. Pay attention to the time reference in each case.**

9 WRITING **Choose two of the sentences in Exercise 7 and use them to write mini dialogues of four to six lines.**

A *You should think carefully about the offer.*
B *Really? I wasn't very impressed with it.*
A *You won't get a better one, I promise.*
B *That's where I disagree. I think I will.*
A *Well, I hope you don't end up regretting it.*
B *I won't.*

→ workbook page 55

VOCABULARY
Fame

10 **Match the sentence halves.**

1 She's enjoyed *being in the*
2 He's an *up-and-*
3 The *paparazzi* couldn't
4 She doesn't like attention and tries
5 She was followed everywhere
6 My sister has a *celebrity*
7 She is *the face*
8 The party was amazing. All the *A-list*

a *coming* comedian. He's going to be huge!
b *celebrities* were there.
c she went by a *stalker*.
d *crush* on Chris Hemsworth.
e *of* an expensive new perfume.
f take any photos of her because she hid her face.
g to *keep a low profile*.
h *limelight* since she was in the school play aged six.

11 SPEAKING **Complete the sentences with the missing words. Then work in pairs and discuss the questions.**

1 Which famous people can you think of who like to keep … ?
2 Who are the A-… celebrities in your country?
3 Do you enjoy being in the … ? Why/Why not?
4 What punishment should a … get for following a celebrity?
5 Is it normal to have a … on an actor/actress?

→ workbook page 56

WRITING
An essay

12 INPUT **Read these essay titles.**

- Famous people have a right to privacy. Discuss.
- Some people will do anything for fame. Discuss.
- The media is too focused on celebrities. Discuss.

13 PLAN **Your class had a discussion on the third title. You made the notes below. How could you organise them into an essay structure?**

- Famous people sell newspapers.
- They're a distraction from all of the horrible things happening in the world right now.
- Our children are growing up wanting to be famous. There needs to be a balance.

14 PRODUCE **Your teacher has asked you to write one of the essays from Exercise 12. Write your essay in 220–260 words.**

Activity idea Role play

Set up a role play in which a celebrity is interviewed about their career. Divide students into two groups, A: journalists and B: celebrities. A students should write questions to ask the celebrity using expressions from Exercise 10. B students should think about their life as a celebrity and decide how they will explain their successes/failures. Give students time to prepare with a member of their own group before pairing off ABAB for the interview. Listen to some of their questions and answers during whole-class feedback and encourage further group discussion.

TH!NK more

Practice Extra
Unit 6 Practise it!

Workbook
Grammar p55, Ex.5–7
Vocabulary p56, Ex.2–4
Vocabulary Extra p57, Ex.1–3
Developing Writing p59

Worksheets
Grammar Worksheets 6
Vocabulary Worksheets 6

Warmer

Revise modals by dividing the class into groups of three. Give each student one of three situations (going camping; going to the beach; climbing a mountain) and tell them not to show it to their group. Give students time to write sentences about their situation using *should*, *shouldn't*, *must*, *mustn't* or *can't*, without directly naming the situation. Students then take turns to read their sentences for their group to guess the situation. The winner is the student who reads the most sentences before their partner guesses the situation. If students enjoy the activity, ask them to repeat the activity with situations of their own choice.

1 **6.05** Tell students to cover the dialogue and discuss the question in pairs before listening to check.

2 **6.05**
1 She is concerned that Becky is spending too much time on her phone and her school work is suffering.
2 Tell her mum she is playing tennis this evening.
3 That Becky should have other interests.

3 To encourage speed-reading, you could do this as a race and ask students to find the expressions as quickly as possible.
1 Mum 2 Mum 3 Becky 4 Mum 5 Mum 6 Mum
Students' own answers

4 During feedback, say the sentences for students to repeat. Check pronunciation and intonation.
1 Come on
2 for a change
3 Fat chance
4 Just out of curiosity
5 You might have told me
6 by any chance?

DEVELOPING SPEAKING

1 6.05 **Look at the photos. Who do you think the girl is talking to? Who is the tennis player? What's the connection between the girl and the tennis player? Read, listen and check your ideas.**

Mum: So, at the weekend, let's have a picnic in the park. I'm tired of always being indoors. I want to do something outside for a change. What do you think, Becky?
Becky: Sure, Mum. Whatever. Oh no! Seriously?
Mum: Becky? Just out of curiosity, what are you doing on your phone? No, let me guess. You're reading her feed on Instagram, aren't you?
Becky: Well, if by 'her' you mean Naomi Osaka – yes, I am. What's the big deal, Mum?
Mum: Tennis, tennis, tennis. It's always tennis. And always following Osaka on social media. But seriously, … it's all you ever do.
Becky: Oh, come on, Mum. That's so not true.
Mum: It *is* true, Becky. I think it's great you like playing tennis, but constantly following players on your phone … Haven't you got anything else to do with your time? I'm worried your schoolwork's suffering.
Becky: Oh, Mum, give me a break, please! I really don't need this right now.
Mum: Well, have you finished your project work, by any chance?
Becky: No, but I can do that this evening, after the match.
Mum: Match? What match?
Becky: Um, well, I'm playing mixed doubles with Steve this evening, at the club. Six o'clock.
Mum: Well you might have told me, Becky. And what about your dinner?
Becky: Sorry, Mum, I forgot. Don't worry, I'll be back by seven thirty.
Mum: Fat chance of that! You'll never finish a match and get back home in an hour and a half.
Becky: OK. I'll call off the tennis, do my project work and then have dinner. Happy now?
Mum: There's no need to be like that. And don't call off your match. It's just … I think you should have other interests, that's all.

2 6.05 **Read and listen to the dialogue again. Answer the questions.**
1 What are Becky's mum's concerns about her?
2 What has Becky forgotten to do?
3 How does Becky's mum feel at the end of the conversation?

Phrases for fluency

3 **Find these expressions in the dialogue. Who says them? How do you say them in your language?**
1 for a change
2 Just out of curiosity
3 Come on
4 …, by any chance?
5 You might have told me
6 Fat chance

4 **Use the expressions in Exercise 3 to complete the dialogues.**
1 A Have you tidied your bedroom? I want that done before you go out.
B … , Dad, I haven't got time. I'll do it later.
2 A We always eat Italian. Why don't we try Japanese food … ?
B But I don't really like Japanese food.
3 A Do you think we're going to win today?
B … . They're way better than we are.
4 A … , can I ask you why you're looking so happy?
B I've just had the most fantastic news!
5 A Joan? Listen, sorry, I can't make it tonight.
B What? … earlier. I've just finished getting ready!
6 A Can you lend me ten pounds, … ?
B Sorry, I haven't got ten pounds.

FUNCTIONS
Complaining

5 **Write the phrases in the correct column.**

But seriously, … it's all you ever do. | ~~Give me a break …~~
Haven't you got anything else to do with your time?
I really don't need this right now.
I really haven't got time for this now. | ~~It's always tennis~~

Making a complaint	Responding to a complaint
It's always (tennis)	*Give me a break …*

6 ROLE PLAY **Work in pairs. Student A plays the part of Jake. Student B plays the part of Jake's father. Use the expressions from Exercise 5 in your conversation. Then switch roles.**

Jake is mad about horses. He's about to go horse-riding. His dad thinks he spends too much time on his hobby.

66

5 *Making a complaint: It's always (tennis) But seriously … it's all you ever do. Haven't you got anything else to do with your time?*
Responding to a complaint: Give me a break … I really don't need this right now. I really haven't got time for this now.

6 Allow students six to eight minutes to prepare their stories. Encourage them to use the key language. Tell students to stay in character to make the activity interesting and fun. Give them time to practise in pairs before asking more confident students to act in front of the class.

Activity idea Extension

Disappearing sentences: you'll need to write out the dialogues in Exercise 4 on the board or project them on the IWB. Make A/B pairs. Students practise the dialogues in their pairs. Cover a small section of the dialogue, beginning from the right-hand side of the screen or board. Students repeat the dialogues in their same A/B pairings trying to remember the whole thing, including the parts they can no longer see. Cover more and more of the dialogue, with students practising at each stage, until eventually nothing is left on the board. Ask for volunteers to perform for the class or have all As and all Bs perform in unison.

TH!NK more

Workbook
Phrases for fluency p60

Life Competencies

Warmer

Write *wide range of interests* on the board and elicit the meaning *(a large number of things you are interested in)*. Ask students to give themselves a mark for each of the hobbies they have or have had. Do they have a wide range, or are their interests all in one area?

▶ 17 Life Lessons: Having a wide range of interests

1 ▶ 17 birdwatching; photography; film-making; acting; vlogging; writing

2 ▶ 17 Ask students to try to answer the questions from memory before watching the video again to check.

3 **Check/clarify:** *obsessed, revolves around, empathise, pregnant, fanaticism.*
1 football
2 He doesn't get a job because his only interest is football, he has a strained relationship with his mother and his girlfriend leaves him.
3 His girlfriend gets pregnant.

4 **Check/clarify:** *fanatical.*

5 If you are short of time, you could put students in groups to share ideas on one idea.

6–7 If space allows, encourage students to walk around the classroom to find someone who is also interested in their big hobbies, or someone who knows a lot about something they'd like to know more about. Ask students to report their findings and encourage them to use the phrase '*So does he/she/*[student's name].' etc.

Homework

Ask students to make a presentation about one of their big hobbies or interests. If students do not have interests, they can research something they would like to know more about. Encourage them to make a list of at least two ways they could expand or have expanded their interest. As a follow-up, ask students to give their presentation to the class.

LIFE COMPETENCIES

It's good to have an interest or a hobby that you really love, but you should be careful about becoming obsessed with one thing. Having a wide range of interests can bring advantages.

1 ▶ 17 **Watch the vlog. Which hobbies has Will had at some point in his life?**

acting | birdwatching | computer gaming | film-making | photography | politics | vlogging | writing

2 ▶ 17 SPEAKING **Watch the vlog again. Work in pairs. Discuss these questions using your answers to Exercise 1.**
1 How did Will go from being a birdwatcher to a vlogger?
2 How is Will's life story a good example of the vlog theme?

3 **Read the book review and answer the questions.**
1 What is Paul's obsession?
2 What problems has this caused him in his life?
3 When does he start to realise there are other things in life?

4 SPEAKING **Work in pairs and discuss the questions.**
1 What other things/interests do people sometimes become fanatical or obsessive about?
2 Do you know of any other characters in films or books or TV programmes who are obsessive?

5 **Choose one or two of the following areas of interest. Think how the interest could be expanded.**

films | literature | mobiles | music | sport

music: singing / playing an instrument / listening to music / history of music / music photography / ...

Fever Pitch (1997)

The film *Fever Pitch* is based on the novel by Nick Hornby. The story is set in London and concerns Paul Ashworth, a schoolteacher who is obsessed with football and the team he supports, Arsenal. He has been obsessed since he was 11 years old, when his father took him to his first match. Paul eats, drinks and sleeps football (he is the coach of the school football team) and Arsenal. Paul's life revolves around Arsenal and their games – he goes to every home game. However, he starts a relationship with another teacher, Sarah, who knows nothing about football and cares about it even less.

As the film develops, we see the extent of Paul's obsession, for example, when he is interviewed for a more senior position at the school, he is asked about his interests and can only say 'football'. (He doesn't get the job.) He also has a strained relationship with his mother because of football. We also see how Sarah at first cannot understand Paul's passion for the game – at one point she leaves him because of it. However, she slowly begins to empathise with him and helps him to see that there's more to life than one thing. When she becomes pregnant, Paul gets excited about starting a new life as a father and husband and starts to behave a little differently. Sarah shares his happiness at the end when Arsenal win the championship.

The film is an interesting examination of fanaticism, and looks at the importance of having as many interests as possible in order to lead a fulfilling life.

Me and my world

6 **Complete the lists for yourself.**
- My big hobbies
- Things I have a bit of interest in
- Things I'd like to know more about

7 SPEAKING **Work in pairs. Use your lists to discuss your interests with your partner and to give advice about how they could expand their interests.**

TIPS ON HAVING A WIDE RANGE OF INTERESTS

- **Think about people that you have something in common with. The things they are interested in might interest you as well.**
- **If most of your interests are to be found indoors, think of one or two outdoor pursuits you might like to try (and vice versa).**

Culture notes

Nick Hornby is an English novelist and screenwriter. His novels include *Fever Pitch* (1992), *About a Boy* (1998) and *Just like You* (2020), some of which have been made into films. His novels mainly focus on music, sport and the difficulties of human relationships.

Fever Pitch: A Fan's Life is an autobiographical novel. Each chapter relates various events in Hornby's life with a football match that he watched at Arsenal stadium around that time. The book was made into a film in 1997.

Arsenal FC is a football club based in London, England.

TH!NK more

Practice Extra
Unit 6 Master it!

Worksheets
Life Lessons: Having a wide range of interests

Tests
Unit, extension and skills test 6
End of term test 2

Units 5 & 6
GET IT RIGHT!

1 Make sure students understand the difference between a participle and a gerund, and then go through the examples as a class. After doing the exercise, ask students to explain their choice in each sentence.
1 Jumping 2 Discovered 3 Caught
4 Seen 5 confused 6 compared

2 1 ~~Writting~~ Writing
2 ~~Loosing~~ Losing
3 ~~swiming~~ swimming
4 ~~studing~~ studying
5 ~~embarassing~~ embarrassing
6 ~~disapearing~~ disappearing

3 Do the first example in open class and then ask students to complete the exercise in pairs.
1 If Jenny wears that outfit tonight she ~~would~~ will be the centre of attention!
2 Although I'm interested in reading about celebrities, I ~~will~~ would not describe myself as obsessed.
3 When people suffer from Celebrity Worship Syndrome, they ~~won't~~ can't function properly in their normal lives.
4 You ~~wouldn't~~ won't find much difference between those two celebrities. They're both famous for doing very little!
5 I asked if she ~~can~~ could help me stay out of the limelight at the party.
6 You ~~will~~ may / might be an up-and-coming child actor, but you still have to do your homework!

GET IT RIGHT! UNITS 5 & 6

Participles and gerunds

Learners often use a gerund when a past participle should be used and vice versa.
✓ ***Cooked*** *properly, Brussels sprouts can taste really nice.*
✗ *~~Cooking~~ properly, Brussels sprouts can taste really nice.*
✓ ***Talking*** *loudly, the students walked down the corridor.*
✗ *~~Talked~~ loudly, the students walked down the corridor.*

1 Choose the correct option.
1 *Jumping / Jumped* out of her chair, she said, 'Let's go!'
2 *Discovering / Discovered* in time, a lot of serious illnesses can be cured.
3 *Catching / Caught* outside in the thunderstorm, we ran for shelter under some trees.
4 *Seeing / Seen* from far away, the mountain path didn't look that long.
5 All this noise is making me *confusing / confused*.
6 The new stuntman is a real daredevil *comparing / compared* with the last one.

Learners often make spelling mistakes with gerunds.
✓ *My sister really likes* ***running*** *in the evening.*
✗ *My sister really likes ~~runing~~ in the evening.*

2 There is one spelling mistake in each sentence. Find the mistakes and correct them.
0 Thank you for puting the plates back in the right place.
Thank you for putting the plates back in the right place.
1 Writting a travel blog is a fun way to record your travel adventures.
2 Loosing my tickets and passport was the worst thing that happened to me.
3 We really enjoyed swiming in the waterfall.
4 They travelled deep into the jungle, studing insects and plants that they encountered along the way.
5 None of us could speak their language and it was quite embarassing.
6 The group stood on the river bank as they watched the boat disapearing into the distance.

Modals

Learners often confuse the different modals – *may, might, can, could, will, won't.*
✓ *I hope you* ***will*** *like it.*
✗ *I hope you ~~would~~ like it.*
✓ *You* ***won't*** *believe it when you see it.*
✗ *You ~~can't~~ believe it when you see it.*

3 Correct the error and rewrite the sentences.
0 I will be grateful if you could help me tomorrow.
I would be grateful if you could help me tomorrow.
1 If Jenny wears that outfit tonight she would be the centre of attention!
2 Although I am interested in reading about celebrities, I will not describe myself as obsessed.
3 When people suffer from Celebrity Worship Syndrome, they won't function properly in their normal lives.
4 You wouldn't find much difference between those two celebrities. They're both famous for doing very little!
5 I asked if she can help me stay out of the limelight at the party.
6 You will be an up-and-coming child actor, but you still have to do your homework!

68

1 In C1 Advanced Reading and Use of English Part 7, candidates have to read a longer text with six numbered spaces, then decide which of the seven paragraphs provided belongs in each gap.

This part of the exam tests whether candidates can follow the narrative of a text, the development of ideas and understand how a well-structured text is formed.

Encourage your students to do the following when they approach this task:

- Read the whole text to understand the narrative.
- Look at each numbered space and choose one of the sentences to complete each gap.
- After choosing a sentence, check the other six options and decide why they are wrong.
- Check that each letter has been used only once and there is one paragraph that is not used.
- Read the completed text again to make sure it makes sense.

1C 2F 3E 4G 5A 6D

Workbook p61

TOWARDS C1 Advanced

READING AND USE OF ENGLISH
Part 7: Gapped text

→ workbook page 61

1 **You are going to read an extract from a magazine article. Six paragraphs have been removed from the extract. Choose from the paragraphs A–G the one which fits each gap (1–6). There is one extra paragraph that you do not need to use.**

FAN BEHAVIOUR

While it may seem understandable that an athlete becomes attached to teammates and to being part of a team, it's clear that sports spectators can also become extremely passionate about their team, to the point that it becomes part of their identity and can affect their well-being.

1

Team identification is the extent to which that fan feels a psychological connection to a team, and the team's performances are viewed as relevant on a personal level, according to Daniel Wann, Professor of Psychology at Murray State University.

2

As with these other aspects of identity, people are investing a lot of who they are in their identity as a fan of a team. As Professor Wann explains: 'A huge part of who they are, where they derive a lot of their positive and negative feelings, is from what their team is doing.' Perhaps the most basic question is why people follow sports so ardently. What is it about watching sports that makes people scream, obsess over statistics, and paint their faces, particularly when they know that there's a very good chance that their team won't achieve success?

3

In other words, it's a voluntary activity where a large proportion of consumers aren't going to like the product when they've finished consuming it. As Wann says: 'You wouldn't go see a movie if you thought there was a fifty-fifty chance you wouldn't like it.'

4

Perhaps no fans demonstrate what these must be better than followers of the Chicago Cubs. The Cubs haven't won the World Series for nearly 100 years, yet the team has a legendary community. Ask a Cubs fan why they like the team and they won't say because of the championships.

5

The senior vice president of Marketing for the Cubs agrees. 'We're marketing the experience more than other teams,' he says. 'Here, it's about the unique mystique of the Chicago Cubs. What resonates the loudest with the fanbase is the experience.'

6

'When we look at motivation for following a sports team, group affiliation is one of the top ones,' says Wann. 'Identifying strongly with a local team where other fans are around – that's a benefit to social-psychological well-being.'

A 'They'll say, "I love Wrigley Field – I love the community here," ' says Wann. So it's evident that identification is not simply a matter of results; it has far more to do with an experience.

B Fans who watched their team win, however, reported significantly higher estimates of the team's future performance, their own task performance and personal self-esteem than those who watched their team lose.

C A fan may be affected in this way because, watching the action, the individual does identify with the team, and for some fans, this becomes important for their sense of self.

D People report many reasons for following a favourite team, but social connectedness is one of the most frequently mentioned aspects of the experience, as Wann finds in his research on college and professional sports fans.

E Sports fan researchers acknowledge the irony in this: sporting events are competitions in which it's assumed that one team will generally lose, which means that around half of those watching won't see their desired result. In other activities, those odds might not seem like a worthwhile investment of one's time.

F The research he's carried out there has shown similarities between a fan's identification with a sports team and how people identify with their nationality, ethnicity, or even gender.

G So being a fan can't be all about a team's winning performance. 'Everyone is eventually going to lose,' says Wann. 'It's clear there have to be other benefits.'

69

1 1 on 2 kick 3 hot 4 daredevil 5 in 6 worshipped 7 with 8 shoulder 9 risk 10 crush

2 1 take 2 should 3 might 4 Inspired 5 can't 6 Having

3 1 ~~Walking~~ Having walked all morning, we were extremely hungry when we arrived home.
2 I heard the telephone ~~ringing~~ ring three times before it stopped.
3 She's just had a baby. She ~~can~~ must be very tired.
4 They ~~must~~ can't be very famous – I've never heard of them.
5 Leaving my office, ~~the telephone rang~~ I heard the telephone ring. / When I was leaving my office, the telephone rang.
6 I looked up and saw the bus ~~crashing~~ crash into the car.

4 1 see; Point
2 mind; suppose
3 always; break
4 accept; see

TEST YOURSELF UNITS 5 & 6

VOCABULARY

1 Complete the sentences with the words in the list. There are four extra words.

A-list | cold | crush | daredevil | for | hot | in | kick | on | risk | shoulder | stunt | with | worshipped

1 He's fixated … getting into the football team. He talks about nothing else.
2 I really get a … out of travelling. I find going to new places so exciting.
3 I told him he was wrong and he got … under the collar. He obviously didn't agree.
4 My sister's a bit of a … . She isn't scared to try any kind of extreme sport.
5 He doesn't really like being … the limelight and tries to keep away from the cameras.
6 My mum … a group called ABBA when she was young. She still has all their albums.
7 My two-year-old has got a fascination … wheels. He loves anything that moves.
8 She apologised to her friend, but all she got was the cold … .
9 I think we should assess the … before we attempt the jump.
10 I'm a huge fan of Selena Gomez. She's always been my celebrity … .

GRAMMAR

2 Complete the sentences with the words in the list. There are two extra words.

can't | having | inspired | inspiring | might | should | take | taking

1 He's lying about the chocolates. I saw him … the last one.
2 You … take your children to see this film. They'll love it.
3 It … be warm now, but it'll get cold later, so make sure you take a coat.
4 … by the concert, I decided to start piano lessons.
5 His team haven't won all year. They … be very good.
6 … lived in a cold climate most of my life, I found Brazil extremely hot.

3 Find and correct the mistake in each sentence.

1 Walking all morning, we were extremely hungry when we arrived home.
2 I heard the telephone ringing three times before it stopped.
3 She's just had a baby. She can be very tired.
4 They must be very famous – I've never heard of them.
5 Leaving my office, the telephone rang.
6 I looked up and saw the bus crashing into the car.

FUNCTIONAL LANGUAGE

4 Choose the correct options.

1 A The way I *understand* / *see* it, we'll never get anywhere if we keep on disagreeing.
B OK. *Point* / *Idea* taken. Let's make some decisions.
2 A To my *opinion* / *mind*, we should spend less money on defence and more money on hospitals.
B I *suppose* / *agree* you're right, but defence is also very important.
3 A You're *always* / *only* watching TV. If you aren't watching it, you're talking about it.
B Give me a *rest* / *break*, Mum. I'm trying to watch my show.
4 A I don't *accept* / *admit* that young people are responsible for most of our crime.
B That's not how I *see* / *observe* things either. It's too easy to just blame them.

MY SCORE
22–30 | 10–21 | 0–9

The Cambridge Life Competencies Framework

Collaboration
Agreeing success criteria
Watch this video for a tip on developing your students' collaborative skills. Scan the QR code here.

Warmer

Tell students they are going to play a game called *ABSTRACT*. Ask them to get into pairs and tell them they have three minutes to think of as many abstract nouns (e.g. *beauty*) as they can. The pair who can think of the most words wins. Once the time is over, brainstorm as a whole group and write all the abstract nouns on the board. Explain any words that students do not know.

▶ 18 Get TH!NKing

Ask the question. Get students to compare their ideas in groups. Play the video and then ask students for feedback.

1 Ask students what they can see in the painting. Does it remind them of any paintings they know? What is most striking about it? Does it make them feel anything? Ask them if they like it or not, and encourage them to explain why.

2 Put students into small groups and ask them to come up with five ideas for what, in their view, makes a work of art beautiful. Then work as a whole class and share ideas. Ask students to suggest examples of works of art that they think are especially beautiful. They could use the internet to find images of their favourite works of art to show to the other students.

3 Get students to finish the following statements: *Art needs to be beautiful because …* and *Art does not need to be beautiful because …* Share ideas as a whole class and write up the suggestions on the board. Have a vote on which one of the completed statements is the students' favourite.

Objectives

Functions Language of persuasion
Grammar Substitution (*the ones, so, that of, do*); ellipsis
Vocabulary Fads; emotional responses
Values Valuing the beauty around us
Literature Three poems

Resources for this unit

All available online

Videos

- Get **TH!NK**ing: *What does beauty mean to you?*
- Grammar video!: Substitution (*the ones, so, that of, do*)

Tests

- Unit, extension and skills test 7

Worksheets

- Grammar and vocabulary: Basic, Standard and Extension Worksheets
- Project: Beauty awareness
- Communication: Beauty is in the eye of the beholder
- Grammar presentation: Substitution & Ellipsis
- Literature Worksheets: *Jane Eyre*; *Desiree's Baby*
- Get **TH!NK**ing and Grammar video! video Worksheets

Warmer

Write the following adjectives on the board: *bushy, square, full, sharp, hooked, long*. Ask students to guess which facial features they can be used to describe. Discuss whether they are positive or negative.

Answers: eyebrows, jaw, lips, cheek bones, nose, eyelashes/nose.

1 Put a copy of the three pictures on the board and do the exercise as a class before students open their books.

2 Clarify that the question is about students' opinions – there are no right or wrong answers.

3 **7.01 Check/clarify:** *constitutes, state of affairs, hair transplants, stomach reductions, trendy, fads, derogatory comments, twisted, flattered, compassionate*.
Before playing the audio, ask students to answer as much as they can from memory.

1 She found women's beauty salons, hair, cosmetics, etc. She also found images of women, mostly western, who conform to the current idea of beauty.
2 Our ideas of beauty are different from our grandparents, great-grandparents and people in the Middle Ages.
3 The beauty industry focuses too much on how we look and is damaging, leading to a depressing state of affairs.
4 There is no connection between a good personality and a beautiful appearance.
5 Being kind, funny, generous and compassionate.
6 Inner beauty doesn't fade. If you achieve inner beauty, it will remain with you for the whole of your life.

4 Encourage students to speak at length and to use vocabulary from the article.

A

B

C

READING

1 SPEAKING **Work in pairs. Discuss the questions.**

1 Which of the people in the photographs
   a look really interesting?
   b would you like to meet and talk to?
2 What can you say about the people just by looking at them?

2 SPEAKING **Quickly scan the article on the next page. Choose the best title. Compare your ideas with a partner.**

a Inner beauty is just as important as physical beauty
b Why worry about beauty at all?
c Our confused notions of beauty
d How beauty has changed over the centuries

3 7.01 **Read the article again and listen. Answer the questions below.**

1 What did the writer discover by searching for 'beauty' online?
2 What does she say about changing ideas of beauty?
3 What is her opinion of the current beauty industry?
4 What does she say about the connection between appearance and personality?
5 What examples does she give of what 'inner beauty' involves?
6 Why does she disagree that 'beauty fades'?

4 SPEAKING **Work in pairs and discuss the following questions.**

1 The writer lists some examples of what people these days do to improve their physical appearance. What do you think about these examples?
2 Note something the writer says that you agree with and something you disagree with.
3 To what extent, in your country, do you think that there is a concentration on physical beauty rather than personality?

Train to TH!NK

Understanding irony

Irony is a technique used in speaking and writing to create a contradiction between what people say and what they mean. Ironic remarks can sound humorous, but can also sound sarcastic or unkind.
Here's an example from the article: Isn't it a wonderful world?
Explanation: This is an ironic remark. It's clear from everything else the writer says that she doesn't think it's a wonderful world at all.

72

5 Check/clarify: *irony, ironic remark, sarcastic.*
Do the first one with the class as an example if necessary. Ask them to think about how the people might feel and react when they hear the ironic statements. Check answers in open class and give examples of how sentences a to c might be said for students to repeat and get an understanding of ironic intonation. Tell students that we should be careful when using irony as it could be seen as quite rude in certain circumstances.
1c 2a 3b

6–7 Encourage students to practise responding so that the irony does not sound rude. Listen to some of their responses in open class as feedback and ask the rest of the class to decide if the answers sound authentic.

Homework

Ask students to keep a journal for two or three days, with a record of what ironic comments they have heard or made.

Activity idea Mixed-ability

In Exercise 7, give weaker students some situations and ask them to think of ironic remarks. Stronger students may be able to think of several ironic remarks for a situation and create a dialogue.

Activity idea Extension

Write the following ironic remarks on the board.

I can't think of anything I'd rather be doing than writing a 1000-word essay.

Of course, do you want me to wash up when I've finished?

No problem, I didn't want it anyway.

I love housework. I spend most of my spare time cleaning.

Ask students to work in pairs to think of a situation when people might say the sentences, then create short dialogues around two of them. Listen to some of the best examples in open class as feedback.

Communication
Using appropriate language and register for context
Uses a variety of language and communication strategies to achieve a desired effect.

A THING OF BEAUTY? UNIT 7

Gemma Stanley wonders if we've got our priorities straight.

Try this: pick a search engine (it doesn't matter which one) and type in the word 'beauty'. I guarantee that the first 20 hits will be to do with women's beauty salons, hair, cosmetics, and so on. This is true even if you live, as I do, in a country where the first language isn't English. After that, click on 'Images'. Guess what the first hundred images will be of? You probably don't even need me to tell you that it will be the faces of women, mostly western, who conform to the current idea of what a beautiful woman looks like (and who are frequently photographed to promote a 'beauty' product of some kind).

Our society's concentration on beauty as physical appearance is nothing new, of course. And there has always been a 'beauty industry' tagged on to this. Our idea of what constitutes beauty is quite different from that of our grandparents, let alone our great-grandparents or people in the Middle Ages. But our age of magazines, Hollywood and social media seems to have resulted in what I consider to be a rather depressing state of affairs. Now, we have plastic surgery; we have facial makeovers; we have hair transplants; we have stomach reductions; and a whole lot more. There are endless numbers of must-have clothes or accessories, and trendy fads and treatments, urging people (women and girls in particular) to spend money they perhaps don't have on things that, deep down, they don't really need. Isn't it a wonderful world?

This all leads me to ask: why are we so obsessed with appearance and with gender ideals as defined by the media and beauty industry? Why are we taken in by these messages? Haven't we got everything upside down?

Not long ago I saw something on social media about a famous person (no names) who had made some derogatory comments about another person's appearance. But that same person, who is very beautiful facially, apparently had a website all about how we should focus on people's inner beauty. How twisted is that?

In my life, I've met all kinds of people, some of whom are outwardly stunning. As we all know, though, that has nothing to do with what a person is truly like. I know physically lovely people who I like, and several that I don't. And I know many physically ordinary people who are kind, funny, generous and compassionate. They're the ones I want to spend time with.

Don't get me wrong. I like to look good, too, or as good as I can anyway. I like elegant clothes, I use make-up, I try to look after my hair, I'm flattered if someone says I look cool. But that can't compare to knowing that someone enjoys my company, or that they turn to me for advice, or that they like being with me because I'm interesting to be with.

Some people say that beauty fades, but I don't think so; physical beauty simply changes over time. But more importantly, inner beauty remains. If you can achieve any level of inner beauty, it's likely to stay with you throughout your life. Instead of worrying how your hair looks or if you could be slimmer, think about how you can be more kind-hearted, more compassionate. So, to my kids, my friends, my readers, I'd like to say: Try to be less concerned about how you look. Pay attention to who you are. Think about how to be as positive a presence as possible in the world. As Khalil Gibran said, 'Beauty is not in the face; beauty is a light in the heart.'

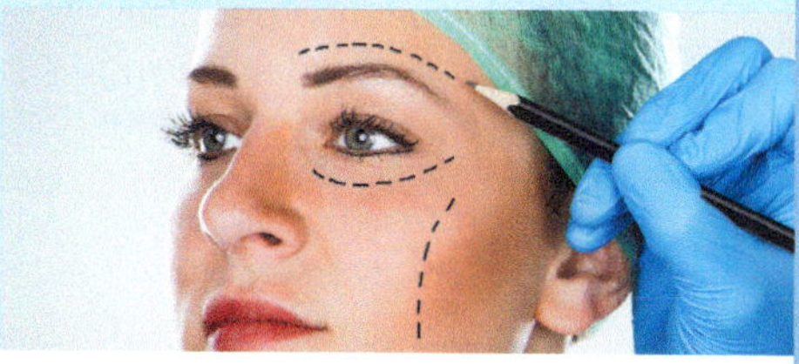

5 Match the situations 1–3 with the ironic remarks a–c below.

1 Mr Brown is in a hurry and has been patiently queuing up in a bank. Just as it's his turn, the assistant asks if he'd mind if she made a phone call before serving him. He says: ...
2 It's Monday morning. Joanne leaves the house and gets her bike out of the shed to ride it to school, but then notices it's got a flat tyre. She says: ...
3 Ken drives a brand new sports car. He notices a little stain on the front window and complains about it. His friend Carol drives an old car. She says: ...

a 'Brilliant. Today couldn't have started any better!'
b 'My goodness! How can you ever think of getting into that filthy car again?'
c 'Sure. Why on earth would you think I'd mind?'

6 SPEAKING Work in pairs. Think of an ironic remark people might make in each of the following situations.

1 It's a beautiful Sunday morning. Sally and her friend have decided to go to the beach. Ten minutes after the girls arrive at the beach, it starts raining heavily. Sally says: ...
2 Nick always leaves home early. He hates being late. One day, he arrives at the station half an hour before the train leaves. He sits down on a bench and starts reading a book. He loves the story so much that he completely forgets about the train and misses it. When he notices the train has gone, he says: ...
3 Mr Miller has had his new suit cleaned. When he puts it back into the wardrobe, he notices that there are several stains that weren't there before. He says: ...

7 WRITING Now, in pairs, write down two more situations and think of ironic remarks that you could make about them.

73

Language notes

It can be difficult for students to understand the difference between irony and sarcasm and they are often confused. In general terms, sarcasm is a type of irony but not all irony is sarcasm.

Irony can be written or spoken. It can be sad and tragic, or it can be funny and suspenseful. It is when something appears to be a certain way, but is actually different. It is often used for comedy and drama.

Sarcasm is only spoken. It is only used with the intent to insult or ridicule, such as mocking an idea.

TH!NK more

Worksheets

Project Beauty awareness
Communication Beauty is in the eye of the beholder
Get **TH!NK**ing *What does beauty mean to you?*

Warmer

Ask: *Can you think of five things people do to improve their appearance?* Students work in pairs to make a list. Make a list on the board for later in the lesson.

▶ 19 Grammar video! Substitution (*the ones, so, that of, do*)

1 Ask students to say what *that, ones, so* and *do* refer to in the sentences.
1 do 2 that 3 ones 4 so
RULE: 1 formal 2 informal
3 phrase 4 auxiliary

2 Where more than one answer is possible, ask students to explain any subtle differences in meaning.
1 that of 2 so 3 those / the ones
4 do 5 neither/nor does my best friend / my best friend doesn't either
6 so is my sister / my sister is too.

3 If you're short on time, set this for homework. Do the first item with the whole class as an example.
A Have you heard of Tough Mudder?
B Yes, I have. It sounds too tough for me though. I wouldn't want to run a mile waist-deep in mud.
A And neither would I. / Nor would I.
B The good thing is there aren't any winners or losers. You have to work as a team and help each other. I think that's a great idea.
A I think so, too. / I do too. And the company sounds really cool. I've heard their employees can take as much holiday as they like.
B That's good from a company perspective, too. Apparently, studies have found that high-performing employees take more holiday than those who aren't performing so well.

Workbook p64

GRAMMAR

Grammar video ▶19

Substitution (*the ones, so, that of, do*)

1 Read the sentences from the article on page 73. Complete them with *that, ones, so, do*. Then choose the correct options in the rule.

1 This is true even if you live, as I … , in a country where the first language isn't English.
2 Our idea of what constitutes beauty is quite different from … of our grandparents.
3 They're the … I want to spend time with.
4 Some people say that beauty fades, but I don't think … .

RULE: We use substitution to avoid repetition.
The cosmetic industry today is a lot stronger than ***that of (the cosmetic industry)*** *100 years ago.*
Your new hairstyle is much nicer than ***the one (the hairstyle)*** *you had before.*
Many people say beauty is skin-deep, and I ***think so (think it's skin-deep)****, too.*
Will those new clothes make me feel good? –
I certainly ***hope so (hope they make me feel good)****.*
I don't like him very much and ***neither do my friends (my friends also don't like him very much)****.*
- The words *that of/those of* tend to be more [1]*formal / informal.*
- The words *the one/the ones* tend to be more [2]*formal / informal.*
- The words so and *do/did* replace a [3]*word / phrase.*
- The words *so/neither/nor* include the meaning 'also'. Here, we invert the subject and [4]*auxiliary / main* verb.

2 Rewrite the sentences, substituting the underlined words. Sometimes more than one correct answer is possible.

1 Today's idea of beauty is very different from <u>the idea of beauty of</u> 200 years ago.
2 A Are you going to try that beauty treatment?
B No, I don't think <u>I'm going to try that beauty treatment</u>.
3 I don't think the clothes shops in this city are as good as <u>the clothes shops</u> in my previous town.
4 A I really like his new hairstyle.
B I <u>like his new hairstyle</u>, too.
5 My brother doesn't like my new glasses, and <u>my best friend doesn't like my new glasses either</u>.
6 I'm keen on doing a course about make-up, and <u>my sister is keen on it, too</u>.

3 Read the dialogue and find the repetitive sections. Then rewrite the dialogue using substitution to replace these sections.

A Have you heard of Tough Mudder?
B Yes, I have. It sounds too tough for me, though. I wouldn't want to run a mile waist-deep in mud.
A And I wouldn't want to run a mile waist-deep in mud.
B The good thing is there aren't any winners of Tough Mudder and there aren't any losers of Tough Mudder. You have to work as a team and help each other. I think that's a great idea.
A I also think that's a great idea. And the company sounds really cool. I've heard their employees can take as much holiday as they like.
B That's good from a company perspective, too. Apparently, studies have found that high-performing employees take more holiday than employees who aren't performing so well.

→ workbook page 64

VOCABULARY

Fads

4 Match the sentence halves.

1 The retro look
2 The latest smartphone quickly
3 We have seen many rather *short-lived*
4 The pilates class was full,
5 Can you remember when
6 Long hair for men was
7 I don't think jeans

a fitness crazes over the years.
b ripped jeans became *a thing*?
c so I'm doing yoga, which is *the next best thing*.
d will ever *go out of fashion*.
e *really in* in the '70s.
f established itself as the new *must-have* device.
g is *bang on trend* at the moment.

5 Choose the correct words to complete the sentences.

1 Wide-legged trousers are *really in / short-lived*.
2 Everybody's got a selfie stick nowadays. It's a *really in / must-have* device.
3 You can't always take your guitar with you. The Pocket Strings is *a thing / the next best thing*.
4 Cafés with odd chairs and tables were *bang on trend / must-have* in London in 2019.
5 It was *a thing / short-lived* in 2019 to drink out of jam jars.
6 Do you think gyms will ever *be the next best thing / go out of fashion*?

→ workbook page 66

Get it Right!
Substitution

Student's Book p90

4 Check/clarify: *fads.*
Before students do the exercise, ask them to work in pairs and think of some recent fads in fashion, music, etc. When students have completed the exercise, encourage them to guess the meanings of the words in italics from the contexts.
1 g 2 f 3 a 4 c 5 b 6 e 7 d

5 1 really in 2 must-have 3 the next best thing 4 bang on trend 5 a thing 6 go out of fashion

Workbook p66

Activity idea Extension

Write the sentences on the board. Students decide on the correct answer.
1 The mountains in France are not as high as *that / those* in Tibet. (those)
2 Will it take a long time to read? Well, it might *do / do so*. (do)
3 Is Peter coming on Wednesday? *I hope not / I don't hope so*. (I hope not.)
4 I didn't want to go to Scotland and *so / neither* did my brother. (neither)

TH!NK more

Workbook
Grammar p64, Ex.1–4
Vocabulary p66, Ex.1–2
Vocabulary Extra p67, Ex.1–3

Worksheets
Grammar Worksheets 7
Grammar presentation Substitution & Ellipsis
Vocabulary Worksheets 7
Grammar video! Substitution (*the ones, so, that of, do*)

6 🔊 **7.02 Check/clarify:** *leech, pomegranates, a snail.*
Nominate individuals to describe what they can see. Students discuss in pairs.

7 🔊 **7.02 Check/clarify:** *confront, wasp venom, ritual, suck, sceptical, illusion, excrement, dung, peel, sumac.*
1 F (A well-known American actor uses leeches to purify his blood.)
2 T 3 T 4 T 5 T
6 F (It was considered beautiful and correct for married women to have black teeth.)

8–9 Check/clarify: *tummy tuck, face lift, teeth-whitening, steroids.*
Refer back to the list of answers from the Warmer. How many of the things are mentioned? At the end of Exercise 9, listen to some of the students' ideas and encourage discussion.

10 Before students look at the exercise, write the first sentence on the board with brackets at the front: *(…) not heard that one before.* Elicit what words might be missing from the beginning (*I have*). With books open, ask what the sentences have in common (they all have words left out). Explain that this is called ellipsis and that it is mostly used in informal conversations, especially when the speakers know each other very well.
1 e 2 f 3 c 4 a 5 b 6 d
RULE: 1 informal 2 subject 3 verbs

11 🔊 **7.03** If you're short on time, set this exercise for homework.
1
Peter Do you fancy another game, Matt?
Matt I would love one.
Peter What about you, Jamie?
Jamie Sorry, there is not enough time. I have got to be home by five.
Peter See you at the same time tomorrow, then?
Jamie That would be great.
2
Helen Have you got a minute? I need to talk to you.
Mike No, I'm sorry, I'm busy now. Maybe we can talk later.
Helen That is no problem.
3
Emma Do you want a coffee?
Jake I'd love one.

Workbook p65

LISTENING

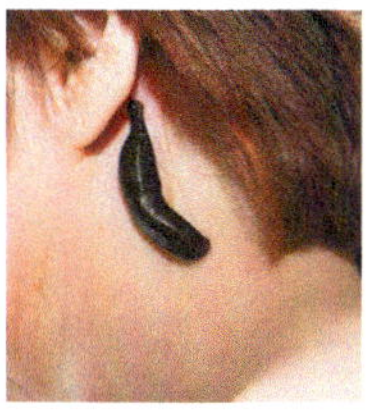

6 🔊 7.02 **Look at the photos. How do you think these things relate to beauty? Listen and check your answers.**

7 🔊 7.02 **Listen again. Are the statements T (true) or F (false) according to what the historian says? Correct the false statements.**

1 An American actor is reported to use the venom from a snake to purify his blood.
2 People are prepared to spend money on beauty treatments which lack scientific corroboration.
3 Media stories make us think that we can buy beauty.
4 Certain ingredients used in facemasks in Ancient Rome and Egypt were difficult to find.
5 Japanese women rubbed nuts against their teeth to make them black.
6 Having black teeth in 19th-century Japan signalled that you wanted to get married.

8 **Read the list of things people do to improve or change their looks. Check the meaning of the words and phrases. Can you add two more things?**

- have plastic surgery, for example a tummy tuck or a face lift
- dye their hair
- buy expensive cosmetics
- have a facial treatment
- cut down on sugar
- have a teeth-whitening treatment
- take steroids
- take up bodybuilding and/or exercise regularly
- …
- …

9 SPEAKING **Work in pairs. What do you think about each of the things listed in Exercise 8?**

It's a safe way to change your looks.
It can be fun.
It poses a serious health threat.
It's ridiculously expensive.
It doesn't have any long-lasting effects.
It may be worth trying.

GRAMMAR
Ellipsis

10 **Read these sentences (1–6) from the listening. Match them with the omitted words (a–f). Then complete the rule with *subject, informal* and *verbs*.**

1 Not heard that one before.
2 Want to hear another example?
3 Fancy trying any of these yourself?
4 Unbelievable!
5 Why black teeth?
6 Some examples?

a That's
b did they want
c Would you
d Can you give
e I have
f Do you

RULE: We often leave words out, especially in [1]… spoken English. This is known as 'ellipsis'. We can omit [2]… pronouns, articles, auxiliary [3]… or, in fact, any verb when it's clear from the context what the verb is.
Would you like more ice cream? ➜ *More ice cream?*
I would love some. ➜ *Love some.*

11 🔊 7.03 **Read the three dialogues and find the words that can be omitted. Then listen and check your answers.**

1 **Peter** Do you fancy another game, Matt?
Matt I would love one.
Peter What about you, Jamie?
Jamie Sorry, there is not enough time. I have got to be home by five.
Peter See you at the same time tomorrow, then?
Jamie That would be great.
2 **Helen** Have you got a minute? I need to talk to you.
Mike No, I'm sorry, I'm busy now. Maybe we can talk later.
Helen That is no problem.
3 **Emma** Do you want a coffee?
Jake I'd love one.

➜ workbook page 65

Homework

Ask students to research a fad from history. As a follow-up, students can present this fad in the next lesson. If students are struggling, suggest the following to research: *mantua dress, chopines, hacky sacks, shoulder pads, slap bracelets, leg warmers, mullets, citizens band radio, deely boppers, Atkins diet, Tamagotchi, rah-rah skirts, fidget spinners.* If students do not have access to the internet, they can create their own ideas. After each presentation, encourage the rest of the class to ask questions.

Culture note

The Meiji era was from 1868 to 1912, under Emperor Meiji, or Mutsuhito. This period saw huge transformation in Japanese society and social, economic and military power was completely restructured. A revolution returned political power to the Emperor and the capital moved from Kyoto to Tokyo.

TH!NK more

Practice Extra
Unit 7 Practise it!

Workbook
Listening p70, Ex.1–3 Grammar p65, Ex.5–8

Worksheets
Grammar Worksheets 7

Warmer

Tell students about something you think is beautiful. Tell them there is an old song with the lyrics *Everything is beautiful in its own way*. Ask students: *Do you think it is true that everything can be beautiful?* Students discuss the question in pairs and then compare their ideas with another pair.

1 If students are struggling to think of ideas, point out that they might choose a smell, music, a place, a person, an animal, etc. Divide the class into small groups to share their ideas and decide which of the things is the most beautiful.

2 **Check/clarify:** *murmuration, The Northern Lights.*
Before students open their books, put a copy of the six pictures up on the board and ask them to work in pairs to describe the pictures.

3 **7.04** Set a three-minute time limit to encourage students to read quickly and focus on the task rather than on trying to understand every word.
A2 B5 C8 D6 E1 F4

Pronunciation
Connected speech feature: assimilation
Student's Book p138

4 **Check/clarify:** *pirouettes, tiptoe, swirling, shivers, spine, goosebumps, tummy, tears* /tɪəz/.
If students disagree, encourage them to try to persuade their partners to change their scores.
1 The blog asks readers to tell them, in no more than 60 words, about something the reader thinks is beautiful.
2–4 Students' own answers

READING

1 Make a list of five things that you find beautiful.

2 SPEAKING Work in pairs. Look at the photos. Where is the 'beauty' in each one? Discuss.

I think this shows the beauty that's there in nature.

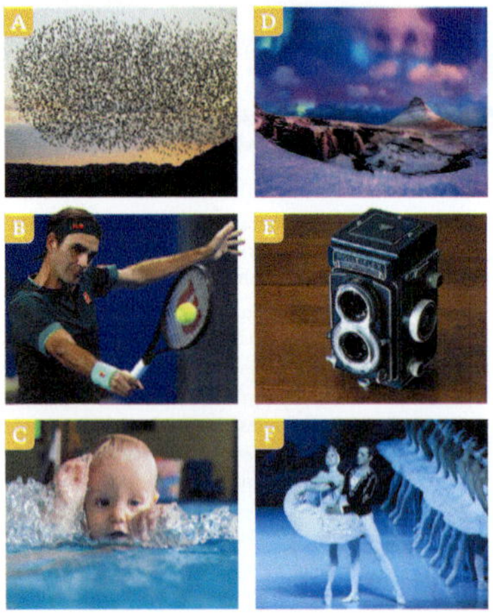

3 7.04 Read and listen to the blog. Match each photo with a post.

PRONUNCIATION
Connected speech feature: assimilation
Go to page 138.

SPEAKING

4 Work in pairs and discuss the questions.
1 What did the blog ask readers to do?
2 Which of your ideas in Exercise 1, if any, were mentioned?
3 Find some of the positive words and expressions used in the posts (that you liked).
4 Read each post again and give it a score from 0 to 5 according to how much you liked it. Then discuss your scores in pairs.

I didn't like number 5. I thought it was pretentious.

My favourite is number 3. I'd never thought that it was possible to find mathematics beautiful.

76

What's beautiful for you?

We asked you to tell us, in no more than 60 words, about something you think is beautiful. And we got a great range of answers. Here are some that we really liked. Which one do you like the best? Write and let us know.

1 In 1932, my great-grandfather bought a camera. My grandfather had it, then my mother, now it's mine. It sits on a shelf in my office, a bit battered but still working and still lovely – a beautiful piece of old technology, and part of my family history. I look at it and it brings a smile to my face.

2 A bird flying is already a lovely thing. But sometimes, in the evening, thousands of starlings come together and make an immense cloud of birds, a cloud that swirls and dances in the air. I saw it once and it set my heart racing. It's beautiful to watch and has a beautiful name: a 'murmuration'.

3 People are always surprised when I say I'm a mathematician. They're even more surprised when I talk about the beauty of mathematics. But I agree with the man who said, 'mathematics, rightly viewed, possesses not only truth, but supreme beauty'. Equations, mathematical shapes – they're like music to me, or art. It's the beauty of understanding, perhaps.

4 The most wonderful thing in my world is to watch professional ballet dancers. My dream was always to dance, but illness prevented me. The music, the grace, the seemingly effortless movement. Doing pirouettes and standing on tiptoe, spinning and swirling. It makes my heart soar and do pirouettes when I watch!

5 The right leg moves across the left, knees bent, perfect balance, eye on the ball. The racket swings back. The crowd gasps as he hits the ball, his right arm finishing high over his right shoulder. Federer's backhand is a wonderful shot to watch, perhaps the best ever. It sends shivers down my spine to think of it.

6 Last year, we took a winter cruise on the coast of Norway, up to the Arctic Circle, to see the aurora borealis. Our second night there, it happened – those magical waves of green and blue light, flashing in the sky. It gave me goosebumps all down my arms. Unfortunately, we didn't see it again on the cruise.

7 When he comes home and smiles and I look into his eyes, I always think of that Peter Gabriel song: 'In your eyes, the light, the heat. In your eyes, I am complete.' That describes perfectly how I feel about my husband's beautiful, smiling eyes. He's older now, but the light is still there.

8 When our little girl was born, my husband said we should take her to the local swimming pool. It's what his parents did with him when he was a baby. I could not believe it as she splashed happily in the water, with his hand under her tummy. It brought tears to my eyes!

Culture notes

Aurora Borealis, also known as The Northern Lights, is a natural phenomenon caused by electrically charged particles released from the Sun that enter the Earth's atmosphere colliding with gases such as oxygen and nitrogen. The lights are seen around the magnetic North Pole, Finland, Sweden, Norway, Iceland and Greenland. Galileo is thought to have coined the term in 1623. A similar phenomenon can be seen in regions of the South Pole.

Peter Gabriel, born in 1950, is an English singer-songwriter, musician and humanitarian activist. He rose to fame as the lead singer of the prog rock band *Genesis*. In 1975 he left the band for a solo career and developed a deep interest in world music, leading to the founding of the WOMAD (World of Music, Arts and Dance) festival in 1982. His video for *Sledgehammer* was voted 'best video of all time' by *Rolling Stone* magazine.

TH!NK more

Workbook
Reading p68, Ex.1–4
Pronunciation p120

5 1 *It* = seeing a murmuration; heart
2 *It* = Federer's backhand; spine
3 *It* = seeing the writer's daughter in the swimming pool; eyes
4 *It* = looking at the writer's family camera; face
5 *It* = watching professional ballet dancers; heart
6 *It* = watching the aurora borealis; arms

6 Monitor to encourage students to use the expressions.

7 If you're short on time, you can set this exercise for homework. Alternatively, it could be done as a collaborative writing activity in class.

Workbook p66

8–9 When students are ready, you could put students into new pairs to report back on their first conversation.

10 Copy the table onto the board and do an example with the class.

11 Ask students to think about the following questions:

Who do you want to aim your campaign at?

Where and when will you campaign?

Will you need to campaign more than once?

What outcome do you want?

When the plans are completed, students can present their campaigns to another pair and give each other feedback.

12 1 d 2 f 3 h 4 a 5 g 6 b 7 c 8 e

Critical TH!NKing
Solving problems and making decisions
Identifying and understanding problems.

Critical TH!NKing
Generating ideas
Comes up with many options.

Critical TH!NKing
Generating ideas
Builds on others' ideas.

Social Responsibilities
Understanding global issues
Demonstrates awareness of [environmental] issues around the world.

Social Responsibilities
Understanding global issues
Identifies ways in which personal habits and behaviour have the capacity to affect the environment.

Critical TH!NKing
Solving problems and making decisions
Examines possible solutions to a given problem and states how effective they are.

VOCABULARY
Emotional responses

5 What does *It* refer to in each of these sentences from the posts on page 76? Complete the sentences with the missing parts of the body. Then read and check.

1 *It* set my … racing.
2 *It* sends shivers down my … to think of it.
3 *It* brought tears to my … !
4 *It* brings a smile to my … .
5 *It* makes my … soar and do pirouettes when I watch!
6 *It* gave me goosebumps all down my … .

6 SPEAKING Work in pairs. Discuss what gives you the feelings described in each of the sentences in Exercise 5. Then make a list and share your ideas with another pair.

7 WRITING Now choose one of the ideas and write your own post about something you find beautiful for the blog.

→ workbook page 66

TH!NK values
Valuing the beauty around us

8 SPEAKING Work in pairs. Look at the photos and discuss.

1 In what ways are the photos similar?
2 How are they different?
3 Do sights like these bother you? How do they make you feel?

9 SPEAKING Work in groups. Make a list of four things you could do to tackle the environmental problem shown in one of the photos.

10 SPEAKING Work in pairs. Make a list of four 'ugly' sights in the town where you live and copy and complete the table.

Place	Issue	Cause	Solution

11 Choose one of the sights and talk about the advantages and disadvantages of using each of the different media below to raise awareness about the problem. Decide on the best one and, using your notes from Exercise 10, plan a campaign.

- a video
- banners
- social media

FUNCTIONS
Language of persuasion

12 Match 1–8 with a–h to complete the expressions.

1 *I strongly*
2 *Try our brand*
3 *This revolutionary new*
4 *This offer*
5 *Have you always*
6 Five million *people* worldwide
7 *We understand that*
8 *Imagine*

a *is limited.*
b *have already discovered* Nutrawheat.
c your health is important.
d *recommend* trying this treatment.
e having perfect sight again.
f new product.
g *dreamed of* owning a sports car?
h system is easy to use.

13 What is the aim of the expressions above?

14 7.06 Now complete the advert with six of the expressions in italics in Exercise 12. Then listen and check your answers.

Smile and the world smiles with you – or does it?

[1]… having a perfect smile? Well, now you can. If you want a confident smile, try our brand new, almost invisible tooth-straightening device. [2]… device is easy and comfortable to wear, and it fits perfectly. 'I always tried to hide my teeth when I smiled, but now I show them,' said Karen. 'If you feel the same way, [3]… trying Smile-Align.' '[4]… being able to smile for a photo again,' says Max. 'After using Smile-Align, I can do that.' [5]… the price is important, so we have a great offer for you today. The process usually costs £2,000, but we're offering it to you for just £1,500. But hurry, [6]… and must end soon.

15 WRITING Now create your own advert for a beauty gadget or piece of exercise equipment. Then present your advert to the class.

13 to persuade people to buy or to consider something

14 7.06 Before filling the gaps, ask students to quickly read through the dialogue to get a general understanding and to answer the question: *What product is being sold?* (a teeth-straightening device).
1 Have you always dreamed of 2 This revolutionary new 3 I strongly recommend 4 Imagine 5 We understand that 6 this offer is limited

15 Tell students that they should use the advert in Exercise 14 as an example. Encourage them to be creative! At the end of the presentations, hold a class vote to decide which gadgets they feel are the best.

TH!NK more

Workbook
Vocabulary p66, Ex.3–4

Worksheets
Vocabulary Worksheets 7

Warmer

Show students a picture of William Shakespeare. Ask: *Can you list five things you know about Shakespeare? Who can name the most Shakespeare plays?* (Hamlet, Romeo and Juliet, Macbeth, A Midsummer Night's Dream, Othello, King Lear, Twelfth Night). Students discuss the questions in pairs. Listen to some of their answers as a class.

1 🔊 **7.07** Before students do the task, point out that the poems and extracts from plays were written quite a long time ago, so the language may seem quite strange at first. Tell them not to worry about unknown vocabulary, but to focus on the task.
a 3 b 2 c 1

2 Look at the example with students and elicit differences between the two sentences. During feedback, ask students to refer to the extract and describe how the language has been paraphrased.
5, 9, 6, 10, 7

3 Before students do the exercise, write the highlighted words on the board. Tell students to find the words in the extract as quickly as possible. When they have seen them being used in context, ask them to try to work out the meaning of the phrases. Compare their meanings with the definitions in the book.
1 paced 2 sorrows 3 glowing 4 overhead 5 pilgrim 6 murmur 7 nodding 8 fled

Literature

1 🔊 7.07 **Read and listen to the extracts from three poems. Which one:**

a talks about how someone's beauty will never die?
b talks about remembering beauty and a love that was not fulfilled?
c talks about seeing someone beautiful for the first time?

2 Look at the first extract. Match these sentences to lines 5–10.

- And when I take her hand, my poor hand will be very fortunate.
- A white bird looks like this when it walks in the middle of a group of black birds.
- Have I ever been in love before? My eyes say no!
- How this woman stands out amongst the other women.
- Tonight is the first time I've ever seen someone really beautiful.
- When the dancing finishes, I'll watch where she stands.

3 VOCABULARY **Look at the second extract. Match the highlighted words with their definitions.**

1 walked backwards and forwards while feeling nervous
2 sadness, unhappiness
3 producing a warm light
4 above (your head)
5 someone who makes a long and difficult journey to a special place
6 speak or say something quietly
7 falling asleep
8 ran away

1

Romeo and Juliet
William Shakespeare

Romeo:
O, she doth teach the torches to burn bright!
It seems she hangs upon the cheek of night
Like a rich jewel in an Ethiope's ear;
Beauty too rich for use, for earth too dear!
So shows a snowy dove trooping with crows,
As yonder lady o'er her fellows shows.
The measure done, I'll watch her place of stand,
And, touching hers, make blessed my rude hand.
Did my heart love till now? forswear it, sight!
For I ne'er saw true beauty till this night.

2

When you are old
William Butler Yeats

When you are old and grey and full of sleep,
And **nodding** by the fire, take down this book,
And slowly read, and dream of the soft look
Your eyes had once, and of their shadows deep;
How many loved your moments of glad grace,
And loved your beauty with love false or true,
But one man loved the **pilgrim** Soul in you,
And loved the **sorrows** of your changing face;
And bending down beside the **glowing** bars,
Murmur, a little sadly, how Love **fled**
And **paced** upon the mountains **overhead**.

3

Sonnet 18
William Shakespeare

Shall I compare thee to a summer's day?
Thou art more lovely and more temperate.
Rough winds do shake the darling buds of May,
And summer's lease hath all too short a date.
Sometime too hot the eye of heaven shines,
And often is his gold complexion dimmed;
And every fair from fair sometime declines,
By chance, or nature's changing course, untrimmed;
But thy eternal summer shall not fade,
Nor lose possession of that fair thou ow'st,
Nor shall death brag thou wand'rest in his shade,
When in eternal lines to Time thou grow'st.
So long as men can breathe, or eyes can see,
So long lives this, and this gives life to thee.

78

Culture notes

William Shakespeare, born 1564, was an English poet, playwright and actor. A prolific writer during the Elizabethan and Jacobean era of British theatre, he wrote at least 38 plays, 154 sonnets and a number of poems, although no original manuscripts of the plays are known to exist. Originally from Stratford-upon-Avon, most of his career was spent in London as a member of a group of actors called *The King's Men*. He is often considered the greatest dramatist of all time.

William Butler Yeats, born 1865, was an Irish poet, playwright and author. He helped found the Abbey Theatre in Dublin, one of the country's leading cultural institutions. Political from a young age, he became a politician in 1922 and was a member of the Irish Senate for six years. Yeats won the Nobel Prize for Literature in 1923 and is considered by some as the greatest English-language poet of the 20th century.

Writing

4 Encourage students to cover the definitions and look at the third extract and try to guess the meaning of the phrases in context.
13, 7, 14, 9, 10

5 Monitor and encourage students to answer in full sentences and to justify their answers.

1 Tell students not to worry about unknown vocabulary, or to choose between adverbs at this stage.
She is upset that the models were not racially or culturally diverse and that they all represented one particular body shape. She hopes the newspaper will take note of her comments and include more diverse models in another edition in the future.

2 Let students compare their answers with a partner before feedback.
1 especially 2 thoroughly 3 remotely 4 arguably 5 equally

3 Elicit/clarify the meaning of the adverbs before students do the exercise.
Students' own answers

4 **Check/clarify:** *making amends.* Ask students to underline the parts of the letter that support their answers.
2, 1, 4, 3

5 To interest students in the topic, show students some images of photoshopped models on the internet or in magazines.

6 If you're short on time, students can do the preparation in class and complete the writing at home. Alternatively, this could be done as a collaborative writing activity in class with pairs of students of a similar level working together.

4 **Look at the third extract. Match these phrases to the lines which mean:**
- summer does not last very long
- as long as there are people in the world
- everything that is beautiful loses its beauty at some time
- this poem will live on, and will keep you alive
- you will not die
- you will not lose the beauty that you have now

5 SPEAKING **Work in pairs and discuss the questions.**
1 Which of the three poems do you like most? Why?
2 Which poem was easiest to understand, and which was the most difficult? Why?
3 Do you know any poems or songs, in English or in your own language, about beauty? Tell the class about it/them.

WRITING
A formal letter

1 INPUT **Read the letter. What two issues is Clara upset about and how does she hope the newspaper will respond?**

2 **Complete the letter by choosing the best option for each adverb.**

3 **Complete the sentences with your own ideas.**
1 Although she has made several great films, her latest is arguably ...
2 I have to admit I found the book thoroughly ...
3 He's a talented singer, but he's an equally ...
4 The last chapter of the book is especially ...
5 Not being a football fan, I wasn't remotely ...

4 ANALYSE **Match the paragraphs (1–4) with their functions.**
- This paragraph outlines the issue (what is wrong).
- This paragraph gives the background information.
- This paragraph proposes a solution.
- This paragraph explains why this situation is wrong.

5 PLAN **While reading a fashion magazine, you noticed that several of the models have been photoshopped to make them look perfect. You decide to write a letter about this. Use the structure of Clara's letter to help you organise your ideas.**

6 PRODUCE **Write a letter to the magazine complaining about this issue. Use your notes to help you.**

Dear Madam,

1 Being a student in my final year at the London School of Fashion, I was [1]*equally / especially* looking forward to the special fashion edition of your newspaper's weekend magazine. At first glance, I was not disappointed. The clothes that you featured were as original as they were exciting.

2 However, while I was [2]*arguably / thoroughly* enjoying the featured fashion, something did not feel quite right. I was trying to work out what it was when suddenly it dawned on me. Of the 12 different models you used for your shoot, ten were white, one was Asian and one was black – hardly reflective of the multicultural society in which we live. Furthermore, all of the models were what the media like to refer to as size zero. None of them were even [3]*remotely / thoroughly* approaching the shape or size of the majority of your female readership.

3 I have to say that I was particularly disappointed that your paper, which normally prides itself on its forward-thinking articles, should fall into the trap that less progressive magazines are keen to promote, i.e. that women should aspire to unreasonable, and [4]*arguably / especially* unhealthy, body sizes. I was [5]*remotely / equally* upset that you did not take the opportunity to portray a fair representation of the women who actually inhabit this world.

4 I do not imagine that you will consider making amends by offering us another fashion special in the next few weeks which features more diverse models. However, I do hope you will take note of my comments and observations, and make sure that in the future you present us with a fashion edition I know you are capable of producing.

Yours faithfully,

Clara Bowen

79

Homework
If you are short on time, students can do Writing Exercise 6 for homework. If you have done this in the class, ask students to exchange their letters with another student for them to read and give feedback on content and structure. Students could check if the letter uses the same structure as the template.

Activity idea Extension
There have been many film, TV and theatre versions of *Romeo and Juliet* that you could watch in class. One of the most popular was *Romeo + Juliet* directed by Baz Luhrmann with Leonardo DiCaprio as Romeo and Claire Danes as Juliet, released in 1996. The film has a modern-day setting but maintains the original language.

TH!NK more
Practice Extra
Unit 7 Master it!
Workbook
Developing Writing p69
Tests
Unit, extension and skills test 7

Life Competencies

Warmer

Write *The Natural World* on the board and make three columns headed *Positive*, *Neutral* and *Negative*. Brainstorm words and ask students to place them in the correct column, giving reasons for their choices.

▶ 20 Life Lessons: Appreciating the natural world

1 ▶ **20** Ask students to compare their ideas.
Suggested answers: seeing nature first hand, appreciating the power of nature, understanding how things work

2 ▶ **20** Ask students to suggest answers to Questions 1 and 2 before watching again.
Suggested answers: 1 Field trips don't give you a real feeling of what nature is. 2 to explain that extreme weather is also part of the natural world

3 **Clarify/check:** *hiking, sentimental, push myself, middle of nowhere.*
Students discuss their ideas together.

4 When answering these questions, students will probably be looking for language to express their ideas. Highlight useful language for giving opinions.

5 Students discuss the question in groups. With the whole class, elicit theories that address the questions and write them on the board. Try to establish an answer that everyone more or less agrees with.

6 Give students five minutes to note down their ideas. Give an example from your own experience for Question 1.

7 Monitor and help with any difficulties, but avoid interrupting if possible. You could highlight good examples of students exchanging opinions, disagreeing or agreeing respectfully.

LIFE COMPETENCIES

The natural world existed for millions of years before humans arrived and will (hopefully) be here long after we're gone. It is all around us – but how often do we really stop to appreciate it?

1 ▶ 20 **Watch the vlog. What did Annie appreciate about her experience working on a farm?**

2 ▶ 20 SPEAKING **Watch the vlog again. Work in pairs. Discuss these questions.**
1 What point is Annie making when she talks about field trips?
2 Why do you think Annie talks about the way nature can be dangerous?

We asked people what the natural world means to them. Here are some of their replies.

- My little garden. Although I live in a town, I grow my own tomatoes and potatoes. Food you grow yourself really does taste better! (Andrea/teacher)
- I go hiking every weekend. For me, it's a place where I can be myself and get away from the routine of working in an office. It's a place where I can breathe. (Paul/banker)
- It's my work. I produce food, I sell it and that's how I make a living. I respect nature, but I'm not sentimental about it. (Sandra/farmer)
- A world of magic and mystery! There's always something new to discover – it might be an amazing landscape or a tiny insect I've never seen before. (Alix/photographer)
- A challenge. I've been climbing mountains since I was a teenager. I try to push myself to do more difficult climbs and that gives me a great sense of achievement. It's a fantastic feeling when you reach the top. (Daniel/designer)
- Holidays. No homework! Seeing old friends and making new ones. I go to a little village in the middle of nowhere – it's where my parents grew up. I'm there for a month but it feels like a couple of days. (Samantha/student)

3 **Read the text with people's views about the natural world. As you read, think about this question: which opinion do you find the most interesting? Why?**

4 SPEAKING **Work in pairs and discuss the questions.**
1 What do you think Paul means when he says, 'It's a place where I can breathe'?
2 Do you think the food Andrea grows really tastes better than the food she can buy in a shop? Why/Why not?
3 Why might it be important for farmers like Sandra not to be sentimental?
4 Why is it important for Alix to look carefully at nature? How carefully do you look at nature?

5 SPEAKING **Why do you think activities such as hiking and climbing are popular ways of interacting with nature?**

Me and my world

6 **Make notes with your ideas about the following.**
1 Can you think of an occasion when you enjoyed the natural world? What happened? How did you feel?
2 A lot of people feel very strongly about protecting nature. Do you think they can make a difference?
3 Which of the ideas from the vlog and reading text describe or reflect your own ideas?

7 SPEAKING **Work in pairs. Compare your ideas and discuss to what extent they are similar or different.**

TIPS ON APPRECIATING THE NATURAL WORLD

- **Set aside time each week to be somewhere outdoors in nature. Use this time to reflect and be at one with yourself and your immediate surroundings.**
- **Remember, you don't have to go far to get in touch with the natural world. Even if you are in a city, there are parks and gardens – even your balcony – where you can enjoy nature.**

80

Activity idea

Using any of the ideas explored through the lesson, students work in pairs and write a questionnaire about the natural world designed to find out people's opinions.

Homework

Students interview around five people (friends and family) using their questionnaire. In class, students work in small groups and summarise the answers they received. With the whole class, ask what general conclusions we can draw from the information.

Unit Opener

Warmer

Write *Ipx bsf zpv?* on the board and tell students you are using a code to communicate with them. Give them one minute to try to guess in pairs how the code works. If the students haven't worked it out, explain that each letter used in the secret message corresponds to the following letter in the alphabet – so the message reads: *How are you?*

Ask them to create a coded message in pairs, using the same instructions. Ask for volunteers to come out to the board to write their coded messages, or ask students to spell out the letters for the rest of the class to decipher.

▶ 21 Get TH!NKing

Ask the question. Get students to compare their ideas in groups. Play the video and then ask students for feedback.

1 Ask students to think of codes in our daily lives (like the one shown in the picture). Why are they important? What impact can they have on our daily lives? Ask students to share what they think of the picture. How do they feel about it? Then discuss the students' ideas as a whole group.

2 Ask students if it's important to know how to code (i.e. to use a computer language to write programs). Can any of the students do this? Ask them to think of as many types of computer language as they can.

3 Draw two columns on the board and write *Learning to code* at the top of one and *Learning a language* at the top of the other. Elicit ideas from students and write them in the two columns. Are there any similarities between learning to code and learning a language?

8 CRACKING THE CODE

Get TH!NKING
Watch the video and think:
how many different codes do you know?

OBJECTIVES
FUNCTIONS:
saying that you don't understand or didn't fully hear
GRAMMAR:
relative clauses with determiners and prepositions; *however, wherever, whatever*, etc.
VOCABULARY:
language and communication; personality (2)

Work in pairs. Look at the photo and discuss the questions.
1 What things in life are controlled by this kind of code?
2 How important is it to know how to code?
3 Do you think learning to code is like learning a language? Why/Why not?

81

Objectives

Functions Saying that you don't understand or didn't fully hear
Grammar Relative clauses with determiners and prepositions; *however, wherever, whatever*, etc.
Vocabulary Language and communication; personality (2)
Values Learning another language
Culture Extinct languages

Resources for this unit

All available online

Videos
- Get TH!NKing: *How many different codes do you know?*
- Grammar video!: Relative clauses with determiners and prepositions
- Culture: Language Extinction

Tests
- Unit, extension and skills test 8

Worksheets
- Grammar and vocabulary: Basic, Standard and Extension Worksheets
- Project: Speak up!
- Communication: It's all Greek to me!
- Literature Worksheets: *Jane Eyre*
- Get TH!NKing and Grammar video! video Worksheets

Reading; Pronunciation; Train to TH!NK

Warmer

Write on the board: *J mjlf cbobobt cvu J epo'u mjlf bqqmft.* Ask students to work in pairs to guess what the sentence means. If they have difficulties, change the first letter to *I*, then the second letter to *L* until students understand that you have used the same code as previously (replacing each letter with the letter following it in the alphabet). Students race to be the first pair to decipher the sentence (I like bananas, but I don't like apples.). Ask: *Who uses codes? When are codes used?* Students discuss in pairs. Listen to some of their answers as a class and write any interesting vocabulary on the board.

1 Put a copy of the three pictures up on the board and do the exercise as a class before students open their books.
A The Rosetta Stone
B hieroglyphics
C Egyptian Pharaoh statue

2 Set a three-minute time limit to encourage students to read quickly. Encourage them to concentrate on answering the question rather than on trying to understand every word.
Egyptian hieroglyphics, Egyptian Demotic script and Ancient Greek

3 **8.01 Check/clarify:** *inscribed, scholars.*
Tell students not to worry about difficult vocabulary at this stage as this will come up later. Ask students to underline the parts of the text that helped them choose their answers.
1 f 2 d 3 b 4 e 5 h 6 g

4 Monitor to help with vocabulary, but do not interrupt to correct errors unless they impede communication. For further speaking practice, regroup students to compare their answers.

Pronunciation
Stress in multi-syllable words
Student's Book p138

A

B

C

READING

1 SPEAKING Work in pairs. Look at the photos. Tell your partner what you can see in them.

2 Read the article quickly. What three languages appeared on the Rosetta Stone?

3 8.01 Read the article again. Match the headings to the paragraphs 1–6 in the article. There are two you won't use. Then listen and check.

a Time to reconsider
b A language lost forever?
c Changing times
d A key to the past
e The story it told
f A chance discovery
g The final breakthrough
h First steps

4 SPEAKING Work in pairs. Discuss your answers to the questions.
1 What other important objects do you know of that people have discovered and used to learn about the past?
2 Imagine you were burying a piece of text for civilisations in the far future to discover and learn about your language. What text would you bury and why?

PRONUNCIATION
Stress in multi-syllable words Go to page 138.

Train to TH!NK

Making logical deductions about unknown words

When reading, we may sometimes come across words with which we are not familiar. If we look carefully at the context, we can often make logical deductions to help us understand the meaning of these words.

82

Reading

Culture notes

Napoléon Bonaparte was a French military leader who played a key role in the French Revolution of 1789 and crowned himself Emperor of France and King of Italy. He established *The Napoleonic Code*, a set of civil laws, which stated that government jobs must be given to the most qualified. It remains a model for governments worldwide.

The Rosetta Stone is a slab of granite stone, approximately 112 cm x 76 cm, featuring a written decree issued in 196 BCE by a group of Egyptian clergy and Egypt's then ruler, Ptolemy V, describing his generosity and beliefs. The decree is written in three ways and the stone became an essential tool for helping researchers understand the code of hieroglyphics.

Jean-François Champollion was a French linguist who deciphered the Rosetta Stone and cracked the hieroglyphic code. He is considered the founding father of Egyptology.

5 During feedback, elicit which part of speech *deciphering* is (verb: *to decipher*) and ask students to paraphrase the sentence.
1 the scholars 2 their knowledge of Ancient Greek 3 the writing on the Rosetta Stone 4 to find out the stories and secrets from the ancient culture

6 Suggested answer:
to discover the meaning of something written badly or in a difficult or hidden way

7 Explain that students have to come up with <u>questions</u> rather than a definition for now. Students can discuss in pairs and then also come up with a definition. During feedback, check that they're placing stress on the correct syllable (on the first syllable in *baffled* /'bæf.əld/ and *breakthrough* but on the second in *unravel*).
Suggested answers
baffled: to be completely unable to understand or explain something
breakthrough: an important discovery or event that helps to improve a situation or provide an answer to a problem
unravel: to become known or understood

Communication
Facilitating interactions
Guesses or coins a 'new' item of language based on existing knowledge.

THE ROSETTA STONE

CRACKING THE CODE UNIT 8

1 In 1798, the French emperor Napoleon Bonaparte invaded Egypt. Napoleon was particularly interested in art and education, and one of his missions in Egypt was to take anything that might be of cultural importance. In 1799, a group of French soldiers, one of whom was called Pierre-François Bouchard, was rebuilding a fort near a town called Rosetta. While digging in the sands, Bouchard came across an unusual slab of black rock. It was about 120 cm long and 75 cm wide. On closer inspection of the rock, he could see that it was inscribed with ancient writing. Knowing about his emperor's interest in such things, he took it back to show him.

2 As soon as the scholars looked at the stone, they knew they were looking at something very important. The Rosetta Stone, as it became known, had three layers, and on each layer there was a different language inscribed. The top layer contained ancient Egyptian hieroglyphics and the second layer was written in the later Egyptian Demotic script, neither of which anyone knew how to read. Luckily, the third layer was written in Ancient Greek, a language which was familiar to many of the scholars.

3 For many years, scholars had been <u>baffled</u> by the inscriptions they had found on the walls of Ancient Egyptian buildings. They knew these series of repeating images were a kind of language, in which case they must be saying something, but what? There were clearly pictures of birds, beetles and body parts, among many other things, but what did they mean? This ancient language, which they called 'hieroglyphics', had not been used for over 1,600 years and it seemed there was no way of ever being able to interpret it. The Rosetta Stone was about to change all that.

4 The first thing the scholars did was to translate the Ancient Greek passage on the stone, all of which they learned had been written by a group of priests in 196 BC to praise a pharaoh called Ptolemy V, who ruled over Egypt at that time. The passage contained a list of all the great things the pharaoh had done for his country. It also said that there should be a statue of the leader in every temple in the land, along with a copy of the text written on the Rosetta Stone. The passage in Greek was easy; the difficult part was what was written in the other two unknown scripts.

5 The first <u>breakthrough</u> came when scholars realised that all three passages said the same thing. Using the Greek translation, they now had the tools to start working on deciphering the hieroglyphics. Over the years, language experts, many of whom came from the world's most famous universities, studied the Rosetta Stone to try and crack its code, but it proved to be really difficult. It wasn't until 1822, when a Frenchman called Jean-François Champollion started studying the stone, that progress really started to happen.

6 Champollion had been fascinated with the Rosetta Stone since the age of 12. He became a scholar of languages and set about learning Latin, Greek, Hebrew, Arabic, Syriac, Persian, Aramaic and, most usefully of all, Coptic, which was a later form of the Egyptian language. But hieroglyphics was to prove his greatest challenge. It was a language compared to which all the others he knew seemed easy. However, slowly he was able to identify seven signs that the Coptic script shared with the Demotic script (that was also on the stone) and identify their meanings. He used this to start working out what several individual hieroglyphics meant. He was then able to make educated guesses about other signs and slowly the code began to <u>unravel</u>, unlocking stories and secrets from one of the world's most fascinating ancient cultures.

5 Look at the sentence from the article and answer questions about the underlined word.

Using the Greek translation, the scholars now had the tools to start working on <u>deciphering</u> the hieroglyphics.

1 Who is doing the deciphering?
2 What are they using to do the deciphering?
3 What are they deciphering?
4 What do they hope to achieve by deciphering?

6 Use your answers in Exercise 5 to write a definition for *decipher*, and then compare with a partner.

7 Find the following underlined words in the article and write questions that will help you arrive at a logical definition for each one.

1 baffled 2 breakthrough 3 unravel

83

Homework

If you are short on time, students can write the questions for Exercise 7 for homework. If you have done this in the class, ask students to exchange their questions with another student for them to read at home and write a definition.

TH!NK more

Worksheets
Project Speak up!
Communication It's all Greek to me!
Get **TH!NK**ing *How many different codes do you know?*

Warmer

Play 'vocabulary tennis'. Teams take turns to say a determiner (*a few, a, an, all, any, both, each, either, enough, every, half, her, his, least, less, many, more, most, much, my, neither, no, one, two, three, our, several, some, such, that, the, their, these, this, those, what, which, whose, your*). Elicit one or two in whole class to check students are clear about what a determiner is. If a team makes a mistake or takes more than five seconds to think of a determiner, the other team scores a point. As well as acting as an introduction to this language point, this game will give you an idea of the extent of students' knowledge of determiners.

▶ 22 Grammar video! Relative clauses with determiners and prepositions

1 1 one of whom 2 neither of which 3 in which case 4 all of which 5 many of whom 6 compared to which
RULE: 1 end 2 beginning 3 whom 4 begins

2 1 Grammar is something about which I know nothing.
2 She is a woman to whom I have never spoken.
3 Language is something to which we all give great importance.
4 Translation is the profession to which he has dedicated his life.
5 He's a friend from whom I almost never hear.

Workbook p72

Get it Right!

Relative pronouns with determiners

Student's Book p90

GRAMMAR

Relative clauses with determiners and prepositions

Grammar video ▶22

1 **Complete the sentences from the article on page 83 using the phrases in the list. Then complete the rule by choosing the correct options.**

all of which | compared to which | in which case | many of whom | neither of which | one of whom

1 A group of French soldiers, … was called Pierre-François Bouchard, was rebuilding a fort.
2 The top layer contained ancient Egyptian hieroglyphics and the second layer was written in the later Egyptian Demotic script, … anyone knew how to read.
3 They knew these series of repeating images were a kind of language, … they must be saying something, but what?
4 The first thing the scholars did was to translate the Ancient Greek passage on the stone, … they learned had been written by a group of priests.
5 Over the years, language experts, … came from the world's most famous universities, studied the Rosetta Stone.
6 It was a language … all the others he knew seemed easy.

RULE: Typically, prepositions go at the [1]*beginning / end* of a clause, for example 'Egyptian hieroglyphics, Egyptian Demotic and ancient Greek were the languages (which) the Rosetta Stone was inscribed with.'
In writing or in very formal spoken contexts, we can put the preposition at the [2]*beginning / end* of a relative clause, for example 'Egyptian hieroglyphics, Egyptian Demotic and ancient Greek were the languages with which the Rosetta Stone was inscribed.'
In this case, the relative pronoun is always [3]*that / whom* for people.
Sometimes the relative clause [4]*begins / ends* with a determiner, for example *all, some* or *none*.

2 **Rewrite the sentences in more formal language.**

0 Coptic is a language that few people are familiar with.
Coptic is a language with which few people are familiar.
1 Grammar is something that I know nothing about.
2 She is a woman that I have never spoken to.
3 Language is something we all give great importance to.
4 Translation is the profession that he has dedicated his life to.
5 He's a friend that I almost never hear from.

→ workbook page 72

VOCABULARY

Language and communication

3 **Read the paragraphs. Which one isn't about spoken language?**

A When I'm in France I like to try to practise my language skills. However, my **broken French** is so poor that sometimes I **can't make myself understood** and so it ends in a complete **communication breakdown**. I do my best to **pronounce** things clearly, but of course I'm not a **native speaker** or anywhere approaching that level, so people often **misunderstand** me.

B The other day, I met someone from another part of the country who had such a **strong accent** that at times I found him virtually **incomprehensible**. It was hard to believe that we shared the same **first language**, to be honest. And it wasn't just the accent – he was actually speaking a different **dialect** and using slang words that meant I just couldn't **follow** him. We had to get someone to **interpret** for us!

C When you travel, there's sometimes a **language barrier** that makes communication difficult. But I've found that **body language**, while obviously not exactly the same around the world, is sufficiently universal to mean that we can 'talk' to other people. **Gestures** and **facial expressions** allow you to show people that you don't understand, that you want a particular thing, or whatever.

4 SPEAKING **Work in pairs. Discuss the meaning of the words and phrases in bold. Use a dictionary to help you.**

5 **Use expressions from Exercise 3 to complete the text.**

I'll always remember the first time I went to the north-east of England. People there speak with a really [1]… and there are some vocabulary differences, too, which means it's really a different [2]… of English. More than once, people said things to me and I just couldn't [3]… them. And sometimes they [4]… me, too. It's strange when there seems to be a [5]… between people who share the same [6]… !

→ workbook page 74

SPEAKING

6 **Work in pairs. Give examples of:**

1 a time when you couldn't make yourself understood.
2 a slang expression in English.
3 a dialect that someone in your family speaks.
4 mistakes people often make when writing your language.
5 someone you know who speaks with a strong accent.

84

3 Tell students not to worry about difficult vocabulary at this stage and encourage them just to concentrate on answering the question.
C

4 Encourage students to guess the meanings from context first. Say the words and phrases for students to repeat and check pronunciation. Pay close attention to the stress of multi-syllable words.

5 Ask students to quickly read through the paragraph to get a general understanding and to answer the question: *What is the problem?* (The writer had trouble understanding people in the north-east of England).
1 strong accent 2 dialect 3 follow 4 misunderstood 5 communication breakdown 6 first language

Workbook p74

6 Encourage students to use some of the words and phrases in Exercise 3.

Activity idea Fast finishers

Ask students to write sentences describing their own language ability and communication skills using some of the phrases in Exercise 4.

TH!NK more

Workbook
Grammar p72, Ex.1–3
Vocabulary p74, Ex.1–2

Worksheets
Grammar Worksheets 8
Vocabulary Worksheets 8
Grammar video! Relative clauses with determiners and prepositions

Functions; Listening; Grammar

7 Before students do the exercise, mumble some incomprehensible sentences and elicit reactions from students. Ask: *What do you say if you can't hear somebody clearly?*
1 c 2 a 3 f 4 e 5 d 6 b

8–9 Make sure students are translating the meaning of the expression rather than a literal translation of the individual words.

10 Suggested answers: Morse code, barcode, access code, genetic code, semaphore

11 🔊 **8.03**
An unidentified male found on a beach in Adelaide / Nobody knows who he was. It remains a mystery.

12 🔊 **8.03 Check/clarify:** *grisly, non-random order, infiltrated, spies.*
1 He had been on the beach all night.
2 He had no identification on him and his clothes weren't suited to the Australian weather.
3 He had no identification, nobody knew who he was and his fingerprints were not in the fingerprint database.
4 A piece of paper (with the words 'Tamám Shud' written on it).
5 A man came forward and said he had found a book in his car. It was a copy of a Persian poem (*The Rubaiyat* by Omar Khayyam).
6 The ripped-out piece of paper that was in the Somerton Man's pocket came from the book and there was some sort of code inside the cover of the book.
7 Experts have been unsuccessful.
8 The book went missing in the 1960s.

13 Point out that *however* is followed by an adjective.
1 c 2 b 3 a
RULE: 1 some 2 important

14 1 Whatever you say, he won't like it.
2 Whenever we leave, the roads will be full of traffic. / Whenever we leave, the roads are always full of traffic.
3 Whichever way you say it, it means the same thing.
4 However strong your accent is, everyone will understand you.

15 You could ask students to write three sentences that are true for them and one that is false. Their partner has to guess which sentence is false.

Workbook p73

Get it Right!
however, wherever, whatever, etc.

Student's Book p90

FUNCTIONS
Saying that you don't understand or didn't fully hear

7 **Match the beginnings (1–6) with the correct endings (a–f).**

1 Sorry, there was a bus going past.
2 He was using all sorts of technical jargon,
3 His argument isn't very clear.
4 She hasn't explained it very clearly.
5 That was a bit of a complicated explanation!
6 The teacher said that I needed to 'use some elbow grease',

a so I **didn't quite get** what he said.
b but I wasn't **familiar with** that expression.
c I **didn't catch** what you said with all the noise.
d I'm afraid **you've lost me**. Can you explain it more simply?
e I **don't quite see** what she means.
f I **don't follow** him at all.

8 **How do you say the expressions in bold in your language?**

9 **Answer the questions about the expressions in Exercise 7.**

1 Which one(s) do you like most?
2 Which one(s), if any, do you not like at all?
3 Which one(s), if any, could you see yourself using?
4 Which one(s), if any, would you not feel very comfortable using?

LISTENING
Codes

10 SPEAKING **Work in pairs. Discuss the question.**
What famous codes can you think of?

11 🔊 8.03 **Listen to the radio programme. Who was the Somerton Man?**

12 🔊 8.03 **Listen again and answer the questions.**

1 How long had the man been on the beach when he was found?
2 Why did the police think he wasn't local?
3 Why were they not able to find out his identity?
4 What did they find in his pocket?
5 How did the case develop from this discovery?
6 What two things were odd about the book?
7 How successful have experts been in solving the code?
8 Why can't the book be used to solve the code now?

GRAMMAR
however, wherever, whatever, etc.

13 **Match the beginnings and endings of the sentences from the listening. Then choose the correct options to complete the rule.**

1 However hard they tried,
2 Whoever the police asked,
3 Whatever he'd been doing on the beach

a would remain a mystery.
b no one seemed to know who he was.
c the experts could not crack it.

RULE: We can add *-ever* to *how* and [1]*all / some wh-* words: *however/whatever/whoever/wherever/whenever/whichever.*
We use *whatever/wherever/however,* etc. to mean it isn't [2]*important / necessary* what/where/how because the result is always the same.
The word order is *-ever* word + (adjective) subject + verb.

14 **Rewrite these sentences. Start each one with an *-ever* word.**

0 It doesn't matter when you arrive – we'll be here.
Whenever you arrive, we'll be here.
1 It doesn't matter what you say – he won't like it.
2 It doesn't matter when we leave – the roads are always full of traffic.
3 It isn't important which way you say it – it means the same thing.
4 It doesn't matter how strong your accent is – everyone will understand you.

15 SPEAKING **Complete the sentences, and then compare with a partner.**

1 Whatever I decide to do after I leave school, ...
2 Whenever I have free time, ...
3 Wherever I go to university/on holiday ... , ...
4 However expensive it ... , ...

→ workbook page 73

Homework
Ask students to research a code or cipher. They can find a picture and write a description of code and how it works or how/why/when it was created, in English. If students do not have access to the internet, they can create their own ideas. As a follow-up, students can present their code to the class.

Language note
Point out the following variations in form:
however + adjective + subject + verb
whoever + verb (*whoever* can be the subject of a sentence – *Whoever told you that is wrong*)
whatever is often used to show disinterest – A: You need to study more. B: Whatever.

TH!NK more
Practice Extra
Unit 8 Practise it!
Workbook
Listening p78, Ex.1–2
Grammar p73, Ex.4–6
Worksheets
Grammar Worksheets 8

Warmer

Ask: *What percentage of the world's population are:*

a) monolingual (know only one language) – 40%

b) bilingual (can use two languages) – 43%

c) trilingual (three languages) – 13%

d) multilingual (four or more) – 3%

Students work in pairs to guess the percentages. Check answers with the class and give a point to the pair who get closest to each answer.

1 During feedback, find out who knows the person who can speak the most languages and what they are.

2 Set a three-minute time limit to encourage students to read quickly and focus on answering the question rather than on trying to understand every word.

3 **8.04 Check/clarify:** *verbal, aggression, domination, guilt, peers, traits, inherent.*
Give students time to read through 1–6 and check they understand. Encourage them to underline the key information in the sentences that will help them place them in the text.
A3 B6 C4 D2 E1
Not used: 5

4 When students have completed the exercise, you may like to regroup students and ask them to repeat the exercise with new partners. As well as maximising speaking practice, this is often motivating for students as they are able to express themselves more fully at the second attempt.

Multilinguals have multiple personalities

Between 2001 and 2003, linguists Jean-Marc Dewaele and Aneta Pavlenko asked over a thousand bilinguals whether they 'feel like a different person' when they speak different languages. [A]

Susan Ervin, a sociolinguist at the University of California, Berkeley, set out to explore the differences in how bilinguals represent the same stories in different languages. She recruited 64 French adults who lived in the US and were fluent in both French and English. On average, they had spent 12 years living in the US; 40 were married to an American. On two separate occasions, six weeks apart, Ervin showed her subjects a series of illustrations [B]. In one session, the volunteer and experimenter spoke only in French, [C].

One of the illustrations Ervin used in her first experiment

Ervin then analysed the stories, and she identified some significant topical differences. The English stories more often featured female achievement, physical aggression, verbal aggression towards parents, and attempts to escape blame, while the French stories were more likely to include domination by elders, guilt, and verbal aggression toward peers.

[D] This time, Ervin looked at Japanese women living in the San Francisco area. Ervin had a bilingual interviewer give the women various verbal tasks in both Japanese and in English, and found – as she expected – important differences.

For instance, when the women were asked to complete the following sentences, their answers differed depending on the language in which the question was asked:

1 **When my wishes conflict with my family …**
(Japanese) it is a time of great unhappiness.
(English) I do what I want.

2 **I will probably become …**
(Japanese) a housewife.
(English) a teacher.

Scholars have also used more qualitative methods to try to understand language's impact on personality. In 1998, Michele Koven spent a year and a half carrying out ethnographic research with bilingual Parisian adults whose parents had immigrated from Portugal. All of her subjects were fluent in both French and Portuguese, and most maintained close ties to Portugal while living in France. Koven focused specifically on how her subjects represented themselves in narratives of personal experience, which she elicited by asking them to recount various life events in both languages. Koven saw that her subjects emphasised different traits in their characters, depending on which language they were speaking. For instance, the women in the French stories were more likely to stand up for themselves, whereas the female characters in the Portuguese narratives tended to cede to others' demands. [E] One girl, Koven writes, sounded like 'an angry, hip suburbanite' when she spoke French, and a 'frustrated, but patient, well-mannered bank customer who does not want attention drawn to the fact that she is an émigré' when she spoke Portuguese. Whether that's due to the different context in which she learned French and Portuguese, an inherent difference between the two languages, or some combination of the two, researchers have yet to figure out.

86

READING
Multilingual people

1 SPEAKING **Do you know anyone who is multilingual? Tell your partner about them.**

2 **Look at the title of the article. What do you think it is going to say about multilingual people? Read it quickly to check your ideas.**

3 8.04 **Read and listen to the article again. Put these sentences/phrases into the correct place in the article, A–E. There is one that you won't use.**
1 And their own personas changed, too.
2 In 1968, Ervin designed another experiment to further explore her hypothesis that the content of bilinguals' speech would change along with the language.
3 Nearly two-thirds said they did.
4 while the other session was conducted entirely in English
5 She believed that the content of bilinguals' speech would change along with the language.
6 and asked them to make up a three-minute story to accompany each scene

4 SPEAKING **Work in groups. Discuss the questions.**
1 To what extent do you feel 'different' when you speak English (or another language that isn't your first language)?
2 In what other way(s) could you test the effect that language has on someone's personality?

Culture notes

Jean-Marc Dewaele is Professor of Applied Linguistics and Multilingualism at Birkbeck, University of London. In 2010, he published a study on emotions in multiple languages. He won an award for Excellence in Second Language and Bilingualism Research in 2016.

Aneta Pavlenko is Professor of Applied Linguistics at the University of Oslo, specialising in the relationships between bilingualism and cognition and emotion, and an expert consultant in forensic linguistics.

Susan Ervin-Tripp was a psycholinguist and Professor Emerita of Psychology at the University of California at Berkeley whose pioneering studies focused on bilingualism and language development in children, native Americans and immigrants.

Michele Koven is a Professor at the University of Illinois researching the relationships between identity and language practices in migrant communities.

TH!NK more

Workbook
Reading p76, Ex.1–4

Activity idea Mixed-ability

Give weaker students time to work together and make notes on their answers in Exercise 4 before regrouping students for discussion. Stronger students can discuss the questions without any preparation time.

Vocabulary; TH!NK Values

5 Encourage students to scan the article quickly.
patient, well-mannered

6 Tell students not to worry if they do not understand some of the phrases in bold, but to try to work them out from their context.
assertive: to behave confidently and not frightened to say what you want or believe
forceful: expressing opinions strongly and demanding attention or action
self-conscious: nervous or uncomfortable because you are worried about what people think about you or your actions
expressive: showing what you think or feel
modest: not usually talking about or making obvious your own abilities and achievements
conceited: too proud of yourself and your actions and abilities
impulsive: showing behaviour in which you do things suddenly without any planning and without considering the effects they may have
self-assured: having confidence in your own abilities

7 *1 conceited 2 impulsive 3 self-conscious 4 assertive / forceful 5 modest 6 expressive*

8 As they make notes of their answers, encourage them to think of specific situations and anecdotes.

9 Monitor and help with vocabulary as necessary. Try the 'silent tick' – writing a tick on a student's notebook if they speak well.

Workbook p74

VOCABULARY
Personality (2)

5 **Look back at the article on page 86 and find two words to describe personality.**

6 SPEAKING **Here are some people talking about language and personality. Work in pairs. Discuss the meaning of the words in bold. Use the context to help you.**

1 I tend to be a bit afraid to say what I think in a foreign language. I can be a lot more **assertive** and **decisive** in my own language.
2 I feel really **self-conscious** if I speak another language, like everyone is listening and thinking I'm not very good at it, so I often don't even try.
3 I love speaking other languages – I feel much more **expressive** than I do in my own language and my true personality comes out.
4 I'm usually a **modest** person, but when I speak another language I feel like I get a bit **arrogant** and start to behave as if I think quite highly of myself!
5 I've got a friend who's more **impulsive** when he isn't speaking his native language – he just says whatever he's thinking!
6 Maybe speaking more than one language helps you become more confident and **self-assured**?

7 **Use a word from Exercise 6 for each space. There may be more than one possibility.**

1 He thinks he's wonderful – he's so … !
2 She often acts without thinking – she's really quite … .
3 It's difficult for me to talk to new people – I always feel a bit … .
4 Don't let other people tell you what to do! You have to be a bit more … .
5 He's a very well-mannered and … child. He never boasts about his achievements.
6 It's captivating watching her tell a story. Her facial expressions are amazing. She's so … .

8 **Which (if any) of the statements in Exercise 6 do you identify with? Think of examples and make notes. Compare ideas with a partner.**

9 SPEAKING **Work in pairs and discuss the questions.**

1 What's your favourite word in any language other than your own? Why do you like it?
2 What other languages have you heard people speak? How would you describe how they sound? Do you think that they suggest a certain kind of personality?
3 What gestures do native speakers of your language use to help them communicate more expressively? What gestures have you noticed speakers of other languages use?
4 Do you feel different in any way when you speak English compared to when you speak your first language?
5 What do you think are the advantages and disadvantages of being able to speak more than one language?

→ workbook page 74

TH!NK values
Learning another language

10 **Which of these statements do you agree with?**

A good reason to learn another language is to …
be able to communicate when travelling;
learn about another culture;
improve my job prospects;
be able to talk to foreigners in my country;
be able to read books, magazines and newspapers in another language;
develop myself personally.

11 SPEAKING **Work in a group of six to eight. Find out from the other students which they agreed with. Did anyone agree with the same statements as you?**

12 **Make a graph or chart like the one below to show how your group feels.**

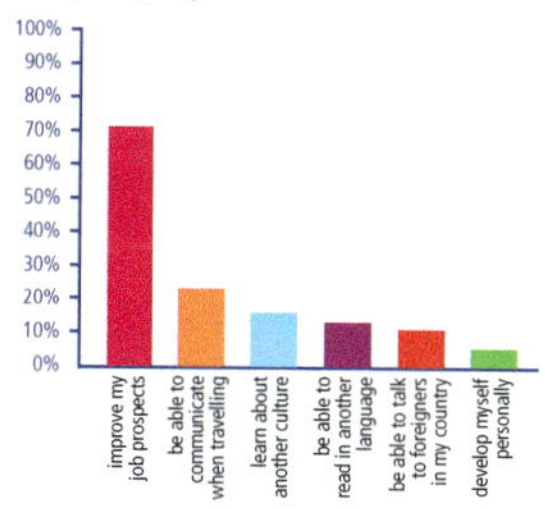

10–11 If space allows, encourage students to walk around the classroom to find someone who agrees with the same statements. Ask students to report their findings back to the class and encourage them to use the phrase 'So does he/she/[student's name] …'.

12 Ask all students to draw the chart. When they have completed the exercise, regroup students to compare their charts.

Homework

Encourage students to watch part of a film or TV show they are familiar with, but with a different language audio. Can they still understand it? Does it help to have subtitles in their own language, or in the other language? As a follow-up, students can discuss what they saw and how easy or difficult they found it.

Collaboration
Taking personal responsibility for own contribution to a group task
Makes relevant suggestions.

Collaboration
Taking personal responsibility for own contribution to a group task
Volunteers to take on a specific role.

Collaboration
Encouraging effective group interaction
Helps other students put their ideas across.

TH!NK more

Workbook
Vocabulary p74, Ex.3–5
Vocabulary Extra p75, Ex.1–3

Worksheets
Vocabulary Worksheets 8

Warmer

Ask students: *Did you speak an invented language when you were younger? Can you still remember any of it?* Students discuss in pairs. Can anyone teach the class some words? You may like to give an example of your own to get students started.

Alternatively, you could give them an example of 'Pig-Latin' which is a fun language some children in the UK use: move the consonant cluster from the start of the word to the end of the word, and then add 'ay'. When the word begins with a vowel, add 'ay' or 'yay' to the end instead. For example, 'Pig Latin' would translate as *Igpay Atinlay* and 'Let's learn a new language today' would be *et'slay earnlay ayay ewnay anguagelay odaytay.* (There are Pig Latin translators on the internet that you can refer to!)

▶ 23 TH!NK
Language extinction

1 Before students open their books, put a copy of the four pictures up on the board and write the names, mixed up. Ask students to match the pictures with the names and then answer the question.

2 🔊 **8.05** Tell students not to worry about difficult vocabulary at this stage as this will come up later.
Hunnir does not have a photo because there is no documentation of the language.

TH!NK Language extinction

Culture

Extinct languages – or are they?

1 Look at the photos. What do you think these languages have in common?

2 🔊 8.05 Read and listen to the article and check your ideas. Which of the languages does not have an accompanying photo? Why is this?

Languages are dying out all the time. There are currently approximately 7,000 languages spoken across the world and that's fewer than there were two years ago. Here are five languages that were once widely spoken but these days are classified as 'dead' languages.

Middle English

Middle English was spoken in England between the 12th and 15th centuries and is very different to the English we use these days. In the past, England, along with Scotland and Wales, was a country that had been invaded by several different nations, and this was reflected in its language, which was highly influenced by Norman French and Old Norse. Middle English also included a lot of Germanic vocabulary. There are very few **manuscripts** in Middle English as it was much more fashionable in those days to write in French. Perhaps the most famous document that has survived is *The Canterbury Tales* (or *Tales of Caunterbury*, as it was originally known), which was written between 1387 and 1400 by the poet Geoffrey Chaucer. Middle English gave way to early modern English, which is popularly associated with Shakespeare.

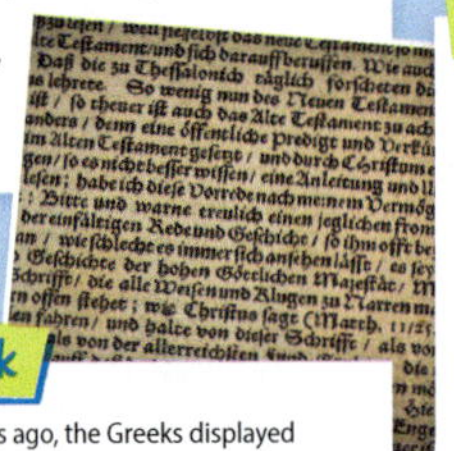

Old Norse

Old Norse was spoken and written by the Vikings from the northern countries of Europe from about the 7th century. It belongs to the Germanic group of languages and was used in countries as far apart as Iceland and parts of Russia. It used a complex system of characters known as runes to depict individual letters and sounds. Much of our knowledge of Norse mythology comes from stories written down in runes. The Vikings were also famous for their **raids** on neighbouring countries, and so it is not surprising that Old Norse had an influence on the languages of the places they raided, including English. For example, English words such as 'egg', 'gift', 'anger', 'want', 'trust' and 'score' are all **derived from** Old Norse. Although it is no longer spoken, it is still possible to learn runes.

Latin

Back in 5 BC, there were many different languages spoken in Italy. In an area called Latium, which included Rome, the people spoke Latin, so as Rome became more and more important, Latin spread throughout the country until it became the principal language. But Rome's influence did not stop in Italy. As the Roman Empire spread across Europe, it took its language with it and gradually Latin became the **lingua franca** for much of the continent. Latin was spoken mainly by the noblemen and **aristocrats**, but there was another form of the language known as Vulgar Latin which was used by ordinary people. When the Roman Empire collapsed in the 5th century, it took Latin with it. However, its huge influence can still be found in many modern European languages, including French, Italian, Portuguese, Spanish and English.

Ancient Greek

More than 4,000 years ago, the Greeks displayed great knowledge in philosophy, maths, literature and politics. They also spoke a very **sophisticated** language known today as Ancient Greek, and developed the first alphabet to contain vowels. Indeed, the English word 'alphabet' is taken from the first two letters of the Greek alphabet: *alpha* and *beta*. The ancient Greeks wrote a lot of historical accounts and philosophical essays. They also wrote many plays which are considered to be the forerunners of modern theatre. Although the language is no longer spoken anywhere, it continues to be studied by scholars around the world and, along with Latin, is regarded as one of the most important languages of all time.

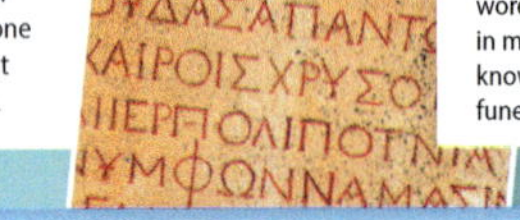

Hunnir

Hunnir is the most mysterious of the languages on our list, because it is the one that the least is known about, as no documentation of the language exists. The Huns were a **tribal** community that spread across much of eastern Europe in the 4th and 5th centuries. The most famous of the Huns was Attila, a warrior famous for his raids in western Europe. Despite the Huns' success in expanding their **empire**, their language was never written down, which is why we have very little knowledge of it today. The few words that are known are mainly names, which are similar to names used in modern Turkey and Mongolia. Apart from these, only three words are known: *medos*, *kamos* (both types of drinks) and *strava* (a feast served at funerals).

88

Culture notes

Geoffrey Chaucer, born around 1340, was an English poet, diplomat and civil servant. He is best known for writing *The Canterbury Tales*, which is considered one of the greatest poetic works in English. He was buried in Westminster Abbey, London and his grave became the centre of Poets' Corner – a place where many other famous British writers and cultural icons have been interred.

The Canterbury Tales is a collection of stories by Chaucer. The common theme is of a pilgrimage to the shrine of Thomas Becket in Canterbury and those who make the journey have a storytelling contest to pass the time as they travel.

William Shakespeare: see Culture Note on page T78.

The Vikings were Norse people who came from Scandinavia. During 700–1100 CE many travelled to other countries, particularly Britain and Ireland. They have a reputation as violent warriors, starting fierce battles with the Anglo-Saxons but many in fact came peacefully to settle. They were farmers and kept animals and grew crops. Over the years they took control of almost the whole of Britain.

The Huns were nomadic warriors who terrorised much of Europe and the Roman Empire in the 4th and 5th centuries CE. They were expert horse riders, learning to ride from three years old and living off the land as hunter-gatherers.

3 **Check/clarify:** *forerunners, runes, mythology, noblemen, raids, funerals.*
1 b 2 c 3 d 4 a 5 e

4 When they have seen the highlighted words being used in context, ask them to try to work out the meaning of the phrases. Compare their meanings with the definitions in the book.
1 aristocrats 2 tribal
3 sophisticated 4 raids
5 derived from 6 empire
7 manuscripts 8 lingua franca

5 Monitor and help with vocabulary and ideas, as necessary. After students have discussed in pairs, put them into small groups for students to report back on their discussions and share opinions. At the end of the exercise, listen to some of the students' ideas and encourage open-class discussion.

1 Set a two-minute time limit to encourage students to read quickly to find the percentages. This can be done as a class competition with pairs competing to be first to complete the graph. Encourage them not to focus on every word for now.
Inability to maintain motivation – 16%
Budgetary constraints – 11%
No or limited access to good learning materials – 5%
Lack of time – 24%
Various other difficulties – 18%

2 Ask students to underline the parts of the report that support their answers and refer to these during feedback.
a 2 b 1 c 4 d 3

3 Tell students they are looking for five more verbs and ask them to underline them in the report.
cited, reported, stated, put forward, mentioned

4 Encourage students to make notes in preparation for writing their report. Encourage them to use some of the vocabulary from the report, but not to copy large chunks of it.

5 If you're short on time, you can set this exercise for homework. The report could be done as a collaborative writing activity in class with pairs of students writing their essays together.

3 **Match the statements and the languages according to the information in the article.**
1 Hardly any words have survived from this language.
2 Many educational documents were written in this language.
3 There were two forms of this language.
4 It's the most 'modern' language on the list.
5 It used a system of signs called runes.

a Middle English c Ancient Greek e Old Norse
b Hunnir d Latin

4 VOCABULARY **Match the highlighted words or phrases in the article to the definitions.**
1 people of a higher social class
2 belonging to a group of people
3 intelligent or designed in a complicated way
4 attacks or invasions
5 comes or develops from
6 many countries controlled by one ruler
7 written documents
8 the common, shared language

5 SPEAKING **Work in pairs and discuss the questions.**
1 Why do you think languages die out?
2 Do you think it's important to save these dying languages? Why/Why not?
3 What do you think can be done to help save dying languages?

WRITING
A report from a graph

1 INPUT **Read the report and complete the empty spaces in the graph.**

Difficulties in learning another language

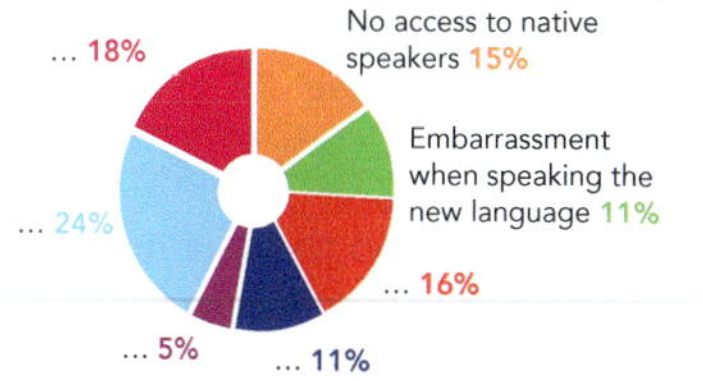

1 A lot of people around the world are keen to gain some level of proficiency in another language. Many people start their learning motivated to succeed but then experience numerous difficulties along the way which can hamper their enthusiasm. A recent study was carried out in the US among adult and teenage learners who were taking a foreign-language course outside of their normal school to find out what difficulties they had encountered.

2 By far the most widely cited difficulty was a lack of time, which 24% of respondents reported as their main obstacle – especially (but not exclusively) the adults. Of those surveyed, 16% stated that an inability to maintain motivation was their main problem, while 15% claimed that it was not being able to meet and converse with native speakers.

3 Other problems encountered included budgetary constraints impeding their ability to continue their course, which 11% of learners put forward as a reason for giving up. Finally, a meagre 5% of respondents, especially those who were learning less frequently studied languages, such as Bulgarian or Farsi, stated that they had either no or limited access to good learning materials. Various other difficulties were mentioned by 18% of people.

4 It seems, then, that difficulties are far from rare among language learners. However, of the respondents, only 17% said that the difficulties had made, or might make, them give up, since the benefits of doing a foreign language course far outweighed the drawbacks.

2 ANALYSE **Which paragraph of the report:**
a starts the presentation of the data?
b introduces the subject of the information in the graph?
c pulls the ideas together and adds a concluding comment?
d adds further data?

3 **Read the report again. Find different words which the writer uses to refer to what people said.**
said, claimed, ...

4 PLAN **You are going to work with the data you gathered in the Values activity on page 87. Look at it again and:**
- remind yourself of the topic and the information you gathered.
- think about how you can introduce the topic.
- decide in what order to present the main findings.
- decide how you might draw the report to a close and any final comments you might make.

5 PRODUCE **Write a report from the graph you drew (180–220 words).**

Homework
You could set the writing task for homework. As a follow-up in the next lesson, ask students to exchange their essays with another student for them to read and make comments and suggestions. Tell them not to correct every error, but to look for the following:
Did they follow the correct structure?
What further information would you like?
In what ways could vocabulary be improved?

Activity idea Extension
Ask students to work in pairs to create a peer feedback checklist and use it to comment on each other's writing so they're also feeding back on things like content and organisation, as well as accuracy.

TH!NK more
Practice Extra
Unit 8 Master it!
Workbook
Developing Writing p77
Tests
Unit, extension and skills test 8

1 Remind students of other words that can be used for substitution and look at the examples in the box.
1 ~~I'm not someone who finds those activities fun~~ I'm not one of those people.
2 … and ~~the teachers didn't exercise more than twice a week~~ neither did the teachers.
3 … ~~or on a child's face~~ or that of a child's …
4 … when I watch a horror film and so does Becca.
5 … ~~and also Sally doesn't agree with people having plastic surgery~~ and Sally doesn't either.
6 B ~~Yes I think you'll lose weight if you take up running~~ Yes, I think so.

2 Focus students on the examples in the box and elicit why the second sentence is wrong.
1 … most of ~~who~~ which …
2 … both of ~~what~~ which …
3 … compared to ~~whom~~ which …
4 … one of ~~which~~ whom …
5 … in ~~what~~ which case …
6 … the job to ~~whom~~ which …

3 Focus attention on the examples and point out that when the *wh-* word with *-ever* refers to the object of the sentence, the object appears immediately after the *wh-* word. When it refers to the subject of the sentence, this inversion doesn't happen.
1 However hard you try, you will not be able to break their code.
2 Whatever mistakes you make, you must try again.
3 However loudly I spoke, they could not hear me.
4 Whatever problems they encountered, they always carried on.
5 Whenever people greeted us, they invited us to visit their homes.

GET IT RIGHT! UNITS 7 & 8

Substitution

Learners at this level often avoid using substitution with words such as *so, neither, either, that, those, ones.* This can make sentences sound repetitive.
✓ *People's idea of beauty is very different to* ***that*** *of 100 years ago.*
✗ *People's idea of beauty is very different to ~~their idea of beauty~~ 100 years ago.*
✓ *I didn't pass the exam and* ***neither*** *did Clara.*
✗ *I didn't pass the exam and Clara ~~didn't pass the exam~~.*

1 Rewrite the sentences using substitution.

0 Fiona is going to buy some new trainers this weekend. She's going to buy the trainers she saw on sale. (ones)
Fiona is going to buy some new trainers this weekend. She's going to buy the ones she saw on sale.
1 Some people find these kinds of activities fun, but I'm not someone who finds these activities fun. (those)
2 The survey revealed that none of the students exercised more than twice a week and the teachers didn't exercise more than twice a week. (neither)
3 It brings a smile to my face when I see the delight on a baby's face or on a child's face when they eat chocolate for the first time. (that)
4 I get shivers down my spine when I watch a horror film and Becca gets shivers down her spine too. (so)
5 Tom doesn't agree with people having plastic surgery for cosmetic reasons and also Sally doesn't agree with people having plastic surgery. (either)
6 **A** Do you think I'll lose weight if I take up running?
B Yes I think you'll lose weight if you taking up running. (so)

Relative pronouns with determiners

Learners often confuse the different relative pronouns *who, whom* and *which.*
✓ *I'm the one* ***who*** *would be the best person to do that.*
✗ *I'm the one ~~whom~~ would be the best person to do that.*

2 Rewrite the sentences correctly using *who, whom* or *which.*

0 There were about 100 people at the conference, many of who came from Russia.
There were about 100 people at the conference, many of whom came from Russia.
1 He spoke in broken English, most of who I was unable to understand.
2 As well as speech, people communicate with gestures and facial expressions, both of what can greatly aid understanding.
3 My grandad spoke a northern dialect compared to whom standard English might seem like a different language!
4 I met several people at the party, one of which was the most conceited person I've ever met!
5 Mandy might have brought her hairdryer with her, in what case I'll borrow it from her.
6 Oliver has had many jobs, but interpreting for the United Nations was the job to whom he dedicated himself the most.

however / wherever / whatever, etc.

Learners often make mistakes with word order when using *wh-* words with *-ever*.
✓ ***Whatever languages you study****, it helps you to understand more about other people.*
✗ *~~Whatever you study languages~~, it helps you to understand more about other people.*

3 Each sentence contains an error in word order. Rewrite the sentences correctly.

1 However you try hard, you will not be able to break their code.
2 Whatever you make mistakes, you must try again.
3 However I spoke loudly, they could not hear me.
4 Whatever they encountered problems, they always carried on.
5 Whenever greeted us people, they invited us to visit their homes.

90

1 In C1 Advanced First Reading and Use of English Part 6, candidates have to read four short texts, on a related theme, and four questions. Candidates have to match the specific information in the text with the questions. This part of the exam tests whether candidates can recognise opinion and attitude and identify agreement and disagreement between the writers.

Encourage your students to do the following when they approach this task:

- Skim the texts to find out the general attitude of each writer to the subject being discussed.
- Read each question carefully.
- Underline parts of each text which give an opinion or attitude and identify if this is positive or negative.
- Underline the key words in each question to identify which aspect of opinion is being tested.
- Look at all the writers and identify similar or different opinions.
- Check that the answer to the question is reflected in the text.
- Do not assume an answer must be correct simply because it contains a word that is also in the text. Some of the options may be correct for more than one question.
- After choosing an answer, check the other options and decide why they are wrong.

1 B 2 A 3 C 4 A

Workbook p79

TOWARDS C1 Advanced

READING AND USE OF ENGLISH

Part 6: Cross-text multiple matching → workbook page 79

1 You are going to read four extracts from reviews of a book on the subject of cosmetic surgery. For questions 1–4, choose from the reviewers A–D. The reviewers may be chosen more than once.

Cosmetic Surgery by Sean Calston

Reviewer A

In his book on the supposed misuses of cosmetic surgery, Calston makes the point that it meets the needs of a certain sector of society in which people are so obsessed with their appearance that this obsession could be considered a form of illness. Although he is rightly critical of those in the medical profession who make enormous profits from the trade in plastic surgery, and he has a point when he says the industry should be more tightly regulated, I don't go along with his main thesis. He dismisses the view that such surgery could actually help to alleviate mental-health problems, but frustratingly he doesn't really explain why. Calston's book has attracted a lot of media attention, but it's hardly a gripping read. I'd got the point by chapter two after which the same ideas just get recycled with tedious examples.

Reviewer B

A vital part of being human is the ability to express yourself freely and fearlessly, and I, for one, wouldn't want to live in a society where freedom of expression was limited or legislated against, which is what Calston seems to be suggesting when he calls for laws to control what he sees as the 'misuses' of plastic surgery. Sure, cosmetic surgery is big business, but that in itself doesn't make it wrong. Calston's book isn't exactly an engaging read, although he does illustrate his points with some relevant examples – my problem is that I just don't agree with his main arguments. One point where I thought it fell down badly, however, was when he disagrees with those who claim that cosmetic surgery can be a therapy in the treatment of depression. I wanted to know more about the rationale behind that view, but we don't get one.

Reviewer C

Sean Calston seems to be a writer who can turn his hand to any subject and he's never shy about giving us an opinion. His latest book on cosmetic surgery is no exception. His direct journalistic style makes the subject very accessible and readable – and the wealth of fascinating examples is it's real strength. Calston gives us quite a negative view of those who make a living out of cosmetic surgery, and he does seem to have a point. He's also quite justified in questioning the rather dubious notion that cosmetic surgery is actually therapeutic for people with some forms of mental illness. He makes a convincing case why this isn't a serious proposition. Less convincing, however, is his idea that the cosmetic surgery industry needs to be more strictly governed by legislation – to my mind what he's suggesting would be a step too far.

Reviewer D

I found it quite difficult to get through Sean Calston's book on cosmetic surgery. Much as I like his style, I got rather bogged down in all the long-winded anecdotes and examples. I think I got the main points he was making, but it was a struggle to keep going to the end. It's difficult to argue, however, with what he says about the commercial aspects of cosmetic surgery – there is certainly money to be made from the vulnerable and this may be open to abuse. Calston is right, therefore, to suggest that it might well be time for us to introduce laws to control the abuse of what remains a medical procedure. He also deals sensitively and thoroughly with the issue of whether such surgery could help mental-health patients, although he clearly doesn't agree with it.

Which reviewer ...

1 has a different opinion to Reviewer A regarding Calston's attitude to the business side of cosmetic surgery.

2 shares Reviewer B's opinion of how well Calston deals with the question of whether cosmetic surgery could be used to treat mental illness.

3 has a different view to the others regarding how easy Calston's book is to read.

4 shares reviewer D's opinion of Calston's suggestion that there should be more laws regulating cosmetic surgery?

91

1 1 forceful 2 in 3 spine 4 communication 5 impulsive 6 arms 7 broken 8 must-have 9 conceited 10 short

2 1 However 2 most of whom 3 think so 4 Wherever 5 hope so 6 all of which

3 1 Some people say it's a dangerous sport, but I don't ~~hope~~ think so.
2 I have three brothers, one of ~~who~~ whom lives in Argentina.
3 Whatever ~~do you~~ you do, don't say anything.
4 She has three phones, ~~both~~ all / two of which are broken.
5 I'll follow you ~~whatever~~ wherever you go.
6 I'm not sure we'll win, but I hope so.

4 1 dreamed 2 follow 3 brand 4 lost 5 limited 6 familiar 7 strongly 8 see

TEST YOURSELF UNITS 7 & 8

VOCABULARY

1 Complete the sentences with the words in the list. There are four extra words.

arms | arrogant | broken | communication | decisive | heart | impulsive | in | modest | must-get | must-have | short | slang | spine

1 He's quite … . He's always able to make decisions quickly, even when they're difficult!
2 Loom bands were really … a few years ago.
3 That scene at the end of the film sent shivers down my … .
4 I think we've got a … breakdown here. We're really not understanding each other.
5 He's a bit … and often acts without really thinking first.
6 Are you cold? You've got goosebumps all down your … .
7 I make lots of mistakes, but I can just about get by in Brazil with my … Portuguese.
8 Are smartwatches really going to be the next … item?
9 She thinks she's better than everyone else. She's so … .
10 Nobody knows this band anymore – their fame was rather …-lived.

GRAMMAR

2 Complete the sentences with the words/phrases in the list. There are two extra words/phrases.

all of which | hope so | however | in which case | most of whom | think so | whatever | wherever

1 … hard I try, I never really understand what he says.
2 I have a lot of friends on social media sites, … I rarely see in person.
3 Many people think this film will win an Oscar, but I don't … .
4 … he goes, people recognise him.
5 Do you think it'll be sunny this weekend? I … because I'm planning to go to the beach.
6 She has two jobs and three children to bring up on her own, … means she never has any time to herself.

3 Find and correct the mistake in each sentence.

1 Some people say it's a dangerous sport, but I don't hope so.
2 I have three brothers, one of who lives in Argentina.
3 Whatever do you, don't say anything.
4 She has three phones, both of which are broken.
5 I'll follow you whatever you go.
6 I'm not sure we'll win, but I hope.

FUNCTIONAL LANGUAGE

4 Choose the correct options.

A Have you always [1]*dreamed / hoped* of an easier life?
B I'm sorry? I don't quite [2]*follow / catch* you.
A An easier life. If you try our [3]*brand / known* new product, you'll save hours every week.
B I'm afraid you've [4]*got / lost* me. What product are you talking about?
A Lush 2.0. It's on offer. But only for a [5]*narrow / limited* time.
B I'm sorry, but I'm not [6]*known / familiar* with Lush 2.0. What is it exactly?
A Lush 2.0 – our most advanced washing powder yet. I [7]*powerfully / strongly* recommend you give it a go.
B Washing powder?! I don't quite [8]*see / follow* why I'd be interested in washing powder. I'm only 13 years old.

MY SCORE
22–30 | 10–21 | 0–9

92

The Cambridge Life Competencies Framework

Communication
Comparing communication strategies
Watch this video for a tip on developing your students' communication skills.
Scan the QR code here.

Warmer

Ask students to write down five words related to the picture. Put them in groups of two or three and ask them to choose their favourite three words and write definitions for each one of them. Then put them together with another group. They should take turns reading out their definitions and guessing each other's words. As an additional activity you could ask them to spell out the words for the other students in the group to write down. What was the most popular word?

▶ 24 Get TH!NKing

Ask the question. Get students to compare their ideas in groups. Play the video and then ask students for feedback.

1 Elicit what the students think is happening in the photo. What does it show? In what situations would people hold up signs like the one in the picture? What is the objective of doing this? Have students ever held up a sign to complain about something? Share ideas as a whole group.

2 Ask them to look at the title of the unit and the picture of the girl holding the sign. Ask them what they know about protests like this. Are these becoming more common? Have students ever gone on a protest themselves? What do they think about this?

3 Ask students to think of other social issues that are important to them. Make a list on the board as they call them out, and then ask students what can be done to protest against injustice and to improve society.

Objectives

Functions Talking imprecisely about numbers
Grammar Negative inversion; spoken discourse markers
Vocabulary Court cases; fairness and equality
Life Competencies Standing up for your beliefs

Resources for this unit

All available online

Videos

- Get **TH!NK**ing: *How do you decide what's fair?*
- Grammar video!: Spoken discourse markers
- Vlog: Standing up for your beliefs

Tests

- Unit, extension and skills test 9
- End of term test 3

Worksheets

- Grammar and vocabulary: Basic, Standard and Extension Worksheets
- Project: Crazy crimes
- Communication: Is it fair?
- Grammar presentation: Negative inversion
- Literature Worksheets: *Jane Eyre; Ozymandias, The New Colossus; Desiree's Baby*
- Get **TH!NK**ing, Grammar video! and Life Lessons video Worksheets

Warmer

Write *That's not fair.* on the board. Describe a situation when you might have said the sentence. For example: *People with blue eyes are allowed to finish work at 3 pm, people with brown eyes have to work until 5 pm.* Ask students to work in pairs and think of at least two real or imaginary situations when they might use the sentence.

1 Write a few of the students' ideas on the board, but do not comment at this stage.

2 1 A situation in which someone is punished by the law courts for a crime that they have not committed.

3 **Check/clarify:** *innocent, convicted, jury, intervened, prosecutors, imprisonment, verdict, prosecution, ordeal, alibi, incarceration, innocence, confessed, interrogation, retracted, miscarriage of justice.* These words could be elicited/clarified through inclusion in a description of a court case. Tell students that they should try to guess any unknown vocabulary from context, but that they can use dictionaries if absolutely necessary.

4 **9.01** To encourage 'long-turn' speaking, ask students to take turns to answer all of the questions for their text, rather than taking turns to answer each question individually.

5 Encourage students to give reasons for their answers, to develop answers with examples where possible and to try to use a range of vocabulary to add interest.

Pronunciation

Unstressed syllables and words: the /I/ phoneme

Student's Book p138

READING

1 SPEAKING **Work in pairs. Discuss your answers with a partner.**

1 What do you think a *miscarriage of justice* is?
2 Can you think of any famous miscarriages of justice?

2 **Look at the photos, read the headline and introduction on page 95 and check your answers to Exercise 1 question 1.**

3 **Work in groups of three. Read your text and the questions, and note down your answers.**

Student A: read text 1
Student B: read text 2
Student C: read text 3

1 What was the person/were the people convicted of?
2 What was the evidence that was used to convict them?
3 How were they set free, and after how long?
4 What happened to them after their release from prison?

4 9.01 SPEAKING **Tell your group what you learned. Use your notes to help you. Then listen and read the texts to check.**

5 SPEAKING **Work in pairs and discuss the questions.**

1 Which of the three cases do you think describes the worst miscarriage of justice? Why?
2 In your country, what kind of punishment is given for:
- shoplifting?
- dangerous driving?
- fraud? (getting money by deceiving people)
- murder?
3 Which of the crimes in question 2 do you think a person should go to prison for? Why?
4 What other crimes should a person go to prison for? Why?

PRONUNCIATION
Unstressed syllables and words: the /ɪ/ phoneme
Go to page 138.

94

6 During feedback, ask: *Do you think there is any truth in any of the statements?*
1 The Guildford Four 2 Rubin 'Hurricane' Carter 3 Sally Clark

7 You may like to brainstorm a list of different social groups on the board to get students started.

Homework

Ask students to look back at the reading text and choose ten words to research and write definitions for. In the next lesson, students can peer-teach the words to each other.

Activity idea Extension

Ask students to work in pairs and think of three different ways in which teenagers are victims of the *ad hominem* fallacy. For example, teenagers say they have too much homework. However, as 'all teenagers are lazy', they must be saying that to avoid work. Regroup students into small groups to share their ideas. Ask: *Do you think there might be some truth in some of the accusations? For example, are teenagers sometimes lazy?*

Culture notes

Rubin Carter was a middleweight boxer who fought 40 bouts, winning 28. He was convicted of murder in 1967 but the conviction was overturned in 1976. However, a second trial found him guilty again. Numerous appeals failed until, in 1985, he was freed when the judge ruled that the conviction had been due to racism. From 1993 to 2005, Carter served as executive director of the Association in Defence of the Wrongly Convicted.

Bob Dylan is an American singer-songwriter who became one of the most influential voices in American popular music of the 1960s. He has been awarded the Nobel Prize for Literature.

FAIRNESS MATTERS UNIT 9

Miscarriages of JUSTICE

Imagine – one day, out of the blue, you are arrested, accused of a crime that you didn't commit, found guilty and sent to prison. Even in the best legal systems, innocent people can find themselves convicted by judge and jury and sentenced to years behind bars.

1 Sally Clark (UK)

Sally Clark was a lawyer and mother of two. Her first son was born healthy in 1996, but died suddenly when he was just three months old. In 1998 she had another son, but he too died aged just two months and in the same circumstances. At this point, social services intervened and Mrs Clark was subsequently put on trial for murder.

The prosecutors based their evidence on the findings of a medical expert, who claimed that the chances of two babies from the same family dying a natural death in identical circumstances were virtually nil. Despite protesting her innocence, Clark was found guilty on the basis of that evidence and sentenced to life imprisonment. She appealed the verdict and after three years in jail, she was released when it emerged that evidence proving that one of the children had died from natural causes had been withheld from her defence lawyers. Furthermore, the statistical evidence on which the prosecution was based was shown to be invalid. One doctor commented that rarely had statistical evidence been so misused in a trial. Sally Clark never fully recovered from her ordeal and she died in 2007, aged only 43.

2 Rubin 'Hurricane' Carter (US)

Rubin Carter was born in 1937 in New Jersey. He was convicted of several crimes before he became a professional boxer in 1961. Nicknamed 'Hurricane' because of his lightning-fast fists, he was a promising boxer who was on the way to winning the middleweight world championship. But in 1966, Carter and his friend John Artis were arrested and prosecuted for the murder of three people in a bar. The evidence was weak – two witnesses said they'd seen Carter and Artis running away from the crime but later they changed their story. Not only did Carter and Artis have no motive, but they also had alibis. Moreover, it was never proven that their guns were the ones used in the murders. Nor were any fingerprints taken at the crime scene. Despite all of this, both Carter and Artis were convicted in 1967 and given life sentences. Throughout his incarceration, Carter campaigned for his release, always protesting his innocence. Various people campaigned on his behalf and singer Bob Dylan even wrote a song about his case. Finally, in November 1985, the case was thrown out of court and Rubin Carter was finally released after having spent 18 years behind bars. Artis had already been released four years earlier. Carter died in 2014 at the age of 76. His story was made into an Oscar-nominated film, *Hurricane*, in 1999, starring Denzel Washington.

3 The Guildford Four (UK)

In the 1970s, the Irish Republican Army (IRA) ran a bombing campaign in the UK to protest against British military presence in Northern Ireland. One bomb, in 1974 in a town called Guildford, killed several soldiers and their girlfriends. No sooner had the bombing taken place than four young people – Gerry Conlon, Patrick Armstrong, Carol Richardson and Paul Hill – were arrested and charged. All four of them confessed under police interrogation, but they later retracted their confessions. In 1975, they were sent to prison for life. None of the four had the typical profile of a bomber and furthermore, the prosecution withheld evidence that proved that Conlon had been in London at the time of the bombing. Later, the IRA itself stated clearly that none of the four had been involved in the Guildford bombings. Nevertheless, it took until 1989 for them to be released, fifteen years after their arrest. Conlon went on to become a campaigner against miscarriages of justice both in the UK and abroad. He died in 2014. A film, *In the Name of the Father*, was made about him in 1993, starring Daniel Day-Lewis.

Train to TH!NK

The *ad hominem* fallacy

'Ad hominem' *means 'against the man'. The* ad hominem *fallacy describes a situation where instead of using logic or evidence to argue against an opinion, claim or point of view, you attack an opponent's character. Often the* ad hominem *fallacy uses stereotypes and encourages prejudice. For example, a man complains to the police about his noisy neighbours. The neighbours defend themselves saying that they aren't surprised about the complaint since he's a really grumpy man and is always complaining about things. Their comments about his personality don't necessarily mean that his complaint isn't valid.*

6 **Look at the texts again. Which of the victims do these remarks refer to?**
1 They're young. They must be guilty.
2 He's a violent man. He must have done it.
3 I don't trust lawyers so I'm sure she's guilty.

7 SPEAKING **Work in pairs. What examples can you come up with of people (individuals or groups) who often unfairly find themselves victims of the *ad hominem* fallacy?**

95

The Irish Republican Army (IRA) is a paramilitary organisation seeking the end of British rule in Northern Ireland and the reunification of Ireland. It was created in 1919 and employed guerrilla tactics to force the British government to negotiate. In 1981, the political wing (Sinn Féin) began to play a more prominent role. In 1998 the participants in the peace talks approved the 'Good Friday Agreement' which linked a new power-sharing government in Northern Ireland with decommissioning of the IRA and normalising of cross-community relations.

Denzel Washington is an American actor and director. He has won two Academy Awards, three Golden Globes and was ranked the greatest actor of the 21st century (so far) by the *New York Times* in 2020.

Daniel Day-Lewis is an English actor. He won his first Academy Award in 1989 for his role in *My Left Foot*. He has also won Academy Awards for *There Will be Blood* and *Lincoln*.

Critical TH!NKing
Evaluating ideas and arguments
Identifies evidence and its reliability.

Social Responsibilities
Understanding global issues
Demonstrates awareness of human rights issues around the world.

TH!NK more

Worksheets
Project Crazy crimes
Communication Is it fair?
Get TH!NKing *How do you decide what's fair?*

Warmer

In pairs, give students three minutes to brainstorm as many ways of expressing negativity as possible, for example *no, none, nowhere, nothing, nobody, nowt, naught, zero, zilch, etc.*

1 1 rarely 2 Not only 3 No sooner

2 Ensure students are clear on the meaning of each adverbial phrase, giving example sentences as required.
RULE: 1 negative 2 beginning 3 more 4 normal statement 5 written

3 1 Never have I 2 Not only were they 3 had the case finished 4 could they

4 Use the answers to clarify the changes in word order if necessary.
1 On no account should we discuss this in front of other people.
2 Never have I read such an appalling story.
3 Not only was he innocent, but so were the others.
4 Rarely are innocent people released from prison following a miscarriage of justice.

Workbook p82

Get it Right!
Negative inversion

Student's Book p112

5 Ask students to cover 1–10 and read through the definitions a–j. Students work with a partner to try to guess the words for each definition. Students can then uncover the definitions to check their ideas and complete the exercise.
1 d 2 h 3 g 4 a 5 i 6 j 7 c 8 f 9 b 10 e

6 1 a confession 2 retracted 3 gave 4 the prosecution 5 the defence 6 found guilty 7 sentenced 8 appealed 9 evidence 10 found innocent

Workbook p84

TH!NK more

Workbook
Grammar p82, Ex.1–4
Vocabulary p84, Ex.1–2

Worksheets
Grammar presentation Negative inversion
Grammar Worksheets 9
Vocabulary Worksheets 9

GRAMMAR
Negative inversion

1 Complete the sentences from the texts on page 95.

1 One doctor commented that … had statistical evidence been so misused in a trial.
2 … did Carter and Artis have no motive, but they also had alibis.
3 … had the bombing taken place than four young people […] were arrested and charged.

2 Here are the same ideas written in a more usual form. What differences do you notice? Think about meaning and form. Then choose the correct options in the rule.

1 One doctor commented that statistical evidence had never been so misused in a trial.
2 Carter and Artis not only didn't have a motive, but they also had alibis.
3 The bombing took place and immediately afterwards, four young people were arrested and charged.

RULE: We can bring [1]*positive / negative* and limiting adverbs and adverbial phrases, such as *rarely, little, not only … but (also), no sooner … than, never, under no circumstances, on no account* to the [2]*beginning / end* of a sentence to make it [3]*more / less* emphatic. The rest of the sentence follows the pattern of a [4]*normal statement / question.*
In present and past tense forms of non-modal verbs, we use the auxiliary *do* or *did* and invert the auxiliary and the subject. With other verb tenses or modals, we use the auxiliary that's already there (for example *is, are, have, can, will*).
We use this structure much more often in [5]*written / spoken* English. We can use it in speech when we want to add dramatic effect.

3 Choose the correct options.

1 *Never have I / Never I've* read about such disturbing cases.
2 *Not only they were / Not only were they* innocent, but they weren't even at the scene of the crime.
3 No sooner *the case had finished / had the case finished* than the judge set them free.
4 Under no circumstances *could they / they could* be the criminals.

4 Rewrite the sentences. Use the word(s) in brackets at the start of the new sentence.

0 The film finished and we immediately left. (No sooner … than)
No sooner had the film finished than we left.
1 We should not discuss this in front of other people. (On no account)
2 I've never read such an appalling story. (Never)
3 He was innocent and so were the others. (Not only … but)
4 Innocent people are not often released from prison following a miscarriage of justice. (Rarely)

→ workbook page 82

VOCABULARY
Court cases

5 Match the words with the definitions.

1 to be found guilty/innocent
2 to appeal a verdict
3 a witness
4 to make a confession
5 to retract a confession
6 the defence
7 the prosecution
8 to give evidence
9 to withhold evidence
10 to be sentenced to life imprisonment

a to say that you committed a crime
b to not give information that is important in a trial
c the lawyers who try to prove that someone is guilty
d to have a court say that you did/didn't commit a crime
e to be told that you will spend the rest of your life in prison
f to give information in a court
g someone who says in court what they know or saw
h to ask to go to a higher court for another trial
i to say that the confession you made before wasn't true
j the lawyer(s) who try to prove that someone is innocent

6 Complete the text using words and phrases from Exercise 5 in the correct form.

The woman was arrested for murder and she made [1]… , but three days later, she [2]… it. However, the case went to court. During the trial, about 20 people [3]… evidence. A witness for [4]… said he had seen the woman at the scene of the crime. But the lawyer for [5]… claimed that that wasn't possible. In the end, she was [6]… and she was [7]… to life imprisonment. The defence [8]… the verdict and, in the subsequent retrial, it was shown that the prosecution had withheld [9]… . The woman was [10]… and released.

→ workbook page 84

96

Language note Negative inversion

Common mistakes when using negative adverbials are to use a double negative, e.g. **On no account must you not say a word to anyone. *Never haven't I seen such a boring film.*

Point out to students that as the adverb is negative, the use of *not* creates a double negative and it is therefore not used.

Pay special attention to the use of *than* with *no sooner*, as students will often make the mistake of using *when* instead, e.g.

No sooner had I sat down when the phone rang. This is grammatically incorrect, but is actually a common mistake made by native speakers.

Activity idea Fast finishers

Ask students to put the words from Exercise 5 on a timeline, from to *make a confession* to *life imprisonment*, for example. Elicit answers to the board after feedback on Exercise 5.

Listening; WordWise; Writing

7–8 🔊 **9.03** During feedback, encourage students to explain why they chose their answers and why other answers are not possible.
1 a 2 d 3 c 4 b

9 Do the first item with the whole class as an example.
1 Chris's 2 Chris's 3 Daniel's 4 Daniel's

10 At the end of the exercise, listen to some of the students' ideas and encourage open-class discussion.

11 During feedback, elicit or explain the meaning of the five phrases and give further examples as necessary to clarify meaning.
1 on trial 2 on the way 3 on good terms 4 on his behalf 5 on the basis

12 During feedback, work on pronunciation and intonation of the sentences.
1 on trial 2 on the way 3 good terms 4 behalf 5 basis

Workbook p84

13 Before students do the exercise, ask: *What do you need to do to write a good discursive or 'for and against' essay?* and think of ideas as a class. Elicit that such essays should look at both sides of the argument, including two or three arguments for and against, and finish with a conclusion giving the writer's opinion.

14 Encourage them to discuss and decide which are the best arguments to include in their essays.

15 If you're short on time, students can do the preparation in class and complete the writing at home. This can be done as a collaborative writing activity in class with pairs of students of a similar level working together to complete the exercise.

LISTENING

7 SPEAKING **Look at the cartoons. What do you think is happening in each one? Discuss with your partner.**

8 🔊 9.03 **Listen to a radio programme about how two fathers, Daniel and Chris, discipline their teenagers and choose the correct answers.**

1 How do you think Daniel's three sons feel when Daniel uses his punishment?
 a embarrassed
 b proud
 c disappointed
 d furious
2 What does Daniel do to cause this reaction?
 a tell the boys to sing a song
 b act out a scene from a play
 c do a dance routine from a famous musical
 d perform a song from a musical
3 What had Chris' children done to upset him?
 a They hadn't tidied their rooms when he asked them to.
 b They had gone into his study and left it untidy.
 c They had taken something from his desk.
 d They had hidden their doors.
4 What did Chris decide to do?
 a He didn't let them go to sleep.
 b He took away the doors to their bedrooms.
 c He didn't give them their mobile phones or laptops for a week.
 d He made them swap bedrooms.

9 SPEAKING **Who do you think might say these things later – Daniel's or Chris' children? Why? Compare your ideas with a partner.**

1 'It made me feel very insecure. I hated it.'
2 'It feels really strange going to sleep without it.'
3 'We need to make sure we don't have any arguments in the supermarket again.'
4 'If we're good and we don't act up, he'll keep quiet.'

10 SPEAKING **Work in pairs and discuss the questions.**

1 In your opinion, which parent's punishment is the most effective– Daniel's or Chris'? Discuss and give your reasons for your choice.
2 What is the most effective punishment that you have ever received from your parents? Tell your partner.

WordWise
Expressions with *on*

11 **Look at these sentences from the unit so far. Complete them with the phrases from the list.**

on good terms | on his behalf
on the basis | on the way | on trial

1 She was put … for murder.
2 He was a promising boxer who was … to winning the middleweight world championship.
3 My three sons are usually … with each other.
4 Various people campaigned … and singer Bob Dylan even wrote a song about his case.
5 She was found guilty … of that evidence.

12 **Choose the correct options.**

1 It must be awful to be put *on the way / on trial* for something you didn't do.
2 I'm saving up and I'm well *on the way / on the basis* to having enough money for a new tablet.
3 He isn't my best friend, but I'm on quite *good terms / behalf* with him.
4 She couldn't be at the ceremony, so her husband accepted the award on her *behalf / basis*.
5 You'll be given marks on the *basis / behalf* of the progress you make.

→ workbook page 84

WRITING
An essay

13 PLAN **Note down three arguments in favour of the statement below, and three arguments against it. (You can use your own ideas or any from the unit.)**

Prisons should be decent, comfortable places for prisoners.

For	Against
1 …	1 …
2 …	2 …
3 …	3 …

14 **Compare your ideas with a partner.**

15 PRODUCE **Use your notes to write an essay of around 150–200 words.**

Homework

Ask students to write six sentences of their own using negative inversions. Write the following sentence beginnings on the board and ask students to complete them in their own words.

Under no circumstances would I … *Rarely do I …*
Never have I seen … *No sooner had I …*
Not only can I … but I can also … *Little did I know …*

As a follow-up, listen to some of the best examples as a class.

Activity idea Mixed-ability

To simplify Exercise 8 for weaker students, for each question, tell them one option which isn't correct.

TH!NK more

Workbook
Listening p88, Ex.1–2
WordWise p84, Ex.4
Developing Writing p87

Warmer

Ask: *What do you spend money on? If you were a billionaire, what would you spend money on? Would you give any of your money away? Who would you give it to?* Ask students to work with a partner and discuss the questions. During feedback, make a note of any interesting answers on the board.

1 Ask students to repeat the exercise again with a different partner.

2 Set a two-minute time limit to encourage them to read quickly. Tell them not to worry if they do not understand every word, but to focus on choosing the best summary.
3

3 🔊 **9.04 Check/clarify:** *life expectancy, infant mortality rate, social mobility, obesity, chronic health problems.*
Ask students to underline the parts of the text that helped them find the answer.
1 Countries that have more equality in terms of wealth.
2 Inequality causes shorter, unhealthier and unhappier lives.
3 A more equal distribution of income.
4 He questions the link between a country's high murder rate and its level of income. He also questions the link between average life expectancy and income inequality.

4 If space allows, encourage students to walk around the classroom to find someone who agrees with the same statements. Encourage students who disagree on a statement to try to convince their partners that their opinion is the 'right' one. Ask students to report their findings back to the class and encourage them to use the phrase 'So does he/she/[student's name]'.

THINK more

Workbook
Reading p86, Ex.1–4

READING

1 Which of these statements do you agree with?

A huge gap between the earnings of rich and poor people in society leads to …
1 more crime.
2 people being unhappier.
3 people having shorter and unhealthier lives.

2 Read the book review quickly. Which of these is the best summary of the review? The book …
1 is about ways to increase wealth and happiness in society.
2 is about ways to prevent violent crime in society.
3 shows that inequality is the cause of most problems we face in society.

3 🔊 9.04 **Read the review again and listen. Answer the questions.**
1 Which countries are the happiest and healthiest?
2 What examples does the writer give of things that inequality leads to?
3 What would every country benefit from?
4 What does Peter Saunders question in his report on the book?

SPEAKING

4 Work in small groups. Discuss your responses to the statements. Are there any that you all agree or disagree with?
1 'I believe that I will have a better life in Sweden than in the US.'
2 'There is more crime in countries where there is a bigger gap between the incomes of the richest and the poorest.'
3 'Poverty is the only cause of ill health.'
4 'People with a higher income live longer.'

BOOK REVIEW
The Spirit Level
by Richard Wilkinson and Kate Pickett (2010)

A few months before his election as British Prime Minister, David Cameron said: 'Research by Richard Wilkinson and Kate Pickett has shown that among the richest countries, it's the more unequal ones that do worse according to almost every quality of life indicator.'

The then Labour leader Ed Miliband also seemed to make a reference to *The Spirit Level* when he proclaimed that, 'The gap between rich and poor does matter. It doesn't just harm the poor; it harms all of us.'

These political leaders are just two of many people across the world who have been influenced by *The Spirit Level*, the surprise bestseller which has sold over 200,000 copies.

The Spirit Level claims that income inequality is bad not only for the poorest in society, but also for the wealthiest, and that an equal society benefits both the rich and the poor. And let's face it, inequality causes shorter, unhealthier and unhappier lives. The authors' claims are based on statistical evidence, which they say shows that more unequal countries (and within the US, more unequal states) suffer from higher crime rates, a lower than average life expectancy, increased infant mortality rates and less social mobility. In fact, almost every social problem from obesity to crime has one root cause: inequality. Because of this, their conclusion is that we would all benefit from a more equal distribution of income, and to be honest, I agree with them. *The Spirit Level* was praised by politicians on both the left and the right, and it seemed the book was proof that economic inequality leads to chronic health and social problems for everyone, including the rich.

I found the book so interesting that I then did some more research and came across Peter Saunders' report, *Beware False Prophets*. It looks again at the arguments made in *The Spirit Level* and finds that only one of the 20 statistical claims (the association internationally between infant deaths and income inequality) truly supports their theory. For example, Saunders points out in his report that the claim that a country's murder rate is linked to its level of income inequality depends entirely on the high murder rate in the US, while the claim that average life expectancy is linked to income inequality rests entirely on the long lives of the Japanese. Across the other 22 countries analysed, there was simply no association.

I strongly recommend reading both the book and the report and coming to your own conclusions.

98

COMMENTS

James Inkworth
I went to a talk given by Richard Wilkinson and I can assure you that he is as convincing in a lecture theatre as he is in this book. Inequality and widening inequality is dangerous for every level of society – not just the worst-off. This book should be on everyone's bookshelf.

Margaret Baker
An extremely interesting read. I highly recommend this book. To tell you the truth, it shows how almost everything – from life expectancy to mental illness, violence to illiteracy – is affected not by how wealthy a society is, but how equal it is.

Martin Wiseman
In general, it is an excellent read. However, I would recommend skipping the first 12 chapters and reading the last few chapters for their brilliant conclusion and excellent recommendations.

Gemma Hunter
A thorough and brilliant evidence-based analysis of the many reasons why it would be wise for us to look to Scandinavia and not to the US as our role model for how to build a healthier and happier society.

Kim Fletcher
The more unequal our world becomes, the more problems we face, and if you ask me, this book provides the evidence to confirm this. That said, it is not impossible to believe, especially in the age of AI, that a universal income could be introduced and we could have equality. I give it six stars.

Culture notes

The Spirit Level: Why More Equal Societies Almost Always Do Better by Richard Wilkinson and Kate Pickett has sold more than 150,000 copies in English. It was chosen as one of the top ten books of the decade by *The New Statesman* and one of the top 100 books of the century by *The Guardian* newspaper.

Kate Pickett is a British epidemiologist and political activist who is Professor of Epidemiology at the University of York, UK.

Richard Wilkinson is a British social epidemiologist, author and political activist. He is Professor Emeritus of Social Epidemiology at the University of Nottingham, UK.

David Cameron was a British Conservative politician and Prime Minister of the United Kingdom from May 2010 until July 2016. His premiership was dominated by the referendum on whether the UK should remain a member of the European Union. He resigned from the post of prime minister within hours of the vote result in favour of leaving.

Ed Miliband is a British politician and he has been an MP since 2005. He was Leader of the Opposition between 2010 and 2015.

Beware False Prophets: Equality, the Good Society and The Spirit Level by Peter Saunders was published by Policy Exchange in 2010. Peter Saunders is Professor Emeritus of Sociology at the University of Sussex, UK. He has written a number of reports on poverty and family policy.

5–6 Ask students to discuss the meaning of the words and phrases in bold and try to deduce their meanings from context.

7 This could be done as a competition with pairs racing to be first to complete the exercise correctly. During feedback, say the nouns for students to repeat and check pronunciation.
1 violence 2 society 3 politics
4 equality 5 generalisation
6 obesity

8 Check/clarify: *confrontations.*
1 violent 2 equality
3 generalisation 4 obese
5 evident 6 society

Workbook p84

▶ 25 Grammar video!
Spoken discourse markers

9 1 That said 2 Because of this
3 Let's face it 4 However
RULE: a 2 b 3 c 1 d 4

10 During feedback, elicit/give examples of the usage of each discourse marker. Point out that, while all of the discourse markers can be used to start a sentence, *because of/as a result of* are more commonly used between two clauses in a sentence.
Cause and result: because of, as a result of
Contrast: nevertheless, actually, however, mind you, on the other hand, that said, while
Opinion: personally, actually, at the end of the day, for a start, if you ask me, let's face it, the thing is, to be honest, to tell you the truth
Topic change: anyway, by the way
Concession: while, on the other hand, that said

11 Check/clarify: *unethical, corruption.*
1 They all knew it was unethical. Nevertheless, / However, they went ahead and did it.
2 I left in the middle of the film. Let's face it, / To tell you the truth, it was awful.
3 The company director resigned because of / as a result of accusations of corruption.
4 I'll listen to your thoughts. But at the end of the day, it's my decision.
5 It wasn't at all good. To be honest, / Let's face it, / To tell you the truth, / If you ask me, it was the worst idea ever.

Workbook p83

VOCABULARY
Fairness and equality

5 SPEAKING **Work in pairs. Read the sentences below. Discuss and check the meaning of the words and phrases in bold.**

1 We live in an **unfair** society with a widening gap between the richest and the poorest.
2 It is **evident** that poverty does, in some cases, lead to crime.
3 Cases of **violent** crimes using knives and guns are on the increase.
4 Poverty can lead to **social** problems such as bad health and unhappiness.
5 The authors of *The Spirit Level* have medical rather than **political** motives for writing the book.
6 People are not born **equal**. Some people have greater opportunities than others.
7 In **general**, people are happier and healthier in Japan than in the US.
8 People are **obese** because they cannot afford to buy healthy food.

6 SPEAKING **Work in pairs or small groups. Think of examples of:**

1 how society is unfair.
2 violent crimes being committed in your country.
3 people who have a political motive for doing something.
4 people who aren't born equal into society.

7 Complete the noun related to the adjectives in Exercise 5.

0 evid*ence*
1 viol...
2 soc...
3 polit...
4 equal...
5 general...
6 obes...

8 Write the correct form of the word in brackets.

1 There were no ... confrontations at the protest today. (VIOLENCE)
2 I hope that one day we will see ... for everyone. (EQUAL)
3 I think it is a ... to say poverty causes crime. (GENERAL)
4 The number of ... children in developed countries has been on the rise in the last decade. (OBESITY)
5 It was ... from the meeting that many politicians want to stop climate change. (EVIDENCE)
6 Every ... needs a fair justice system. (SOCIAL)

→ workbook page 84

GRAMMAR
Spoken discourse markers

Grammar video ▶25

9 Complete the sentences from the book review and comments on page 98 and then complete the rule with the correct sentence numbers.

1 ... , it is not impossible to believe, especially in the age of AI, that a universal income could be introduced and we could have equality.
2 Almost every social problem from obesity to crime has one root cause: inequality. ... , their conclusion is that we would all benefit from a more equal distribution of income.
3 ... , inequality causes shorter, unhealthier and unhappier lives.
4 In general, it is an excellent read. ... , I would recommend skipping the first 12 chapters.

RULE: We use discourse markers to:
- talk about a result. Example sentence [a]...
- show the writer's opinion. Example sentence [b]...
- introduce a concession. Example sentence [c]...
- introduce a contrast. Example sentence [d]...

10 Copy and complete the table below, writing the discourse markers in the correct column. Some may go in more than one column.

actually | anyway | as a result of | at the end of the day | ~~because of~~
by the way | for a start | however | if you ask me | let's face it
mind you | ~~nevertheless~~ | on the other hand | ~~personally~~ | that said
the thing is | to be honest | to tell you the truth | ~~while~~

Cause and result	Contrast	Opinion	Topic change	Concession
because of	*nevertheless*	*personally*	*anyway*	*while*

11 Rewrite each sentence. Remove the word in bold and use a discourse marker from Exercise 10 to replace it. (There are several possibilities.)

0 I knew it was wrong. **So** I didn't do it.
I knew it was wrong. Because of this, I didn't do it.
1 They all knew it was unethical. **But** they went ahead and did it.
2 I left in the middle of the film. **I thought** it was awful.
3 The company director resigned. **There were** accusations of corruption.
4 I'll listen to your thoughts. But **finally** it's my decision.
5 It wasn't at all good. **I think** it was the worst idea ever.

→ workbook page 83

Homework

Ask students to complete the following sentence starters with ideas of their own using the vocabulary from Exercise 5:

We live in an unfair society because ...

It is evident that poverty ...

Cases of violent crimes ...

People are not born equal because ...

In general, people are happier when ...

People are obese because ...

TH!NK more

Practice Extra
Unit 9 Practise it!

Workbook
Vocabulary p84, Ex.3
Vocabulary Extra p85, Ex.1–3
Grammar p83, Ex.5–7

Worksheets
Vocabulary Worksheets 9
Grammar Worksheets 9
Grammar video! Spoken discourse markers

Developing Speaking; Phrases for fluency; Functions

Warmer

Revise discourse markers from the previous lesson by giving students the first letters of selected markers from the box in Exercise 10 on page 99 and asking students to complete them. For example, *a t e o t d – at the end of the day.* Students continue in pairs.

1 🔊 **9.05** Tell students to cover the dialogue and discuss the question in pairs before listening to check their answers.

2 🔊 **9.05**
1 He was found guilty of stealing money from his company's pension plan and sentenced to five years in prison.
2 He was earning roughly 300 times more than his average employee and he has left over 100 people without a pension in the future.
3 Because he's rich and could probably afford a really expensive lawyer to help him.

3 To encourage speed-reading, you could do this as a race and ask students to find the expressions as quickly as possible and underline them.
1 Michelle 2 Steve 3 Michelle
4 Steve 5 Michelle 6 Steve

4 During feedback, say the sentences in the dialogues for students to repeat.
1 I'd have thought
2 Apparently
3 if I'm not mistaken
4 more to the point
5 That's news to me
6 when you put it like that

DEVELOPING SPEAKING

1 🔊 9.05 **Look at the photos. What do you think Steve is angry about? What do you understand from the newspaper headlines? Read, listen and check your ideas.**

Steve: This makes me really angry. It's just so completely unfair! Only five years?! After what he did!
Michelle: What are you talking about? Let me see. Oh, that guy. He's the one who took the money from his company's pension plan, if I'm not mistaken.
Steve: 'Took'?! Stole! And he's been found guilty. But he only got a five-year jail sentence. Apparently, it could be only three years or so if he gets time off for good behaviour.
Michelle: That's news to me. And it certainly doesn't sound like a strong enough sentence.
Steve: It absolutely isn't. I'd have thought around 20 years would have been more appropriate. I mean, he's left over 100 people with no pension in the future. It's two crimes, in a way: not just stealing money, but stealing people's futures.
Michelle: Well, when you put it like that, it does seem really bad.
Steve: It's worse! Do you know, as the boss of the company, he was earning roughly 300 times more than his average employee?
Michelle: Seriously? And he isn't so old, is he? Only 40ish, by the look of it.
Steve: More to the point, if you're making that kind of money, why do you need to steal from the pension plan?
Michelle: Yes. And you know, I think maybe he didn't get a more severe sentence because he's rich and could afford a really expensive lawyer. That's how it works a lot of the time.
Steve: One law for the rich, another for the poor. And that makes me angry, too!

2 🔊 9.05 **Read and listen to the dialogue again. Answer the questions.**
1 What was the company director found guilty of, and what was his sentence?
2 What do we learn about the director's salary, and about his employees' futures?
3 How does Michelle explain the reason for the 'light' jail sentence?

Phrases for fluency

3 **Find these expressions in the dialogue. Who says them? How do you say them in your language?**
1 …, if I'm not mistaken.
2 Apparently, …
3 That's news to me.
4 I'd have thought …
5 … when you put it like that, …
6 More to the point, …

4 **Use the expressions in Exercise 3 to complete the dialogues.**
1 A This music's horrendous!
B I'm surprised. … you'd like it.
2 A John hasn't turned up yet. Where is he?
B He isn't coming. … , he's very busy or something.
3 A What time does the match start, Sir?
B Eight thirty, … .
4 A We've run out of milk, I think.
B Yes, you're right. But … , who left the empty bottle in the fridge?
5 A Paul Graham's taking on the role of Student Representative. Did you know?
B No. … .
6 A Let's not go out. It's miserable outside.
B Well, … , perhaps a walk really isn't a good idea.

FUNCTIONS
Talking imprecisely about numbers

5 **Complete the sentences from the dialogue.**
1 It could be only three years … if he gets time off for good behaviour.
2 I'd have thought … 20 years would have been more appropriate.
3 He was earning … 300 times more than his average employee.
4 Only 40… , by the look of it.

6 **What are the imprecise expressions in these sentences? Do the numbers come before or after each expression?**
1 It cost around $120.
2 It took something like three years to build.
3 Fifty people turned up, give or take.
4 In the region of 10,000 people live here.

7 **Answer the questions using an imprecise expression.**
1 How many students are there at your school?
2 How much does a bottle of water cost where you live?
3 How far is it from your house to the town/city centre?
4 How long does it take you to get to school every day?

5 Ask students to try to complete the gaps from memory before referring back to the dialogue to check.
1 or so 2 around 3 roughly 4 ish

6 Ask students to underline the imprecise expressions.
1 around – after
2 something like – after
3 give or take – before
4 in the region of – after

7 As feedback, ask the questions in open class to find out who was closest to the correct answer in questions 1 and 2, and who lives furthest/takes longest in questions 3 and 4.

Activity idea Extension

In pairs, students write five questions which require imprecise answers. For example, *How old is* (famous actress)? *I think she's in her early 30s.; How much does a smartphone cost? They cost around 800€.* Regroup students to ask each other their questions.

TH!NK more

Workbook
Phrases for fluency p88

Warmer

Write *Stand up for your beliefs* on the board and elicit the meaning in this context (to defend or support an idea that you are certain about or care about). Ask students to give themselves a mark for their ability to stand up for their beliefs between 0 and 10. Does their ability to do this change depending on who they are interacting with?

▶ 26 Life Lessons: Standing up for your beliefs

1 ▶ **26** Ask students to compare their ideas with a partner.
Annie protested about the park being turned into a car park. It was successful.

2 ▶ **26 Check/clarify:** *mayor.*
Ask students to try to answer the questions from memory before watching the video again to check.
1 Martin Luther King, Emily Pankhurst and Greta Thunberg
2 Annie got people to sign a petition
3 She got very nervous.

3 **Check/clarify:** *agenda, folk.*
After a few minutes, invite students' reactions in open class prompting them to try to explain their answers.
1 That anyone is alone over Christmas.
2 She has managed to draw up an agenda of visits and start a campaign amongst the school pupils, staff and parents to collect small presents that they could take to the elderly people.
3 All her friends and their parents.

4 As a follow-up, discuss as a class and have a quick show of hands to see which issues students feel most strongly about.

5 If students are struggling to think of something, suggest they choose an idea from Exercise 4. Give students time to plan their presentation and then ask the groups to present their ideas to the rest of the class. After each presentation, encourage the rest of the class to ask questions and finally hold a class vote to decide which was the most interesting presentation.

LIFE COMPETENCIES

Most of us will feel strongly about certain issues throughout our lives. But it isn't always easy to stand up and let others know how you feel. Taking the right kind of action is a skill that will lead you to feeling more satisfied and like you can make a difference.

1 ▶ 26 **Watch the vlog. What did Annie protest against? Was the protest successful?**

2 ▶ 26 **Watch the vlog again and answer the questions.**
1 Which of her heroes does Annie talk about?
2 What did Annie do on her protest outside the town hall?
3 What happened to Annie when she met the mayor?

3 **Read the article and answer the questions.**
1 What did Jenny decide was wrong?
2 What two things has she managed to do?
3 Who helped her?

4 SPEAKING **Work in groups. Read through the mini-scenarios. Rank them in order of how strongly you feel about each one (1 = least strong; 4 = most strong).**
- Your town council is planning to sell off the local park to a building company who are going to turn it into a shopping centre.
- The headmaster of your school has decided to ban all mobile phones from the school buildings.
- The government wants to introduce a tax of £500 for anyone who owns a dog.
- Your local hospital is going to close because the local authorities say it is too expensive.

Me and my world

5 SPEAKING **In your groups, think about something you feel strongly about and organise a campaign. Discuss the following questions:**
- What do you want to say?
- Who do you want to say it to?
- How you are going to say it?
- What change do you hope for?

TIPS ON STANDING UP FOR YOUR BELIEFS

- **If you feel strongly that something is wrong, you should try to find the courage to speak out against it, although this is not always so easy.**
- **Think carefully about why you feel strongly, what it is you would like to see changed and the best way to achieve it.**
- **Try to keep a calm head. Aggression rarely achieves anything.**

Teen brings Christmas cheer to elderly

Over 50 elderly people who live alone in the local area are going to get a visit over Christmas, thanks to 15-year-old Jenny Stainsby. Jenny was determined to do something to ensure that the elderly people wouldn't be entirely alone.

'Many old people either have no relatives at all, or else their relatives live too far away to visit them,' said Jenny. 'No one should be alone over Christmas – that's miserable – so we've tried to do something about it.'

'We' means Jenny and around 20 of her co-pupils at the high school. Jenny created a page on social media, asking for the names of elderly people living alone in the area. Then she called on her friends at school to help her to do two things: firstly, to draw up an agenda of visits (i.e. which of them would go and visit who, and when) over the Christmas period; and secondly, to start a campaign amongst the school pupils, staff and parents to collect small presents that they could take to the elderly people. Their campaign was generously responded to, and they will now be able to not only call in on the 50 elderly folk, but also take each of them two small gifts (for example a book, an item of clothing, a small cake).

Jenny said: 'It was my idea at first, but all my friends and their parents have been brilliant. I'm so happy we can do this, and if it's successful, I hope we can repeat the idea every year.'

Homework

Ask students to research someone who has stood up for their beliefs. As a follow-up, students can present this person to the class. If students are struggling to think of someone, you could give them some of the following to research: *Malala Yousafzai* (women's right to education), *Xiuhtezcatl Roske-Martinez* (climate change), *Amariyanna Copeny* (clean water), *Elyse Fox* (mental health awareness), *Mohammed Manan Ansari* (child labour), *Imani Barbarin* (disability rights), *Marley Dias* (literacy and diversity), *Yolanda Renee King* (gun reform), *Shawn DeAngelo* (urban agriculture).

TH!NK more

Practice Extra
Unit 9 Master it!

Worksheets
Life Lessons: Standing up for your beliefs

Tests
Unit, extension and skills test 9
End of term test 3

Warmer

Read through the information. Ask students what the text will be about. Do they think animals can communicate and if so, how?

Culture note

Hector Hugh Munro (1870–1916), more commonly known as Saki, is considered a master of the witty, satirical short story. He was born in Burma (now Myanmar), but after the death of his mother was sent to England to live with his grandmother. His most famous short stories include 'The Interlopers', 'Esme' and 'Tobermory'. Saki's work mocks and challenges the society in which he lived.

1. 9.06 Tobermory is sarcastic and critical of others, and likes spreading gossip. He also seems to have a sense of humour.
2. Tobermory reveals that Sir Wilfrid criticised one of his guests, Mavis, before he invited her to his house. According to Tobermory, Sir Wilfred said that she was 'the most brainless person he knew' (lines 12 and 13).
3. Lady Blemley – she obviously feels uncomfortable with Tobermory there because she suggests he goes for his dinner two hours before he usually eats. (Tobermory has also revealed that Lady Blemley said that Mavis' 'lack of brain power' was the reason she had been invited – she was the only person 'idiotic enough to buy their old car'.)
4. The writer mentions the 'Tom Cat from the Rectory' (line 51) to explain why Tobermory leaves the room without finishing his story, so he probably fears or hates the other cat.
5. Encourage students to think of different scenarios. Accept all sensible answers.
6. Encourage students to answer the questions. They should give examples and justify their answers.

Literature

TOBERMORY
BY HECTOR HUGH MUNRO

A group of people have been invited to spend a weekend at a large country house. One of the guests claims that he can teach animals to talk. The other guests are very surprised when the family's pet cat – Tobermory – learns to speak and starts to answer questions.

1 9.06 **Read and listen to the text and answer the following question: How would you describe Tobermory's personality?**

Another silence fell on the group, and then Miss Resker asked if the human language had been difficult to learn. Tobermory looked seriously at her for a moment. It was obviously a boring question.

'What do you think of human intelligence?' asked Mavis Pellington.

'Of whose intelligence in particular?' asked Tobermory coldly.

'Oh, well, mine for instance,' said Mavis, with a feeble laugh.

'You put me in an embarrassing position,' said Tobermory, whose tone and attitude certainly did not suggest any embarrassment at all. 'When your inclusion in this house-party was suggested, Sir Wilfrid insisted that you were the most brainless person he knew. Lady Blemley replied that your lack of brain-power was the precise quality which had earned you your invitation, as you were the only person she could think of who might be idiotic enough to buy their old car …'

'Would you like to go and see if cook has got your dinner ready?' suggested Lady Blemley hurriedly, pretending to ignore the fact that it was at least two hours to Tobermory's dinner-time.

'Thanks,' said Tobermory, 'not quite so soon after my tea. I don't want to die of indigestion.'

'Cats have nine lives, you know,' said Sir Wilfrid heartily.

'Possibly,' answered Tobermory; 'but only one liver.'

'Adelaide!' said Mrs. Cornett, 'do you mean to encourage that cat to go out and gossip about us in the servants' hall?'

The panic had indeed become general …

Even in a delicate situation like the present, Agnes Resker could not bear to remain too long in the background.

'Why did I ever come down here?' she asked dramatically.

Tobermory immediately responded. 'Judging by what you said to Mrs. Cornett in the garden yesterday, you were out for food. You described the Blemleys as the dullest people to stay with that you knew, but said they were clever enough to employ a first-rate cook; otherwise they'd find it difficult to get anyone to come down a second time.'

'There's not a word of truth in it! I appeal to Mrs. Cornett –' exclaimed the discomforted Agnes.

'Mrs. Cornett repeated your remark afterwards to Bertie van Tahn,' continued Tobermory, 'and said, "That woman would go anywhere to get four good meals a day," and Bertie van Tahn said – '

At this point the story mercifully ceased. Tobermory had caught a glimpse of the big yellow Tom Cat from the Rectory working his way through the bushes towards the house. In a flash he had vanished through the open French window.

Glossary

feeble – weak
discomforted – feel uncomfortable, especially mentally
mercifully – in a way that makes you grateful because something unpleasant has stopped
caught a glimpse – saw something for a very short period of time
in a flash – quickly or suddenly

2 What embarrassing information does Tobermory reveal about Sir Wilfrid?

3 Which of the guests do you think is probably most embarrassed by what Tobermory says?

4 Why do you think the writer mentions the 'Tom Cat from the Rectory'?

5 What do you think is going to happen to Tobermory?

6 SPEAKING **Work with a partner and discuss these questions.**
1. To what extent are animals able to communicate with human beings?
2. Do you think we might one day teach an animal to talk? Why/Why not?

Unit Opener

Warmer

Divide the board into two columns and write *Learning for life* at the top of one and *Learning once* at the top of the other. Give an example of each one (e.g. learning for life: learning a language; learning once: learning how to ride a bike). In pairs, ask students to make a list of examples of *learning for life* and examples of *learning once*. Share answers as a whole class. Ask students what the differences are between the two different types of skill. If necessary, explain that some skills will not be forgotten once learned, while others will require constant effort to maintain or improve.

▶ 27 Get **TH!NK**ing

Ask the question. Get students to compare their ideas in groups. Play the video and then ask students for feedback.

1 Elicit what the students think is happening in the photo. What does it show? How old are these people? What is most striking about the photo? Does the same thing – or similar things – happen in their country? Share ideas as a whole group.

2 Ask them when they last finished a stage of their education, and whether they did anything to celebrate this. Was it the same for previous generations? Is completing a stage of education given too much importance? Or not enough? Share ideas as a whole group.

3 Ask students in groups to think of alternatives to university and to consider the differences between the different options. What is the final goal of each one? Then discuss as a whole class. Do students want to go to university?

10 LEARNING FOR LIFE

OBJECTIVES

FUNCTIONS: reacting to news

GRAMMAR: reported verb patterns (review); passive report structures; hedging

VOCABULARY: higher education; life after school

Get TH!NKING

Watch the video and think: how important is it to learn new things?

Work in pairs. Look at the photo and discuss the questions.

1 How are these people feeling? What are they wearing and why?
2 Do you think it's important to celebrate finishing different stages of education? Why/Why not?
3 How important is a university education? Do you want to go to university?

103

Objectives

Functions Reacting to news
Grammar Reported verb patterns (review); passive report structures; hedging
Vocabulary Higher education; life after school
Literature *Daddy-Long-Legs*

Resources for this unit

All available online

Videos

- Get **TH!NK**ing: *How important is it to learn new things?*
- Grammar video!: Passive report structures

Tests

- Unit, extension and skills test 10

Worksheets

- Grammar and vocabulary: Basic, Standard and Extension Worksheets
- Project: Alternative studies
- Communication: You live and learn
- Literature Worksheets: *Nicholas Nickleby*
- Get **TH!NK**ing and Grammar video! video Worksheets

Warmer

Ask: *What are the good and bad things about the education system in your country? What can you do if you do not like something at your school?* Students discuss the questions in pairs.

1 Encourage students to be as creative and open-minded as possible and to accept all ideas and interpretations equally.

2 Give students two minutes to work individually and make notes before they discuss.

3 **Check/clarify:** *school governors.* During feedback, for question 3, make a list on the board for later use.
1 A meeting for school governors, teachers, parents and students
2–3 Students' own answers

4 **10.01** During feedback, check students' ideas that are on the board.
The financial position of the school was being debated and the question 'Which subject would you never, ever, leave out of the curriculum?' was being answered.

5 **Check/clarify:** *the chair (of the governors), financially viable.* Before reading, ask students to underline key words in the comments that they should look for in the text. Tell them that they should read the article and comments carefully and check that the text matches the information in a sentence *exactly* before deciding if a comment matches.
1 JoBolton 2 Nancy421
3 GrantG 4 RedmanOfYork
5 Ali_Burke 6 JoBolton
7 Nancy421 8 Ali_Burke

6 To maximise communication, give students time to think about their answers prior to their discussions. Encourage them to refer to the blog when they are explaining their answers.

READING

1 SPEAKING **Work in pairs and look at the photos. What might the people be learning from doing these activities? How might they be feeling? In which of the situations would you most enjoy learning? Why?**

2 **Think of a memorable teacher you had in primary school. What made him/her memorable? Write down your ideas. Then compare them with a partner.**

3 **Read the notice and answer the questions.**
1 What kind of meeting is this?
2 Is it the kind of meeting you'd go to? Why/Why not?
3 What do you think the 'school crisis' might be?

> St Jonathan School, Greenway
> Tuesday 12th April
>
> **Meeting with school governors and staff**
>
> *Parents and children are invited to attend this meeting to discuss the current school crisis.*

4 10.01 **Read and listen to the summary of the meeting written by a pupil and the comments which follow. What issue was being debated and what question was being answered by the people who commented?**

5 **Read the comments again. Which of the people who commented on the summary do you think might say the following things?**
1 'The 1979 elections were a turning point for the country.'
2 'I learned so much from playing the part of Biff.'
3 'Now I know what 'blue notes' are, and why they're so common in jazz.'
4 'It's crazy that you spent eight years at school, and you still don't know about phishing.'
5 'I can see why people learning the language might get this wrong, but there's no excuse for native speakers.'
6 'Who was it who said that if you don't remember the past, you'll just repeat the same mistakes?'
7 'I couldn't possibly stand in front of people and act, but I love helping the people who do.'
8 'The worst thing is that when everyone starts making the same grammar mistake, it starts to become OK.'

6 SPEAKING **Work in pairs and discuss the questions.**
1 Should less academic subjects such as Food Technology, Art and Dance be taught in schools? Why/Why not?
2 List the subjects you study at school. Then put them in order from most to least important. Compare your list with your partner, giving reasons for your choices. Then agree together on a final ranking.
3 Imagine one of your subjects was going to be cut from the timetable. Agree on which subject that should be.

7 Check/clarify: *valid, flawed.*

8 Check/clarify: *invalid.*
Divide the class into small groups for students to compare their answers and come to an agreement on which are the most and least valid reasons.

Homework

Write the following situations on the board.

I want to become a vegetarian because …

I am going to leave home when I am 18 because …

I want to sell my bicycle because …

I am not going to go out this weekend because …

Ask students to write a valid or invalid reason for each sentence. As a follow-up in the next lesson, ask students to work with a partner and take turns to read their sentences. If student A gives a valid reason, student B has to respond with an invalid reason. If students enjoy the activity, ask them to repeat the activity with further situations of their own.

Activity idea Extension

Look at the list of topics on the board from question 3 in Exercise 3. Have a quick vote in open class to decide which topics to discuss. Divide the class into groups of four and ask them to discuss the topics. In order to maximise discussion, tell them one student should be against each topic, one in favour and one undecided. The fourth student should chair the discussion and make notes on the discussion. When students have discussed the topics ask the chair of each group to report back in open class.

Activity idea Mixed-ability

In Exercise 8, put students into pairs roughly according to level. Ask weaker students to focus on one valid and one invalid reason. Stronger students can create three valid and three invalid reasons.

Critical TH!NKing
Solving problems and making decisions
Examines possible solutions to a given problem and states how effective they are.

SCHOOLREPORTER.CO.UK LEARNING FOR LIFE UNIT 10

Home About New reports Community

What to drop?

Last night at our school, there was a meeting of the school governors, and they invited any interested parents to come along. My parents went and I tagged along. The place was packed – governors, teachers, parents, kids – because everyone knew the main topic for the meeting was the school's financial problems. The chair of the governors thanked everyone for coming and confessed that they had to find a way of making savings. Our headteacher, Mrs Grimmond, insisted that the school was doing everything it could, and blamed government spending cuts for putting the school in a bad position. Then the chair of governors said that the only thing left to do was to remove at least one subject from the school curriculum, in order to save on staff salaries. Mrs Grimmond promised to keep working towards making the school more financially viable but, very reluctantly, she agreed that something had to be cut. Then, of course, the discussion moved on to which subject that could be. Mrs Grimmond said that she would not make any suggestions because she had to remain impartial. One parent accused her of being indecisive, but most people agreed with her decision. Then someone suggested cutting Art because it wasn't a life skill for kids. Someone else said, 'Well, if that's true, then you could also cut Music, and maybe PE.' As you might expect, there were arguments for and against every subject put forward, and in the end, the governors decided to organise an online vote. And I was thinking, I know which subject I would *never* cut. But before I tell you what it is, why don't you tell me which school subject you would never, ever leave out of the curriculum?

Comments 5 20 9

I would never leave out History. How can we understand where we are at the present moment – and why – if we don't know how we got here? I think it's vital that children learn the history of not only their own country (incredibly important), but also that of other countries, at least over, say, the last 50 years. And I don't mean just learning historical facts and figures – I mean analysing what's happened and why. Truly important, to my mind.
JoBolton

For me, the most important thing in the school curriculum is English. I don't mean literature – I mean good grammar, spelling, punctuation and so on. I'm horrified when I meet people who don't know when to write 'its' or 'it's', or the difference between 'there', 'their' and 'they're'. Everyone should learn to write and speak their own language properly. Then you've immediately got an advantage.
Ali_Burke

I know a lot of people will think I'm crazy, but for me it's Drama. Not just because I love it, but because I see how being on stage and acting a role gives so many kids confidence and a better understanding of themselves and other people's lives. Drama also involves teamwork, and this is a big plus in an age when we spend so much time working alone on computers, and so on.
Nancy421

I really don't like IT and computing much, but in this day and age it's vital, and it has to be on the curriculum. I think we're going to see (if we aren't seeing it already) a world where anyone who isn't up to speed with what's going on in IT is going to be left behind.
RedmanOfYork

I would keep Music. Learning to play a musical instrument is fantastic for anyone who does it, so I think everyone should do it! It's creative, stimulating and something that you can enjoy for the rest of your life – I don't think you can say that about a lot of other subjects! Even if you don't learn to play, you can start to understand and appreciate music more – what's not to love about that?
GrantG

Train to TH!NK

Doing something for the 'right' reasons

Before taking a particular course of action, we should make sure that any decision we make is based on valid and logical reasons. We must be careful not to be influenced by reasoning that isn't relevant. For example, Mandy says she wants to study Physics next year because the teacher doesn't give much homework. James wants to study Physics next year because he's interested in studying Medicine at university. Whose reasoning is the most valid?

7 SPEAKING **Work in pairs. Read the reasons people give for wanting to go to university. Who has a valid reason? Whose reasoning is flawed? Why?**

I want to go to university after leaving school because …

I can't think what else to do. *Kevin*
All my brothers and sisters went. *Susan*
I want to be in the university football team. *James*
I want to be a lawyer. *Diana*

8 SPEAKING **Work in pairs. Complete this sentence with two valid and two invalid reasons.**

I want to get married before I'm 25 because …

105

Activity idea Extension

Make small groups. Ask students to take it in turns to expand on one of the invalid reasons they came up with in Exercise 8 and try to convince their groups that their argument is correct. They could then go on to discuss their own personal opinions on each statement.

TH!NK more

Worksheets
Project Alternative studies
Communication You live and learn
Get **TH!NK**ing *How important is it to learn new things?*

Grammar; Vocabulary; Speaking

Warmer

Revise reporting verbs. Read out the following sentences and elicit the reason for each statement:

You should buy a new computer. (recommend)
My neighbours make a lot of noise. (complain)
Hello, I'm Brian. (introduce)
I told him your secret. (confess)
What time is it? (enquire)

Write any correct answers on the board. To see how much students know, ask them to transform the sentences using the reporting verb. For example: *You should buy a new computer – He recommended buying a new computer.*

1 At this level, students should have a good awareness of reporting verbs. Ask them to cover the rule box and divide the class into small groups for students to make a list of reporting verbs before they do the exercise.
1 was doing 2 to keep 3 of being 4 to come
RULE: 1 accuse 2 promise 3 insist 4 invite

2 1 The men confessed to hacking into his account and stealing his identity. 2 The education minister denied knowing anything about the Prime Minister's plans to reduce the number of English lessons. / The education minister denied knowing that the Prime Minister was/had been planning to reduce the number of English lessons. 3 The headmaster congratulated Valerie on getting a place at the top university. 4 The project leader suggested discussing this more before making a decision.

GRAMMAR
Reported verb patterns (review)

1 **Read the sentences from the summary on page 105 and complete them with the correct form of the verbs in brackets. Then complete the rule with the reporting verbs (in bold in sentences 1–4).**

1 Our headteacher **insisted** that the school ... everything it could. (do)
2 Mrs Grimmond **promised** ... working towards making the school more financially viable. (keep)
3 One parent **accused** her ... indecisive. (be)
4 They **invited** any interested parents ... along. (come)

RULE: Instead of using *say* and *tell*, we can use other verbs to report what someone said more accurately.

Pattern	Reporting verbs
+ (person) + preposition + gerund	blame/apologise/confess/congratulate/ [1]... *She* ***blamed government spending cuts for putting*** *the school in a bad position.*
+ *to* + infinitive/ *that* clause	decide/[2]... *They* ***decided to organise*** *an online vote.*
+ gerund or *that* clause	recommend/admit (to)/regret/suggest/ deny/[3]... *Then someone* ***suggested cutting*** *Art.*
+ (person) + (*not*) *to* + infinitive	warn/[4]... *They* ***warned us not to take*** *that route.*

2 **Rewrite the sentences, using the reporting verbs in the list.**

~~apologise~~ | confess | congratulate | deny | suggest

0 'We're sorry that we didn't invite Nick to the party.'
They *apologised for not inviting Nick to the party.*
1 'We hacked into his account and stole his identity.'
The men ... .
2 'I didn't have any idea that the Prime Minister was planning to reduce the number of English lessons.'
The education minister ... .
3 'Well done, Valerie! You've got a place at the top university!'
The headmaster ... .
4 'Let's discuss this more before making a decision.'
The project leader ... .

3 ROLE PLAY **Work in groups of four (A, B, C, D). Students A & C: go to page 143. Students B & D: go to page 144. You have five minutes to reach a decision on what the government should invest in. Then work in pairs and summarise the discussion using reporting verbs.**

Marcus suggested that ... *Max convinced Marcus that ...*

→ workbook page 90

VOCABULARY
Higher education

4 SPEAKING **Match the sentence halves. Then discuss the meaning of the expressions and words in italics with a partner.**

1 Margaret *sailed through her* end-of-school
2 She *took a gap year* in India before *starting her undergraduate degree*
3 She *did her master's degree*
4 She *wrote her dissertation* on 20th-century
5 After graduating, she *got*
6 She went to work in Africa

a *full-time* over the course of a year.
b *a scholarship* to do a postgrad course in Toronto.
c economic policy.
d *exams* when she was 18.
e as a *fully qualified* economist.
f in Economics at Newcastle University.

5 **Complete the sentences using the words and phrases in italics in Exercise 4.**

1 She's a ... doctor now. She starts work at her local hospital next month.
2 He graduates today. He ... and got a first.
3 She ... on molecular biology. It's a tough read!
4 He didn't go straight to university after school. He ... volunteering in Laos.
5 She ... in English Literature this year.
6 After graduating, I ... to do a postgrad course at Columbia University.
7 He doesn't want to do his master's part-time. He wants to do it ... and finish within a year.
8 After her undergraduate degree, she went on to ... in Art History at the Sorbonne.

→ workbook page 92

SPEAKING

6 **Choose four of the phrases in italics in Exercise 4 and use them to write three true sentences and one false one about you.**

7 **In small groups, take turns to read out your sentences. Ask follow-up questions to try to work out which sentence isn't true.**

106

3 After five minutes, students work in A/B and C/D pairs to write summaries using reporting verbs. When the majority of students have finished, regroup A/C and B/D for them to compare their summaries.

Workbook p90

Get it Right!
Reporting verbs

Student's Book p112

4 1 d 2 f 3 a 4 c 5 b 6 e

5 **Check/clarify:** *a first.*
Give students time to quickly read the sentences and ask about any difficult vocabulary.
1 fully qualified 2 sailed through his exams 3 wrote her dissertation 4 took a gap year 5 started her undergraduate degree 6 got a scholarship 7 full-time 8 do her master's degree

Workbook p92

6 Give your own example to get students started.

7 Monitor to check vocabulary items are being used correctly.

TH!NK more

Workbook
Grammar p90, Ex.1–5
Vocabulary p92, Ex.1–2
Vocabulary Extra p93, Ex.1–3

Worksheets
Grammar Worksheets 10
Vocabulary Worksheets 10

8 Ask: *What are you planning to do when you finish school?* Elicit answers in open class.

9 🔊 **10.02**
1 Joanna: Yes; Harry: No. He's working in the tax office.; Tanya: No. She's looking for work.
2 Joanna: She didn't want to go straight from school to university and she'd always wanted to see Australia and New Zealand.; Harry: His headteacher encouraged him to take a gap year to decide if he wanted to go to university or not. He worked in the tax office and found the work and the place interesting.; Tanya: She was worried about the expensive university fees and getting into debt. She also read that a degree's almost worthless these days because universities give away degrees to anyone. She also met a girl who had a good job in a bank and that the experience had been important for her.
3 Joanna: She thinks she did the right thing and is enjoying her university course now.; Harry: He loves it.; Tanya: She isn't sure if it was the right decision.

10 🔊 **10.02 Check/clarify:** *university fees, debt.*

11 🔊 **10.03**
1 what kind of person the student is and how they want to spend the gap year
2 He would think it was a positive way to spend the year.
3 Students' own answers
4 Fewer people are seeing gap years as just a year to put their feet up and have fun – they're much more concerned about how they're going to pay for university, and the debt they may have afterwards.

12 Monitor but do not interrupt the conversations unless inaccuracy hinders comprehension.

13 During feedback, say each of the phrases for student to repeat and check pronunciation.
1 took 2 have 3 got; do
4 going to; take 5 doing
6 have 7 got 8 have

14 1 earn money 2 get into debt
3 afford a gap year 4 go straight to university 5 sit an exam 6 pay off a loan 7 pay tuition fees

Workbook p92

Pronunciation
Lexical and non-lexical fillers
Student's Book p138

LISTENING AND VOCABULARY
Life after school

8 SPEAKING **Work in pairs and discuss which of these things are typical choices for school-leavers.**
- travel
- do military service
- get a full-time job
- go to university
- take a gap year
- do an apprenticeship

9 🔊 10.02 **Listen to Joanna, Harry and Tanya talking about life after school and copy and complete the table.**

	Joanna	Harry	Tanya
1 Did they go to university? If not, what are they now doing?			
2 What factors helped them make their decision?			
3 How do they feel now about the decision they made?			

10 🔊 10.02 **Listen again. Which of the three people would you most like to talk to? Why?**

It would be interesting to hear about Joanna's travels.

I disagree. She sounds a bit selfish. I'd rather talk to Harry. He seems the most normal.

11 🔊 10.03 **Listen to a headteacher giving his opinion. Answer the questions. Use your answers from Exercise 9 to help you.**
1 Which two things does he say his answer depends on?
2 What would he think about what Joanna did?
3 Do you think he'd approve of Harry's decision? Or Tanya's?
4 What does he say about current trends in gap years?

12 SPEAKING **Work in pairs and discuss the questions.**
1 Are gap years common in your country at the moment? Have they ever been common?
2 Which of the headteacher's views do you agree with? Which do you disagree with? Why?
3 Would you consider taking a gap year? Why/Why not?
4 How would you spend it? How would you finance it?

13 **Choose the correct option to complete the sentences.**
1 I'm glad I *took / went* a gap year before starting my degree course.
2 I've graduated and I now *have / do* a large loan to pay off.
3 I was very lucky that I *went / got* a scholarship to *do / have* my master's degree.
4 I'm *going to / doing* university next year, but I'd like to *take / have* a year out first.
5 I'm *having / doing* a course in French at the moment and I'm really enjoying it.
6 Lots of young working people live with their parents. This means they *have / afford* a reasonably high disposable income.
7 I *went / got* a part-time job to help finance my university degree.
8 I need to *do / have* the right qualifications for the job.

14 **Match the verbs in Column A with the words and phrases in Column B.**

A	B
1 earn	a gap year
2 get into	straight to university
3 afford	money
4 go	a loan
5 sit	tuition fees
6 pay off	debt
7 pay	an exam

→ workbook page 92

PRONUNCIATION
Lexical and non-lexical fillers
Go to page 138.

SPEAKING

15 **Work in pairs. Choose one of the statements below and try to convince your partner of your opinion. Student A: you agree with the statement. Student B: you disagree with the statement.**
- Being an honest person is more important than being highly educated.
- If more people had access to higher education, fewer people would believe everything they heard and read on the news.

16 **Now discuss your real opinion on the statement with your partner.**

15–16 In preparation for the discussion, you may like to divide the class into A/A and B/B pairs and give students time to think of arguments in favour of or against the statements. Before students speak, remind them of different ways of giving opinions.

Homework
Ask students to report the discussion from Exercise 16, starting: *My partner suggested that …*

Activity idea Extension
Ask students to write sentences of their own using some of the reporting verbs. Listen to some examples after feedback.

TH!NK more
Workbook
Listening p96, Ex.1–2
Vocabulary p92, Ex.3–5
Pronunciation p121

Worksheets
Vocabulary Worksheets 10

Reading

Warmer

Write on the board: *Do you play or know anyone who plays a musical instrument? What do you think the benefits are of learning to play an instrument, other than playing the instrument itself?* Divide the class into pairs or small groups for students to discuss the questions. Listen to some of their ideas in open class as feedback.

1 Write the three summaries on the board to make this a bit easier. Listen to students' ideas but do not comment at this stage.

2 Give students a three-minute time limit to encourage them to read quickly and get the gist in order to choose a summary.

3 **10.05 Check/clarify:** *cortisol, dopamine, soothing, auditory functions*. During feedback, ask students to refer to the parts of the text that support their answers.

1 Cortisol causes stress.
2 Dopamine improves people's mood.
3 It improves memory and abstract reasoning skills which can lead to improved academic achievement.
4 It helps to reduce the effects that ageing naturally brings.

READING

1 **Look at the photo and the title of the article. Which of these summaries do you think is best for the article?**

a The guitar is the best musical instrument to learn.
b There are several benefits to learning to play music.
c Playing a musical instrument helps children with problems.

2 **Read the article quickly and check your ideas.**

3 10.05 **Read the article again and listen. Answer the questions.**

1 What effect does cortisol have on people?
2 What effect does dopamine have on people?
3 What can be improved by learning to play a musical instrument?
4 What evidence is given that not only young people can benefit from learning an instrument?

Pick up your guitar and (learn to) PLAY

George Howard looks at music and learning to play an instrument.

It has been known for quite a long time that listening to music is good for you. Why do people get home from work and put music on, or listen to music while they're going to and from work? Stress reduction, that's why. People working in the area of music therapy have gathered lots of evidence to show that listening to the music you love brings down the amount of cortisol in your body – and it's cortisol that's responsible for most of the stress we feel.

There are other good reasons to listen to music. Listening to classical music (or any soothing music, in fact) for 30 minutes or so before going to bed could help you sleep significantly better. Runners listen to music too, and it seems that doing so improves their performance. And it helps to improve your mood as well – people who listen to music regularly have been shown to be calmer, more patient and more sociable.

But that's just *listening* to music. Great though it is, listening to music is nothing compared to actually *playing* it. If you already play an instrument, well, you probably know already how it can make you feel. But if you don't – well, think hard about learning to play an instrument, because the benefits are fantastic.

First of all, listening to and playing music have something in common, which is the release of dopamine into the brain. Dopamine is a chemical that gets released when we do things we like – eating good food, having fun with friends, getting to the next level in a game like Candy Crush. It's now understood that dopamine also plays an important role with regard to the brain. It stimulates things like motivation and memory, focus and attention, learning and creativity. It improves your mood. And learning to play music gives people a dopamine rush.

So much is involved in playing an instrument such as the guitar – there are motor functions (controlling your fingers), visual functions (reading the music), auditory functions (listening to the sounds you make and judging them), and of course there's the emotional response – hopefully pleasurable – to the music you're making. This is all excellent for the human brain, and helps to reduce the effects that ageing naturally brings. Learning to play an instrument improves things like memory (remembering a sequence of chords, for example) and abstract reasoning skills (understanding what the relationship is between this chord and another one), and this can lead to improved academic achievement, for both children and older people. It is believed to improve language skills, too. In one UK study, kids learning an instrument were found to be far more likely to score well on verbal skills.

Are there other benefits from learning to play an instrument? There probably are. Like anything else, the early stages of learning can be frustrating: it requires some dedication and commitment, and loads of patience. One music company reckons that anyone starting out needs to practise for a year before any clear improvements come. Does that sound terrible? Maybe. But there's a pay-off when you make the breakthrough and become more accomplished at playing. Satisfaction guaranteed – all that effort brings a reward.

So, if you don't already play, get learning. And it's never too late: I know someone who started to learn the guitar at the age of 60, and he loves everything about it – it's me.

TH!NK more

Workbook
Reading p94, Ex.1–4

4 🔊 **10.06** Before listening, give students time to read the headlines and work in pairs to predict what they will hear.
Cuts to education budget – 1
Tests for the very young – 4
Pupils get greener learning – 2
Government announces job losses in education – 3

5 🔊 **10.06** During feedback, write the expressions on the board to clarify which syllables are stressed. Say them for students to repeat and check pronunciation and intonation.
That's outrageous! – 5 ✗
I'm glad to hear it. – 2 ✓
Finally, someone's taking things seriously. – 1 ✓
They've got to be joking. – 7 ✗
They can't do that. – 6 ✗
What will they think of next? – 8 ✗
That's the best news I've heard in ages. – 4 ✓
It's about time they did something about it. – 3 ✓

6 Monitor and help with pronunciation and intonation.

▶ 28 Grammar video!
Passive report structures

7 *RULE: 1 formal 2 not important 3 subject 4 past participle 5 have*

8 Clarify that the agent (scientists, experts, etc.) is not usually needed if it is clear from the context.
1 Music is believed to have beneficial effects on a number of illnesses.
2 Some animals have been found to react strongly to certain types of music.
3 Lots of experiments are said to have been done.
4 The experiments are thought to have been an important breakthrough.

9 Tell students that we often use passive reporting structures to show that we are uncertain. This is known as *hedging*.
1 is believed to improve 2 It seems that doing so 3 could help you 4 There probably are.
RULE: 1 doesn't want

FUNCTIONS
Reacting to news

4 🔊 10.06 **Listen to two people talking about the news. Number the headlines 1–4 in the order you hear them.**
- Cuts to education budget
- Tests for the very young
- Pupils get greener learning
- Government announces job losses in education

5 🔊 10.06 **Listen again and number the functions in the order you hear them. Do the sentences express agreement/satisfaction or disbelief/protest?**
- That's outrageous!
- I'm glad to hear it.
- Finally, someone's taking things seriously. (*1*)
- They've got to be joking.
- They can't do that.
- What will they think of next?
- That's the best news I've heard in ages.
- It's about time they did something about it.

6 ROLE PLAY **Work in pairs. Student A: Go to page 143. Student B: Go to page 144.**

GRAMMAR
Passive report structures

Grammar video ▶28

7 **Read the sentences from the article. Then complete the rule.**
1 **It has been known** for quite a long time that listening to music is good for you.
2 Kids learning an instrument **were found** to be far more likely to score well on verbal skills.

RULE: We use passive report structures in more [1]*formal / informal* contexts to report information when the agent is [2]*not important / very important*. We use passive report structures with verbs such as *say, think, believe, know, find* and *consider*.
Compare these two pairs of sentences.
A *They say that music has a positive influence on humans.*
B *Music is said to have a positive influence on humans.*
A *In a UK study, they thought that learning an instrument improved children's verbal skills.*
B *In a UK study, learning an instrument was thought to have improved children's verbal skills.*
In the passive reporting structure (B), the underlined words are the [3]*subject / object* of the sentence. The word order is:
Present: subject + *be* + [4]… + *to* infinitive
Past: subject + *be* + past participle + *to* + [5]… + past participle

8 **Rewrite the following sentences, using passive report structures.**
0 Experts think a lot more research is needed into the effects of music on humans.
A lot more research into the effects of music on humans is thought to be needed.
1 Scientists believe music has beneficial effects on a number of illnesses.
2 Experts have found that some animals react strongly to certain types of music.
3 They say lots of experiments have been done.
4 Scientists think that the experiments were an important breakthrough.

Hedging

9 **Which option in each sentence expresses uncertainty? Choose the correct words to complete the examples of hedging from the article on page 108. Then complete the rule.**
1 It *is believed to improve / improves* language skills, too.
2 Runners listen to music too, and *it seems that doing so / doing so* improves their performance.
3 Listening to classical music for 30 minutes or so before going to bed *could help you / helps you* sleep significantly better.
4 Are there other benefits from learning to play an instrument? *There are. / There probably are.*

RULE: Hedging refers to cautious or vague language used when a writer [1]*doesn't want / wants* to state something as fact.
We use verb phrases such as: *seems to/that, is thought/believed to be, could be, might be, is said/thought to have been* and adverbs such as: *probably, perhaps* and *possibly.*

10 **Replace the underlined verb in each sentence with the hedging expressions in the list.**

are thought to have been | could help | ~~is believed to make~~ | is said to have been | seems to improve

0 Listening to music makes you learn better.
Listening to music is believed to make you learn better.
1 Playing music in hospital waiting rooms improves patients' moods.
2 My uncle was the best pianist in the country.
3 Early claims about playing music to very young children were exaggerated.
4 Music helps people become better human beings and overcome emotional difficulties.

→ workbook page 91

10 For further practice, ask students to rewrite the sentences using other hedging devices.
1 Playing music in hospital waiting rooms seems to improve patients' moods.
2 My uncle is said to have been the best pianist in the country.
3 Early claims about playing music to very young children are thought to have been exaggerated.
4 Music could help people become better human beings and overcome emotional difficulties.

Workbook p91

Homework
Ask students to think of some myths and theories with no certain answer, then write six sentences using hedging expressions. e.g. *There is thought to be life on other planets.*

TH!NK more
Practice Extra
Unit 10 Practise it!
Workbook
Grammar p91, Ex.6–8
Worksheets
Grammar Worksheets 10
Grammar video! Passive report structures

Warmer

Ask students to make a list of books or films about the adventures of a teenager. Elicit a few and write them on the board. Ask students to work in pairs and look for similarities and common themes in the books/films. Monitor to help with vocabulary as necessary and to make a note of any interesting answers to listen to during whole-class feedback.

1 Give a couple of your own examples before students do the task. Encourage them to give reasons for their choices.
Students' own answers

2 **10.07 Check/clarify:** *daddy-long-legs.*
Before students listen, read through the questions ask students to predict the answers.
Students' own answers

3 Ask students to underline the key information they will need to read for. You could encourage students to try to answer the questions before reading again.
1 Students' own answers
2 I love / I love; very, very happy; singles / singles; happiest / happiest; angel / angel; bright / brighter. They are repeated to focus the attention of the reader.
3 Students' own answers
4 Students' own answers

Literature

1 **Think of the many different ways that we can communicate with other people. Which are the most common and what might be the advantages of some over others? Why are some of the ways we can communicate not so popular now?**

2 10.07 **Read and listen to the extract. Think about these questions.**
1 Do you think Jerusha enjoys writing her letters to Daddy-Long-Legs? Why/Why not?
2 What do we learn about the ways in which Jerusha is different from the other girls at the college?

Daddy-Long-Legs *by Jean Webster*

***Daddy-Long-Legs* is an American novel published in 1912. Jerusha Abbot is a freshman at college (someone in their first year.) She grew up in a home for children who have no parents, but someone offered to pay for her education. His identity is a secret, but Jerusha has to write him a letter every month, so she invents a name for him – Daddy-Long-Legs.**

October 1st.

Dear Daddy-Long-Legs,

I love college and I love you for sending me – I'm very, very happy, and so excited every moment of the time that I can scarcely sleep. You can't imagine how different it is from the John Grier Home. I never dreamed there was such a place in the world. I'm feeling sorry for everybody who isn't a girl and who can't come here; I am sure the college you attended when you were a boy couldn't have been so nice.

My room is up in a tower that used to be the infirmary. There are three other girls on the same floor of the tower – a senior who wears glasses and is always asking us please to be a little more quiet, and two freshmen named Sallie McBride and Julia Rutledge Pendleton. Sallie has red hair and a turn-up nose and is quite friendly; Julia comes from one of the first families in New York and hasn't noticed me yet. They room together and the senior and I have singles. Usually freshmen can't get singles as there aren't many of them, but I got one without even asking. I suppose the registrar didn't think it would be right to ask a properly brought-up girl to room with a foundling. You see there are advantages!

My room is on the northwest corner with two windows and a view. After you've lived in a dormitory for eighteen years with twenty room-mates, it is restful to be alone. This is the first chance I've ever had to get to know Jerusha Abbott. I think I'm going to like her.

Do you think you are?

Tuesday.

They are organizing the freshman basket-ball team and there's just a chance that I shall make it. I'm little of course, but terribly quick and wiry and tough. While the others are hopping about in the air, I can get under their feet and grab the ball. It's loads of fun practising – out in the athletic field in the afternoon with the trees all red and yellow and the air full of the smell of burning leaves, and everybody laughing and shouting. These are the happiest girls I ever saw – and I am the happiest of all!

I meant to write a long letter and tell you all the things I'm learning but the bell has just rung, and in ten minutes I'm due at the athletic field in gymnasium clothes. Don't you hope I'll make the team?

Yours always,

Jerusha Abbott.

October 10th.

Dear Daddy-Long-Legs,

Did you ever hear of Michael Angelo? He was a famous artist who lived in Italy in the Middle Ages. Everybody in English Literature class seemed to know about him and the whole class laughed because I thought he was an angel. He sounds like an angel, doesn't he? The trouble with college is that you are expected to know such a lot of things you've never learned. It's very embarrassing at times. But now, when the girls talk about things that I never heard of, I just keep still and look them up in the encyclopedia.

I made an awful mistake the first day. Somebody mentioned Maurice Maeterlinck*, and I asked if she was a freshman. That joke has gone all over college. But anyway, I'm just as bright in class as any of the others – and brighter than some of them!

[…]

(Dinner bell, goodbye)

Jerusha Abbot.

* A well-known Belgian writer at the time

3 **Read the extract again. Answer the questions.**
1 What impression do you get of Jerusha's personality? Which words or phrases give you this impression?
2 Can you find examples in the letters of words/expressions that are repeated? Why do you think Jerusha repeats these words?
3 What does the text suggest about how Jerusha's social background influences her life at the college?
4 Do you think Jerusha is going to be a popular person with the other students? Why/Why not?

110

Culture note

Jean Webster was the pseudonym of Alice Jane Chandler Webster, an American author born in 1876 and the great-niece of Mark Twain. She was a lifelong supporter of women's suffrage and children's institutional reform and her most well-known books are coming-of-age novels featuring lively and likeable female protagonists. She is most remembered for *Daddy-Long-Legs* and wrote a sequel in 1914 called *Dear Enemy*. She died in childbirth in 1916.

Daddy-Long-Legs, published in 1912, is a novel that was part of a trend of 'college girl' books such as *Anne of Green Gables* and *Little Women* which featured young female protagonists dealing with themes such as college, career and marriage. Although it pre-dates modern views of teenage years and is sometimes criticised for its paternalistic themes, it is still considered relatable and praised for its depiction of everyday life. It is written as a series of letters and follows Jerusha Abbott as she goes to college, paid for by an unknown beneficiary. Webster adapted it into a stage play in 1914.

Writing

4 During feedback, say the words for students to repeat and check pronunciation.
1 dormitory 2 foundling 3 infirmary 4 registrar 5 scarcely 6 wiry

5 Monitor but do not interrupt as this is a fluency activity.

1 **Check/clarify:** *assertion.*
Ask students to read the essay quickly first to get a general overview.
The writer strongly agrees with the assertion.

2 **Check/clarify:** *aside, irrespective, refute, struggling.*
Give students time to read through the phrases before re-reading the essay to find expressions with the same meanings.
1 none more persuasive than 2 Namely 3 While education may be expensive 4 As for the idea 5 To my mind 6 Aside

3 Clarify that students should focus on the purpose of each paragraph rather than the specific content in this essay.
A introduction
B arguments agreeing with the assertion
C arguments disagreeing with the assertion
D conclusion and personal opinion

4–5 If you're short on time, students can do the preparation in class and complete the writing at home. Alternatively, this could be done as a collaborative writing activity in class with pairs of students of a similar level working together.

Homework

If you are short on time, students can do Exercise 5 for homework. If you have done this in the class, ask students to exchange their essays with another student for them to read and give feedback on the content and structure. Students could check if the essay uses the same structure as the template. They should also decide which the most/least interesting part of the essay is.

4 VOCABULARY **Match the highlighted words in the extract with the definitions.**
1 a large room containing many beds, for example in a boarding school
2 a young child who is left by its parents and then found and cared for by someone else
3 a room in a school, prison, etc. where people go when they are sick
4 someone whose job is to keep official records, of students at a university, for example
5 only just/very limited
6 thin but strong, and often able to bend easily

5 SPEAKING **Work with a partner and discuss the questions.**
1 What kinds of challenges are there when you start at a new school or college?
2 Why do you think people become friends? What is it that makes some people want to be friends with others?
3 Nowadays not many people write letters. How would you feel if you received letters from a friend instead of texts or emails?
4 Imagine you had the opportunity to help someone go to college. How would you choose that person?

WRITING
An essay

1 INPUT **Read the essay. Which option is correct?**
1 The writer …
2 slightly agrees with the assertion.
3 strongly agrees with the assertion.
4 is undecided.
5 slightly disagrees with the assertion.
6 strongly disagrees with the assertion.

2 ANALYSE **Find expressions in the essay which have the same meanings as the underlined ones below.**
1 … the most important of which is …
2 For example, it is expensive.
3 Although it's true that education is expensive, it is also a fundamental right …
4 With reference to the argument about salaries …
5 As I see it, there are too many people going to university …
6 Apart from my personal interest …

3 **Read the essay again. Give a short summary of what the writer does in paragraph …**
A …
B …
C …
D …

4 PLAN **Read the essay title and note down your ideas for and against the statement.**
No one should go to university before they are 25.

5 PRODUCE **Write your essay in 200–250 words giving both sides of the argument before presenting your position.**

Further education should be provided free to all who want it

A When my parents went to university in the early 1990s, neither of them had to pay their tuition fees. Sadly this is no longer the case. In a few years, I will probably choose to do a degree knowing that I am likely to leave with debts of around £30,000. It has made deciding to go to university a huge responsibility.

B My own personal interest aside, I can think of a number of reasons why further education should be free for all and none more persuasive than it means that it really is open to all, irrespective of family wealth. Obviously, the government will argue that there are schemes to help those from poorer backgrounds with funding, but clearly those from rich families will never have to take financial factors into consideration when deciding whether to go to university or not.

C Of course there are arguments that refute the assertion that further education should be free for all, namely, that it is costly and that those who go on to graduate are likely to earn higher salaries than those who start working at 18. Each of these will be discussed in turn. While education may be expensive, it is also a fundamental right for citizens of any society. It is an important investment in our country's future and without it our ability to compete on the world stage would diminish. As for the idea that having a degree enhances your earning prospects, this is unfortunately no longer always the case. A rise in the number of people going to university means that competition for high paid jobs is fierce and many graduates are struggling to secure the employment they believed having a degree would assure them.

D To my mind, too many people are currently going to university, and as a result the value of further education is falling. University entrance should be made harder for all and those who are successful should not have to pay tuition fees. But of course, to make things fair, the government should also be looking at how to provide those who leave school at 18 with opportunities to get ahead in the working world.

Activity idea Mixed-ability

In Vocabulary Exercise 4, stronger students could look at the six words in the extract and try to deduce meaning from context before referring back to the definitions and completing the exercise. With weaker classes, you could give students the first letter of each word to guide them.

TH!NK more

Practice Extra
Unit 10 Master it!

Workbook
Developing Writing p95

Tests
Unit, extension and skills test 10

1 Write on the board *Never …*, *Little …*, *Not only …*, *Under no circumstances …* and *Rarely …* and ask students to write complete sentences, reminding them that the sentence starters are negative, restricting adverbs. Check and correct any errors before doing the exercise.

1 Little did the defence lawyer realise that her client would be found guilty.
2 Not only did the witness give false evidence, but also committed the crime himself!
3 Rarely do people think it's fair to be able to pay to jump a queue.
4 Under no circumstances are the children allowed to go in there – it's where I'm keeping all their Christmas presents.
5 Never have I stolen anything from a shop.
6 Not only do they know where you are, but also what you are doing.

2 Focus students' attention on the example in the box. Then elicit different reporting verbs from students and ask them to say what preposition follows each one.

1 Dave apologised for not remembering my birthday.
2 The government agreed ~~for~~ on a change in the school curriculum.
3 Chloe invited Georgina ~~for~~ to the wedding.
4 The researcher confessed to altering the test results.
5 My sister blamed me for not helping her with her studies.
6 My dad insisted ~~in~~ on picking me up after the DeCode festival.

3
1 having
2 taking
3 studying
4 to go
5 going
6 to help

GET IT RIGHT! UNITS 9 & 10

Negative inversion

Learners at this level often avoid using negative inversion or use it incorrectly. Typical learner mistakes relate to word order or the omission of the auxiliary after a negative or restricting adverb.
✓ ***Never have I*** *heard such rubbish!*
✗ *~~Never I have~~ heard such rubbish!*
✓ ***Little does she*** *know he's not who he says he is.*
✗ *~~Little she knows~~ he's not who he says he is.*
✓ ***Not only did she*** *pass, but she also got a distinction.*
✗ *~~Not only she did~~ pass, but she also got a distinction.*

1 Rewrite the sentences beginning with the words given, paying attention to word order and including any necessary auxiliaries.

0 The members of the jury had never heard such a story before.
Never ***before had the jury heard such a story.***
1 The defence lawyer didn't realise that her client would be found guilty.
Little …
2 The witness gave false evidence, but also committed the crime himself!
Not only …
3 People don't often think it's fair to be able to pay to jump a queue.
Rarely …
4 The children are absolutely forbidden to go in there – it's where I'm keeping all their Christmas presents.
Under …
5 I have never stolen anything from a shop.
Never …
6 They know where you are, but also what you are doing.
Not only …

Reporting verbs

Learners often use the wrong preposition, or omit the preposition after reporting verbs.
✓ *He* ***accused*** *me* ***of*** *cheating in the exam.*
✗ *He accused me ~~for~~ cheating in the exam.*

2 Rewrite these incorrect sentences correctly.

0 The President was accused with behaving recklessly.
The President was accused of behaving recklessly.
1 Dave apologised not remembering my birthday.
2 The government agreed for a change in the school curriculum.
3 Chloe invited Georgina for the wedding.
4 The researcher confessed altering the test results.
5 My sister blamed me not helping her with her studies.
6 My dad insisted in picking me up after the DeCode festival.

Learners often make mistakes with verb patterns after reporting verbs.
✓ *They* ***decided to go*** *to the beach.*
✗ *They decided ~~going~~ to the beach.*

3 Choose the correct option.

1 The politician denied *to have / having* promised a reduction in student fees.
2 My teacher recommended not *to take / taking* a gap year before university.
3 I always regretted not *to study / studying* another language at university.
4 Joanna invited us *to go / going* to her party on Saturday night.
5 Helen suggested *to go / going* ice skating for her 18th birthday.
6 They promised *to help / helping* us to find a part-time job.

112

1 🔊 **10.08** In C1 Advanced Listening Part 4, candidates have to listen to five short related texts, each with a different speaker. Candidates must choose the option from a set of eight that matches what each speaker says. This task tests listening for gist, detail, attitude and opinion.

Encourage your students to do the following when they approach this task:

- Read and listen to the instructions to understand the context of the conversations.
- On the first listening, try to understand the gist and choose the best option for each speaker.
- On the second listening, check all the answers carefully.

Task 1 1 F 2 C 3 A 4 H 5 E
Task 2 1 B 2 H 3 E 4 G 5 D

Workbook p97

2 In C1 Advanced Writing Part 1, candidates have to write an essay of about 240 words. There will be a statement or question, which students have to give their opinion about and two prompts to help give students some ideas. This part of the exam tests the candidates' ability to write well-organised texts with a real communicative purpose.

Encourage your students to do the following when they approach this task:

- Read the question/statement and the two prompts carefully, to identify what is required and who it is for, and what kind of information is needed.
- Plan the answer and respond to both prompts.
- Students will need to think of a third idea of their own which is different from the two given prompts. Brainstorm some ideas for this.
- Write a rough draft of the essay before writing the final answer. Make sure that it is well organised and has a range of tenses, expressions and vocabulary.
- Read the essay again to check that it makes sense and that all the content points have been included.

Students' own answers

TOWARDS C1 Advanced

LISTENING
Part 4: Multiple matching

→ workbook page 97

1 🔊 10.08 **You will hear five short extracts in which people are talking about an evening class that they attended.**

Task One

For questions 1–5, choose from the list (A–H) each speaker's main reason for choosing the class.

A to get better at something I'd always enjoyed
B to meet new people
C a love of languages
D to learn the basics of how to make things out of wood
E to fulfil a long-standing desire to learn something
F to improve an existing skill
G a desire to travel
H to be able to better enjoy something else

1 Speaker 1
2 Speaker 2
3 Speaker 3
4 Speaker 4
5 Speaker 5

Task Two

For questions 6–10, choose from the list (A–H) what each speaker disliked about the class they chose.

A There was insufficient time to practise.
B There were too many students in the class.
C Some students asked really difficult questions.
D The teacher's language level was poor.
E The teacher had a tendency to talk too much.
F The teacher's methods were poor.
G It revealed my lack of ability in the subject.
H Some students were not quick learners.

6 Speaker 1
7 Speaker 2
8 Speaker 3
9 Speaker 4
10 Speaker 5

WRITING
Part 1: An essay

2 **You have been to a discussion on which levels of education should receive the most government funding. You have made the notes below:**

Which levels of education should receive the most government funding?

- primary education (4–10 years)
- secondary education (11–17 years)
- college/university education (18 years and older)

Some opinions expressed in the discussion:

'Primary schools are the basis for everything that comes later.'

'Secondary schools are important for training young people to get useful jobs in the real world.'

'Universities shouldn't get much money because they're for the privileged few.'

Write an essay of around 220–260 words discussing two of the levels in your notes. You should explain which level you think is more important for the government to give money to, giving reasons in support of your answer.

You may, if you wish, make use of the opinions expressed in the discussion, but you should use your own words as far as possible.

113

1 1 undergraduate 2 fees 3 judge 4 jury 5 evident 6 wrote 7 gap 8 unfair 9 evidence 10 sailed

2 1 have left 2 Never have 3 on passing 4 meeting 5 have never 6 Rarely does

3 1 ~~Nevertheless~~ Although I really like football, my brother prefers rugby.
2 The thieves are thought to ~~steal~~ have stolen more than $2 million.
3 No sooner had I got home than the phone rang.
4 He's considered to ~~being~~ be the finest guitarist ever.
5 He insisted ~~about~~ on paying for dinner.
6 Because ~~of it raining~~ it was raining / Because of ~~raining~~ the rain, we stayed in all day.

4 1 something; around
2 take; around
3 taking; news
4 next; joking

TEST YOURSELF UNITS 9 & 10

VOCABULARY

1 Complete the sentences with the words in the list. There are four extra words.

evidence | evident | fare | fees | gap | judge | jury
made | sailed | sit | undergraduate | unfair | witness | wrote

1 He did an … degree at the University of Liverpool.
2 I wanted to go to university, but I couldn't afford the tuition … .
3 The … sentenced the thief to six months in prison. We were surprised by the harshness of her sentence.
4 The … took two days to find him guilty.
5 It is … that obesity is a growing problem in modern-day society.
6 He … his dissertation on nineteenth-century American poetry.
7 I really wish I'd taken a … year before I went to university.
8 It's … to keep a bird in a cage, isn't it?
9 No witnesses were found to give … , so the police had to drop the case.
10 He … through his exams. They were no problem at all.

GRAMMAR

2 Complete the sentences with the words/phrases in the list. There are two extra words/phrases.

have left | have never | leave | meeting
never have | on passing | rarely | rarely does

1 The criminals are thought to … the country.
2 … I heard such a terrible story.
3 She congratulated me … the exam.
4 He recommended … a few hours earlier so that we'd have plenty of time to get to the airport.
5 I … actually met him.
6 … he give an interview.

3 Find and correct the mistake in each sentence.

1 Nevertheless I really like football, my brother prefers rugby.
2 The thieves are thought to steal more than $2 million.
3 No sooner had I got home the phone rang.
4 He's considered to being the finest guitarist ever.
5 He insisted about paying for dinner.
6 Because of it raining, we stayed in all day.

FUNCTIONAL LANGUAGE

4 Choose the correct options.

1 A It took *something* / *anything* like 500 men more than ten years to build it.
B And *around* / *area* how much did it cost to build?
2 A We've got half an hour give or *get* / *take* to get to the station.
B That's fine. I reckon it'll take us *around* / *least* ten minutes to walk there.
3 A Finally, someone is *taking* / *doing* things seriously.
B Yes, it's the best *news* / *report* I've heard in ages.
4 A A flying car?! What will they think of *soon* / *next*?
B Really? You've got to be *serious* / *joking*.

114

MY SCORE
22–30 | 10–21 | 0–9

The Cambridge Life Competencies Framework

Social Responsibilities
Understanding another culture
Watch this video for a tip on understanding social responsibilities.
Scan the QR code here.

Warmer

Elicit from students some situations in their daily lives that can cause stress. Write them on the board and discuss as a whole group. When you have listed enough stressful situations, ask students to vote on what they think the most common sources of stress are. Then put students into pairs. Ask them to choose two of the situations and to think of at least three possible ways to reduce the stress caused by each one. Feed back as a whole group. Do the students think any of the ideas to reduce stress are good ones? Do they do any of these already?

▶ 29 Get TH!NKing

Ask the question. Get students to compare their ideas in groups. Play the video and then ask students for feedback.

1 Elicit what the students think the picture represents. What does it show? What type of contradiction is it trying to express? What do students think about mixing the old and the new? When does doing this work and when doesn't it, in their opinion? Share ideas as a whole group.

2 Ask them to describe what a VR (virtual reality) headset is. Have they ever used one? Would they like to? Encourage students who have used one to share their experience.

3 Ask students to get into pairs and make a list of pros and cons for technological advances. Tell them they have two minutes and that they should list the same numbers of advantages and disadvantages. Feed back as a whole group and make a list on the board.

11 THE MODERN WORLD

OBJECTIVES

FUNCTIONS
telling someone to keep calm

GRAMMAR:
more on the passive; causative *have* (review); modal passives (review)

VOCABULARY:
(not) getting angry; *-isms*

Get TH!NKING
Watch the video and think: what makes life today stressful?

Work in pairs. Look at the photo and discuss the questions.

1 What does this image mean to you? What do you think it's meant to represent?
2 Have you ever used a VR headset? Would you like to? Why/Why not?
3 Is technological advancement always a good thing?

115

Objectives

Functions Telling someone to keep calm
Grammar More on the passive; causative *have* (review); modal passives (review)
Vocabulary (not) getting angry; *-isms*
Values Modern life
Culture Back in time

Resources for this unit

All available online

Videos
- Get TH!NKing: *What makes life today stressful?*
- Grammar video!: Causative *have*
- Culture: Living in the past

Tests
- Unit, extension and skills test 11

Worksheets
- Grammar and vocabulary: Basic, Standard and Extension Worksheets
- Project: Apps
- Communication: 21st Century living
- Grammar presentation: Causative and passive *have / get*
- Literature Worksheets: *Nicholas Nickleby*
- Get TH!NKing and Grammar video! video Worksheets

Warmer

Ask students: *What do you use social media for?* If your students have mobile devices, ask them to use them to compare answers. Ask: *Do you all use the same apps and networks?* Listen to some of their ideas in open class and encourage discussion.

1 Give your own example before students do the task.

2 Set a three-minute time limit and tell to read quickly and not worry about understanding every word, but just focus on checking their answer to Exercise 2.
Switch off your social media.

3 🔊 **11.01 Check/clarify:** *compassion, traced back, feuds, prejudice, golden rule, thick skin, make your blood boil, block.*
1 i 2 f 3 g 4 h 5 a 6 b 7 e 8 d 9 c 10 j

4 Encourage students to express themselves in English and to use any vocabulary they have learned from the text.

5 **Check/clarify:** *contradicts, hypocritical.*
Before students do the task, give them three pieces of advice. For example, *You should always wash up immediately after eating; You should read at least 20 pages of a novel before going to bed; You should never put your bag on the desk* (when your bag is on the desk). Ask: *What is the difference between the three pieces of advice?* (You don't follow the last one yourself.)

6 Listen to some examples with the class as feedback.

A

B

'THIS IS OUR MOST EFFECTIVE JUNK MAIL FILTER'

READING

1 SPEAKING **Work in pairs. Look at the cartoons on this page. How do the people feel in each one and why do you think they feel this way? Then make a list of things that make you angry about the internet and social media.**

2 **Read the article quickly. What's the author's final solution for dealing with anger on the internet?**

3 🔊 11.01 **Read the article again. Complete it with these missing extracts. Then listen and check.**

a on social media
b get criticised
c or ideally altogether
d and not always good for us
e and forget it
f being a doctor
g for a start
h the level of
i one thing is for sure
j don't be afraid to

4 SPEAKING **Work in pairs and discuss the following questions.**

1 What do you do when you come across angry people online?
2 What do you think can be done to make the internet a friendlier place?

Train to TH!NK

Do as I say, not as I do

When someone says or does something which contradicts what they say they believe, we often find this hypocritical and we can dismiss their advice all too easily as a result. It's important to consider people's advice as separate from their actions. For example, a father who tells his children not to use their phones at the dinner table, even though he may occasionally check his, is still passing on very valid advice.

5 SPEAKING **Work in pairs. Consider these situations. Why is the advice given still valid?**

1 My mother says I shouldn't spend too much time on social media, even though she often uses it.
2 My dad says I shouldn't get angry with my computer, even though I often see him shouting at his.

6 SPEAKING **Think of two situations in which you've been given hypocritical advice, but then on reflection, that advice has proven to be valid. These could be real or imaginary. Tell your partner about them.**

Critical TH!NKing
Solving problems and making decisions
Examines possible solutions to a given problem and states how effective they are.

Homework

Ask students to keep a journal for two or three days, with a record of what made them angry, how long for and how they overcame their anger.

Activity idea Extension

Ask students to work in pairs and make a list of people who give them advice.

Ask: *Who gives you advice most often?*

Whose advice do you follow most?

Does anyone say you should not do things that they did when they were younger?

What is the best/worst piece of advice you have been given?

Do you ever give people advice?

Do you tell people to do things that you do not do yourself?

Students discuss the questions in small groups and try to find as many things they have in common as possible.

INTERNET RAGE

Whether it's moaning about the government and injustices in society, losing your temper with cyclists or simply getting worked up about what someone said or didn't say about your favourite soap actor, [1]… : there's plenty of anger on the internet. Just take a look through the comments after any online news story – for every positive reaction, there are many more negative comments. Let me give you a quick example. A doctor friend of mine was featured in the online version of her local newspaper. Her twin daughters had got sent to different high schools because there weren't enough places at their local one. For every comment offering sympathy for their situation, there were at least three saying that she should stop crying about the situation and that [2]… , she was rich enough to send her children to a private school – and these were just the polite ones. It seemed the general public – complete strangers to my friend – had very little time or compassion for her.

So why exactly is there so much anger on the web? Well, [3]… , anger is a strong emotion – it gets attention. Studies have shown that an angry post is more likely to get shared than a happy one, for example. The message seems to be that if you want to get noticed, get angry.

And then, of course, the internet is a great place for letting off steam, and because we can do it anonymously, we are often tempted to exaggerate [4]… our feelings more than we might do if we knew the comments could be traced back to us.

Not all such displays of anger are done hiding behind an alias. There are plenty of examples of famous people having a go at other celebrities [5]… , and the media is more than happy to publicise these feuds further – after all, they help sell newspapers.

Is all this anger good for us? Of course it isn't. For many of us, the internet is somewhere we go to get informed or meet like-minded people; we aren't looking for hatred and prejudice. Social media is a way of keeping in touch with family and friends and not a place to [6]… or get our heads bitten off by those who might not agree with us.

So what should we do? Well, it starts with ourselves. Before you post anything, ask yourself if there's any chance it might upset someone somewhere; if there is, then ask yourself, 'Do I really need to write this?' Following the golden rule of 'If you haven't got anything nice to say, then don't say anything at all.' is a pretty good place to start. And if something has really annoyed you, bite your tongue [7]… .

That takes care of the 'anger' in your online content, but what about that from others? Well, the simplest thing to do perhaps is to develop a thick skin and stay calm. That, though, may be easier said than done [8]… – if something upsets you, it isn't always healthy to pretend it doesn't.

Perhaps the most effective way of avoiding the stress that internet anger can cause is to try to avoid it as much as possible [9]… . Do you really need to read the comments section after news stories when you know that they'll only make your blood boil? Such behaviour can become addictive and you need to find a way of breaking that addiction. Avoid the sites that attract the most negative comments.
Your life won't suffer.

When it comes to social media, be careful who you choose to include on your friends list and [10]… block those who write unkind comments. You're better off without them in your life anyway.

And if none of this works then there is one easy answer: switch it off.

TH!NK more

Worksheets

Project Apps

Communication 21st Century living

Get **TH!NK**ing *What makes life today stressful?*

Warmer

Elicit reasons for getting angry or frustrated. In pairs, students discuss how often they get angry, what causes them to get angry and what helps them to calm down. Close with a group discussion.

1 During feedback, elicit that we can form the passive with *to get* instead of *to be*.
1 get 2 got 3 get
RULE: 1 informal 2 dynamic 3 an action

2 1 While she was crossing the road, she got hit by a car.
2 The man got taken to hospital by ambulance.
3 My bike got damaged when I got hit by a car.
4 I got shouted at for cycling on the pavement.
5 My jeans got ruined when I fell off my bike.
6 We didn't get hurt in the accident.

Workbook p100

Get it Right!
Passive with *get*

Student's Book p134

3 Point out that all the expressions are informal.
Getting angry: had a go at; shouted at; loses her temper; gets worked up; letting off steam; bit my head off; bit my tongue (feeling angry but not expressing it)
Not getting angry: keeping her cool; stays calm; keep the peace; bit my tongue (feeling angry but not expressing it)
Saying something: had a go at; shouted at; bit my head off

4 1 kept; cool 2 loses; temper 3 keeping the 4 get worked 5 tongue 6 let off

5 Give a couple of your own ideas as examples first.

Workbook p102

TH!NK more

Workbook
Grammar p100, Ex.1–3
Vocabulary p102, Ex.1–3
Vocabulary Extra p103, Ex.1–3

Worksheets
Grammar Worksheets 11
Vocabulary Worksheets 11

GRAMMAR
More on the passive

1 **Complete each sentence from the article on page 117 with one word. Then complete the rule by choosing the correct options.**

1 An angry post is more likely to … shared than a happy one.
2 Her twin daughters had … sent to different high schools.
3 The internet is somewhere we go to … informed.

RULE:
- We can use the verb *get* instead of *be* in passive constructions. This is more common in [1]*formal / informal* English.
- We only use *get* with [2]*state / dynamic* verbs. We <u>don't</u> say *he got believed to be guilty* or *he got loved by his parents.*
- We often use *get* when there is a clear good or bad effect or when something happens unexpectedly or accidentally, for example *he got mugged* or *several things got lost when we moved house.*
- Sometimes *get* is used rather than *be* to make it clear that [3]*a state / an action* is involved, for example *the window was broken* could be a state or an action, but *the window got broken* has to be an action.

2 **Use the prompts to write sentences, using the correct past form of the passive with *get*.**

0 While / we / be / on holiday / we / rob / .
While we were on holiday, we got robbed.
1 While / she / cross / the road / she / hit / by a car / .
2 The man / take / hospital / by ambulance / .
3 My bike / damage / when / I / hit / by a car / .
4 I / shout at / for cycling / on the pavement / .
5 My jeans / ruin / when / I / fall off / my bike / .
6 We / not hurt / in the accident / .

→ workbook page 100

VOCABULARY
(not) getting angry

3 **Read the three passages. Which expressions in bold are about getting angry? Which are about *not* getting angry? Which involve someone *saying* something?**

A Yesterday I was late for work and my boss really **had a go at** me. She **shouted at** me really loudly. I wasn't surprised – she's someone who **loses her temper** quite easily and she **gets** really **worked up** if things don't go her way.
B My mum is great at **keeping her cool**. She always **stays calm**, even when someone else is **letting off steam**. If someone criticises her, she manages to **keep the peace** and not argue back.
C Alex is having a bad day. I asked him to lend me something and he just **bit my head off**, saying I always borrow things and never give them back! I didn't say anything – I just **bit my tongue**.

4 **Complete each space with one word from the expressions in Exercise 3 in the correct form.**

0 If I say something she doesn't like, she *bites* my head *off*.
1 When he shouted at me, I … my … and smiled at him!
2 My aunt's so calm – she never … her … .
3 He's really good at … … peace when an argument starts.
4 It's fine – don't … … up over it!
5 When you're angry, it's good to bite your … and say nothing.
6 When I'm stressed, I run – it's how I … … steam.

5 SPEAKING **Work in pairs. Answer the questions.**

1 Who do you know who always manages to keep the peace when tensions rise in your family?
2 When was the last time you lost your temper and shouted at someone? What was it that made you cross?
3 What do you think is the best way to let off steam, apart from shouting at the person who's upset you?
4 Who was the last person to have a go at you about something? How did you react? How did you feel?

→ workbook page 102

FUNCTIONS
Telling someone to keep calm

6 11.02 **Listen to two conversations. Why is the boy angry in situation one? Why is the girl angry in situation two?**

7 11.02 **Match 1–5 with a–e to make expressions for helping someone who's stressed. Then listen again and check.**

1 Chill	a easy.
2 Take it	b getting worked up about.
3 Don't let it	c get under your skin.
4 He's not worth	d out.
5 Don't let him	e get to you.

8 ROLE PLAY **Work in pairs. Student A: Go to page 143. Student B: Go to page 144.**

118

6 11.02
1 because the bus is late
2 because someone has spoken to her in a way she doesn't like

7 11.02 The aim of these phrases is to tell someone to keep calm, so it is important that students use the correct intonation.
1 d 2 a 3 e 4 b 5 c

8 As feedback, listen to some examples and vote to decide who sounded angriest and who was the best at calming their partner down.

Activity idea Extension

Ask students to complete the sentences using the passive form of one of these verbs: *steal scratch fine tell off pay*

1 *My uncle … for speeding.*
2 *When I came in late, I … by my mother.*
3 *My bicycle … when I left it unlocked.*
4 *My phone … when I dropped it on the floor.*
5 *The workers didn't … last week.*

1 got fined 2 got told off 3 got stolen 4 got scratched 5 get paid

9 Put a copy of the four pictures up on the board and do the exercise as a class before students open their books. During feedback, write some of their answers on the board to refer to when they have listened to the recording.

10 🔊 **11.03**
A 4 B 3 C 1 D 2

11 🔊 **11.03** Ask students to correct any false statements.
1 T
2 F (he tries to have it delivered when he knows he'll be in, but he always seems to miss them by five minutes.)
3 F (She finds it difficult to remember some of her passwords.)
4 T 5 T 6 T
7 F (… he had to take the train into work – something he'd never done before.)
8 F (It was an uncomfortable journey but he had nowhere to sit.)

12 Give some examples of your own to get students started. For example: poor internet connection; advertisements on websites. Encourage them to think of at least five.

13 As a follow-up, discuss as a class and come up with a definitive list.

Pronunciation
Intonation: mean what you say

Student's Book p138

▶ 30 Grammar video! Causative *have* (review)

14 To check understanding at this point, elicit a few more examples from the class of things they might have done for them by somebody else.
Sentence 1
RULE: 1 have 2 past participle

15 1 having my hair cut
2 had it repainted
3 'm having my motorbike fixed
4 Have; had something valuable stolen
5 to have my blood pressure checked

16 Sentences 0 and 4

17 Clarify that one list should contain things they have paid for or wanted to happen, and the other list things they have not wanted to happen.

18 When students have compared lists, re-group students and ask them to report their findings to their new partners.

Workbook p100

LISTENING
Stresses and strains of modern life

9 SPEAKING **Work in pairs. What's happening in each of the pictures? How are the people feeling? Discuss with your partner.**

10 🔊 11.03 **Listen to the radio phone-in. Number the pictures in the order you hear about them.**

11 🔊 11.03 **Listen again. Are the statements T (true) or F (false)?**

1 Matt, the radio host, does a lot of online shopping.
2 He can't choose the time of the deliveries.
3 Daisy finds it difficult to remember any of her passwords.
4 Matt only has one password.
5 Matt doesn't understand what 'flex' means.
6 Ryan's friend was disappointed with his exam results.
7 Andy usually takes the train to work.
8 Andy complains about the uncomfortable train seats.

SPEAKING

12 **The radio host talks about modern problems, i.e. things that your grandparents, for example, would not have had to face. Make a list of these.**

13 **Work in pairs. Compare lists and agree together on a ranking from most to least serious problems.**

PRONUNCIATION
Intonation: mean what you say Go to page 138.

GRAMMAR
Causative *have* (review)

Grammar video ▶30

14 **Read the three sentences from the listening. Which sentence talks about something the person wanted another person to do? Then complete the rule.**

1 I try to have it delivered when I know I'll be in.
2 A friend of mine had her social media account hacked.
3 My car got broken into the other day.

RULE: This structure is formed with the verb [1]… + object + the [2]… of the main verb.
We can use it:
- when we ask or pay someone to do something for us (example sentence 1).
- when someone (often not known) does something unpleasant to us (example sentences 2 and 3).

We can also use *get* instead of *have*. This is more informal but doesn't change the meaning: *We got the car fixed last week.*

15 **Complete each sentence using causative *have*.**

0 Last week, I *had my phone stolen* on the bus. (phone, steal)
1 This afternoon at 3.00, I'll be in town … . (hair, cut)
2 They didn't like the colour of the house, so they … . (it, repaint)
3 Next week, I … . I can take the bus until then. (motorbike, fix)
4 … you ever … ? (something valuable, steal)
5 Tomorrow I'm going to the clinic … . (blood pressure, check)

16 **Which sentences in Exercise 15 talk about unwanted events?**

17 SPEAKING **Work in pairs. Make a list of as many examples as you can of:**
- something you/someone in your family often have done (intentionally).
- something you/someone in your family once had done to you.

18 SPEAKING **Work in groups. Compare lists and ask each other follow-up questions.**

→ workbook page 100

Get it Right!
Causative *have*

Student's Book p134

Homework
Ask students to imagine they were given a lot of money a month ago and that they haven't seen their classmates since then. They write a text using causative *have* to explain the things they have done in the last month using the money.

Activity idea Extension
After Exercise 15, ask students to write the active form of each of the sentences. For example: *Somebody stole my phone on the bus last week.* This will emphasise the fact that the person doing the action is unknown.

TH!NK more

Workbook
Listening p106, Ex.1–2
Pronunciation p121 Grammar p100, Ex.4–5

Worksheets
Grammar Worksheets 11
Grammar video! Causative *have*
Grammar presentation Causative and passive *have / get*

Reading

Warmer

Revise phrases for *(not) getting angry* by giving students an incomplete phrase from page 118 Exercise 3. They must then say a sentence including the full phrase. For example, *had a go (beep) – had a go at. My mum had a go at me for not doing my homework! Correct.* Students continue in pairs.

1 Put a copy of the three pictures up on the board and do the exercise as a class before students open their books. Write a few of their ideas on the board, but do not comment at this stage.

2 **Check/clarify:** *veganism.*
Set a three-minute time limit and tell students to read quickly and not worry about understanding every word, but just focus on checking their answer to Exercise 1.

3 **11.05 Check/clarify:** *poll, animal welfare, consumption, diabetes, salmonella, mercury, nutrients, supplements, dieticians, boycott, exploits, aquarium, circus, sanctuaries.*
Before students read the article again, get them to read the questions through. Ask them to underline key text that supports their answers.

1 A vegan cannot eat any animal products.
2 According to a poll, in the US there has been a 600% rise in the number of vegans over the last three years.
3 The three reasons are that vegans believe animals shouldn't be killed for our consumption, producing red meat is one of the biggest causes of global warming and meat has been linked to health issues.
4 It can bring down stress levels and reduce the risk of heart disease and some forms of cancer. It can also help people lose weight.
5 It may cause a lack of important nutrients.
6 More ready-made vegan food can be found in supermarkets and more restaurants now serve vegan food.
7 Vegans also boycott any form of entertainment that exploits animals.

READING

1 SPEAKING **Work in pairs. Look at the photos. How do you think these things relate to veganism? What else do you know about veganism?**

2 **Read the article quickly and check your ideas.**

3 11.05 **Read the article again and listen. Answer the questions.**

1 What food can a vegan not eat?
2 What evidence is there that veganism is becoming more popular?
3 What three reasons are given to suggest why people become vegans?
4 What health benefits have been linked to veganism?
5 What health issues might veganism cause?
6 Why is it easier to be a vegan these days?
7 What other things, apart from not consuming animal products, do true vegans do?

4 SPEAKING **Do you think you could be a vegan? Discuss in pairs and give your reasons.**

EXPLAINING THE MODERN WORLD: VEGANISM

What is veganism?
Veganism is the avoidance of eating any animal or animal products, such as eggs, honey and cheese. Vegans eat only plant-based foods. They don't wear any clothing that has come from animals and they also refuse to use any product that might have been tested on animals.

Is it new?
Not at all. The Vegan Society was formed back in 1944. In recent years, however, veganism has grown more and more popular. According to one poll in the US, there has been a 600% rise in the number of vegans over the last three years, taking the percentage of US citizens who claim to be vegan from 1% to 6%. But it isn't just in the US; there has been a worldwide increase in the number of vegans. In the UK, for example, 7% of the population identifies as being vegan. The country with the highest percentage of vegans is India with a total of 27% of the population.

So why is it so popular?
To answer this, we need to look at the reasons why people are choosing to become vegan. For many people, animal welfare is their biggest concern. They believe that animals shouldn't be killed for our consumption. It's as simple as that. There are also many people who are worried about the impact that raising farm animals has upon the environment. It is well known that producing red meat, in particular, is one of the biggest causes of global warming. There are also many people who believe that a vegan diet is healthier than one that includes meat, and so they are making the change for health reasons. Red meat has long been connected with health issues such as diabetes and heart disease, while chicken can cause salmonella and fish mercury poisoning.

Is a vegan diet really healthier?
That will probably depend on who you ask. A lot of research has been done to look into this exact question and the general opinion is that a vegan diet can certainly help reduce the risk of heart disease and some forms of cancer. It's also believed to bring down stress levels and it has proven to be an effective way of losing weight for many people who have tried it. However, there is a downside, too: a true vegan diet is often lacking in important nutrients such as zinc, calcium, iron and, perhaps most importantly, vitamin B12 (commonly found in eggs, meat and fish), which supports healthy cell production. These minerals can easily be taken as supplements, though, as many dieticians would recommend.

Avoiding meat – that sounds like a lot of hard work?
It is much easier to be a vegan these days and ready-made vegan food can be found in most large supermarkets. Rather oddly, this food is often versions of the meat cuts they are substituting, such as vegan bacon, vegan chicken fillets and even a vegan burger that 'bleeds' when you bite into it (the blood effect comes from beetroot juice). You can also find vegan restaurants in most reasonably sized towns and many other restaurants will also include vegan options on their menus.

Is there anything else I should know?
To be a true vegan, you should also boycott any form of entertainment that exploits animals. This includes trips to zoos, aquariums or circuses that use animals as part of their show (although this has already been banned in many countries). You should also not get involved in any sport that uses animals, such as horse-racing or dog-racing.

But can I have a pet?
Of course! So long as you are committed to looking after its welfare. In fact, the national vegan society encourages its members to visit and support animal sanctuaries that provide a safe home for animals that have been rescued.

120

4 Invite students to share their answers with the rest of the class during feedback. If you have students who are already vegan, perhaps they could give reasons for why they decided to give up meat and animal products.

Culture note

The Vegan Society is the oldest vegan society in the world and was founded in the UK by Donald Watson, who identified as 'a non-dairy vegetarian'. In 1944, he and a few others formed a non-dairy sub-group of the Vegetarian Society and started a quarterly newsletter called *The Vegan News*. The founding members of this group coined the word *vegan* from the word *vegetarian* by taking its first three and last two letters, making a point about veganism's starting point of vegetarianism, and what they view as its logical conclusion.

TH!NK more

Workbook
Reading p104, Ex.1–4

Grammar; Vocabulary; TH!NK values

5 Ask students to try to answer the questions from memory before referring back to page 120 to check. Ask students to underline the modal verb in each sentence.
1 tested 2 taken 3 found 4 killed

6 1 sentence 1
2 sentences 2, 3 and 4
3 Students' own answers; The person who performed each of the actions in passive structures is unknown, understood or not important.
RULE: 1 be 2 have been

7 If you're short on time, set this exercise for homework.
1 More information can be found on our website.
2 New ideas might be thought up.
3 These things should be re-used.
4 You could have been hurt.
5 Your bike must have been stolen.
6 It may have been put here on purpose.

Workbook p101

8 During feedback, say the words for students to repeat and check pronunciation. Write the words on the board to elicit and mark the stress on each word. Point out the stress on the first syllable.
1 d, capitalist 2 a, pessimist 3 e, optimist 4 b, socialist 5 c, ageist

9 1 ageist 2 capitalist 3 socialist 4 pessimist 5 optimist

10 Give a couple of your own ideas as examples first.

Workbook p102

11 Allow students to add a third option if they disagree with both of the options.

12 Encourage students to give reasons for their answers and ask each other questions to develop conversation.

13 Listen to some answers as a class as feedback.

GRAMMAR
Modal passives (review)

5 Read the sentences from the article. Complete them with the words in the list.

found | killed | taken | tested

1 They refuse to use any product that might have been ... on animals.
2 These minerals can easily be ... as supplements.
3 Ready-made vegan food can be ... in most large supermarkets.
4 They believe that animals shouldn't be ... for our consumption.

6 Answer the questions about the sentences in Exercise 5 and then complete the rule with *have been* and *be*.

1 Which sentence refers to a past situation?
2 Which sentences refer to the present?
3 Who performed each of the actions?

RULE: We can use modals in the passive voice by using these structures:
Present: modal verb + [1]... (infinitive) + past participle
Past: modal verb + [2]... + past participle

7 Write sentences using the passive. Do not include the agent.

0 Someone must know the answer.
The answer must be known.
1 People can find more information on our website.
2 Someone might think up new ideas.
3 People should re-use these things.
4 Someone could have hurt you.
5 Someone must have stolen your bike.
6 Someone may have put it here on purpose.

→ workbook page 101

VOCABULARY
-isms

8 SPEAKING Work in pairs. Match the *-isms* with their definitions. Then write the adjective form of each *-ism*.

1 capitalism *capitalist*
2 pessimism ...
3 optimism ...
4 socialism ...
5 ageism ...

a the tendency to see the worst in situations
b the belief that people should work together for the good of society
c prejudice against older people
d the belief that privately owned companies should control the economy
e the tendency to see the best in situations

9 Use the adjectives from Exercise 8 to describe these people.

1 'You can't have the job because you're too old.'
2 'I'm sure my train would arrive on time if it was owned by a company rather than the government!'
3 'If we all work together, we'll make the world a better place for everyone.'
4 'Why bother applying for the job? I'll never get it. I never get anything I want.'
5 'I have a really good feeling about this game. I'm pretty sure we're going to win.'

10 SPEAKING Work in pairs. Discuss the questions.

1 Are you more of an optimist or a pessimist? Why do you think that?
2 What examples of ageism have you seen?
3 What do you think are the problems of capitalism and socialism?

→ workbook page 102

TH!NK values
Modern life

11 Read the questions and choose your answer: a or b.

1 When something I own breaks, I ...
a throw it away and get another one.
b get it fixed.
2 When a new model of my phone comes out, I ...
a buy it immediately.
b wait until I need a new one.
3 I think that the internet ...
a makes us lazy.
b is the most useful resource ever.

12 SPEAKING Work in pairs. Compare your answers with a partner.

13 SPEAKING How do you think your grandparents would answer the questions in Exercise 11? Would they answer them in the same way as you or differently?

Homework

Ask students to write five more multiple choice questions to ask their grandparents. As a follow-up, put students in pairs to ask each other the questions, with the student answering the questions taking the role of a grandparent. When they have completed the questions, ask them to discuss whether they would answer the questions differently themselves.

Critical TH!NKing
Solving problems and making decisions
Examines possible solutions to a given problem and states how effective they are.

Emotional Development
Showing empathy for the feelings of others
Shows understanding of other people's perspectives and feelings.

TH!NK more

Practice Extra
Unit 11 Practise it!

Workbook
Grammar p101, Ex.6–8
Vocabulary p102, Ex.4–5

Worksheets
Grammar Worksheets 11

Warmer

Ask students to imagine that they could go back in time to any point in history. Ask them what period they would like to visit and why. Does their gender affect the period they would feel comfortable visiting? Allow students time for pairs to discuss. If space allows, encourage students to walk around the classroom to find someone who agrees with them. Hold a class vote to decide which they feel would be the best period in history to return to.

▶ 31 TH!NK
Living in the past

1–2 After a few minutes, invite students' reactions in open class prompting them to try to explain their answers. During feedback write their ideas on the board to refer to after Exercise 3.

3 🔊 **11.06** Tell students not to worry if they don't understand every word and that they should just focus on checking their ideas. During feedback, refer to the ideas on the board to check which were mentioned in the text.

Culture notes

Port Townsend is a city in Jefferson County, in the state of Washington, United States.

The Victorian era was the period of British history under Queen Victoria's reign from 20 June 1837 until her death on 22 January 1901.

The penny-farthing was the first machine to be called a 'bicycle'. It became popular in the 1870s but by the late 1880s was no longer manufactured. The name came from the British penny and farthing coins which were very different in size, just like the wheels on the bike, but the name only came to prominence towards the end of its time. The height of the bike made it fairly dangerous and the trend was short-lived, being replaced by lower, chain-driven 'safety bicycles'. However, the penny-farthing became a symbol of the late Victorian era and coincided with the birth of cycling as a sport.

TH!NK
Living in the past

Culture

BACK IN TIME

1 SPEAKING Work in pairs. Why are people interested in the past? Write down as many reasons as possible.

2 How might people explore a period of history they are interested in?

3 🔊 11.06 Read and listen to the article. Which of your ideas are mentioned?

Whether it is enjoying hearing our grandparents talk about how life was when they were young or finding History the most fascinating subject at school, most of us have at least a little interest in the past. But how far would you take this? Would you be willing to give up all the comforts of modern life to live in the world that your ancestors would have recognised? Meet three people who have made that very decision.

When Gabriel Chrisman goes out for a bike ride around his hometown of Port Townsend in Washington, he's always sure to turn a few heads – after all, it isn't every day you get to see someone riding high up on a penny-farthing. With his wife Sarah riding alongside him, both of them dressed in clothes their great-grandparents might have worn, the pair are affectionately known locally as 'the Victorian couple'. As a young girl, writer Sarah dreamed of living in the late 1800s, and when she met like-minded Gabriel, they set about making this dream a reality. Their house is decorated and furnished with items from the era, they make and wear their own clothes based on those from Victorian times, and they even cook and eat the same food their distant relatives would have eaten. They do have electricity for the lighting, which is something that came in at the end of the 19th century, but they usually only use this when they have visitors; normally, they will just light their oil lamps when it gets dark. All appliances in the house are manual and they don't miss their modern gadgets at all. The couple was drawn to the Victorian age because it was a time of immense change and optimism. Great inventions were constantly being unveiled to the public and people really believed they could make the world a better place. It is a spirit that the couple would like to see more of in the modern world. And do they mind when people stop and stare at them in the street? Not at all! They just hope they can be an inspiration to anyone who has a dream they'd like to make come true, even if it might make them stand out a little from the crowd.

Across the Atlantic Ocean, in Cambridgeshire in the UK, 35-year-old Brit, Ben Sansum, shares this passion for living in the past, albeit in a somewhat more modern era than that of the Chrismans. Ben earns his living working as cabin crew for an international airline, but when his shift is over, he swaps his temporary homes in the hotels of New York and Sydney for a life in 1946 rural Britain. Ben had been interested in the post-war years since he was at school, when his fascination with the cars, fashion and music of the times began. Ben always dreamed of living in the past as a way of making sure life in the olden days is not forgotten.

When he left home, started working and bought his own house, he set about transforming it into a living monument to the 1940s. Much of his furniture is even older, with some pieces (including his outdoor mangle and the range in his kitchen) dating back to the Victorian times. He does, though, have a modern fridge, which he keeps hidden behind a cloth curtain. For Ben, keeping his food fresh is the one sacrifice he will make!

Ben is no great fan of the modern world and feels that everything these days moves far too fast. He believes that our addiction to technology, such as mobile phones, has made us become detached from real life. He hopes that by surrounding himself with reminders of when life was simpler, he'll be able to reconnect with the more important things in life. The view from his bedroom is of the local church and graveyard – a view that hasn't changed for over a hundred years. It's just a shame that when he looks down at the road below, he is brought swiftly back to reality with his neighbours in their modern cars all fighting for somewhere to park.

122

4 Check/clarify: *era, immense, albeit, rural, mangle, range.*
Tell students to underline information in the text that helped them answer each question.
1 Because they ride a penny-farthing.
2 They use oil lamps.
3 It was a time of immense change and optimism.
4 He wants to make sure the olden days are not forgotten.
5 He thinks the modern world moves too fast and people are addicted to technology.
6 He can see the local church and graveyard, but the modern cars spoil the view.

5 Before students do the exercise, write the highlighted words on the board. Tell students to find the words in the article as quickly as possible. When they have seen them being used in context, ask them to try to work out the meaning of the phrases. Compare their meanings with the definitions in the book.
1 appliances 2 cabin crew
3 monument 4 ancestors
5 graveyard 6 unveiled
7 like-minded 8 shift

6 Encourage students to express themselves in English and to use any vocabulary they have learned from the text.

1 Set a time limit of two minutes to encourage quick scanning. Students tick the pictures.
A and C are mentioned.

2 Regroup students to compare their ideas with a different partner.

3 Check/clarify: *willingly.*
1 fixedly 2 laboriously
3 reluctantly 4 shrilly 5 readily
6 desperately

4 Ask students to read the blog without the adverbs to get a feel for the difference they make.

5–6 Divide the class into small groups so that they can share ideas before writing individually (they could do this for homework). Students make notes in preparation for writing their article. Allow students six to eight minutes to write their notes. Monitor to make sure all students are on task.

4 According to the article:
1 why might people stop and stare at the Chrismans?
2 how do the Chrismans light their house?
3 what attracts them most to the Victorian era?
4 why is Ben keen to live in the 1940s?
5 what does he dislike about modern life?
6 what can he see from his bedroom window and what spoils the view?

5 VOCABULARY Match the highlighted words in the article to the definitions.
1 objects in a house such as a washing machine, TV, dishwasher, etc.
2 the people who ensure the passengers on a plane are safe and looked after
3 a building specially built to remember someone or some event from the past
4 your relatives from the past
5 a place where people are buried
6 to show something for the first time
7 to think the same way as someone else
8 the period of time when you work

6 SPEAKING Work in pairs. Discuss the questions.
1 If you could meet Gabriel, Sarah or Ben, what would you like to ask them?
2 What time in history interests you most and why?
3 Would you like to live in that time? Explain your answer.

WRITING
A blog post

1 INPUT Sam has a blog and in her latest post, she imagines life in 1966, when her grandparents were teenagers. Read the blog post and look at the photos. Which of the things does she mention?

2 What other differences do you think Sam might notice in 1966?

3 ANALYSE Which of the underlined adverbs means:
1 intently, without moving?
2 in a way that requires a lot of effort?
3 without really wanting to?
4 in an unpleasantly loud way?
5 quickly and willingly?
6 in an extremely worried way?

4 None of the underlined adverbs is completely necessary in the blog. Why do you think Sam uses them?

5 PLAN You're going to write a blog post, imagining that you're in the year 2036. Make notes on the following:
1 What different technology exists?
2 What everyday things have been replaced by technology?
3 How do you feel about all of this technology? Is there any technology from your normal life that you miss?

6 PRODUCE Use your ideas to write a blog post (200–250 words). Use adverbs to make it as interesting and involving as possible.

Sam's blog: imagine 1966!!

Here I am. It's 1966, and I'm spending a day hanging out here just to see what things are like and how different everyday life is.

First of all, I wake up to a bell ringing shrilly – it's an alarm clock, not my smartphone. After my shower, I head off for breakfast. I'd like to find out what's been happening in the world, and hunt around a bit desperately for my tablet. No, I have to get my news from a newspaper.

I need to get in touch with my friend Alex, so I pick up the phone and dial his number – and I mean – I have to laboriously dial his number, using my index finger in those holes on the front of the telephone. Since it's the weekend, Alex suggests we go into Manchester for the day and I readily agree. He says to meet him at the corner of Argyle Street. OK, so all I have to do is buy a train ticket online – whoops, no, I'll have to do that at the station. I'd use my credit card, but I haven't got one and neither have my parents. Anyway, Dad reluctantly gives me five pounds and off I go to the station.

On the train I'm thinking: 'Argyle Street? Where's that?' I'd normally check it on the GPS on my phone, but naturally I can't, so when I get off the train I ask someone where it is. It's quite nice, actually – talking to someone rather than just staring fixedly at my screen.

more – click for page 2

A

B

C

Homework

If you are short on time, students can do Exercise 6 for homework. If you have done this in the class, ask students to exchange their texts with another student for them to read at home and give feedback on content and structure. Students could check if the report uses the same structure as the model. They should also decide if the solution to the outlined problem is a good one or not.

Activity idea Extension

On completion of the writing task, ask pairs to swap blog posts and read and evaluate each other's writing on the basis of **content** (How interesting was the blog post?); **organisation** (Did the blog post follow the organisation of the model text?); and **language** (Did they use a variety of adverbs?)

TH!NK more

Practice Extra
Unit 11 Master it!

Workbook
Developing Writing p105

Tests
Unit, extension and skills test 11

Warmer

Read through the information and ask students if they have read any spy novels or if they like films about spies. Ask them to discuss as a whole group.

Culture note

G. K. Chesterton (1874–1936) was an English writer. He was a prolific author, producing over 80 books, around 200 short stories and hundreds of poems. He is considered a master of paradox – he often made contradictory statements that undermined what people typically thought.

1 🔊 **11.07** Throughout most of the text Syme seems to be fearful of what the Professor might find out. He tries to hide his fear by smiling and joking, but by the end he's become angry.

2 Suggested answer: Syme manages to convince the Professor with his answers until the end of the passage.

3 The Professor probably suspects Syme because he thinks he looks like a policeman.

4 Examples include: 'shook his head' (line 18); 'The old man struck his hand angrily on the old table' (line 25); 'leaning across to him' (line 31); 'He leant his elbow far across the table, and raised his large loose hand to his ear' (lines 34 and 35); 'Professor de Worms fell back in his chair' (line 37); 'Syme jumped straight up, sending back the bench behind him with a crash' (lines 39 and 40). The author uses these words to set the scene and show the reader that there is an uncomfortable atmosphere between the two men.

5 Students' own answers

6 Put students in groups and encourage them to give examples and justify their answers. Then discuss the questions as a whole group.

Literature

THE MAN WHO WAS THURSDAY: A NIGHTMARE
BY G. K. CHESTERTON

Gabriel Syme is working for the New Detective Corps, a part of the British secret police. He has joined an organisation that the police believe is dangerous for society. There are seven people in the organisation. Each one has a code name, which is a different day of the week. After one of the organisation's meetings, Syme is followed by Professor de Worms (Friday), who wants to ask Syme some questions.

1 🔊 11.07 **Read and listen to the text and answer the following question: Which emotions does Syme experience during his conversation with the professor?**

Professor de Worms asked suddenly, without any sort of preparation—

'Are you a policeman?'

Whatever else Syme had expected, he had never expected anything so brutal and direct as this. Even his great <u>presence of mind</u> could only manage a reply by trying to sound amused and confident.

'A policeman?' he said, laughing vaguely. 'Whatever made you think of a policeman in connection with me?'

'The process was simple enough,' answered the Professor patiently. 'I thought you looked like a policeman. I think so now.'

'Did I take a policeman's hat by mistake out of the restaurant?' asked Syme, smiling wildly. 'Have I by any chance got a number stuck on to me somewhere? Have my boots got that suspicious look? Why must I be a policeman? Do, do let me be a postman.'

The old Professor shook his head with a seriousness that gave Syme no hope.

'Are you in the police service?' said the old man, ignoring all Syme's comments. 'Are you a detective?'

Syme's heart turned to stone, but his face never changed.

'Your suggestion is ridiculous,' he began.
'Why on earth – '

The old man struck his hand angrily on the old table, nearly breaking it.

'Did you hear me ask a plain question, you spy?' he <u>shrieked</u> in a high, crazy voice. 'Are you, or are you not, a police detective?'

'No!' answered Syme, like a man waiting to be <u>condemned</u>.

'You swear it,' said the old man, leaning across to him. 'You swear it! You swear it! You are not in the British police?'

He leant his elbow far across the table, and raised his large loose hand to his ear.

'I am not in the British police,' said Syme calmly.

Professor de Worms fell back in his chair.

'That's a pity,' he said, 'because I am.'

Syme jumped straight up, sending back the bench behind him with a crash.

'Because you are what?' he said angrily.
'You are what?'

'I am a policeman,' said the Professor with his first broad smile, and smiling through his spectacles. 'I am in the British police force; but as you tell me you are not in the British police force, I can only say that I ought to arrest you.' And with these words he laid on the table before Syme the same blue card which Syme had in his own waistcoat pocket, the symbol of his power from the police.

Glossary

presence of mind – the ability to think quickly in a difficult situation
shrieked – gave a short, loud, high cry, especially one produced suddenly as an expression of a powerful emotion
condemned – going to be killed as a legal punishment for a very serious crime

2 **In your opinion, how effective are the answers Syme gives to the professor's questions?**

3 **Why do you think the professor suspects Syme?**

4 **Look for examples of physical movement in the text. What words does the writer use to describe them? Why do you think he includes these words?**

5 **Do you think the professor is telling the truth when he says he is a policeman? Why/Why not?**

6 SPEAKING **Work with a partner and discuss these questions.**

1 What kind of person do you think makes a good undercover police officer or spy?
2 What do you think happens next in the story?

Warmer

Write *HERO* on the board. Ask students to get into small groups and tell them they have two minutes to think of as many adjectives as possible to describe a hero. Give them an example if necessary (e.g. *courageous*). Then ask them to choose three of their adjectives and write definitions for them (e.g. *courageous*: having or showing the ability to control one's fear when faced with danger). Put each group together with another one and ask them to take turns reading out their definitions for the other group to guess. Feed back as a group. Did any of the groups think of any very unusual words?

▶ 32 Get TH!NKing

Ask the question. Get students to compare their ideas in groups. Play the video and then ask students for feedback.

1 Elicit what the students think the photo represents. What does it show? What is most striking about the photo? What do the students think is the main idea? Can a pet become a hero? Do they know any stories of pets being heroes?

2 Give students an example of someone who is a hero for you and explain why you admire this person. Ask students to do the same in their groups. Are there common characteristics that heroes have? Could a fictional person be a hero for someone?

3 Give students examples of heroic things that people might do in everyday life (doing voluntary work, helping someone in need, showing someone support ...). Ask students what heroic things they do or have done, and elicit answers. Discuss as a group.

Objectives

Functions Expressing anticipation
Grammar Future perfect; future continuous (review); future in the past
Vocabulary Awards; success and failure
Life Competencies Avoiding temptation

Resources for this unit

All available online

Videos

- Get **TH!NK**ing: *What makes someone a hero?*
- Grammar video!: Future in the past
- Vlog: Avoiding temptation

Tests

- Unit, extension and skills test 12
- Final test

Worksheets

- Grammar and vocabulary: Basic, Standard and Extension Worksheets
- Project: Comic book heroes
- Communication: Unsung heroes
- Grammar presentation: Future in the past
- Literature Worksheets: *Nicholas Nickleby*
- Get **TH!NK**ing, Grammar video! and Life Lessons video Worksheets

Warmer

Ask: *Can you name ten superheroes? Why are they called superheroes?* Students discuss in pairs. Listen to some of their answers as a class and write any interesting vocabulary on the board.

1 Put a copy of the three pictures up on the board and do the exercise as a class before students open their books.

2 Give some examples of your own to get students started on this. If students are struggling to think of people, you could give them the categories from the next exercise as prompts.

3 Clarify that students can choose different categories if they wish. As feedback, write examples from each category on the board.

4 🔊 **12.01** Tell students not to worry about understanding every word for now, but to focus on listening to match the people with the categories.
A courage, inspiration, fighting disease, building communities, saving lives
B inspiration, building communities, helping the environment
C courage, inspiration, saving lives , fighting disease, building communities

5 **Check/clarify:** *in the public eye, nominees, Polio, paralysed, tuberculosis, epidemic.*
Ask students to try to answer the questions from memory before reading again to check.
1 B
2 C
3 A

6 Ask students to underline the part of the text which helped them decide.
1 millions of people 2 the footballers with disabilities 3 a group of runners (GoodGym) 4 people from a different generation 5 Dr Megan's family and friends
6 a group of local volunteers

7 Encourage students to go into detail in their answers and refer to the blog when they are explaining their answers.

A

B

C
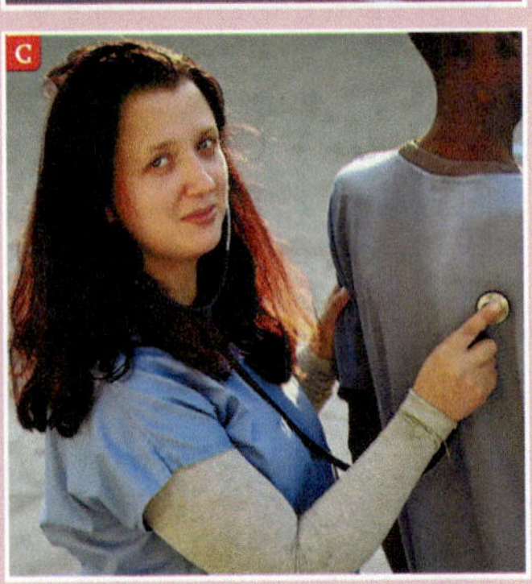

READING

1 Look at the photos. What are the people doing? Why might they be considered heroes?

2 SPEAKING Work in pairs. Make a list of five people who you think are heroes from people you know locally or at school, people from history, the news, music or sport.

3 SPEAKING Work with another pair and compare lists. Categorise your heroes according to their achievements, for example *courage, inspiration, fighting disease, building communities, helping the environment, saving lives*. Some may go in more than one category.

4 🔊 12.01 Read and listen to the online posts. Which of your categories would each of the three people fall into?

5 Match the title to each post (A–C).
1 Doing good while working out
2 Saving lives in difficult circumstances
3 Playing for a better future

6 Who or what does *they* refer to in each sentence (1–6)?
1 Until recently, *they* got this horrible disease. [*Text A*]
2 Through this sport, *they* found hope for a new start. [*Text A*]
3 *They* get fit by helping people in the community. [*Text B*]
4 When you have a conversation with them, *they* teach you a lot. [*Text B*].
5 *They* think she's crazy to give up her research position to go to Haiti. [*Text C*].
6 *They* survived tuberculosis and are now helping others. [*Text C*].

7 SPEAKING Work in pairs. Discuss the questions. Which of the three heroes in the online posts do you admire most? Why? If you could do something heroic to make a difference to other people's lives, what would it be?

126

Culture notes

Polio, or poliomyelitis, is a serious viral infection which spreads through contaminated water. It usually affects children under five and can lead to paralysis. It used to be very common worldwide until routine vaccination programmes were introduced.

Musbahu Lawan Didi is co-founder of Nigeria's Association of Polio Survivors and campaigns for the rights of those with polio. He is also the founder and President of the Para-soccer Federation of Nigeria.

Ivo Gormley is the founder of GoodGym. In 2009, he directed the documentary film *Us Now*, an exploration of participatory culture. GoodGym currently runs around 60 locations across the UK.

Tuberculosis (or TB) is a bacterial infection spread through breathing in tiny droplets from the coughs or sneezes of an infected person. It has killed more people than any other infectious disease worldwide.

Dr Megan Coffee is Clinical Assistant Professor in the Department of Medicine at New York University, USA. In 2011, she started the non-profit organisation *Ti Kay Haiti* to raise awareness, treat and stop the spread of tuberculosis and HIV.

Haiti is a country in the Caribbean Sea. The country, whose population is almost entirely descended from African slaves, won independence from France in 1804.

WANTED: real-life heroes

We're looking for ordinary people who have made a difference – people who aren't in the public eye, but who have changed the world around them for the better. Who do you think deserves to win our real-life hero trophy and £10,000 prize? Read about the first three nominees, and then let us know your views.

A rowan0719

Polio is an awful disease that, until recently, millions of people suffered from. Today, not many people get it, and there is hope that in the next ten years, this disease will have disappeared completely.

My hero is a polio survivor named Lawan Didi, from Nigeria. I'd like to put him forward for the award. He got polio at the age of three and it left him paralysed and unable to walk. Even travelling to school was difficult and he needed help from his brothers. As a teenager, he loved sport – football in particular – and in 1988, he invented the game of para-soccer with the support of six friends. It is a football-style game for people with disabilities. When they first started playing, the players crawled on the ground, but now they sit on specially adapted roller skates so the players can move faster and play better.

In addition to this, Lawan campaigns for the use of the polio vaccine. Just a few drops of vaccine can prevent a child from getting the disease. Lawan's wish is that one day we can end polio in Nigeria and across the world – he made his dream of playing soccer come true, and he believes we can make this one come true, too. Even if he doesn't win, I hope they will shortlist him for the award – he definitely deserves it.

B helpinghand_23

I'd like to nominate Ivo Gormley for a local hero award. He set up GoodGym, which is a group of runners that gets fit by helping people in the community. It's now operating in 28 areas across the UK.

I've joined a group in my area. On some days, we clear parks of leaves or paint community centres. Next week we will be planting trees in our local park. We run there, do the job and then we run back home again. The whole session takes about 90 minutes, so it's the equivalent of a session in a gym. As well as getting fit and helping out, it's a really good way of getting to meet other people in your area. By the time I get home in the evening, I will have run several kilometres and I will have helped my local community, too.

We also help the elderly in the community. I do the weekly shopping for an elderly lady called Edith. I do her shopping and then run to her house. I stay and chat for half an hour and then I run home again. We chat about all kinds of things and we have some very interesting conversations. Now it's turned into a friendship and I can talk to her about anything. There is so much you can learn from people from a different generation.

Ivo Gormley should be in the running for the award, and I hope that by the time you read this article, he will have won.

C w_raven_peak

My candidate for the competition is Dr Megan Coffee. I don't know if you remember, but there was a terrible earthquake in the Caribbean country of Haiti in 2010. Many people needed urgent medical care and there was a risk of a tuberculosis epidemic spreading across the country. Dr Megan Coffee, an infectious disease specialist, got on a plane to Haiti to help. She gave up a research position at Berkeley in the US and went to work in Haiti for no pay. Her family and friends still think she's a little mad for choosing Haiti over Berkeley. I think it was very brave of her to go there in spite of the danger, and she has inspired me to think about volunteering. In September, after I graduate, I will be going to Ghana to work in a hospital there.

A group of local volunteers, many of whom survived tuberculosis because of Dr Megan, is now helping to take care of other infected men, women and children. She has inspired so many people and that's why I'm voting for her.

Train to TH!NK

Appropriate sampling

In order to reach a relevant and informed conclusion, it's important to conduct research. However, this research should always be done responsibly. One danger is that the research sample is not entirely representative. For example, research might claim that 90 percent of people believe that the government should give a lifetime achievement award to the manager of their country's national football team. If the survey was based on the views of the readers of a footballing magazine, we cannot claim that this result represents all people.

8 **Would these people agree or disagree with this statement?**
'We need to protect the habitats of our wildlife.'

building developer | farmer
member of the national bird society

9 WRITING **Work in pairs. You have been asked to find a *Hero of Our Times*. To do your research responsibly, who would you ask to choose the hero? Choose five people who are representative of the population and write a list of questions to ask them.**

10 SPEAKING **Work in pairs. How would the answers differ across the different people in your list? Discuss with your partner.**

PRONUNCIATION
Shifting word stress Go to page 138.

8 Before students do the exercise, ask: *Do you believe all the information on the news or in newspapers? What about statistics in news articles, for example, if you read that 80 percent of students love doing homework, would you believe the information? Why (not)?* Listen to some of their ideas as a class.

9 Clarify that if students want their survey to be representative of the whole population, they should ask a variety of people questions.

10 Give a couple of your own ideas as examples.

Pronunciation
Shifting word stress

Student's Book p138

Homework

Ask students to research a 'hero' from around the world or from their local community. They can find a picture and write a description of the person and what they did. They can use the blog posts on page 127 to help them. Students can present their person to the class in the next lesson.

Critical TH!NKing
Solving problems and making decisions
Gathers information from reputable sources to understand different perspectives on an issue.

Emotional Development
Showing empathy for the feelings of others
Shows understanding of other people's perspectives and feelings.

Critical TH!NKing
Evaluating ideas and arguments
Gives reasons for an arguments plausibility.

TH!NK more

Worksheets
Project Comic book heroes
Communication Unsung heroes
Get TH!NKing *What makes someone a hero?*

Warmer

Write *Awards* on the board and elicit a definition. Ask students: *Have you ever won an award?* If you have access to the internet, show students a clip of an awards ceremony. Ask: *What was the process before the person was given the award? Who decided this person would be given an award? How did they decide?* Listen to some of their answers in open class and write any interesting words on the board.

1 Before students open their books, copy the three sentences onto the board and ask students to explain which tense is used in each. Students work together to describe when we use the two tenses. During feedback, draw a timeline to show the difference between the future perfect and future continuous.

Future perfect

I ***will have done*** *my homework by 8pm.*

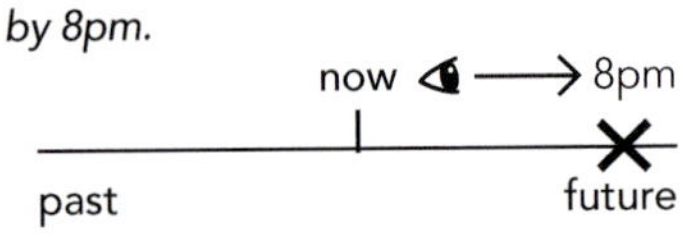

Future continuous

I ***will be doing*** *my homework this evening.*

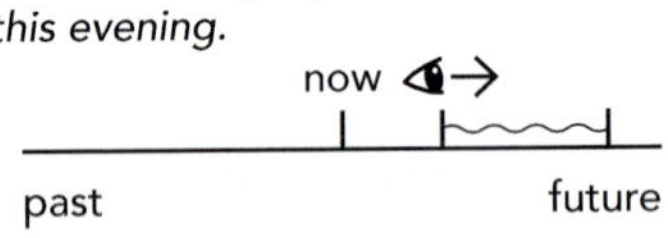

1 future perfect 2 future perfect
3 future continuous
RULE: 1 present participle
2 past participle

2 Go through the first item to make sure students are clear on what they have to do.

1 'll have gained 2 will have had; 'll have made 3 'll have done; 'll be waiting 4 'll have bought; 'll … be driving

Workbook p108

GRAMMAR
Future perfect; future continuous (review)

1 Read the sentences from the online posts on page 127. Which are examples of the future continuous, and which are examples of the future perfect? Then complete the rule with *present participle* and *past participle*.

1 In the next ten years, this disease **will have disappeared** completely.
2 By the time I get home in the evening, I **will have run** several kilometres.
3 In September, after I graduate, I **will be going** to Ghana to work in a hospital there.

> **RULE:** We use *will be* + [1]… to talk about actions that will be in progress at or around a time in the future.
> We use *will have* + [2]… to talk about actions that will be finished by a certain time in the future.

2 Complete the sentences using the future continuous or future perfect of the verbs in brackets.

1 The project will help students who want to study abroad. By the time those students return to their home countries, they … important insights into other cultures. (gain)
2 By the end of next year, 2,000 young people from all over the world … the chance to live abroad and they … new friends. (have, make)
3 A week from today, we … our exams and we … for the results. (do, wait)
4 A Do you think he … his new car by the time he comes to see you?
B No, I think he … still … his old car. (buy, drive)

→ workbook page 108

VOCABULARY
Awards

3 Choose the correct options to complete the definitions.

1 **nominate someone:** *show a preference for / officially suggest* someone for an honour, a position, a job or an election
2 **put oneself/someone forward for something:** *suggest / search for* oneself/someone for other people to consider
3 **vote for someone:** make your *choice / recommendation*, typically by marking a paper or by raising your hand in a meeting
4 **elect someone:** *choose / reject* someone for an official position
5 **campaign for something/someone:** organise a series of activities to try to *help / convince* people to do something or support someone
6 **be in the running for something:** *have a chance of winning / be likely to lose* a competition
7 **shortlist people:** select a(n) *increased / reduced* number of candidates for final consideration for something

4 Complete the sentences with the correct form of the words and phrases from Exercise 3.

1 Jack's decided to *shortlist me / put me forward* for the position.
2 Anna *is in the running / voted* for the award. I think she's got a good chance of winning.
3 My class is *nominating / campaigning* for our Maths teacher to win the Teacher of the Year prize by putting up posters around the school.
4 Gemma's cat cartoon has been *nominated / campaigned* for best animated film. I hope she wins!
5 Mehmet's among the five people that have been *in the running / shortlisted* for the book award. He now stands a good chance of winning the prize.
6 Who is Tim *voting for / electing* in the elections?
7 Amy's class *elected / shortlisted* her as their class prefect and she's done a brilliant job so far.

→ workbook page 110

SPEAKING

5 Imagine your class is planning to give awards to the teachers at your school. What three awards do you think should be given? Make notes.

most inspiring teacher
best public speaker
funniest teacher, etc.

6 Work in pairs. Compare ideas and agree on just one award category together.

7 Share your idea for an award with the class. Hold a class vote and choose a winner for each award category.

3 Check/clarify: *honour, consideration.*
1 officially suggest 2 suggest 3 choice 4 choose 5 convince 6 have a chance of winning 7 reduced

4 1 put me forward 2 is in the running 3 campaigning 4 nominated 5 shortlisted 6 voting for 7 elected

Workbook p110

5–6 Give students time to work individually to think of more examples of awards that could be given to some of the teachers before working in pairs to find a single category.

7 Write the students' ideas on the board and ask them to work in pairs or small groups to decide which teacher should win each award. Hold a class vote for each award and nominate individuals to give reasons for their choices.

TH!NK more

Workbook
Grammar p108, Ex.1–5
Vocabulary p110, Ex.1

Worksheets
Grammar Worksheets 12
Vocabulary Worksheets 12

Activity idea Fast finishers

Ask students to work in pairs to place the expressions in Exercise 3 on a timeline from *put someone forward* to *elect*. Listen to some of their ideas after feedback.

8 12.03
He did it to raise money for charity.

9 **12.03 Check/clarify:** *incurable, cancer, passed away, bowel cancer, legacy.*
1 Medicine 2 cancer gene 3 feel sorry 4 (bucket) list 5 public speaking 6 politicians 7 Facebook page 8 heroic

Culture notes

Wembley Stadium is a football stadium located in London and hosts England's home matches, live music concerts and other sporting events. Sports have been played there since 1880 but the first stadium was built in 1923. In 2003, it was demolished and a new stadium was built on the same site, which opened in 2007. It has a capacity of 90,000 and is the second largest stadium in Europe.

Teenage Cancer Trust was established in 1990 by a group of women who fundraised for a children's intensive care heart unit at Guy's Hospital, London. It was set up to provide a 'teenage environment' to help young people with cancer who were, up until then, being treated alongside older people on an adult oncology ward. In 1990, Teenage Cancer Trust's first specialist cancer unit at the Middlesex Hospital in London was officially opened.

The Neon Brotherhood are a group of 40 people who recorded a single titled *Hope Ain't a Bad Thing* as a fundraiser for Teenage Cancer Trust in memory of Stephen Sutton. Within 24 hours of its release, the song reached Number 2 in the UK iTunes Charts.

10 **Check/clarify:** *adversity, pursue.* Allow students to use dictionaries to confirm answers if necessary. Check answers as a class, but do not discuss meaning at this stage.
1 a 2 h 3 f 4 d 5 g 6 c 7 b 8 e

Re-create the table on the board for completion during feedback. Say the expressions for students to repeat and check pronunciation.
Succeed: fulfil an ambition, overcome adversity, pull off a victory
Fail: (one's plans) fall through, fail spectacularly, give up on one's dreams
Neither: be recognised as, pursue one's dreams

LISTENING

8 12.03 **You're going to listen to a presentation about the young man in the photos. He did a skydive, but not just for fun. For what other reason do you think he did it? Discuss. Then listen and check.**

9 12.03 **Listen again. Complete each sentence with one or two words.**

1 Stephen did very well at school and had wanted to study ... at university.
2 Stephen's mother feared that his father had passed the ... on to their son.
3 Stephen was shocked and saddened by his diagnosis, but decided not to ... for himself.
4 Stephen came up with a ... of 46 things to do while he still could.
5 Stephen wanted to write a book, have a go at ... in front of lots of people, break a world record and see a football match live at Wembley.
6 Lots of people from all over the world supported Stephen's cause, including well-known actors, sports people and ... .
7 Stephen's mother keeps his ... updated.
8 A local band recorded a song, for which the inspiration was Stephen's ... life.

VOCABULARY
Success and failure

10 **Match the sentence halves. Then copy and complete the table with the expressions in italics. Use the infinitive form of the verbs.**

1 When it was announced that John would play the lead role in *Hamlet*,
2 Readers often feel inspired by people
3 Dede *is recognised as* one of the
4 They had great hopes for the project, but *their plans*
5 When he learned about his illness, he wasn't
6 If you really want *to pursue your dreams*, you
7 It's ironic that he believed he was the best and
8 My team wasn't playing well, but they still

a his lifelong *ambition* of performing on stage *had been fulfilled*.
b then *failed* so *spectacularly*.
c mustn't waste any time and you have to study hard.
d *fell through* at the last minute.
e managed to *pull off a* last-minute *victory*.
f most talented singers in our country.
g prepared to *give up on his dreams*.
h who manage to *overcome adversity*.

Succeed	Fail	Neither
fulfil an ambition		

11 SPEAKING **Work in groups. Think about these questions and note down your answers. Then compare your ideas with your classmates.**

1 Would you rather pursue big dreams and risk failing spectacularly, or not dare to 'think big' at all?
2 Think of someone who has managed to overcome adversity. What adversity did they overcome? What did they achieve? What personal qualities helped them to succeed?
3 If you could pursue only one dream for your future, what would it be?

12 WRITING **You've decided to pursue one of your dreams. Write a diary entry detailing your plans and how you feel. Include at least three expressions from Exercise 10.**

→ workbook page 110

11 If you want to give students extended speaking practice, ask them to repeat the exercise with a different partner. They can improve their answers from the first attempt.

12 Students can write their diary entry in Exercise 12 for homework. Give an example answer of your own to get them started.

Workbook p110

Homework

Ask students to choose one of the heroes in the pictures on page 126 and write six sentences using the future continuous and future perfect.
For example: *At 3 pm I will be playing football.*

Activity idea Fast finishers

Ask students to close their books and write as many of the collocations from Exercise 10 as they can remember before opening their books to check.

TH!NK more

Workbook
Listening p114, Ex.1–2
Vocabulary p110, Ex.2–3
Vocabulary Extra p111, Ex.1–3

Reading

Warmer

To revise the awards vocabulary from the last lesson, ask students to take turns to read out one of the definitions from Exercise 3 on page 128. Their partner has to say the word.

A: to officially suggest someone

B: to nominate someone

1 Before students do the exercise, ask: *Can you think of five reasons why people would write a letter?* Students work with a partner to make a list. Listen to some of their ideas in open class. Ask: *Why might somebody write a letter to a magazine?* Nominate individuals to give answers.

Martin was helped by lots of people and Mandy helped lots of people.

2 **12.04 Check/clarify:** *frame, anonymously, burden, (homeless) shelters, single mother, make ends meet, coupons.*

Encourage students to underline the parts of the text that helped them find their answers.

1 Matt was trying to raise money for an operation to help him walk.
2 Matt gave his money away to a young boy, Jamie, so he could have an operation to help him walk.
3 Martin became homeless because he lost his job.
4 Tara set up a GoFundMe page to raise awareness of Martin's story.
5 Mandy started collecting coupons to help her mum save money on food shopping.
6 She donated all the food she'd bought to a charity which helps disadvantaged families.

3 Allow students six to eight minutes to prepare their role plays. Monitor to make sure all students are on task. Encourage students to remain in character and add detail to their discussions. In order to make conversations sound more authentic, ask students to repeat their conversations with either the same partner or a new partner.

I just wrote to say … THANK YOU!

In our special Saturday column, we give our readers an opportunity to thank someone who's done something special for them. Someone who they never managed to say thank you to at the time. Send us your stories. If we choose yours, we'll send you a £30 book voucher.

READING

1 **Read the article quickly. Who was helped by lots of people and who helped lots of people? Was it Matt, Martin or Mandy?**

2 12.04 **Read the article again and listen. Answer the questions.**

1 Why was Matt trying to raise some money?
2 Why did Matt decide to give all his money away?
3 How did Martin become homeless?
4 What did Tara do to help Martin?
5 Why did Mandy start collecting supermarket coupons?
6 Why did Sally call her a 'generous young woman'?

3 ROLE PLAY **Work in pairs. Choose one of the stories. Role play a conversation between the person who wrote in and the person they want to thank.**

A ticket to walk

When Matt was 12 years old, he was very badly injured in a cycling accident. Two years after the accident, he began raising money for an operation which could help him to walk again. Some time later, he read a story in a newspaper. It was about a five-year-old boy called Jamie, who had only ever walked with the aid of a frame. Jamie's parents were raising money for an operation to help their son walk without the frame.

Matt knew how it felt not to be able to walk and he felt sorry for the little boy. He contacted the newspaper and he arranged for all the money he had raised to be given to Jamie's parents. He did this anonymously. Jamie's parents were able to take Jamie to America where he had the operation. Today he walks to school and he plays with friends – thanks to the remarkable generosity of this now 29-year-old stranger.

'I felt that Jamie had a better chance of walking than I did, and I wanted to help him,' said Matt. 'Hearing that Jamie could walk was amazing. It made giving the money away worth it.'

A big thank you to Matt from Jamie and his parents. They are eternally grateful to you. It was going to take them years to raise the money. Then you gave it to them. Thank you, Matt.

The streets are paved with notes

New York accountant, Martin Goldberg, had some bad luck which resulted in him losing his job and then his home. He didn't want to be a burden on his relatives, so he moved to another town where he spent seven years living on the street and in shelters. He thought he was going to spend the rest of his life homeless. Then, one day, he found a backpack containing money totalling more than $50,000.

Martin decided not to keep this windfall. Instead, he handed it all to the police. They returned it to the grateful owner and the story of the 'good Samaritan' was reported in a local newspaper.

A stranger, Tara White, read the story and she set up a GoFundMe page to raise a reward for Martin. Donations flooded in from around the world, and the page raised $120,000 in no time. This was enough for Martin to rent a house and sort his life out.

Martin is very grateful to Tara and he has asked us to say that he would love to be able to thank you in person one day.

130

The coupon kid

Mandy Eastwood from Streatham in South London is not your usual 16-year-old. Last year, her single mother Hannah, 43, was struggling to make ends meet on her nurse's salary, so Mandy started finding and collecting supermarket coupons. She saved her mother £2,000 at the supermarket that year. That Christmas, she decided that she would like to help other families, too.

'I didn't have any particular people in mind. I just wanted to help as many people as I could,' she said. 'And I wanted to show them that it's possible to shop very cheaply if you know how.'

She carefully collected 465 coupons for her local supermarket. Then she filled three shopping trolleys with discount food, including meat, vegetables, fruit, cheese and desserts.

'I didn't know exactly what the total would be,' she said. 'It's hard to work it out in your head. I was very surprised when it came to just 10p. That's a saving of £565.10!'

Mandy donated the contents of all three trolleys to a charity which provides food to disadvantaged families.

'She's a very generous young woman,' said Sally, who works for the charity. 'Her act of kindness has helped a lot of families and they would all like to thank her.'

Culture notes

GoFundMe is an American for-profit crowdfunding platform founded in 2010.

Crowdfunding is a method of raising capital through the collective efforts of friends, family, customers and individual investors. Although it has more recently come to prominence via new technology and social media, the principles have a history which dates back centuries. Modern crowdfunding sites give the entrepreneur a single platform to showcase the project and present a pitch. They also have greater reach and efficiency than traditional forms of fundraising. There are generally three types of crowdfunding – donation based, rewards based and equity based.

TH!NK more

Workbook
Reading p112, Ex.1–4

▶ 33 Grammar video! Future in the past

4 To check understanding of these uses of comparatives, say some sentences, some of which are grammatically incorrect, and ask students to decide if they are correct or incorrect. For example, *I was sure that they would win the game.* (correct), *I thought he would going to pass the exam* (incorrect).
RULE: 1 going to 2 would 3 was 4 wasn't 5 would

5 1 would; be 2 was going to be 3 wouldn't be able/wasn't going to be able 4 were going to meet 5 would/was going to snow 6 was going to be/would be

6 During feedback, ask check questions to clarify understanding. For example: *Did Kirsty get home early? Why not?*
1 She wasn't going to leave the country, but then it became too dangerous to stay.
2 He thought he would teach the children to read and write, but he hadn't really thought it through. / He was going to teach the children to read and write, but he hadn't really thought it through.
3 They were going to use football to give the boys more confidence, but then they decided to set up basketball teams instead.
4 She was going to set up a charity to promote the values of tolerance and unity, but so far she hasn't been able to do so.
5 They said they would/were going to offer free healthcare to children, but then it became clear that the government had other priorities.

Workbook p109

Get it Right!
Future in the past

Student's Book p134

7 Monitor to make sure students are using *was going to* and *would* correctly.

8 1 in the public eye 2 in particular 3 in spite of the 4 in no time 5 in mind

9 **Check/clarify:** *soft drinks.*
1 the public eye 2 spite of 3 mind 4 particular 5 no time

Workbook p110

GRAMMAR
Future in the past

Grammar video ▶33

4 **Read the sentences from the article and then complete the rule.**

1 It **was going to** take them years to raise the money.
2 He thought he **was going to** spend the rest of his life homeless.
3 I didn't know exactly what the total **would** be.

RULE: When we want to talk about the future as seen from the past, we use *was/were* [1]… or [2]… .
When we talk about actions that were planned for the future but then our plans changed, we often use [3]… / *were* or [4]… / *weren't going to* … . For example: *I was going to go out last night but I was too tired in the end.* We use *was/were(n't) going to* when a plan was definite.
We use [5]… or *wouldn't* when a plan was less likely to happen or when it was just a possibility or idea.

5 **Complete the sentences with the correct form of the verb in brackets. Use *was/were going to* or *would* to talk about the future in the past. Sometimes there's more than one correct answer.**

1 Last Friday, our teacher announced that the grammar test … probably … on Tuesday, but that she hadn't decided yet. (be)
2 There … a match on Saturday. Then it rained and the match was cancelled. (be)
3 Lily just texted to say she thought she … to come to your party, unfortunately. (not be able)
4 You … Sarah. Why didn't you? (meet)
5 I knew it was going to be cold, but I didn't think it … . (snow)
6 I didn't expect any problems with the test, but I didn't realise it … so easy. (be)

6 **Rewrite the sentences using *was/were going to* or *would*.**

0 Kirsty planned to get home early, but then she had to stay late at work.
Kirsty was going to get home early, but then she had to stay late at work.
1 She didn't intend to leave the country, but then it became too dangerous to stay.
2 He had an idea to teach the children to read and write, but he hadn't really thought it through.
3 Their plan was to use football to give the boys more confidence, but then they decided to set up basketball teams instead.
4 She intended to set up a charity to promote the values of tolerance and unity, but so far she hasn't been able to do so.
5 They talked about offering free healthcare to children, but then it became clear that the government had other priorities.

→ workbook page 109

SPEAKING

7 **Work in pairs. Think about the last two weeks. What things were you going to do that you didn't do? Ask and answer questions and say why you didn't do them.**

I was going to study for the Maths test.
Why didn't you?
I had too much work to do for English so I didn't have time. What about you?
I was going to have my hair cut.
Why didn't you?
I missed my appointment.

WordWise
Expressions with *in*

8 **Complete these sentences from the unit so far with phrases from the list.**

in mind | in no time | in particular
in spite of | in the public eye

1 We're looking for ordinary people who aren't … .
2 As a teenager, he loved sport – football … .
3 I think it was very brave of her to go there … the danger.
4 Donations flooded in from around the world, and the page raised $120,000 … .
5 I didn't have any particular people … .

9 **Choose the correct options.**

1 Not all famous people like being in *mind / the public eye.*
2 We got there on time in *spite of / no time* the terrible traffic.
3 I want to go somewhere tonight, but I haven't got anywhere special in *particular / mind.*
4 I really love soft drinks, lemonade in *mind / particular.*
5 I'll have this work finished in *no time / spite of*, and then we can go out.

→ workbook page 110

Homework

Ask students to change the 'was going to' forms in the sentences in Exercise 5 from affirmative to negative (or negative to affirmative) and make any other necessary changes to the sentences so that they make sense. For example:
1 Last Friday, our teacher announced that the grammar test ***probably wasn't going to be*** *on Tuesday but she hadn't decided yet.*

Activity idea Extension

Do a teacher–student role play. Ask students to write sentences containing mistakes with future in the past forms. Students pass their sentences to a partner. The partner has to act as the teacher, explain the problems with the sentences and elicit the correct answer from the student.

TH!NK more

Practice Extra
Unit 12 Practise it!

Workbook
Grammar p109, Ex.6–8
WordWise p110, Ex.4

Worksheets
Grammar Worksheets 12
Grammar presentation Future in the past
Grammar video! Future in the past

Warmer

Revise expressions with *in* by giving students the sentences in Exercises 8 and 9 on page 131 with a beep in the gap and eliciting the expression with *in*. For example,

Not all famous people like being ***in*** *(beep).* – ***in the public eye***

As a teenager, he loved sport – football ***in*** *(beep).* – ***in particular***

I think it was very brave of her to go there ***in*** *(beep) the danger.* – ***in spite of***

Donations flooded in from around the world, and the page raised $120,000 ***in*** *(beep).* – ***in no time***

I didn't have any particular people ***in*** *(beep).* – ***in mind***

1 🔊 **12.05** Tell students to cover the dialogue and discuss the question in pairs before listening to check their answers.
They are going to Brighton. There's a problem with the bus.

2 🔊 **12.05**
1 They took the bus because it is cheaper, more comfortable and you can see the countryside.
2 They want to see the sea, have a look around and eat fish and chips and ice cream.
3 Meg uses an app to get a car to pick them up and take them to Brighton.

3 To encourage speed-reading, you could do this as a race and ask students to find the expressions as quickly as possible. At the end of the exercise, listen to some of the students' ideas and encourage open-class discussion.
1 Jake 2 Meg 3 Meg 4 Jake 5 Meg 6 Jake

4 During feedback, point out the use of question marks and exclamation marks and say the expressions for students to repeat.
1 for ages 2 do you fancy 3 What's not to like 4 How; is that 5 the question is 6 How should I know

DEVELOPING SPEAKING

1 🔊 12.05 **Look at the photos. Where do you think the two people are going and what problem do they have? Read, listen and check your ideas.**

Jake: This is brilliant. I haven't been on a day trip for ages. And Brighton! I'm really looking forward to seeing the sea again. We can't get there soon enough!
Meg: And I'm glad we took the bus, not the train: cheaper, more comfortable, you can see the countryside – what's not to like? Oh, I'm so excited!
Jake: Me too. Remind me what time we get there?
Meg: 10.30. Gives us a couple of hours to look around before we eat. What do you fancy having for lunch?
Jake: Well, at the English seaside, it has to be fish and chips, doesn't it?
Meg: Ha, that's right! I'm dying to have some ice cream, too. Well, perhaps I should avoid that temptation! Wait a minute – the bus is pulling over. But it's non-stop. Why have we stopped, Jake?
Jake: How should I know? Hang on, the driver's going to say something.
Driver: I'm afraid there's a problem with the bus and I can't fix it. They'll send another one to take you all to Brighton, but it won't be here for a couple of hours. Sorry!
Meg: Oh no! How unlucky is that? Now we won't get there until after lunch!
Jake: The question is, how do we not let this ruin our day out?
Meg: I know. My mum gave me some spending money for today, and I think I know a good way to use it. Just let me open this app. There we go. I can get a car here in five minutes, and it'll get us to Brighton in another twenty. Costs a bit, but that's what money's for, right?
Jake: Meg, you're my hero! Thanks for doing that. And the fish and chips are on me, OK? And the ice cream, too!

2 🔊 12.05 **Read and listen to the dialogue again. Answer the questions.**
1 Why did they choose to travel by bus?
2 What plans do they have for Brighton?
3 How does Meg solve their problem?

Phrases for fluency

3 **Find these expressions in the dialogue. Who says them? How do you say them in your language?**
1 ... for ages.
2 What's not to like?
3 ... do you fancy ...?
4 How should I know?
5 How [unlucky] is that?
6 The question is, ...?

4 **Use the expressions in Exercise 3 to complete the dialogues.**
1 A Do you know where Jenny is?
B Sorry, I haven't seen her ... .
2 A Let's go out somewhere.
B OK. Where ... going?
3 A I love those trousers.
B Me too. They're comfortable and such a great colour! ... ?
4 A *Bring Me The Horizon* is on TV tonight.
B I know! ... fantastic ... ?
5 A We've missed the last train.
B That's right. So, ... , how are we going to get home?
6 A Why hasn't she got here yet?
B ... ? Call and ask her.

FUNCTIONS
Expressing anticipation

5 **Which of these are said by a) Jake, b) Meg, c) neither of them?**
1 This time tomorrow, I'll be ...
2 It's going to be amazing.
3 I'm so excited!
4 I'm really looking forward to ...
5 I'm dying to ...
6 We can't get there soon enough!

6 SPEAKING **Work in pairs. Talk about some of the things you've got planned for the future that you're eager to do. Use the phrases above.**

WRITING

7 **Write your own entry (150–200 words) for the article on page 130. It can be a true story or one you've made up. For example, you could imagine that you were homeless like Martin and somebody like Tara gave you the money to sort your life out. Think about and make notes on:**
- who you want to thank
- what they did for you.

132

5 1 c 2 c 3 b 4 a 5 b 6 a

6 To extend the discussion, tell students they get a point each time they use one of the phrases in their discussion.

7 If you are short on time, students can do the preparation in class, and complete the writing at home. They should organise their work to follow a similar format to the examples on page 130.

Activity idea Extension

Disappearing sentences: you'll need to write out the dialogues in Exercise 4 on the board or project them on the IWB. Make A/B pairs so that half of the class are A and half are B. Students practise the conversations in pairs. Cover a small section of the dialogue, beginning from the right-hand side of the screen or board. Students repeat the dialogues in their same A/B pairings trying to remember the whole thing, including the parts they can no longer see. Cover more and more of the dialogue, with students practising at each stage, until eventually nothing is left on the board. Ask for volunteers to perform for the class or have all As and all Bs perform in unison. This activity involving lots of repetition is a fun way for students to memorise useful lexical chunks.

TH!NK more

Workbook
Phrases for fluency p114

Life Competencies

Warmer

Write *avoiding temptation* on the board and elicit the meaning in this context (*stop yourself doing something that you probably shouldn't do even though you want to*). Ask students to give themselves a mark for their ability to avoid temptation between 0 and 10. Does their ability to do this change depending on who they are interacting with or what the temptation is?

▶ 34 Life Lessons: Avoiding temptation

1 ▶ **34** Ask students to compare their ideas with a partner.
Will is tempted to eat a chocolate bar. He doesn't resist the temptation well at all because he eats the chocolate bar.

2 ▶ **34**
1 wind up his little brother; check his messages at the dinner table; copy his friend's homework
2 Big temptations: hurting his little brother; cheating in an exam; stealing from a shop.
Small temptations: watching too much TV; drinking milk from the bottle; eating chocolate.
3 Students' own answers

3 Elicit at least five different types of temptations, big and small, from students. Then ask them to rank them in terms of size or seriousness. If it helps the discussion, students can match the temptations to the pie charts, e.g. the bigger the slice, the bigger the temptation.

4 **Check/clarify:** *glance, resume.*

5 At the end of the exercise, listen to some of the students' ideas and encourage open-class discussion.
1 Situation 1: The temptation is to cheat by looking at the other student's answers; Situation 2: The temptation is to not say anything and keep the change; Situation 3: The temptation is to eat the chocolate.
2–4 Students' own answers

6 Give students four or five minutes to think about their questions.

LIFE COMPETENCIES

Temptation is when you really want to do something but you know you shouldn't do it. Temptation is hard to resist, but if we give in to it, we have to live with the consequences.

1 ▶ 34 **Watch the vlog. What is Will being tempted by? How well does he resist temptation?**

2 ▶ 34 **Watch the vlog again and make notes on the following:**
1 three things he wishes he could do
2 the examples he gives of big and small temptations
3 the consequences that would have happened if he had given in

3 SPEAKING **Work in pairs. Decide what temptations might fit these pie charts.**

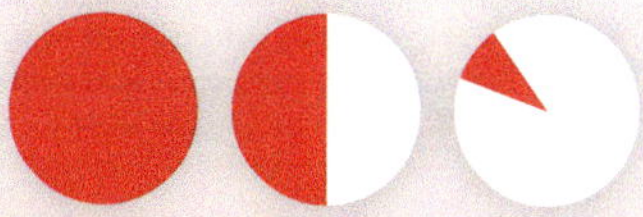

TIPS ON AVOIDING TEMPTATION

- Temptation is a part of everyday life, but it can range in seriousness. Borrowing your brother's T-shirt without asking is not the same as stealing one from a shop.
- Think about the consequences of giving in to a temptation. Would it really make you feel any better?
- Occasionally, it is only natural to give in to a small temptation. But when you do, just try to enjoy it!

4 **Read the quiz and choose your answers.**

1 **You are struggling in your end-of-year Maths test. You are sitting next to the cleverest kid in the class. Her answers are clearly visible on the page. What do you do?**
a Copy down all her answers.
b Glance occasionally at her answers just to check your answers.
c Don't look at her answers, even though it means you'll probably fail the test.

2 **When buying a magazine for £2, you're given change for £10 instead of the £5 you gave the assistant. What do you do?**
a Put the money in your pocket and walk away.
b Spend time thinking about what you should do, then decide it's too late to go back in now.
c Go back to the assistant, show her the mistake and return the money.

3 **You have decided to get yourself healthier. This means running every day and avoiding all fattening food. When visiting your grandmother, she gives you chocolate. What do you do?**
a Eat it! You don't want to upset her and you can resume your diet tomorrow.
b Take it and decide that you will reward yourself with a piece from it every time you go for a run.
c Thank your grandmother, but explain your situation and ask her to take it back.

5 SPEAKING **Work in pairs. Compare your answers.**
1 Identify the temptation in each situation 1–3.
2 Discuss how you might feel if you chose a different option a–c in each situation.
3 Which of situations 1–3 is the least serious? Why?
4 Which is the most serious? Why?

Me and my world

6 WRITING **Write a new question for the quiz.**
1 Think of a situation where you were tempted to do something wrong. Write this situation as a question.
2 Write down three possible options – a, b and c.

7 SPEAKING **Work in groups of five or six.**
1 Take turns to pick a new quiz question at random and read it out to the group.
2 Discuss the options for each question.
3 Finally, try to guess who wrote the question and ask them to talk more about the situation and what they did.

7 Monitor and prompt students to keep talking, but as this is a fluency activity, do not interrupt to correct mistakes.

Homework

Ask students to interview members of their family, friends or neighbours about their temptations and how they avoid them. As a follow-up, students can present any good ideas for how to avoid temptation in the next class.

Activity idea Mixed-ability

In Exercise 6, stronger students write two questions. Weaker students could work in pairs.

TH!NK more

Practice Extra
Unit 12 Master it!

Worksheets
Life Lessons: Avoiding temptation

Tests
Unit, extension and skills test 12
Final test

1 Remind students we can use *get* in passive sentences only with active verbs.
1 (correct)
2 (correct)
3 Which road user is more liked – the cyclist or the motorist?
4 After a week at the sports camp I'm sure we'll be exhausted by all this exercise.
5 Mrs Summers was disappointed with her son. He had promised to give her a lift to the station, but he didn't turn up.
6 The film was enjoyed by all who watched it.

2 Remind students that they have to rewrite them using causative *have* so that the new sentences suggest that somebody else did the action for us.
1 We are going to have our house painted.
2 Jenny has just had her hair cut.
3 I had my bike stolen from outside the school gates.
4 Tony hasn't had the roof fixed on his house yet.
5 I had my passport checked five times going through airport security.
6 I need to go to the dry cleaner's to have my favourite jacket cleaned.

3 Do the example in open class and ask students to complete the esto f the exercise in pairs.
1 Jack and Chloe were going to eat at the Italian restaurant, but they changed their minds and went to the Chinese instead.
2 (correct)
3 (correct)
4 If I'd known I was going to fail so spectacularly, I wouldn't have bothered trying!
5 Did Mike really think that I would invite him to my party?
6 Sally and Jim were going to go on a round-the-world trip, but their plans fell through when Sally's father fell ill.

GET IT RIGHT! UNITS 11 & 12

Passive with *get*

Learners often use *get* in passives, using it with stative verbs or adjectives where *be* should actually be used.
✓ *The baby **was** loved by its parents.*
✗ *The baby ~~got~~ loved by its parents.*

1 Rewrite the incorrect sentences.

0 Tom gets thought to have a bit of a temper, but he's actually quite calm.
Tom is thought to have a bit of a temper, but he's actually quite calm.
1 Anthony got knocked over by a cyclist the other day.
2 The fence got broken by a motorist who crashed his car.
3 Which road user gets more liked – the cyclist or the motorist?
4 After a week at the sports camp, I'm sure we'll get exhausted by all this exercise.
5 Mrs Summers got disappointed with her son. He had promised to give her a lift to the station, but he didn't turn up.
6 The film got enjoyed by all who watched it.

Causative *have*

Learners sometimes use active voice for actions that should be expressed using causative *have*.
✓ *I took my car to the garage to **have it repaired**.*
✗ *I took my car to the garage to ~~repair it~~.*

2 Rewrite each sentence using causative *have*.

0 Our car broke down and we repaired it.
Our car broke down and we had it repaired.
1 We are going to paint our house.
2 Jenny has just cut her hair.
3 Someone stole my bike from outside the school gates.
4 Tony hasn't fixed the roof of his house yet.
5 They checked my passport five times going through airport security.
6 I need to go to the dry cleaner's to clean my favourite jacket.

Future in the past

Learners often make errors when referring to the future from a past perspective, using *will* instead of *would* or *is/are going to* instead of *was/were going to*.
✓ *I thought I **would** be sick.*
✗ *I thought I ~~will~~ be sick.*
✓ *Everyone believed he **was going to** leave school, but he didn't.*
✗ *Everyone believed he ~~is going to~~ leave school, but he didn't.*

3 Rewrite the incorrect sentences.

0 I thought that I am going to be sick.
I thought that I was going to be sick.
1 Jack and Chloe are going to eat at the Italian restaurant, but they changed their minds and went to the Chinese instead.
2 You said there would be plenty of legroom, but there wasn't.
3 He is going to leave school, but not until he's taken his exams.
4 If I'd known I am going to fail so spectacularly, I wouldn't have bothered trying!
5 Did Mike really think that I will invite him to my party?
6 Sally and Jim are going to go on a round-the-world trip, but their plans fell through when Sally's father fell ill.

134

1 **Check/clarify:** *human endeavour, strive, provoke, bricks.*
In C1 Advanced Reading and Use of English Part 8, candidates have to read a longer text or up to six shorter ones, and ten questions. Candidates have to match the specific information in the text with the questions. This part of the exam tests whether candidates can recognise opinion and attitude and locate specific detail.

Encourage your students to do the following when they approach this task:

- Skim the text to find out the topic and general meaning.
- Read each question carefully and identify what information to look for in the text. It is often useful to underline key words in the questions.
- Check that the answer to the question is reflected in the text.
- Do not select an answer just by matching a word in the question with a word in the text.
- Check that the answer is a paraphrase of the whole question, not just one part of it.
- After choosing an answer, check the other options and decide why they are wrong.

1D 2B 3A 4E 5D 6C 7A 8C 9B 10A

Workbook p115

TOWARDS C1 Advanced

READING AND USE OF ENGLISH

Part 8: Multiple matching

→ workbook page 115

1 **You are going to read five people's opinions on modern art. For statements 1–10, choose from the people (A–E). Each person may be chosen more than once.**

Which person expresses each of the following opinions?

I have personal experience of how artists have developed their abilities.	1
There are things that people can do far better than machines can.	2
The value of a work of art is not only a question of the work itself, but also of one's personal taste.	3
True art does not need to be explained.	4
Art will always reflect how people, in any period in history, live their lives.	5
The ordinary things that we see every day do not deserve to be called art.	6
There is no requirement for people to hold the same views about a work of art.	7
Art now is not as good as it was in the past.	8
The move towards less representational art is not difficult to explain.	9
If you look at a work of art and have neither positive nor negative feelings, then it is not art.	10

Person A
People have different ideas when it comes to defining 'art'. My personal opinion is that if something evokes a reaction in the person who sees or hears it, then it can be called 'art'. That said, there's the question of whether the viewer or listener likes it or not, and that's essentially subjective. Beauty is in the eye of the beholder, after all, and that's why I don't have the right to say that what they choose to like isn't 'art'. If you like it and I don't (or vice versa), then we simply disagree.

Person B
Most contemporary art is abstract, and I believe there's a simple reason for that. Since the invention of the camera, people are less and less inclined to devote hours of their time and talent to producing a realistic image, which can be done in a second at the push of a button. So art has evolved, necessarily, into something different from what it once was. To me, this is a positive thing – technology, after all, isn't so good at producing abstract images, whereas humans excel at it. Art today is a matter of interpretation, whether you like it or not.

Person C
Most of what is on display in galleries these days is simply not art. Art should reflect beauty and as such, represent the very best of human endeavour. Thus, it should strive to improve our lives and also to improve itself – to develop and become better. These days, what we are seeing is a progressive reduction in the quality of life and also of art. Art is something that should always provoke positive reactions in the human soul, and nowadays, the stresses and strains of life require more than ever that art should provide an enrichment of our experience, and be something remarkable and admirable. A pile of bricks does not do this.

Person D
Art changes with the times and that is necessarily a good thing. The things that people experience in their lives in the 21st century are distinctly different from what our ancestors experienced. Artists are people too and so the changing human experience will inevitably be reflected in art. Many critics of modern art state that it does not require technique to produce but I would dispute that. As an artist myself, I know that all my contemporaries have studied drawing, colour and so on. Now, whether or not they choose to apply those techniques in what they produce is a matter entirely for them.

Person E
I firmly believe that art has to represent something of value to human beings. Something cannot be called art unless it fulfils a number of criteria, and it is not art if it does not require talent and technique on the part of the artist, if it is merely intended to shock an audience, or if it needs some art critic or other to engage in lengthy justifications of its existence. When I look at the products of self-proclaimed artists such as Hirst or Emin, and hold those criteria in mind, then I, for one, am unable to term them art.

135

Culture notes

Tracey Emin CBE, RA, born in 1963, is a British artist known for her autobiographical and confessional artwork. She studied at the Royal College of Art and came to prominence in the 1990s as part of a group of contemporary artists popularly referred to as YBAs (Young British Artists). She produces work in a variety of media including drawing, painting, sculpture, film, photography, neon text and sewn appliqué. In 1998, Emin was nominated for the Turner Prize, for *My Bed*. She had her first solo exhibition in the US in 1999. Between 2011 and 2013, she was Professor of Drawing at the Royal Academy, London.

Damien Hirst, born in 1965, is a British contemporary artist originally from Bristol, UK. He studied at Goldsmith's College in London and rose to prominence, as a contemporary of Emin, in the 1990s. His varied practice explores the complex relationships between art, religion, science, life and death. His most famous artworks are his *Natural History* series, in which he displayed a 'zoo of dead animals' in glass tanks filled with formaldehyde. The shark from the series remains one of the most iconic symbols of modern British art and popular culture of that decade. He was awarded the Turner Prize in 1995.

1 1 steam 2 nominate 3 ageist 4 tongue 5 failed 6 temper 7 pessimist 8 put 9 vote 10 through

2 1 had 2 has 3 can 4 must 5 will 6 would

3 1 My dad ~~dyes his hair~~ has his hair dyed at the barber's.
2 Police say the fire may have been caused deliberately.
3 The song ~~got~~ was written by all of the members of the band.
4 They will ~~be~~ have been together for 20 years in August.
5 They've just won the cup. Fans ~~would~~ will be singing and dancing in the streets all night.
6 For a few scary moments, I thought I ~~am~~ was going to die.

4 1 time; can't
2 easy; calm
3 dying; forward
4 skin; get

TEST YOURSELF UNITS 11 & 12

VOCABULARY

1 Complete the sentences with the words in the list. There are four extra words.

ageist | failed | head | nominate | optimism | out | pessimist | put | shortlist | steam | temper | through | tongue | vote

1 Don't take him too seriously. He's just letting off a bit of … .
2 I'd like to … my dad for the 'local hero' award.
3 I don't think that joke about old people using technology is very funny. It's just … .
4 He likes to take the opposite view, but I just bite my … and ignore him.
5 His attempts to learn the guitar … spectacularly and he gave up after two lessons.
6 Be careful what you say. She loses her … very quickly.
7 Teresa is such a … . She always thinks the worst is about to happen.
8 I'd like to … myself forward for class president.
9 Do you think people over 16 should be able to … in the elections?
10 We wanted to go camping for the weekend, but our plans fell … at the last minute.

GRAMMAR

2 Complete the sentences with the words/phrases in the list. There are two extra words/phrases.

can | had | has | have | must | were going to | will | would

1 We've … our house broken into three times now.
2 She normally … her hair cut by her mum. Her mum's a great hairdresser.
3 Most phones … be used as cameras, too.
4 I think your cake … have been eaten by the dog. He isn't looking too well now.
5 I've got the worst memory. By the next time we meet, I … have forgotten your name.
6 The ship set sail from England six weeks before it … finally arrive in Australia.

3 Find and correct the mistake in each sentence.

1 My dad dyes his hair at the barber's.
2 Police say the fire may caused deliberately.
3 The song got written by all of the members of the band.
4 They will be together 20 years in August.
5 They've just won the cup. Fans would be singing and dancing in the streets all night.
6 For a few scary moments, I thought I am going to die.

FUNCTIONAL LANGUAGE

4 Choose the correct options.

1 A This *moment / time* tomorrow, we'll be on our way to France.
B I *can't / must* wait.
2 A Take it *easy / simple*. It isn't the end of the world.
B Don't tell me to *cool / calm* down. I'm really angry about this.
3 A I'm *dying / living* to meet Anne's new boyfriend.
B Me too. I'm really looking *ahead / forward* to it.
4 A Don't let him get under your *skin / head*. He's just not worth it.
B I know – you're right. I don't know why I let him *bother / get* to me.

MY SCORE
22–30 | 10–21 | 0–9

The Cambridge Life Competencies Framework

Critical Thinking
Ranks and scales
Watch this video for a tip on developing your students' critical thinking skills.
Scan the QR code here.

PRONUNCIATION

UNIT 1
Intonation: showing emotions

1 1.03 **Listen to the speakers and decide if they are feeling angry (A), cheerful (C), disappointed (D), enthusiastic (E), puzzled (P) or sympathetic (S).**

0 She can be mean to me, but she's still my sister. C
1 But you haven't got a ticket – how did you get in?
2 The homework was difficult, so I'll give you an extra week.
3 My cousin was going to phone, but I still haven't heard from her.
4 I need to move out, Mum. I want to be independent!
5 I'm your best friend, Clara. Why didn't you tell me?

2 1.03 **Listen, repeat and practise.**

UNIT 2
Different ways of pronouncing *c* and *g*

1 **Look at the sentences, paying attention to the pronunciation of the letters c and g in blue. Write the correct phoneme /k/, /s/, /ʃ/, /g/ or /dʒ/ in each word.**

0 There is concern (/k/, /s/) that teenagers (/dʒ/) are not getting (/g/) sufficient (/ʃ/) sleep.
1 Girls (/.../) are especially (/.../) in danger (/.../) of not getting (/.../) the necessary (/.../) hours of sleep.
2 Experts agree (/.../) that sleep and exercise (/.../) are beneficial (/.../) for your health.
3 The causes (/.../) of their anti-social (/.../) sleeping habits are biological (/.../, /.../).

2 2.02 **Listen, check and repeat.**

UNIT 3
Unstressed words in connected speech

1 3.02 **Read and listen to the dialogue. What do you notice about the pronunciation of the words in blue?**

Jane How did you meet your wife, Rob?
Rob It's a funny story. My sister crashed into her car. She wanted to apologise, and she asked me to go with her.
Jane And when you met Petra it was love at first sight!
Rob That's right. If it hadn't been for the accident, we wouldn't be married now!

2 **What types of word are unstressed?**

3 3.02 **Listen, repeat and practise.**

UNIT 4
Telling jokes: pacing, pausing and punchlines

1 4.04 **Read and listen to the ending of joke 3 from the listening on page 41. What does P indicate?**

'What on earth are you doing?' he says. 'Running shoes? You can't run faster than this bear!' P And the other man replies: P 'I don't have to run faster than the bear. P I just have to run faster than you.'

2 4.04 **Listen, repeat and practise.**

UNIT 5
Connected speech feature: elision

1 5.02 **Read and listen to the sentences. Then practise saying the linked words in blue.**

1 Commuters in New York City stopped their mad dash to work to look up in the sky.
2 Since the authorities thought anyone attempting such a death-defying feat must be crazy.
3 First they shot an arrow across to a contact on the roof of the other tower.

UNIT 6
Modal stress and meaning

1 6.02 **Read and listen to the sentences. One of the modal verbs in each pair of sentences is stressed and the other is not. Write S (stressed) or U (unstressed) for each modal verb.**

1 A I may watch the film tonight – I'll see how I feel. S
B They may be rich and famous, but are they happy?
2 A I might go to the beach – but it looks like it could rain.
B Kate might want to get a lift with us – it's a long walk to the beach.
3 A We could have a problem. We need to look into it.
B My dad could solve most problems.

2 **Choose the correct option to complete the rule.**

We stress the modal verb (rather than the main verb which follows it) when we want to emphasise *certainty / uncertainty*.

3 6.02 **Listen, repeat and practise.**

UNIT 7
Connected speech feature: assimilation

1 7.05 **Read and listen to the sentences closely. In the pairs of words highlighted in blue, the final sound of the first word changes. How does this sound change in each sentence?**

1 'London Bridge' is a really good book – everyone's reading it.
2 The meditation class was full, so I'm doing yoga instead.
3 Listen to this all-woman band – they're brilliant!
4 We had sunshine on the day of our garden party.
5 After the robbery, she saw a green car speeding away from the bank.

2 **Practise saying the linked words in blue.**

UNIT 8
Stress in multi-syllable words

1 8.02 **Read and listen to the sentences. Find and write all of the words with three or more syllables. Then draw a circle above the stressed syllable in each word.**

0 While digging in the sands, Bouchard came across an <u>unusual</u> slab of black rock.
1 Knowing about his emperor's interest in such things, he took it back to show him.
2 The top layer contained ancient Egyptian hieroglyphics.
3 For many years, scholars had been baffled by the inscriptions.
4 The first breakthrough came when scholars realised that all three passages said the same thing.

2 8.02 **Listen, repeat and practise.**

UNIT 9
Unstressed syllables and words: the /ɪ/ phoneme

1 9.02 **Read and listen to the sentences, paying attention to the words in blue. Can you hear the /ɪ/ phoneme? This is often used in unstressed syllables and words.**

1 Of the three cases I think the worst miscarriage of justice is the first one.
2 Imagine – she was convicted because of a bullet the police found in her pocket!
3 Since they had no motive, they must have been sent to prison because of prejudice.

2 9.02 **Find the unstressed /ɪ/ phonemes in the words in blue. Then listen and check.**

UNIT 10
Lexical and non-lexical fillers

1 10.04 **Read and listen to these extracts, paying attention to the fillers, shown in blue. How can fillers help you when speaking?**

Well, I didn't really want to go, like, straight from school to university, and I'd always wanted to see Australia and New Zealand, so I decided to take a year off, but split it, you know, so the first six months I worked and saved some money.

The headteacher said, 'Look, why not take a gap year and then decide.' Erm … And I thought, well, that's, like, good advice!

Um, at first, I was thinking about going to university to do an Economics course, you know, but then I kind of stopped to think. I mean, university fees are so expensive and you come out in debt.

2 10.04 **Listen, repeat and practise.**

UNIT 11
Intonation: mean what you say

1 11.04 **Read and listen to the same sentence said in two different ways. In which sentences (A or B) is the tone of voice appropriate? In which sentences is it inappropriate?**

1 A It isn't a problem – don't worry about it, OK?
B It isn't a problem – don't worry about it, OK?
2 A Don't let him get under your skin – he didn't mean it.
B Don't let him get under your skin – he didn't mean it.
3 A Calm down. Shouting won't do any good.
B Calm down. Shouting won't do any good.

2 11.04 **Listen, repeat and practise.**

UNIT 12
Shifting word stress

1 12.02 **Read and listen to the sentences. Decide which is the stressed syllable in each of the words in blue.**

1 A When giving a presentation, you must project your voice so everyone can hear you.
B Jo's really excited about her science project.
2 A The author was happy to sign the new contract.
B Children in poorer countries contract illnesses which could be prevented.
3 A We had to record our voices to practise our English pronunciation.
B She broke a world record at the last Olympics.

2 12.02 **Listen, repeat and practise.**

GRAMMAR REFERENCE

UNIT 1

Talking about habits

1 To talk about things that are generally (but not always) true, we can use the verb *tend to* + verb.

2 We can also use the modal verb *will/won't* + infinitive. In this use, *will* does not have a future reference. This use often refers to how we expect people to behave.

3 When someone has a habit or does something repeatedly, and it annoys us, we can use the present continuous + *always*.

4 We often talk about past habits using *used to* + infinitive or *would* + infinitive.

Adverbs to express attitude

We use words like *unfortunately, admittedly, hopefully, understandably, surely, honestly* and *obviously* to show how we feel about the situation or action we're describing. They usually come at the start of the sentence.

UNIT 2

Past tenses with hypothetical meaning

1 With some expressions, for example, *it's time, I'd rather, I'd prefer (it if), I wish, If only* we use a past tense to talk about how we would like situations to be different.

2 We use *It's time* + past tense to say that something needs to happen soon.

3 We use *I'd rather* + subject + past tense, or *I'd prefer it if* + past tense, to talk about how we'd prefer things to be.

4 With *It's time* and *I'd prefer* we use the infinitive when the subject of the second verb is the same as the subject of *It's time / I'd prefer*. If the subject is different, we use the past tense structure.

5 We use *I wish / If only* + past tense to talk about how we would like a present situation to be different.

6 We use *I wish / If only* + past perfect tense to talk about how we regret a past situation or action.

Adverbs for modifying comparatives

1 To make a contrast stronger, we can use *much* or *a lot/ lots*. We can also use adverbs such as *considerably, far, significantly, notably, way* and *drastically*.

2 There are differences in register amongst these words. *Notably* and *Significantly* are used in more formal spoken contexts and in writing.

3 To make a *not as … as* construction stronger, we can use *not nearly, nothing like* and *nowhere near*.

UNIT 3

Mixed conditionals

1 If we want to connect a hypothetical (imaginary) past with a present action or situation, then the *if* clause follows the pattern of a third conditional and the consequence clause follows the pattern of a second conditional.

2 If we want to connect a hypothetical (imaginary) present with a past action or situation, the *if* clause follows the pattern of a second conditional and the consequence clause follows the pattern of a third conditional.

Alternatives to *if*

1 We can use other words apart from *if* when we want to talk about (real or imaginary) actions and their consequences. Some common ones are: *as long as, otherwise, provided that, suppose, imagine* and *unless*.

2 We use *as long as* and *provided (that)* to mean 'on the condition that'. We use these mainly in first conditional sentences, and usually (though not exclusively) when we are negotiating something with someone.

3 We use *imagine* and *suppose* in second and third conditional sentences when we are hypothesising about imaginary (present or past) situations. They are used at the beginning of sentences and are often used to introduce questions.

4 *Unless* has the meaning of *if not*. It can be used in all conditional structures.

5 We often use *otherwise* when we want to warn someone about what will happen if a condition is not met. We typically use this in first conditional sentences but we can use it in other conditionals too.

UNIT 4
Emphatic structures

1 When we want to write or say something with emphasis, we can use a cleft sentence, using *what*, *it* or *all*.

2 We use the word *it* when we want to focus attention on the information at the beginning of the sentence, often to correct what someone else has said or to offer an alternative opinion or idea.

3 The word *what* is used in this way to mean 'the thing that'. We use *what* in this way when we want to emphasise what comes at the end of the sentence.

4 If we want to focus on one particular thing, we can use the word *all* to mean 'the only thing that'.

5 The form of these structures is as follows:

What / *All* + clause + *be* + clause
It + *be* + noun phrase + relative clause

Boosting

1 We use adverbs such as *certainly*, *undoubtedly*, *unquestionably* and *definitely* to make what we say sound more certain and forceful. This is known as boosting. Other common adverbs include *undeniably*, *clearly*, *absolutely*, *utterly*, *entirely*, *essentially*, *literally* and *totally*.

2 Remember the usual positioning of adverbs:

After the verb *to be*:
It was unquestionably the most difficult test we'd ever done.
Before the main verb:
They undoubtedly expected to win the match.
After auxiliaries:
They have clearly not understood the instructions.

UNIT 5
Participle clauses

In participle clauses, we use the present or past participle form of the verb, or the perfect participle, to combine two clauses that share the same subject.

1 We use them to talk about two events that happen(ed) at the same time.

2 We use them to talk about an action that happened before the other action in the sentence.

3 Remember, the subject of both clauses must be the same.

4 With passive structures, we use the past participle.

5 We can also use participle clauses to give reasons for something.

6 Note that participle clauses are more common in writing than in spoken language.

Verbs of perception with infinitive or gerund

1 Verbs of perception (e.g. *see*, *feel*, *hear*) can be followed by another verb either in the gerund or in the infinitive.

2 If we follow with a gerund, it suggests that we saw (or felt or heard) part of an ongoing action.

3 If we follow with an infinitive, it suggests that we saw (or felt or heard) a complete action from beginning to end.

UNIT 6
Modal verbs

Modal verbs each have more than one use / meaning.

1 *Will* and *won't* can be used to state a belief about the future.

Will can also be used to talk about habitual behaviour in the present.
Won't can be used to express refusal.

2 To hypothesise or to talk about present and future possibilities, we can use *may* / *might* / *could*.

3 *Can* and *may* can also be used to ask for or give permission. Here, *may* is more formal than *can* and so it is less frequent.

4 *Can* is also used to talk about general ability, and about tendencies or theoretical possibility.

5 As well as talking about present or future possibilities, *could* describes general past ability.

6 *Should* is used either to give advice, to make recommendations, or to talk about expectations.

7 *Must* is used to make a deduction, for strong advice, or for strong obligation.

8 *Mustn't* is used for prohibition.

9 *Can't* is used for lack of ability, or to say that something is impossible, based on deduction.

10 We can also use *might* / *may* to express concession.

UNIT 7

Substitution

1 In formal situations and sometimes in written English, we can avoid repetition of nouns by using *that (of) / those (of)*. When we are referring to people we must use *those*.

2 We can avoid repeating verb phrases by using *do / did / think / hope + so*.

3 To avoid repeating ideas, we can use *so / neither, nor*. The phrases take on the meaning of 'also'. The subject and object are inverted.

Ellipsis

We often leave words out in English. This is known as 'ellipsis' and is especially true of informal spoken language. The words that are most frequently omitted are subject pronouns (*I / you*) and auxiliary verbs (e.g. *do / did / are / is*, etc.). When the context is very clear, we often leave out verbs as well.

UNIT 8

Relative clauses with determiners and prepositions

1 In relative clauses, if there is a preposition, it usually appears at the end of the clause.

2 However, in formal written or spoken language, we can put the preposition before the relative pronoun. In this case the only two possible relative pronouns are *whom* (for people) and *which* (for things). In normal spoken language, we tend not to use the relative pronoun *whom* as it can sound overly formal.

3 Sometimes the relative clause begins with a determiner e.g. *all of whom / some of which / none of whom / in which case*.

however / wherever / whatever, etc.

1 We can add *-ever* to *wh-* words to form the words *whatever, whoever, wherever, whenever, whichever* and *however*.

2 When we do this, the result is to create words which mean 'no matter what' (*whatever*) or 'no matter who' (*whoever*) and so on.

3 *Whatever, wherever, whoever* and *whenever* are normally followed by a verb phrase.

4 *Whichever* is usually followed by a noun phrase. *Whatever* can also be followed by a noun phrase.

5 *However* is followed by an adjective or adverb.

UNIT 9

Negative inversion

1 Sometimes we bring negative or limiting adverbs and adverbial phrases to the beginning of a sentence in order to emphasise something.
This is much more common in written than in spoken language but can be used in both for dramatic effect.

2 The word order of the sentence is inverted to follow the pattern of a question. When this inversion happens, we insert the auxiliary *do, does* or *did*, and we invert the auxiliary and the subject. With *be* and modal verbs, we use the auxiliary that's already there (e.g. *is / are / can / will*, etc.) in the appropriate tense.

3 Some of the more common negative or limiting adverbial phrases are: *never (before) / rarely / not only ... but also / under no circumstances / on no account / no sooner ... than.*

Spoken discourse markers

1 We use a lot of discourse markers in spoken language for a number of different purposes.

2 If we want to make it clear that we are talking about a result or outcome, we can use phrases like *as a result*.

3 To show we are giving an opinion we can use a phrase like *as far as I'm concerned, to be honest, to tell you the truth* or *if you ask me*.

4 To show that we're changing the topic of a conversation, we can use a phrase like *by the way*.

5 We can show a contrast using a phrase such as *on the other hand, nevertheless* or *that said*.

UNIT 10

Reported verb patterns

1 There are many verbs which can be used to report what someone said – for example, *say, tell, promise, suggest, persuade, admit, recommend, apologise*. However, the patterns that follow these verbs vary.

2 Some reporting verbs are followed by (person) + preposition + gerund – for example, *accuse / blame / apologise*.

3 One very common pattern is *that* + clause – this happens with verbs like *say, claim, tell, argue, emphasise*, etc.

4 Some verbs (for example, *promise, refuse, decide*) are followed by an infinitive + *to*.
However, *promise* and *decide* can also be followed by *that* + clause.

5 Some verbs (for example, *suggest, deny, regret*) are normally followed by a gerund.

6 Some verbs (for example, *invite, encourage, advise, warn*) are followed by object pronoun + *(not) to* + infinitive.

Passive report structures

1 Passive report structures occur with verbs such as *say, think, believe, know, find* and *consider.*

2 We use passive report structures to report information when the agent is unknown, understood or not important.

3 For reporting information about the present, the structure is subject + *be* + past participle of reporting verb + *to* + infinitive.

4 For reporting information (in the present) about something that happened in the past, the structure is subject + *be* + past participle of reporting verb + *to have* + past participle.

Hedging

Hedging is vague or cautious language that we use in order not to sound forceful or overly certain of something. Phrases that are often used in hedging include: *seem, appear, is believed, thought, said to*; modal verbs like *may, might, could*; and adverbs like *probably, possibly, perhaps.*

UNIT 11

The passive with *get*

1 We sometimes use the verb *get* instead of *be* in passive constructions, especially in informal speech and writing.

2 We only use *get* in passive constructions with dynamic (action) verbs.

3 We usually use the *get* passive when there is a clear good or bad effect.

4 Sometimes *get* is used rather than *be* to distinguish active from stative meaning of a verb and therefore make it clear that an action is involved.

5 *Get* is also used in passive constructions when something happens unexpectedly or accidentally.

Causative *have*

1 This structure is formed with the verb *to have* + object + the past participle of the main verb.

2 It is used to make it clear that another person performs an action for us because we asked them to, or paid them to.

3 It is also used when a person (often an unknown person) does something unwanted and/or unpleasant to us.

4 It is also possible, in informal language, to use the verb *get* instead of *have* – the meanings are the same.

Modal passives

1 To form a present passive using a modal verb, we use modal verb + *be* + past participle.

2 To form a past passive using a modal verb, we use modal verb + *have been* + past participle.

UNIT 12

Future perfect; future continuous

1 We use the future perfect tense when we have a certain moment in the future in mind as we describe / reference an action that happened before that moment. It is formed with *will* + *have* + past participle.

2 We use the future continuous tense to refer to an action that will be in progress at or around a specific time in the future. It is formed with *will* + *be* + gerund.

Future in the past

1 When we want to talk about the future as seen from the past, we can use *was/were going to* or *would.*

2 We tend to use *would* or *wouldn't* when we are referring to a future possibility or an idea.

3 We tend to use *was/were going to* when we are referring to a definite plan for the future.

4 There is more certainty that the future plan or event will take place with *was/were going to* than with *would.*

Unit 1

1.02

Emma ... OK, Joss. Great to talk to you. Look after yourself, OK, and give my love to Steve. What? Yes, of course I will. I'll call you next weekend. Take care! Bye! Joss sends you her love.

Jack Thanks. Is she all right?

Emma Yeah, she's fine. A few problems at college, but nothing too much. Hang on. I know that look, Jack. What's the matter?

Jack Emma, we're supposed to be going out. Remember? Meeting up with Jan and Alex at seven thirty? Well, it's seven forty-five now. And you've been on the phone with your sister for almost an hour! An hour!

Emma Oh, I'm really sorry Jack. I completely forgot. And I lost track of the time. Why didn't you say something?

Jack Because I know what it's like, that's why. If I say anything at all, it's, 'But it's my sister!' What *we've* got planned, well, that can wait, can't it?

Emma But it *is* my sister, Jack, I don't understand. I'm sorry we're going to be late but ...

Jack No more buts, Emma. I'm tired of this family. I'm tired of always waiting while you talk to your sister, and if it isn't your sister it's your little brother. You're all adults now – why do you have to talk to each other *all* the time? Why can't you just get on with your own lives!

Emma Well, they're important to me, Jack. And frankly, getting on with my life includes my family. I'm sorry you haven't got any brothers or sisters ...

Jack That's got nothing to do with it! Even if I had a brother or sister, you can be sure I wouldn't phone them every single day!

Emma And I don't phone my sister every day either. Or my brother. You're just exaggerating because you're in a bad mood. Come on, let's not argue. Let's go and meet Jan and Alex.

Jack I don't want to go anymore. I really don't. I'll message Alex and tell him it's off.

Emma Seriously? Jack, I made a phone call and forgot the time. That's all. Why make such a big deal out of it?

Jack Because ... well ... more and more, I'm feeling that it's never you and me together. We've only just got married! No matter where we go or what we're doing, at any moment there's going to be a phone call or something from your sister or your mother or ...

Jack Tell me it isn't someone in your family!

Emma I have to answer, Jack. I have to. Hello? Simon, look, this really isn't a good time, can you maybe ... just a minute. Jack? Jack! Where are you going? ...

Unit 2

2.03

Today on 'Health Matters', we're looking at insomnia, the inability to fall asleep easily. When I can't get to sleep, I find that baking a cake seems to work. ... And we want to know what tips *you* have, so please text them in and I'll read the best out later. But before that, I'd like to share with you the amazing story of Randy Gardner, the world record-holder for staying awake the longest.

Now, if you want to get yourself into the Guinness World Records, I wouldn't recommend trying to beat that particular record. It might seem like an easy one, but you'd be wasting valuable time! The Guinness World Records no longer accepts any new attempts as it considers the challenge too dangerous. If you really want to set a record, you might want to consider doing something easier – how about organising the world's largest sleepover party (currently standing at 2,004 participants) or making the world's largest sleeping bag (7.5 metres times 16.5 metres). Try not to get lost in it, though!

Back in 1963, 17-year-old Randy Gardner decided to see how long he could stay awake for. With the help of two friends, he recorded the results as part of their entry for their high school's science competition.

His experiment was picked up by the local newspaper, and his story soon made the national news, where it caught the attention of a sleep researcher called Dr William Dement. Dement was so interested in the attempt that he went to offer Randy and his friends some help. He devised a series of tests to monitor the effect of sleeplessness on Randy's sensory and cognitive abilities.

After 48 hours, Randy was finding it difficult to recognise objects by feeling them and he was having trouble with tongue-twisters. Interestingly, he reported an increase in his sense of smell.

As he entered the fifth day of the experiment, Randy was having problems remembering things that had happened only a short while before and he also started hallucinating. However, not everything was bad news. As part of helping him stay awake, his friends would involve him in physical activities and they noticed that his basketball skills actually seemed to improve the more tired he got.

In the end, Randy managed to stay awake for an incredible 11 days and 25 minutes before he jumped into bed for a well-deserved sleep, which surprisingly only lasted for 14 hours. Randy and his friends won the science fair competition and it seemed that Randy himself had managed to escape without any serious side effects. However, as the years passed, Randy started to have more and more trouble getting to sleep, which he blamed on the experiment. These days, he has a more reliable sleep pattern but still rarely sleeps for more than six hours a night. Would things be different if he hadn't stayed awake for a week and a half when he was a teenager? There's probably no way anyone can be sure.

Unit 3

3.03

Presenter Today on Sunnybank School's weekly chat show, our topic is: Luck and lucky charms. And Holly, Nick and Antony are here to tell us their favourite 'luck' stories. Let's start with you, Holly. What's your story?

Holly Well, as Antony and Nick know, I want to be a writer and my story is about a very famous author. His name's Charles Dickens. He was an insomniac. Apparently, he carried a compass everywhere he went.

Presenter Was that because he was always getting lost?

Holly No. He used the compass to position his bed and desk so he could always face north while he slept and wrote. Many people in the late nineteenth and early twentieth centuries believed that it was good for your health if you slept in a bed with your head pointing north, and Charles Dickens believed that, too.

Presenter And have you tried to sleep with your head facing north, Holly?

Holly Yes, and I have to say I sleep better that way. I'd say definitely give it a go!

Presenter Thank you for that interesting little glimpse into the life of one of our most famous authors. Now Nick, what's your story?

Nick My story is about another author. He isn't quite as famous as Charles Dickens. Have you heard of Roald Dahl?

Presenter Of course! He wrote *Charlie and the Chocolate Factory*.

Nick Yes, that's right. But do you know how he became an author?

Presenter No, but I'm guessing you're going to tell me?

Nick It was luck really. You can read about it in one of his autobiographical short stories, *Going Solo*. Roald Dahl was a pilot during the Second World War. One time, when he was flying his plane over the desert in Libya, he was shot down. Against all the odds, he survived and was rescued. He was then sent to America. As luck would have it, while he was there, the famous author C.S. Forester asked him to write a story about the crash. Dahl wrote down everything he could remember and sent it to Forester, who wrote back, 'Did you know you were a writer?' The story was published in the newspaper and that's how Roald Dahl became a writer – all because of good luck!

Presenter Fascinating stuff! Now we've just got time for one more quick story. Antony, what's yours?

Antony It isn't really a story. I read about how some sports people have little lucky routines. For example, if Richard Gasquet wins a point, he asks to use the same ball for the next game because he thinks it will bring him luck. I think that's cool.

Unit 4

🔊 4.02

Narrator One.

Speaker 1 Sally meets her friend Graham on the street one day. 'Hi, Graham,' she says. 'Have you lost one of your gloves?' And Graham says, 'No, why?' Sally says, 'Oh, because you've got a glove on your right hand but not on your left. Why's that?' Graham replies, 'Ah, well, this morning I listened to the weather forecast.' Sally says, 'The weather forecast?' 'Yes,' says Graham, 'and they said that on the one hand it might be warm, but on the other hand there might be some cold winds.'

Narrator Two.

Speaker 2 An old man goes to a doctor and says, 'My wife can't hear very well anymore and I'm worried she's going deaf. What should I do?' The doctor says, 'Well, we need to do a test. Go home, and stand about 10 metres behind her. Ask her something and if she doesn't answer, walk two metres closer and ask again. Repeat this until she can hear you, then come and tell me how far away you were standing.' The old man is very worried about his wife, so he tells the doctor he'll do it. When he gets home, he sees his wife cooking in the kitchen. He stands ten metres behind her and says, 'What's for dinner?' No answer. The man goes two metres closer and asks again: 'What's for dinner?' No answer. The man does this once more and now he's standing only about four metres from his wife. He tries for the fourth time, 'What's for dinner?' His wife turns round and says, 'I've told you three times already – we're having chicken!'

Narrator Three.

Speaker 3 Two men go on a trekking holiday together, walking in the mountains and forests. One day they are walking through part of a forest when suddenly, an enormous bear appears in front of them. It starts to growl and walk towards them. The men don't have a gun, and they don't know what to do about this hungry-looking bear. Then one of them takes off his backpack, takes out a pair of running shoes and starts to put them on. His friend looks at him in astonishment. 'What on earth are you doing?' he says. 'Running shoes? You can't run faster than this bear!' And the other man replies, 'I don't have to run faster than the bear. I just have to run faster than you.'

🔊 4.07

Presenter So, our topic this week is luck and the role that plays in people's lives. With me to discuss the issue is the actor Daniela Merchant who's read a book on the subject. Tell us about it, Daniela.

Daniela Sure. Well, the book's by a guy called Ed Smith, who was a famously unlucky cricketer. Chapter One focuses on how he was once chosen to play for England but missed his chance to do well because of a bad umpiring decision. Now, this was doubly unfortunate: not only was he the victim of someone else's incompetence, but if it'd happened today he could've used technology to review the decision and maybe get it changed. Anyway, as it was he never played for England again. You feel this piece of misfortune lies behind Smith's interest in the subject, but for me the story didn't really hang together. He's obviously told this tale many times, and seems to assume that the reader's familiar with it – and with the rules of cricket – which left me feeling that I might've missed something.

Presenter Sure. But the book goes on to discuss other ideas, like the difference between luck and fate, doesn't it?

Daniela Yes – he relates other moments from his life. We hear how his cricketing career was ended by injury, which was certainly unlucky, but hardly unusual. However, the main event in the book concerns how he first met his wife by purest chance on a train that neither he nor she'd been planning to take. Other people might call this fate, but he puts it down to luck and defines the two concepts quite neatly for us. His most convincing argument is that we tend to downplay luck and talk up things like fate, because we don't like the way luck makes us feel incidental to our own lives. Smith thinks accepting the role of luck is essential for keeping a sense of perspective, particularly for those who like to claim the credit for all their own success, when it's largely a matter of chance.

Presenter But that's not a very acceptable view these days, is it? I mean, we tend to think that it's talent that gets rewarded in life; that if you have it but don't achieve your goals, it's because you lack focus or determination or because you get things wrong.

Daniela Well, that's right. But Smith debunks that view. Earlier in his life, he believed totally in hard work, lots of practice, thinking that that's what determines whether you'll be successful or not. Then things happened that made him rethink his position. Now he's able to see how luck influences just about everything, even things that we think of as not at all related to it at all.

Presenter And he develops these ideas in the second half of the book, doesn't he?

Daniela Yes, he points to how we don't choose our parents or grandparents, nor our genetic make up – but how those things have a profound effect on the course of our lives. And not just that: he stresses the significance of things like the country where we're born, whether we're male or female, what's going on in the world at the time – all these things can be terribly important. And, of course, we have no control over such things. Very often, we like to think that it's our choices in life that make the difference – and, of course, there's an element of truth there, that's part of the story, but Ed Smith shows us that it's far from being the whole story.

Presenter Do you think, then, looking at your own life, that Smith is right – that luck matters?

Daniela Well, I can't help but think that at least some things depended on my abilities – my talent, if you like – but that there's always an element of simply being in the right place at the right time. I mean, the acting school I went to – a month before I went there, the main teacher got sick and they brought in a stand-in. She was superb and taught me so much. Later, I met the original teacher, and I just knew that I wouldn't have done so well under him. I'm reminded of something one great actor said – that he'd go to watch young actors at work and see people who were just as talented as him, if not more so. So he'd had to conclude that he'd got lucky – talent alone couldn't explain his success.

Presenter OK, but back to the book. What's your overall rating?

Daniela Well, I think that Smith's best when he's talking about sport. Some of the things he says about the role of luck in politics and economics, for example, don't seem to me to hold up quite as strongly as the arguments he makes about chance in other areas. And, you know, overall, I can't help thinking that his argument is a bit overstated – he takes it a bit too far. I mean, let's go back to the chance meeting with his future wife. All it means is that they got married to each other rather than to someone else, right? Though I have to admit that their children, if they have any, will no doubt be grateful that they did meet. And I think they'll be grateful that they've got a father who's as smart, witty and empathetic as Ed Smith seems to be.

Unit 5

5.03

Radio host Today we're joined by psychologist Dr Ron Davis, who's going to talk to us about thrill-seeking. Welcome to the programme, Dr Davis.

Psychologist Thanks for having me.

Radio host It's a pleasure … And let's get straight to the point. Why do people get a thrill out of bungee jumping, roller coaster rides and the like?

Psychologist That's an interesting question, and the answer is surprisingly complex. Some people enjoy the thrills they get from activities that stimulate their brain in such a way that they perceive themselves to be in physical danger. We know that there's a certain type of person who actually seeks physical danger by doing dangerous activities like skiing down extreme slopes or parachuting. When you ask one of these risk-takers if they're scared while doing their sport, their answer is usually that that's exactly why they do it in the first place. In other words, they kind of need the adrenalin rush that they experience when doing extreme sports.

Radio host I see, but there's a difference, isn't there, between doing a dangerous and extreme activity – such as jumping out of a helicopter without a parachute – and going on a roller coaster, which isn't really that dangerous at all?

Psychologist Absolutely, and that's exactly the point. The roller coaster doesn't, in all likelihood, offer the same level of risk, but it simulates true danger. In other words, it creates the illusion of having faced a great danger, and that's a deeply satisfying feeling. The danger isn't real, as such, but we behave as if it is – as if we have achieved something great and overcome our fear. Research has shown that after a bungee jump, or after having just been on a roller coaster ride, people feel great – almost as great as if they'd survived something far more dangerous.

Radio host And then, of course, there are others who couldn't care less about getting an adrenalin rush … who really wouldn't dream of risking their lives by going diving or climbing, or even going on a roller coaster ride. What makes daredevils different from them?

Psychologist Well, it seems that there are certain personality types, often referred to as 'thrill seekers', that thrive on this kind of risk-taking. What we know about them is that they love adventure, and they need the kick they get out of facing dangerous situations again and again. If you aren't this kind of person, then all these audacious activities may just seem ridiculous to you.

Radio host I see. And do we know what causes a person to have the type of personality you've just mentioned?

Psychologist That's a good question. One theory holds that in order to really feel excited, thrill seekers usually need more stimulus than the average person. We're talking biochemical processes in the brain here. When those people are involved in dangerous activities, certain chemicals, such as adrenalin, start flowing in their brains, and only then do they get a feeling of being truly alive.

Radio host That's fascinating.

Psychologist Yes, isn't it? And there's another theory along similar lines that basically says that thrill seekers like what they do mostly because it enables them to forget about everything else – all the problems they might have in their daily lives, their everyday worries, and so on. As long as they're involved in an activity that requires their full concentration – because of the need to survive a danger, for example – other things fade into the background. I was talking to an extreme climber once and when I asked him what he enjoyed most about his sport, he answered that as soon as he starts climbing, all the problems 'down there' as he described them – you know, the problems in his normal life, so to speak – become really small.

Radio host Why is it, then, that …

🔊 5.05

Narrator Dialogue One.

Male 1 Have you heard this? An 85-year-old has climbed Mount Everest. To my mind, that's ridiculous. This person was probably risking not only their own life, but those of other people, too.

Female 1 Yes, I suppose you're right. It could have been dangerous … but I don't accept that only young people should be allowed to do daring things. The way I see it is that if a young person does this kind of thing, it could be dangerous, too.

Male 1 Hmm. I hadn't thought of that.

Narrator Dialogue Two.

Female 2 It must be thrilling to drive one of those extremely fast cars.

Male 2 That's not how I see things. I think fast cars are dangerous, pollute the environment and are a waste of money.

Female 2 True. I'd go along with that. But do you never do something just because you get a kick out of it?

Male 2 OK. Point taken. There are things I'd do just for fun. But riding in a fast car? No way.

Unit 6

🔊 6.03

Presenter From Indonesia to Rwanda, from Bogotá to Baghdad, Liverpool F.C. has 770 million followers on social media platforms and millions of loyal supporters, and this makes it one of the most widely supported football clubs in the world. The subject of tonight's programme is Liverpool Football Club. First, I'd like to welcome Steve March, a specialist in the global marketing of football teams. Good evening, Steve.

Steve Good evening.

Presenter My first question, Steve, is what do you think has turned Liverpool Football Club into such a huge global brand?

Steve The rise of social media, of course. Players are now on Twitter and Instagram, and the club has a high profile on all social media platforms. That has definitely had a huge effect on their global popularity.

Presenter Liverpool has fans in so many different countries around the world. How do you market the team to individual countries?

Steve Of course, there are differences between our campaigns in different countries. For example, the ones we run at different times of year, to coincide with special holidays, celebrations and events. In China, for example, we do a lot of advertising around Singles Day and the Chinese New Year, and in the US, we have a massive marketing campaign around Thanksgiving.

Presenter Does the team's success or failure in a match have any effect on the sale of merchandise?

Steve No, actually, it doesn't, because losing a match doesn't affect the fan's loyalty to their team. What can affect sales of merchandise is a country's economy, currency fluctuations, and even the weather.

Presenter We have a fan now with a question for you, Steve. It's David Gomez and he's in Colombia. David, I have a few questions for you. Firstly, do you have other friends or family who support Liverpool, too?

David No, I don't. In fact, I used to have to watch matches on my own. But now, through social media, I've met Liverpool fans in Colombia, as well as in Mexico, Uruguay and Argentina. We've formed a social group in Colombia and we arrange get-togethers in different cities to watch matches. The only thing that makes it difficult is the time difference – some games start at 6 am.

Presenter David, I take it that you've never seen them play at Anfield. Do you think you ever will?

David We all dream of going to Anfield and watching the Reds play in their iconic stadium, but for most of us, we know that will never become a reality.

Presenter And finally, David, what's your question for Steve?

David At the moment, we can buy the team's football strip in Colombia, but we can't buy any other merchandise. Are there plans to distribute the merchandise to South America?

Steve Yes, we're always looking for merchandising partners, so I hope we'll find a partner soon.

Presenter Well, David, I hope that answers your question. Now, before you go, do you have any words for other fans out there in Colombia?

David Just this: maybe your friends and family don't understand why you support Liverpool, but there are plenty of fans out there – fans in every country of the world on social media – who do understand. So if you support Liverpool, as their motto says, 'you'll never walk alone'!

Unit 7

🔊 7.02

Host And with us in the studio is Marcia Hope. Marcia is a student at Moreland University, and has just written her thesis on 'Beauty Across the Centuries'. Thanks for joining us, Marcia.

Marcia Thanks for having me.

Host Marcia, would you agree that we're slightly obsessed with celebrities and their beauty regimes nowadays?

Marcia Yes, if you look on social media, or take a glance through any popular lifestyle magazine, you'll inevitably be confronted by beauty tips from celebrities. And there are all kinds of claims being made. For example, I read the other day that one British female celeb's beauty is apparently down to some kind of wasp venom …

Host Not heard that one before.

Marcia Well, she's by no means the only one to follow a bizarre beauty ritual. A well-known American actor, according to my research, uses leeches to suck and cleanse his blood. And I've heard an actress looks after her skin by letting snails crawl over her face.

Host Marcia, fancy trying any of these yourself?

Marcia No, thanks! But what is interesting is that we seem to believe all these claims, despite the lack of proof. There's no scientific evidence that these things do what they promise, but there are always people who are prepared to pay large sums of money in the hope that they will.

Host But how come? People tend to be sceptical in many other areas of life. Why not when it comes to beauty?

Marcia Well, I think most people wouldn't go for the more extreme things anyway, probably because they couldn't afford them. But these stories always create the illusion that if you're rich, you can buy yourself beauty. Generally, though, people tend to believe these things because they want to believe them. Buying the expensive cream that helps Person X to be so attractive gives us the feeling that we can be equally beautiful. And of course our cultural history is full of this kind of thing.

Host Some examples?

Marcia Well, there have always been claims that certain animal products work miracles on the skin. Perhaps the most bizarre example is from the Ancient Greeks and Romans. They used a special ingredient in their mud baths to tone the body: crocodile excrement.

Host No! Really?

Marcia Yes, really! They used a mixture of earth and freshly collected crocodile dung as an anti-aging face-mask. Of course, this was only for people who could afford it, as crocodile dung wasn't easy to get your hands on!

Host Unbelievable!

Marcia I know. Want to hear another example? TV commercials are full of people with perfect white teeth, aren't they, and we all want to have them too, right?

Host Right ...

Marcia Well, in the Meiji era in late nineteenth-century Japan, married women wanted black teeth.

Host Why black teeth?

Marcia Because in that culture, at that time, it was considered beautiful and correct for married women. So what did they do? First, they got pomegranate peel, and rubbed it against their teeth. Then they'd get some dye made from the nuts of a particular tree, the sumac tree, and apply it to their teeth. The dye didn't smell very nice. And they had to repeat the procedure every three days or so to make sure it worked.

Host So this is something that goes ...

Unit 8

8.03

Residents of Somerton Beach on the outskirts of Adelaide, Australia, woke up to a grisly discovery on the morning of the first of December, 1948. A body lay lifeless on the golden sands. As the news spread, several people came forward to say they had noticed the man the evening before. They assumed he had been taking a nap and didn't want to disturb him.

The man was well dressed. His clothes were not suited to the warm southern Australian summer and certainly not for the beach. There was no identification on his body. The best the police could determine from this was that he was probably not local. Whoever the police asked, and despite a wide media campaign, no one seemed to know who he was. Searches through the fingerprint database and dental records also drew a blank. The Somerton Man, as he became known, was a complete mystery and whatever he'd been doing on the beach would also remain a mystery. The only thing that police were able to determine was that the man had been murdered. In fact, he had been poisoned by an unknown substance. Rumours quickly spread that he had been a Russian spy, but they were never proven.

However, the intrigue didn't end there. Several months later, on a more thorough examination of his clothes, detectives came across a small piece of paper hidden in his trouser pocket. On it were written the words 'Tamám Shud'. Initially, it meant nothing to the detectives, but after some thorough research they discovered these words meant 'ended' in the Persian language.

When the new information was made public in the local newspaper, a man approached the police with some new evidence. He had been on Somerton Beach on the same night the man had died. He had gone for a walk and he had left his car unlocked. On his return, he had discovered on the front seat a copy of a poem called the 'Rubaiyat' by the Persian poet Omar Khayyam. Luckily, he had kept hold of the book and when the police examined it, they found that the piece of paper in the man's pocket had been torn out of this exact book. Furthermore, it was a very rare book.

The ripped-out piece of paper was not the only mystery about the book; on the inside cover there was a series of letters that seemed to have been written down in a non-random order, though it made no sense at all. Detectives believed they were looking at a code, and one with no obvious way of cracking it. This added to the speculation that the man was a spy, especially because a top-secret missile base in Adelaide had recently been infiltrated by Russian spies.

If they could solve the code, maybe it would answer all their questions. But however hard they tried, the experts could not crack it. For years it has remained a complete mystery.

Even a recent attempt in 2009, using the most sophisticated computer software, was unsuccessful. Some believe that the book itself may hold the key to solving the code somewhere inside its pages. Unfortunately, whether or not that is the case will never be known as the book went missing in the 1960s.

To this day, the Tamám Shud case remains unsolved and the code that perhaps might finally reveal the mystery remains unbroken.

Unit 9

9.03

Presenter When it comes to disciplining their teenagers, these two fathers have come up with two unique and very creative ideas. Please welcome Daniel Myers and Chris Walker. Now Daniel, let's hear your idea first. Perhaps you could even give us a demonstration.

Daniel Well, I don't think your listeners would be very happy if I gave a demonstration, so I'll just tell you what I do. My three sons are very close in age and usually they're on good terms with each other, but like all teenagers, they argue sometimes, including when we're all out together.

Telling them to stop arguing or asking them to be quiet just didn't work. I had to think of something more creative and this is what I came up with: whenever they were arguing or acting up in public, I would sing very loudly. It was usually something they didn't like, such as a song from an old musical. My favourite – and their least favourite – was *Memory* from the musical *Cats*. Just imagine your dad singing that at the top of his voice in the aisle at the supermarket. In seconds, they are usually silent. 'Dad, please stop! We promise we'll be good. Take our phones, do anything but don't sing.'

Presenter Well, I think all our listeners will agree, that does sound a very effective way of getting the boys to behave. Now let's see if Chris can beat that. Chris, over to you.

Chris This idea came to me suddenly one night. I noticed that a box of chocolates that I had bought for our neighbours had gone missing from the desk in my study. I asked my three kids – all in their teens: 'Which one of you took the chocolates from my desk? If you're honest with me now, we'll pretend that it never happened.'

There was silence. It was ten o'clock. 'I'll give you ten minutes to think about this. If you don't tell me who took them, I'll take your phones away.' Nobody owned up to taking the chocolates so, I confiscated their phones. Next, I confiscated their laptops. At this point, I could see they were getting tired. It was late and they wanted to go to bed, but still nobody admitted to taking the chocolates. I confiscated their pillows and there was nervous laughter. Then I came up with my brilliant idea.

I went downstairs and came back up a few minutes later. I took out my hammer and screwdriver and proceeded to remove their bedroom doors. I carried the three doors downstairs and told them that they would not get them back for a week. They thought I was kidding, but they soon learned that I wasn't. They all went to their rooms, but I could see that they weren't comfortable! Five minutes later, my youngest son came and said, 'It was me, Dad. I'm sorry.' The next day, I gave them back their phones and laptops, but the doors stayed off for a week.

Privacy means a lot to teenagers and losing it was a powerful lesson. Now I only have to say the word 'door' and they will immediately do what I ask them to.

Unit 10

10.02

Joanna Well, I didn't really want to go, like, straight from school to university and I'd always wanted to see Australia and New Zealand, so I decided to take a year off, but split it, you know, so the first six months I worked and saved some money, the second six months I travelled. Umm … and it worked out fine, I mean, I did six months in an office – not very interesting work – but I began to learn about offices, colleagues and bosses and all that, which was great. Erm, and then I travelled, saw great places and made great friends. So all in all, yeah, I think I did the right thing! And now I'm enjoying my uni course, too.

Harry My teachers encouraged me to go to uni. I mean, I did well at school, you know, but I wasn't sure and the headteacher said, 'Look, why not take a gap year and then decide.' Erm … And I thought, well, that's, like, good advice! So I got a temporary job, at the tax office actually – they needed some untrained help … um, and I found the work and the place dead interesting. And I was earning decent money, too. My dad said, 'That isn't a future – go to university, get your degree, then the world's your oyster.' But in fact, the tax office offered me some on-the-job training, you know, and I jumped at it. And here I am … making very good money, and I love it, yeah.

Tanya Um, at first, I was thinking about going to university to do an Economics course, you know, but then I kind of stopped to think. I mean, university fees are so expensive and you come out in debt. And I read somewhere that universities these days, like, they give away degrees to just anyone who turns up – a degree's almost worthless. And I met a girl who had a good job in a bank – she said she'd left school, she'd gone to work in a shop, and that, like, the experience helped her get the job she was in. So why get a load of debt when you can do that? So I took a year off and went. It's just finished – now I'm looking for work. Was I right to do that? To be honest, I'm not sure – let's see, eh?

10.03

Man It's a question that I get asked a lot, both by parents and by pupils. I always say that it really depends, and mostly on the person in question. I've met lots of 17 – and 18-year olds who get to the end of school and they can't wait to get out there, get a job, see the world, maybe both. If that's how they feel, I encourage them to go for it and take a gap year. Sometimes it's in that year that they find out what they really want to do with their lives: do they really want to go to university, and so on. But another thing that counts in this decision is, what are you going to do in that year? I encourage gap-year pupils to do something they think they'll enjoy but that also, crucially, they can learn something from. Another language? Another skill? How to work in a company environment? I think they have to see it as more than just a year to put your feet up and have fun. But fewer and fewer pupils are thinking of this now – they're much more concerned about how they're going to pay for university, and the debt they may have afterwards, too.

10.06

Narrator Dialogue 1

Woman I heard on the news that teachers are going on strike over government spending cuts on education. Finally, someone's taking things seriously.

Man I'm glad to hear it.

Woman The government isn't happy. They're calling the teachers irresponsible.

Man Well, they would, wouldn't they?

Narrator Dialogue 2

Man Finally – some good news.

Woman What is it?

Man They're going to knock down the old school and build a new one.

Woman It's about time they did something about it. It's falling down. It's a disgrace.

Man Apparently, it's going to be the greenest school in the country. State-of-the-art technology. They're going to spend 20 million pounds on it.

Woman That's fantastic! That's the best news I've heard in ages.

Man Hmm… I'll believe it when I see it.

Narrator Dialogue 3

Woman The government are planning to close about 20 state schools, which will mean making more teachers redundant.

Man What?!

Woman I read it in the paper. More than a thousand teachers are going to lose their jobs over the next three years.

Man That's outrageous!

Woman They say they can't afford to keep them on. So I guess that just means more students in every class.

Man They can't do that. It's just not right. Where's that newspaper? I'm going to write an email about this.

Narrator Dialogue 4

Man There's an interesting article in the paper. Apparently, the government thinks that children should have exams at the end of their first year in primary school.

Woman They've got to be joking.

Man They aren't. The education minister claims that it will help teachers to identify students with problems from the very beginning and start thinking of ways to help them.

Woman Five-year-olds doing exams? That's ridiculous! What will they think of next?

10.08

Narrator You will hear five short extracts in which people are talking about an evening class that they attended. Look at Task 1. For questions 1 to 5, choose from the list A to H each speaker's main reason for choosing the class. Now look at Task 2. For questions 6 to 10, choose from the list A to H what each speaker disliked about the class they chose. While you listen you must complete both tasks.

Narrator Speaker 1

Man 1 I did a carpentry class. I've always been interested in carpentry. I think working with wood is a wonderful thing to do, and if I'm honest – and at the risk of sounding immodest – I think I'm quite good at it. But I wanted to try to tackle bigger projects than in the past so I thought I'd better get some proper instruction to help me be able to do things beyond just the basics. And the course was nice. The teacher was good, but there were more than fifteen of us in the class so the teacher couldn't really give a lot of individual attention to each student. Because of that, I think that perhaps I didn't really learn as much as I'd wanted, as much as I'd hoped. But it definitely wasn't the teacher's fault.

Narrator Speaker 2

Woman 1 I decided to do Spanish. I love travelling and I really want to visit Central and South America in the near future, and so some Spanish could be really useful, even though it might not help much in Brazil! But, in fact, my main motivation was simply that I adore anything to do with learning languages. I already speak fairly good French and German, and my Italian isn't bad, so it seemed like the perfect thing to do. I really enjoyed it and I learned a lot, I think. There were a couple of students who really had no language aptitude at all and that often slowed things down – they took forever to understand anything. But the teacher was great – very patient and very clear – and I plan to do the second level of the course next year.

Narrator Speaker 3

Woman 2 Last year, my husband gave me a really smart camera for my birthday. We like travelling and wherever we go, I like to take photos, so I signed up for a photography course. It was nice because I love having the chance to meet new people and learn something new, but mainly I wanted to find out how to capture really good shots. I've never had much ability – I just point and shoot, you know! But I feel like I've learned so much, even though we had a teacher who just loved the sound of his own voice and spent far too much time droning on about when he worked as a photojournalist! I have to say that some of the other students and I did make life a bit difficult for him! We used to try to think of the hardest questions possible to ask him! Still, overall, it was great!

Narrator Speaker 4

Man 2 Well, I did a German course. I'd learned some German when I was at school, but I was always hopeless at it – well, I was fairly hopeless at everything if I'm honest. So I couldn't say I've always had a love of languages, but not long ago, I started to get interested in opera and I went to see a couple of things by Mozart, sung in German, and I just thought how great it would be if I could understand what they were singing without needing the translation. So I signed up. Never again. It was a complete waste of time, frankly. All I found out was that I'm still hopeless at German. The teacher did her best but … well, what can I tell you?

Narrator Speaker 5

Woman 3 There was a course advertised in Ikebana – the Japanese art of flower arrangement. Quite a long time ago, I lived in Japan for a couple of years, and I'd always wanted to learn how to do it, but somehow I never found the time, although I did learn some Japanese and that helped because the Ikebana teacher was Japanese and her English wasn't so good! Sometimes it was really hard to follow what she was trying to say and that could be a bit frustrating, but on the other hand, she was delightful – all smiles – and when she just showed us how to do things rather than explaining them, we could follow quite easily. So I enjoyed the classes enormously because finally I got to learn something that I'd always been interested in.

Unit 11

11.02

Narrator One

Teen boy 1 Oh, it makes me so angry when the bus doesn't come.

Teen girl 1 Chill out, Andy. There'll be one soon, I'm sure.

Teen boy 1 This bus company's just useless!!

Teen girl 1 Yes, you're right, but don't let it get to you, OK?

Narrator Two

Teen girl 2 I hate it when he talks to me like that.

Teen boy 2 Me too, but don't let him get under your skin. He just likes making people angry, that's all.

Teen girl 2 I'm going to tell him what I think!

Teen boy 1 No, don't do that. Just take it easy. He's not worth getting worked up about.

11.03

Presenter Hello, and on today's phone-in, we're talking about the stresses and strains of the modern world – those little things that just pop up every now and then to frustrate you. What is it that drives you round the bend in your daily life? Call, email, text or tweet in now and let us know. And to get us started, let me give you an example. Every time I order something online, which is very often, they always try to deliver it when I'm not in, so I get back from work to find one of those 'Sorry we missed you' cards lying by the front door and that means a visit to the post office and a half-hour wait in the queue. Every time! I try to have it delivered when I know I'll be in, but I always seem to miss them by five minutes. It's very frustrating. Anyway, enough about me. Over to you, and I believe we have Daisy on the line now, from Liverpool. Hello, Daisy.

Daisy Yeah, hi Matt. The thing that really gets me angry is the number of passwords you need for your online life.

Presenter I know exactly what you mean.

Daisy Of course, I know it's important to keep your personal stuff safe. A friend of mine had her social media account hacked and it was terrible, but there are just so many things you need a password for. I can remember the ones for the sites I use every day. The problem is those sites you just use once or twice a year. I can never remember and then I have to go through all the 'forgotten your password' stuff, and it takes half an hour to do anything.

Presenter Exactly. You need to do what I do – just use the same password for everything.

Daisy They say that's the worst thing you can do.

Presenter Well, I'll take my chances. Thank you, Daisy, and next up we have Ryan from Portsmouth.

Ryan Hi, Matt. What really gets me is people who flex on Facebook.

Presenter Flex? You'll have to explain.

Ryan Yeah, flex – show off. Tell you how great they are. But they always do it by pretending to put themselves down. For example, my mate got his exam results: 8 grade As and a B in Art. So he posts a photo of the results on Facebook with the comment, 'I always was bad at Art.' I mean, come on. The only reason for that is to show off how clever he is.

Presenter And he's still your friend?! Thanks, Ryan. Now, Andy, hi. What do you want to complain about?

Andy My car got broken into the other day.

Presenter Street crime. Now that is a terrible thing.

Andy Well, that wasn't the problem. The problem was that I had to take the train into work – something I've never done before and I hope I never have to do again. I mean, the train was half an hour late, it was crowded and there was nowhere to sit, people were playing music on their phone, there was a bunch of young kids using bad language. All in all, it was a really uncomfortable journey.

Presenter Welcome to my world. That describes my journey to work most days.

Andy And they want us to give up our cars and use more public transport! That's never going to happen.

Presenter Well, thanks Andy, but I guess if we really do want to save the planet, we need to start …

Unit 12

🔊 12.03

OK, so here's my presentation about a real-life hero. He's from England, or rather he was. It's the inspiring story of a young man who achieved remarkable things in spite of the fact that he was living with incurable cancer. When he passed away, at the age of only 19, he'd managed to raise £3 million for Teenage Cancer Trust, the charity which had supported him through his four-year cancer journey. Here's the story.

Stephen Sutton was born in 1994 in Burntwood, a town in central England. He was a very active, young person with a love of sport, in particular football and long-distance running. He achieved very good academic grades at school, and it was his dream to become a doctor. He'd already attended interviews at many leading universities, where he hoped to be able to study Medicine, but unfortunately, as his medical condition worsened, he realised that he would not be able to fulfil his dream.

In 2010, when Stephen had just turned 15, he had the first symptoms of the illness. His mum was worried that her son might have inherited the cancer gene from his father, who had twice overcome bowel cancer. She pleaded with doctors to have Stephen scanned for cancer, but their opinion was that it was extremely unlikely that someone of Stephen's age would have bowel cancer. However, six months later Stephen was diagnosed with the condition and underwent treatment. At the age of 17, after all the treatment had failed, Stephen and his parents were told that he had incurable cancer.

Stephen was devastated, but refused to feel sorry for himself. He was determined not to lose any time, and wrote a 'bucket list' of 46 activities he wanted to complete in the time he had left. The first item on the list was to raise ten thousand pounds for the Teenage Cancer Trust. The list also included such things as writing a book, public speaking in front of a huge crowd of people and getting his name in the Guinness World Records, as well as slightly less ambitious things such as watching a football match at Wembley Stadium.

Stephen was an inspiration for other people in the way he lived his life despite having cancer. He didn't want to give in to the pain, and wanted to enjoy the time he had left as much as possible. He never complained about his situation, bravely managing to stay positive.

Stephen created his own website and Facebook blog, 'Stephen's Story', and it became his passion to help other people by raising money for the Teenage Cancer Trust. He inspired thousands of people to donate money to the charity, and a number of celebrities supported his cause, among them famous actors, sports professionals and politicians, including the then UK Prime Minister, David Cameron. In order to raise money himself, Stephen completed a skydive, organised a charity ball and all kinds of other fundraising events. He always uploaded the photos of his activities to his Facebook page, with the 'thumbs-up' gesture that would become his trademark.

Stephen passed away on the fourteenth of May 2014, but his legacy to help young people diagnosed with cancer has lived on. To date, Stephen's fundraising total has exceeded 5.5 million pounds from over 340,000 donors. A quote from his Facebook page, which is now maintained by his mum, says that Stephen's story 'has inspired hundreds of thousands of people across the world with his passion for life and will continue to make a genuine difference for as long as Stephen's legacy continues'. The Neon Brotherhood, a band from Stephen's hometown, even released a single inspired by his heroic life, 'Hope Ain't a Bad Thing', which went to number two in the British top ten.

OK, that's my talk. I hope that you have found this story as inspiring as I have, and I would now …

WELCOME UNIT

A LESSONS IN LIFE

Exercise 1
1 c 2 a 3 d 4 b

Exercise 2
1 Unless you promise not to tell anyone, I won't tell you my secret.
2 You can borrow my phone provided that you don't use all the data.
3 You can go to the party as long as you promise to be back before midnight.
4 Keep the noise down otherwise my neighbour will get very angry.

get used to

Exercise 1
1 I'll never get used to messaging on this phone.
2 It took me a few months to get used to my new school.
3 It might take you a while to get used to using the new system.
4 I've finally got used to getting up early on Saturdays.

Exercise 2
A I'll never get used to wearing this thing.
B I'm still not really used to heights.
C I got used to eating with them when I lived in China.
D You get used to the noise after a while.

Friendship idioms

Exercise 1
1 out 2 out 3 in 4 on 5 on 6 the 7 at 8 the

Exercise 2
1 bury the hatchet 2 clear the air 3 know each other inside out 4 fall out 5 two peas in a pod 6 a house on fire 7 shoulder to cry on 8 joined at the hip

SUMMING UP

Exercise 1
5, 3, 9, 1, 7, 2, 10, 4, 6, 8

B CHALLENGES

Verbs with *-ing* or infinitive

Exercise 1
1 a to meet b meeting
2 a to call b calling
3 a saying b to say
4 a to take b taking
5 a chatting b to chat

Exercise 2
Students' own answers

Issuing and accepting a challenge

Exercise 1
1 bet – e
2 challenge – b
3 reckon – d
4 bet – a

Exercise 2
Students' own answers

Our greatest challenge

Exercise 1
1 worried
2 unsure
3 apprehensive
4 positive
5 feeling
6 believe

Exercise 2
Students' own answers

Phrases for talking about the future

Exercise 1
1 off to
2 about to
3 on the point of
4 likely to
5 certain

SUMMING UP

Exercise 1
1 challenge
2 apprehensive
3 feeling
4 bet
5 right
6 about
7 doing
8 off

C EMPATHISING

Cheering someone up and sympathising about past situations

Exercise 1
1 it get you down
2 shame
3 you
4 up
5 terrible
6 in there
7 dear
8 the bright side

Exercise 2
Students' own answers

Life's ups and downs

Exercise 1
1 didn't live up to my expectations
2 tried my hardest
3 blame
4 let her down
5 my way
6 getting in the way of

Exercise 2
1 5 2 3 3 1 4 4 5 6 6 2

Adjectives to describe uncomfortable feelings

Exercise 1
1 stuck
2 guilty
3 ashamed
4 awkward
5 puzzled
6 desperate

Exercise 2
1 ashamed
2 puzzled
3 guilty
4 stuck
5 desperate
6 awkward

Talking about past ability

Exercise 1
1 d 2 f 3 a 4 b 5 c 6 e

Exercise 2
Students' own answers

SUMMING UP

Exercise 1
1 managed
2 dear
3 succeeded
4 let
5 you
6 ashamed
7 blame
8 bright

D BUT IS IT NEWS?

Introducing news

Exercise 1
1 c 2 e 3 a 4 d 5 b

Exercise 2
Students' own answers

Ways of speaking

Exercise 1
1 recommending
2 confessing
3 complaining
4 introducing
5 announcing

Verb + noun collocations with *make, take, play, do, give*

Exercise 1
make – a deal, a decision, a speech, money, progress
take – a decision, advantage, advice, revenge
play – a part
do – a deal, research
give – a speech, advice, money

Exercise 2
1 make a decision
2 played; part
3 Take; advice
4 doing research
5 give/make a speech
6 make; money

Cause and effect linkers

Exercise 1
1 result
2 Consequently
3 because
4 due

Exercise 2
Students' own answers

Sharing news

Exercise 1
1 let
2 keep
3 get
4 break
5 pass

SUMMING UP

Exercise 1

7 **Dad** That's your problem, not mine.
10 **Dad** No, Sophie. I'm sorry. There are no more chances. From now on, you're on your own in the kitchen.
3 **Dad** Guess what, kids. I have made a decision.
1 **Dad** Everyone, I'd like to announce something.
5 **Dad** I will. Because of the mess that you always leave in the kitchen, I am no longer going to make meals for you.
8 **Will** I don't really think it's a problem. I quite like the idea of cooking for myself.
2 **Will** What is it this time, Dad?
6 **Sophie** That's not fair, Dad. How are we supposed to eat?
9 **Sophie** That's because you don't really care what you eat. But I do. Please Dad. Give us another chance.
4 **Sophie** Come on then. Tell us what it is.

UNIT 1 FAMILY MATTERS

GRAMMAR

Exercise 1

1 ✓ 3 ✓ 4 ✓ 5 ✓ 7 ✓ 8 ✓

Exercise 2

1 past	5 present
2 future	6 present/future
3 present	7 past
4 past	8 present

Exercise 3

1 used to	5 tends to be
2 would	6 are always trying
3 would never	7 always make
4 used to keep	8 will always

Exercise 4

1 always taking my things
2 tends to get our names
3 will often/usually live with
4 didn't use to get on
5 would sometimes have

Exercise 5

Students' own answers

Exercise 6

1 Annoyingly	4 hopefully
2 Honestly	5 Admittedly
3 Surely	

Exercise 7

1 Surely	5 Honestly
2 Hopefully	6 Understandably
3 Admittedly	7 Annoyingly
4 Regrettably	8 Obviously

Exercise 8

1 Hopefully, I'll get chosen for the school play.
2 Obviously, he wasn't happy about what you said.
3 Honestly, I don't really care what you do.
4 Regrettably, they sold all their best players.
5 Admittedly, I didn't really try very hard.
6 Understandably, they were quite upset about their test results.
7 Surely it won't rain again today.

GET IT RIGHT!

1 Hopefully, my brother and I might start to get on better now.
2 Regrettably, my new job just made things worse.
3 Honestly, if Nora doesn't start being more respectful to her teachers, she'll get into trouble.
4 Admittedly, we don't agree on everything, but we are still good friends.
5 Understandably, you're very upset about his inconsiderate behaviour.
6 Obviously, the lazy students were not used to having such a demanding teacher.

VOCABULARY

Exercise 1

1 self-centred	4 respectful
2 rebellious	5 insecure
3 traditional	6 unconventional

Exercise 2

1 h 2 f 3 d 4 b 5 g 6 a 7 e 8 c

Exercise 3

Students' own answers

Exercise 4

1 life	5 word
2 nerves	6 something
3 me	7 things
4 fights	8 put

Exercise 5

a 1 b 5 c 7 d 2 e 8 f 6 g 3 h 4

VOCABULARY EXTRA

Exercise 1

1 e	4 b
2 c	5 d
3 a	

Exercise 2

1 like one of the family
2 set up home
3 run in the family
4 bring up children
5 provide (material things) for a family

Exercise 3

Students' own answers

READING

Exercise 1

They are (identical) twin sisters.

Exercise 2

3, 4, 7, 5, 2, 6, 1, 8

Exercise 3

Students' own answers

Exercise 4

1 A 2 F 3 A 4 F

DEVELOPING WRITING

Exercise 1

1 She's entered a national essay writing competition.
2 Lola's older sister.
3 Because she copes so well with her autism and tries to help others with the same condition.

Exercise 2

refers to her friend's suggestion
tells her friend what's been happening in her life ✓
gives reasons for the delay in her reply ✓
enquires how her friend is ✓

Exercise 3

Family hero: Jennie, (my older sister)
Jennie's challenge: living with autism
What Jennie wants: to help others understand the condition
Examples of how she does this: spoke for 20 minutes in school assembly, works with a charity supporting children who have autistic siblings

Exercise 4

Students' own answers

Exercise 5

Students' own answers

LISTENING

Exercise 1

C

Exercise 2

1 rebellious 2 self-centred 3 respectful

Exercise 3

1 F 2 F 3 DS 4 F 5 T 6 T

Exercise 4

1 question tag
2 phrase
3 rhetorical question
4 question tag
5 emphatic use of auxiliary
6 repetition of a word or phrase
7 emphatic use of auxiliary

DIALOGUE

Exercise 1

11 **Freya** What do you mean? Why would I want to go there?

3 **Freya** You know exactly what: my new trainers. What have you done with them?

9 **Freya** I will and if I find them, there will be trouble.

5 **Freya** I'm sorry but I don't believe you. You're always taking my things without asking.

7 **Freya** So you won't mind if I take a look in your room then, will you?

1 **Freya** OK, Freya, where are they?

8 **Orla** No, I won't. Go ahead. Be my guest.

2 **Orla** Where's what?

6 **Orla** Well this time I'm not guilty. Sorry to disappoint you.

10 **Orla** But before you waste your time, you might want to check in Lucy's room first.

4 **Orla** Nothing. I've done nothing with your stupid trainers.

12 **Orla** Just that maybe your favourite baby sister has something that belongs to you. I'm not always the problem, you know.

Exercise 2

Students' own answers

C1 ADVANCED

Exercise 1

1 used	5 least
2 own	6 of
3 For	7 will
4 new	8 how

Exercise 2

1 been	5 would
2 much	6 from
3 at	7 being
4 one	8 In

UNIT 2 SWEET DREAMS

GRAMMAR

Exercise 1

1 stopped	5 said
2 didn't	6 to turn
3 to text	7 knew, did
4 was	8 had

Exercise 2

1 went	5 didn't play
2 wasn't/weren't	6 could
3 hadn't drunk	7 bought
4 stopped	8 didn't keep

Exercise 3

1 I wish I lived in the countryside.
2 I'd prefer it if we left half an hour earlier.
3 It's time I had lunch. That's why I'm so hungry!
4 If only it would stop raining.
5 I'd prefer to walk to the party.

Exercise 4

Students' own answers

Exercise 5

1 far more
2 a lot
3 more complex
4 far bigger
5 considerably quicker

Exercise 6

1 She's nowhere near as talented as her younger sister.
2 The Eiffel Tower is far taller than I thought it would be.
3 It is way cheaper to take the bus than the train.
4 That rollercoaster is nothing like as scary as it looks.
5 This exam is significantly more difficult than the one you did last week.
6 This situation is drastically more serious than we first thought.

Exercise 7

Students' own answers

GET IT RIGHT!

1 My dream was nothing like as strange as yours. / My dream was not nearly as strange as yours. / My dream was nowhere near as strange as yours.
2 Some countries don't value the importance of sleep nearly as much as other nations. / Some countries value the importance of sleep nowhere near as much as other nations. / Some countries value the importance of sleep nothing like as much as other nations.
3 Working in this office is nowhere near as interesting as my dream job. / Working in this office is nothing like as interesting as my dream job. / Working in this office is not nearly as interesting as my dream job.
4 Nowhere near as many Japanese people take naps as the Brazilians. / Not nearly as many Japanese people take naps as the Brazilians. / Nothing like as many Japanese people take naps as the Brazilians.
5 Sleepwalking isn't nearly as mysterious as it seems. / Sleepwalking is nowhere near as mysterious as it seems. / Sleepwalking is nothing like as mysterious as it seems.

VOCABULARY

Exercise 1

1 g 2 a 3 b 4 h 5 c 6 e 7 d 8 f

Exercise 2

1 fall asleep	5 under the covers
2 take a nap	6 snores; loudly
3 nod off	7 light sleeper
4 lie in	8 fast asleep

Exercise 3

1 oversleep	4 lack
2 enough	5 get
3 skip	

Exercise 4

Students' own answers

Exercise 5

1 It's beyond my wildest dreams.
2 I'd never dream of doing something like that.
3 It's a dream come true.
4 I need to get my beauty sleep.
5 Don't lose sleep over it.
6 In your dreams.
7 Let me sleep on it.
8 It's my dream job.

Exercise 6

1 It's beyond my wildest dreams. / It's a dream come true. / It's my dream job.
2 I'd never dream of doing something like that.
3 don't lose sleep over it
4 I need to get my beauty sleep.
5 Let me sleep on it
6 In your dreams.
7 It's beyond my wildest dreams / It's a dream come true / It's my dream job.
8 It's beyond my wildest dreams / It's a dream come true.

VOCABULARY EXTRA

Exercise 1

1 through 2 over 3 in 4 out 5 off

Exercise 2

1 sleep out 2 sleep off 3 sleep in 4 sleep through 5 sleep over

Exercise 3

Students' own answers

READING

Exercise 1

Suggested answer

B

Exercise 2

1 Huffington	5 J-Lo
2 Obama	6 Cook
3 J-Lo	7 Huffington
4 Obama	8 Cook

Exercise 3

Students' own answers

Exercise 4

Students' own answers

DEVELOPING WRITING

Exercise 1

C more exercise during the school day

Exercise 2

1 It helps us sleep better, it improves concentration and reduces stress.

2 Because they use electronic devices at home and in school spend more time sitting in front of screens or behind desks.

3 Students who did the classes scored higher in tests and exams and were happier and less stressed than those who hadn't done them.

4 Early morning Wake Up and Shake Up; Lunchtime Song and Dance and After-School Yoga

Exercise 3

1 The principal aim of …

2 According to a recent survey …

3 and 4 We understand that/We strongly recommend/ We suggest

Exercise 4

Students' own answers

Exercise 5

Students' own answers

LISTENING

Exercise 1

1 Ingrid
2 –
3 Olivia
4 Bruno

Exercise 2

1 T 2 F 3 T 4 T 5 F 6 T

Exercise 3

1 moving.

2 calling a bird charity

3 get too angry with him.

4 listening to music through headphones

DIALOGUE

Exercise 1

4, 6, 3, 2, 1, 5

Exercise 2

Students' own answers

C1 ADVANCED

Exercise 1

1 C 2 A 3 C 4 C 5 D 6 B 7 C 8 D

CONSOLIDATION UNITS 1 & 2

Exercise 1

She can never do well enough at school for her parents. ✓

Her parents give her younger sister more freedom.

Her parents expect her to act more maturely. ✓

Her parents think she treats her younger sister badly. ✓

Exercise 2

1 F 2 DS 3 T 4 T 5 DS 6 F 7 DS 8 F

Exercise 3

1 I honestly don't know why I said that. / Honestly, I don't know why I said that.

2 If only we didn't have to go to school today.

3 Surely that was / That was surely the worst game of football ever played.

4 It's far quicker to walk there than to take the car.

5 My brother is always trying to get me in trouble.

6 I'd prefer to take a break and finish this tomorrow.

7 The test was nowhere near as difficult as I thought it would be.

8 We used to be friends until he started going out with my sister.

Exercise 4

1 g 2 d 3 a 4 h 5 b 6 f 7 c 8 e

Exercise 5

1 outgoing
2 rebellious
3 insecure
4 self-centred
5 traditional
6 demanding
7 unconventional
8 respectful

Exercise 6

1 Tell me
2 did you
3 light
4 always taking
5 consider getting
6 self-centred

Exercise 7

1 In different periods, including being awake in the middle of the night.

2 They became more comfortable and they were raised/not on the floor.

3 They slept curled up like babies.

4 They were filled with straw or feathers and were more comfortable.

5 They read books or visited friends.

6 They changed because factory schedules were rigid and people had to sleep in a single cycle.

7 Because the light could be controlled, people started to sleep in one single period and not two.

Exercise 8

Students' own answers

UNIT 3 LUCKY FOR SOME?

GRAMMAR

Exercise 1

1 f 2 c 3 h 4 a 5 b 6 d 7 e 8 g

Exercise 2

1 wouldn't, hadn't

2 had, would, wouldn't

3 had, wouldn't

4 was/were, would

5 wouldn't, hadn't

6 weren't, wouldn't

7 would, were

8 wouldn't, had

Exercise 3

1 hadn't spent, would be

2 wouldn't be, had woken

3 was/were, would've gone

4 wouldn't have, hadn't fallen

5 had accepted, would be

6 wouldn't need, had studied

7 would feel, had forgotten

8 hadn't missed, would be

Exercise 4

Students' own answers

Exercise 5

1 *unless* / ~~*if*~~ / ~~*otherwise*~~

2 *Suppose* / *Imagine* / ~~*As long as*~~

3 ~~*suppose*~~ / ~~*unless*~~ / *otherwise*

4 ~~*Unless*~~ / *If* / ~~*Otherwise*~~

5 *as long as* / ~~*unless*~~ / *provided that*

6 ~~*Imagine*~~ / *Provided that* / *Suppose*

Exercise 6

1 unless
2 as long as
3 Suppose
4 Imagine
5 otherwise
6 if
7 provided that

Exercise 7

1 You can come in after 11 pm as long as you tell the porter when you leave.

2 You mustn't leave your bicycle on the lawn unless you are going out immediately.

3 You can have a wakeup call in the morning if you tell the night porter.

4 You can use the kitchen provided that you leave it clean and tidy.

5 Keep your key safe otherwise you might get locked out.

6 Please don't use the college phone unless it is an emergency.

GET IT RIGHT!

1 Unless you play the lottery, you don't have a chance of winning it!

2 – ✓

3 Juan's going to miss the beginning of the film unless he turns up in the next two minutes.

4 – ✓

5 Sophia never travels on a Friday unless she absolutely has to.

VOCABULARY

Exercise 1

A	T	J	M	O	K	I	L	V	B	I	X	H
O	R	A	C	T	B	J	P	U	R	F	1F	X
J	K	H	P	E	V	D	3W	L	2S	T	A	Y
I	D	B	C	G	O	4C	O	M	E	N	L	J
M	E	G	O	F	K	I	R	W	T	Y	L	Z
F	G	N	L	5P	I	C	K	J	B	F	Z	L
A	U	Q	D	U	Q	R	E	S	E	D	A	L
H	J	6T	U	R	N	E	D	U	P	M	D	Y
E	U	U	W	M	A	H	L	J	O	C	G	E
K	S	R	F	L	K	I	E	S	A	R	K	S
7R	A	N	C	B	G	H	R	U	N	Q	B	K

Exercise 2

1 worked out
2 pick up
3 ran away
4 came to
5 're staying on
6 turned back
7 set off
8 turned down

Exercise 3

1 bad
2 pushing
3 just
4 in
5 bring
6 beginner's
7 have
8 Better

Exercise 4

1 6 2 4 3 3 4 7 5 2 6 5 7 8

Exercise 5

1 just over
2 all over again
3 overall
4 all over
5 fall over

VOCABULARY EXTRA

Exercise 1

1 pull
2 get
3 watch
4 come
5 hand

Exercise 2

1 come over
2 watch over
3 pull over
4 Hand over
5 get over

Exercise 3

Students' own answers

READING

Exercise 1

1 c 2 a 3 b

Exercise 2

1 T
2 F
3 DS
4 T
5 F
6 T

Exercise 3

Students' own answers

Exercise 4

Students' own answers

DEVELOPING WRITING

Exercise 1

A 2 B 4 C 3 D 1

Exercise 2

1 She had saved up for them for a long time and thinks it was money well spent.

2 She felt miserable.

3 She realised when she recognised the bus driver.

4 She was surprised and happy.

Exercise 3

1 to get to the point; to cut a long story short

2 I couldn't have been happier.; My heart sank!; I don't think I've ever felt so miserable in my life.; I was speechless, and over the moon.

Exercise 4

Students' own answers

Exercise 5

Students' own answers

LISTENING

Exercise 1

1 3 2 1 3 2

Exercise 2

1 are only available
2 a bit tight
3 luck and knowledge
4 choose their own
5 wet and muddy
6 just over twenty

DIALOGUE

Exercise 1

5 **Gina** Yes, and it didn't come for ages. And when it finally did come, it got stuck in a traffic jam, you know, it being rush hour at that time of day and all.

3 **Gina** Not wrong exactly – just not right! I was hoping I'd be back home in time for my favourite game show on TV, but the bus driver simply went past my stop without pulling over to pick me up! Just my luck.

1 **Gina** Today hasn't been my lucky day.

7 **Gina** No, and my mum didn't think to record it either. And I so badly wanted to see it.

4 **Martha** So you had to wait for the next one?

2 **Martha** Oh? Why's that? Did something go wrong?

8 **Martha** Bad luck. But don't worry, I'm sure they'll show it again before too long and we can record it for you.

6 **Martha** It's always bad after five o'clock, isn't it? But anyway, I'm guessing you didn't make it back home in time for the show?

PHRASES FOR FLUENCY

Exercise 1

1 assuming
2 that is
3 after all
4 now and again
5 What have you got to lose?
6 We'll sort something out.

Exercise 2

1 What have you got to lose?
2 assuming
3 that is
4 now and again
5 We'll sort something out.
6 after all

C1 ADVANCED

Exercise 1

1 A 2 C 3 C 4 B 5 C 6 A

UNIT 4 HAVING A LAUGH

GRAMMAR

Exercise 1

1 All
2 all
3 It's
4 it's
5 What
6 All
7 all
8 what
9 It's

Exercise 2

1 What I like is a joke with a good punchline.

2 It's Jack who's good at telling jokes, not his brother.

3 It's you who wastes your time playing on your computer.

4 All she was saying was that you should take a break.

5 All Olga wants for lunch is a sandwich.

Exercise 3

1
a What you need to say is 'sorry'.
b It's you who needs to say 'sorry'.

2
a It was my dad who forgot the punchline.
b What my dad forgot was the punchline.

3
a What I don't understand is why she said 'no'.
b It's why she said 'no' that I don't understand.

4
a It's cold showers that I hate more than anything.
b What I hate more than anything is cold showers.

Exercise 4

A 3, 7 B 6, 8 C 1, 5 D 2, 4

Exercise 5
1 This is undeniably the best day of my life.
2 I have certainly made the best decision of my life.
3 I am undoubtedly the happiest man on the planet.
4 It's essentially what I've always wanted to do.
5 I definitely can't wait to get started.
6 It is literally the job of my dreams.
7 A chocolate taster! I mean, it's utterly amazing.
8 And this company absolutely makes the best chocolates there are.

Exercise 6
Students' own answers

Exercise 7
Students' own answers

GET IT RIGHT!
1 It's the release of endorphins that makes us feel good when we laugh.
2 It's her sense of humour that I don't get.
3 It's us who will have the last laugh when we win the tournament.
4 It's him that is undoubtedly the best comedian in the country at the moment.
5 It's them who will be laughing on the other side of their faces when their teacher finds out.

VOCABULARY
Exercise 1
1 g 2 f 3 e 4 a 5 d 6 b 7 c 8 h

Exercise 2
How good is your sense of humour?

1 get	3 punchline
2 at	4 giggles; find

Exercise 3

1 laughing	5 Joking
2 laughing	6 joke
3 laughed	7 laughing
4 laughing	8 laugh

Exercise 4
Students' own answers

VOCABULARY EXTRA
Exercise 1
1 chuckle
2 howl with laughter
3 crack up
4 split your sides laughing
5 be doubled up
6 be in stitches

Exercise 2
1 e 2 c 3 f 4 a 5 d 6 b

Exercise 3
Students' own answers

READING
Exercise 1
Stress reduction, muscle exercise, releasing endorphins and reducing cortisol, increase of cells that attack viruses and tumours.

Exercise 2
A 2 B 1 C 5 D 6 E 4

Exercise 3
1 b Relieves stress and anxiety
2 d Muscle tone and cardiovascular function improved; oxygen levels in the blood are boosted
3 a It makes you feel better and improves your state of mind.
4 c Laughter is contagious; it makes other people feel better.

Exercise 4
Students' own answers

DEVELOPING WRITING
Exercise 1
the actors ✓ the soundtrack ✓

Exercise 2
Suggested answers
no one would be entirely / totally surprised if it went on for many more series;
Neither is the grown-up child moving back into the parental home idea absolutely / utterly / entirely / totally / unquestionably original;
But then the show isn't really trying to utterly / entirely / essentially / literally / totally redefine the genre;
What *Fuller House* undeniably / clearly / unquestionably / definitely delivers so well are clever storylines;
One character in particular has undeniably / clearly / undoubtedly / unquestionably / definitely / certainly helped transform the show into such a global hit;
Kimmy has clearly / undoubtedly / unquestionably / definitely / certainly become a firm favourite with fans;
I absolutely / definitely / certainly must admit that it took me a while to get into *Fuller House*;
But I'm entirely / definitely / certainly happy I stuck with it.

Exercise 3
1 The name of the series; the date of the original series
2 To let the reader know that they are aware they may not have seen the series.
3 To give background information on the series.
4 The concept of a family sitcom.
5 The reviewer likes the storylines, the funny jokes and the characters.
6 It teaches us what is important in life and why families and friends are important.

Exercise 4
Students' own answers

Exercise 5
Students' own answers

LISTENING
Exercise 1
1 Harry up and open the door.
2 Because the teacher told them it was piece of cake.
3 Wow! You've got problems.
4 Throw a clock out of the window.

Exercise 2
1 Because Carl had to explain it to her.
2 That they don't have the same sense of humour.
3 Hearing old jokes that they'd forgotten about.
4 He gets them online.
5 Her homework.
6 She doesn't find it as funny as her mum does. She feels embarrassed and slightly impatient.
7 He has a reputation for telling terrible jokes.
8 Ella suggest that they throw a clock out of the window at school today to make time fly at school/the day to go more quickly.

Exercise 3

1 don't get it	3 hilarious
2 very funny	4 funny; like

DIALOGUE
Exercise 1
5 **Teacher** OK, let me put it to you differently. If I gave you two apples, and another two apples and another two, how many would you have?
3 **Teacher** No, listen carefully … If I gave you two cats, and another two cats and another two, how many would you have?
1 **Teacher** If I gave you two cats and another two cats and another two, how many would you have?
9 **Teacher** Georgia, where on earth do you get seven from?
7 **Teacher** Good. Now, if I gave you two cats, and another two cats and another two, how many would you have?
4 **Georgia** I've already told you. I'd have seven.
8 **Georgia** For the third time, I'd have seven.
10 **Georgia** Because I've already got a cat!
6 **Georgia** Six apples.
2 **Georgia** Easy. I'd have seven cats.

Exercise 2
Students' own answers

C1 ADVANCED

Exercise 1

1 B 2 C 3 B 4 C 5 D 6 A

CONSOLIDATION UNITS 3 & 4

Exercise 1

Order of mention:

1 Rosie's school bus breaks down.

2 Rosie revises for her test.

3 Rosie finds out that the headteacher is teaching her class.

4 Rosie forgets her packed lunch.

5 Rosie gets injured.

6 Rosie misses the school bus.

7 Rosie is locked out of the house.

8 Rosie's phone runs out of battery.

9 Rosie tries to have a hot bath.

Exercise 2

Chronological order:

1 Rosie revises for her test.

2 Rosie forgets her packed lunch.

3 Rosie's school bus breaks down.

4 Rosie finds out that the headteacher is teaching her class.

5 Rosie's phone runs out of battery.

6 Rosie gets injured.

7 Rosie misses the school bus.

8 Rosie is locked out of the house.

9 Rosie tries to have a hot bath.

Exercise 3

1 If John hadn't bought a new tablet, he'd have some money.

2 Unless we leave now, we'll miss the train.

3 All I liked about the party was the food.

4 If I liked seafood, I would have eaten something at the restaurant.

5 If you don't invite Sasha to your party, she'll be really upset.

6 What I find most annoying about travelling is waiting for hours in airports.

7 It's Henry you need to talk to about the mess.

8 Provided you promise not to tell anyone, I'll tell you my secret.

Exercise 4

1 luck	5 joke
2 laugh	6 luck
3 joke	7 luck
4 luck	8 joke

Exercise 5

1 e 2 b 3 g 4 h 5 f 6 a 7 d 8 c

Exercise 6

13 **Robin** Ha ha! Very funny.

3 **Robin** Of course it does, assuming you believe in these things, that is.

9 **Robin** Don't mention it. Let's call it £5.

5 **Robin** Well, if I didn't have this coin, I certainly wouldn't have passed the mid-term exams.

1 **Robin** Have I shown you my lucky pound coin?

11 **Robin** No, I'm serious. It's a bargain. It really works. What have you got to lose?

7 **Robin** Well you can have this one, if you want.

12 **Jenni** Only £4!

4 **Jenni** I do. I really do. So how has it helped you?

10 **Jenni** £5! Ha! That's a good one, Robin.

6 **Jenni** Really? I could do with something like that.

2 **Jenni** No you haven't, does it work?

8 **Jenni** Wow! Thanks. That's really kind of you.

Exercise 7

1 To attempt to find out what makes us laugh and why.

2 They were asked to submit their favourite joke, answer a questionnaire and rate jokes sent in by others.

3 Many Europeans preferred surreal jokes, but English-speaking countries preferred word-play.

4 The time of day and day of the month during which a joke was found funniest, the perfect length for a joke and the funniest animal in jokes.

Exercise 8

Students' own answers

UNIT 5 WHAT A THRILL!

GRAMMAR

Exercise 1

4 Advised	9 Warned
5 dressed	12 Filmed
8 Encouraged,	

Exercise 2

1 Motivated	5 Trained
2 Paragliding	6 Watching
3 Going	7 Climbing
4 Inspired	8 Surrounded

Exercise 3

1 climbing	5 taken
2 Falling	6 Phoning
3 breaking / having broken	7 interviewed
4 Watched	8 Having

Exercise 4

1 Having watched the video lots of times, he knows what happens.

2 Having been scuba diving, she'd (now) like to try deep sea diving.

3 Having enjoyed caving in Wales, he wants to do it again.

4 Having worked as a stunt person in films, she's used to performing dangerous stunts.

5 Having never been keen on heights, he doesn't think he can do a bungee jump.

Exercise 5

1 Having trained for six months, I was ready to run the marathon.

2 Watching the video reminded me of the parachute jump.

3 Having climbed Mount Kilimanjaro, she was ready to climb Mount Everest.

4 Being afraid of heights, he couldn't look down.

5 Having been trained by an Olympic athlete, he was fit enough to trek across the desert.

6 Having done a bungee jump before, she wasn't worried.

Exercise 6

1 After practising on an indoor climbing wall, I was ready to climb outdoors. / Since practising on an indoor climbing wall, I've been ready to climb outdoors.

2 After signing up for a parachute jump, he wasn't able to sleep. / Since signing up for a parachute jump, he hasn't been able to sleep.

3 Learning that his daughter had won the marathon, he was very proud./ Since learning that his daughter had won the marathon, he has been very proud. / After learning that his daughter had won the marathon, he was very proud. / On learning that his daughter had won the marathon, he was very proud.

4 After breaking his leg he didn't do any more climbing. / Since breaking his leg he hasn't done any more climbing.

5 Before doing her first parachute jump, she had done three practice jumps. / Since doing her first parachute jump, she has done three practice jumps.

6 While watching a film set in the Alps, she decided to join a climbing club. / After watching a film set in the Alps, she decided to join a climbing club. / Since watching a film set in the Alps, she has decided to join a climbing club. / On watching a film set in the Alps, she decided to join a climbing club.

7 After seeing (that) his friend was afraid, he climbed back up to help him. / On seeing (that) his friend was afraid, he climbed back up to help him. / Seeing (that) his friend was afraid, he climbed back up to help him.

Exercise 7

1 blow
2 laughing
3 shining
4 beating
5 falling
6 grip

GET IT RIGHT!

1 Having minimised the risks, the film director decided to go ahead with the stunt.
2 Making his point loud and clear, the teacher told the students that they wouldn't pass the exam unless they revised.
3 Having painted Megan's bedroom, they then bought new furniture for it.
4 Having agreed with us initially, she then told us that she wouldn't do it.
5 Hearing Dan sing made his mother very proud. / Hearing Dan sing, his mother felt very proud.
6 Having done one bungee jump, Saul now can't wait to do another!

VOCABULARY

Exercise 1

1 e 2 c 3 a 4 b 5 d

Exercise 2

1 stunt
2 risk-taker
3 death-defying
4 gets a kick out of
5 minimises
6 audacious
7 assessed the risk
8 daredevil

Exercise 3

1 get a kick out of
2 stunt
3 death-defying
4 daredevil
5 audacious
6 assess the risk

Exercise 4

Students' own answers

Exercise 5

1 in hot water
2 pour cold water on
3 the cold shoulder; hot under the collar
4 leave (him out) in the cold
5 hot and bothered

Exercise 6

Students' own answers

VOCABULARY EXTRA

Exercise 1

1 scared stiff
2 take your life in your hands
3 your heart misses a beat
4 scared out of your wits
5 risk life and limb

Exercise 2

1 risk life and limb
2 stiff; misses a beat
3 out of my wits
4 your life in your hands

Exercise 3

Students' own answers

READING

Exercise 1

A

Exercise 2

1 kayaked over
2 of its kind
3 1400 metres
4 108th floor
5 wear a harness
6 going on rollercoasters

Exercise 3

Students' own answers

Exercise 4

Students' own answers

DEVELOPING WRITING

Exercise 1

1 A thrilling experience she had.
2 She went snowboarding to raise money for a local hospital.
3 She was a bit nervous at first, then scared, and relieved when she finished.
4 One of the greatest experiences of her life; thrilling.

Exercise 2

1 Motivated
2 practising
3 having been given
4 putting
5 Knowing
6 Feeling
7 Having relaxed
8 stopping
9 watching
10 Having experienced

Exercise 3

A 2 B 3 C 1

Exercise 4

1 snowboard, boots, goggles, helmet
2 Her instructor was beside her and was doing it with her.
3 She felt nervous at the top of the mountain waiting for her turn.
4 Her friends.
5 One of the greatest experiences of her life; she can't wait to do it again.

Exercise 5

Students' own answers

Exercise 6

Students' own answers

LISTENING

Exercise 1

a The age of the woman who first attempted to go over the waterfall in a barrel.
b The height (in metres) of the frozen waterfall.
c The speed (in kilometres) of the water flowing over the waterfall.

Exercise 2

1 They climbed up Niagara Falls when it was frozen.
2 They have gone over the Falls in a barrel.
3 She thinks they are very brave.
4 He thinks they are crazy.
5 It took Will about an hour and Sarah a lot longer.
6 He thinks the best thing is seeing the photographs of the ice falls.

Exercise 3

1 I'd go along with that; The way I see it
2 OK, point taken; True; That's not how I see it
3 I hadn't thought of that; Well, to my mind; Yes, I suppose you're right

DIALOGUE

Exercise 1

1 I can't wait to hear all about it.; How come? You're a brilliant actress.
2 Oh no, here we go.; You're turning into a couch potato.
3 I did go to sleep really late last night.; You know what I mean.

Exercise 2

Students' own answers

C1 ADVANCED

Exercise 1

1 D 2 C 3 B 4 B 5 C 6 A

UNIT 6 FAMOUS LIVES

GRAMMAR

Exercise 1

1 GT 2 GT 3 F 4 F 5 GT 6 P 7 GT 8 GT 9 GT 10 P

Exercise 2

1 will
2 can
3 might
4 won't
5 could
6 might not
7 can
8 mightn't

Exercise 3

1 won't
2 can
3 could
4 will
5 might

Exercise 4

Students' own answers

Exercise 5

1 f 2 h 3 j 4 a 5 i 6 b 7 c 8 d 9 e 10 g

Exercise 6

1 S 2 E 3 R 4 A 5 E 6 S 7 A 8 A 9 R

Exercise 7

Students' own answers

GET IT RIGHT!

1 Do you think you could do that for me? I'd be very grateful.

2 That actor won't be invited on the chat show, surely? She's not an A-list celebrity!

3 He would definitely try and keep a low profile if it meant he could keep the paparazzi away.

4 I can't imagine that any celebrity would ever wish to disappear without a trace.

5 Perhaps Julia should see a doctor.about her total fixation on that band. It's not healthy.

6 If Simon wants to keep his friends he shouldn't / mustn't keep boring them with details of his celebrity obsession.

VOCABULARY

Exercise 1

1 fixated	5 huge fan
2 obsession	6 idol
3 addicted	7 centre of attention
4 fascination with	8 worshipped

Exercise 2

1 paparazzi	6 the face of something
2 in the limelight	7 A-list celebrity
3 keep a low profile	8 stalkers
4 up-and-coming	
5 celebrity crush	

Exercise 3

1 celebrity crush	5 paparazzi
2 up-and-coming	6 stalkers
3 in the limelight	7 A-list celebrity
4 keep a low profile	8 the face of

Exercise 4
Students' own answers

Exercise 5
1 f 2 a 3 d 4 b 5 c 6 e

VOCABULARY EXTRA

Exercise 1
break into; take off; take up; make up; turn down; come out

Exercise 2

1 turn down	4 take off
2 make up	5 take up
3 come out	6 break into

Exercise 3
Students' own answers

READING

Exercise 1
a selfie.

Exercise 2
1 F 2 DS 3 T 4 T 5 DS 6 DS 7 F 8 T

Exercise 3
2, 3
Students' own answers

Exercise 4
Students' own answers

DEVELOPING WRITING

Exercise 1
Suggested answer
... laws to protect celebrities and we don't need any more.

Exercise 2

1 As people, like everyone else who feel emotions.

2 royalty, singers, actors and sports stars

3 It would protect their privacy because they might not want to live every minute of their life in the public eye or be the centre of attention all the time.

4 Having their photo taken every time they step outside their house.

5 They might get broken.

Exercise 3

1 their – the celebrities

2 they – the special laws

3 it – the photo

4 that – having your photo taken every time you step outside your house

5 it – a celebrity's job

6 that – the fact that their job is in the public eye

7 others – people/ the public/people with that opinion

Exercise 4
Students' own answers

Exercise 5
Students' own answers

Exercise 6
Students' own answers

LISTENING

Exercise 1
A DAN B – C ELLIE D JOSH

Exercise 2
1 B 2 C 3 A 4 C 5 A 6 B

DIALOGUE

Exercise 1

1 Haven't you got anything else to do with your time?

2 It's actually quite a big deal.

3 It's all you ever seem to do.

4 I really don't need this right now.

5 Maybe you'll learn from this.

6 I really haven't got time for this right now.

7 If I do it for you, you'll never learn to do it yourself.

8 This time you're on your own.

PHRASES FOR FLUENCY

Exercise 1

[3] **Jay** I've looked in my room and it's not there.

[11] **Jay** That's not true, Mum. I've got loads of other interests.

[9] **Jay** You might have told me this would turn into a long moan about the computer. Not again!

[1] **Jay** Have you seen my phone, Mum?

[7] **Jay** I don't know. Last week maybe.

[5] **Jay** Come on, Mum. It's not that bad.

[6] **Mum** Actually it is. Just out of curiosity, when was the last time you tidied it?

[2] **Mum** No, but might it be in your room by any chance?

[12] **Mum** Yes, like playing on your phone. But I guess at least you won't be doing that for a while.

[10] **Mum** I'm just saying it's all you ever seem to do.

[4] **Mum** Fat chance you could find anything in your room, it's such a mess.

[8] **Mum** More like last year. If you spent less time on your computer and more time tidying, for a change, you wouldn't keep losing things.

Exercise 2
Students' own answers

C1 ADVANCED

Exercise 1
1 E 2 A 3 D 4 B 5 F 6 G

CONSOLIDATION UNITS 5 & 6

Exercise 1

1 93

2 Wing walking

3 Scotland

4 Northern Ireland

5 1 hour 27 minutes

6 First person to wing walk over the Channel twice.

7 Oldest man to loop-the-loop while wing walking.

Exercise 2

1 1942	5 2011
2 13 years	6 4 times
3 80	7 85
4 £1.25 million	

Exercise 3

1 Inspired	5 Cooking
2 must	6 won't
3 singing	7 fall
4 can	8 Feeling

Exercise 4

1 with
2 of
3 out
4 over
5 on
6 for
7 in
8 off

Exercise 5

1 stunts
2 paparazzi
3 celebrity crush
4 centre of attention
5 idol
6 daredevil
7 hot under the collar
8 huge fan

Exercise 6

1 talk
2 Come
3 do
4 accept
5 point
6 see

Exercise 7

1 It's a hit Broadway musical show.
2 A teenage *Hamilton* superfan.
3 A video of the show her teacher used in class when she was studying American history.
4 The themes of war and the strong, brave young men in it as well as the raps.
5 They can stream it on TV.

Exercise 8

Students' own answers

UNIT 7 A THING OF BEAUTY?

GRAMMAR

Exercise 1

1 so
2 those
3 do
4 Neither
5 so
6 that

Exercise 2

1 Nor
2 the one
3 those
4 so
5 do

Exercise 3

Students' own answers

Exercise 4

Students' own answers

Exercise 5

1 I'd love one. – e
2 Do you fancy playing a game of tennis? – g
3 Have you got time for a cup of tea? – f
4 I'm sorry but I can't stay. – b
5 Don't worry about it. – d
6 Do you want to listen to another track? – h
7 I haven't seen you here before. – a

Exercise 6

1 Love your new haircut.
2 Like an ice cream?
3 Got any chocolate?
4 Seen Sam today?
5 Not a problem./No problem.

Exercise 7

1 ~~I~~ don't know.
2 ~~I'm~~ not sure.
3 ~~That's~~ nice.
4 ~~I'm~~ not bad.
5 Yes, please. I would ~~like an apple~~.
6 No, ~~I think we had~~ better go home now.

Exercise 8

1 A couple.
2 Great.
3 Interesting.
4 Once.
5 Love some.
6 Love to.

GET IT RIGHT!

1 Rebecca thinks Kathryn needs to run greater distances in training if she's going to complete the marathon and she thinks so, too.
2 Monica hasn't been to a fitness class in ages and Jo hasn't either/neither has Jo.
3 My mum thinks that ripped jeans will soon go out of fashion and my dad certainly hopes so, too!
4 Mark doesn't like the retro look and neither does Finn/Finn doesn't either.
5 Smartphones have become a must-have and so have tablets.
6 Isaac is going to cut down on his screen time and so is George.

VOCABULARY

Exercise 1

1 d 2 g 3 e 4 a 5 b 6 c 7 f

Exercise 2

1 bang on trend
2 really in
3 must-have
4 short-lived
5 the next best thing
6 a thing
7 had gone out of fashion

Exercise 3

1 shivers
2 racing
3 smile
4 tear
5 soar
6 goosebumps

The mystery word is: happiness

Exercise 4

Students' own answers

VOCABULARY EXTRA

Exercise 1

1 d 2 a 3 f 4 e 5 b 6 c

Exercise 2

1 dressed to kill
2 a slave to fashion
3 take pride in your appearance
4 off-the-peg
5 dress for the occasion
6 sense of style

Exercise 3

Students' own answers

READING

Exercise 1

arsenic – pills and soaps
deadly nightshade – eye drops
DNP – slimming pills
lead – make-up

Exercise 2

Suggested answers

1 Who started the fashion for pale skin?
2 What are the symptoms of lead poisoning?
3 Why did arsenic pills make the skin pale?
4 What is deadly nightshade?
5 How did Eloise Aimee Parry get to hospital?
6 Why are people buying unregulated and dangerous health and beauty products over the internet?

Exercise 3

Students' own answers

Exercise 4

Students' own answers

DEVELOPING WRITING

Exercise 1

Vita-Hair shampoo and conditioner

Exercise 2

1 The advert claims to be a revolutionary new product that will give you fuller, thicker hair.
After 3 months, Sally hasn't noticed any difference in the thickness of her hair.
2 The advert promises to give you your dream hair.
The shampoo makes Sally's hair dull and lifeless.
3 The advert says that there are only natural oils in the product.
The shampoo contains several chemicals in it.

Exercise 3

That's rubbish!
This is the worst shampoo I've ever tried.
How can you lie to people like that?

Exercise 4

Students' own answers

Exercise 5

Students' own answers

LISTENING

Exercise 1

a visual style that mixes old and new; modern technology with design ideas from the Victorian age

Exercise 2

1, 2, 5

Exercise 3

1 It relates to the Victorian era and the Industrial Revolution because steam power was at its peak then.

2 He watched a video tutorial on YouTube and worked out how to add parts.

3 Because he had seen big fashion labels designing them, but he couldn't afford to buy them.

4 It was second-hand and he adapted it using an old badge, some goggles and some metal parts from his parent's garage.

5 He should try and sell his clothes and accessories at the craft fair he's going to next week.

DIALOGUE

Exercise 1

1 Have you always dreamed
2 We understand that
3 strongly recommend
4 one million people worldwide
5 This offer is limited
6 revolutionary new
7 This brand new
8 Imagine

Exercise 2

Students' own answers

C1 ADVANCED

Exercise 1

1 to avoid putting
2 ate little/nothing for breakfast except for
3 as a (direct) result of
4 was aware that his illness
5 lost a great deal
6 was (widely) regarded as

UNIT 8 CRACKING THE CODE

GRAMMAR

Exercise 1

1 B – compared to whom
2 D – all of whom
3 A – some of whom
4 F – compared to which
5 E – one of which
6 C – one of whom

Exercise 2

1 both of which
2 one of which
3 none of whom
4 compared to which
5 in which case
6 most of which
7 neither of which

Exercise 3

1 none of which won the prize.

2 most of whom said they could come.

3 one of whom plays basketball professionally.

4 none of whom ever got married.

5 most of which she bought on the internet.

6 many of whom agreed with the proposal, but others didn't.

7 some of which are free, but you have to pay for most.

Exercise 4

1 Wherever
2 However
3 whenever
4 whatever/whichever
5 Whatever
6 whoever
7 whenever
8 However

Exercise 5

1 when
2 where
3 Wherever
4 who
5 whatever
6 what
7 whenever
8 Whoever

Exercise 6

1 Whatever
2 Wherever
3 whoever
4 whenever
5 whatever
6 However
7 Wherever

GET IT RIGHT!

1 It's important to whoever's receiving it.

2 I didn't quite get what he said, but whatever he did say I'm not interested.

3 ✓✓

4 ✓✓

5 I'm going to try to learn either Japanese or Chinese – I'll choose whichever course is cheaper.

6 However fluent you may be, there will always be someone who doesn't follow you.

VOCABULARY

Exercise 1

1 facial
2 native
3 gesture
4 dialect
5 incomprehensible
6 pronounce
7 breakdown
8 accent
9 broken
10 language

Exercise 2

1 incomprehensible
2 first language
3 misunderstood
4 language barrier
5 gesture
6 make myself
7 interpret
8 follow
9 communication breakdown
10 body language

Exercise 3

1 a 2 c 3 d 4 f 5 b 6 e 7 g 8 h

Exercise 4

1 modest
2 impulsive
3 assertive
4 self-assured
5 expressive
6 forceful
7 conceited

Exercise 5

Students' own answers

VOCABULARY EXTRA

Exercise 1

lose your patience; throw a tantrum; take a joke; Come to terms with; swallow your pride; reveal your true character

Exercise 2

1 come
2 lose
3 reveal
4 swallow
5 take
6 throws

Exercise 3

Students' own answers

READING

Exercise 1

1 Brussels; the EU Commission
2 out of curiosity
3 Lithuanian, Gaelic and Maltese

Exercise 2

1 not used 2 F 3 C 4 D 5 A 6 G 7 B 8 E

Exercise 3

Suggested answers

1 Disagree
2 Agree
3 Disagree
4 Agree

Exercise 4

Students' own answers

DEVELOPING WRITING

Exercise 1

B

Exercise 2

1 3, 1, 2, 5, 4, 6

2 cost of travel and subsistence; lack of private accommodation; personal problems; better alternatives in own country

Exercise 3

1 down to
2 account for
3 infer
4 in particular
5 worth noting
6 most significant factor
7 thus
8 coupled with

Exercise 4

Students' own answers

Exercise 5

Students' own answers

LISTENING

Exercise 1

1 B

Exercise 2

1 800
2 remaining native speakers
3 didn't ever really learn English
4 interpret the rules of the language
5 a person's identity
6 as common [here in New York City] as
7 history

DIALOGUE

Exercise 1

1 didn't catch
2 familiar with
3 lost me
4 don't follow
5 don't see
6 didn't get

Exercise 2

Students' own answers

C1 ADVANCED

Exercise 1

1 C 2 D 3 A 4 B

CONSOLIDATION UNITS 7 & 8

Exercise 1

a T-shirt.

Exercise 2

1 baseball boots.
2 Because they don't go well with a black suit and no one's worn them for at least three years.
3 smart black shoes.
4 Because she has deleted most of them.
5 She used to make bracelets and cover her arms with them.
6 band T-shirts.
7 To never [ever] wear band T-shirts.

Exercise 3

1 e 2 a 3 g 4 c 5 h 6 d 7 f 8 b

Exercise 4

1 Whoever
2 none of which
3 However
4 whenever
5 both of whom
6 Neither of them

Exercise 5

1 short-lived
2 tear; eye
3 self-conscious
4 body language
5 strong; accent
6 shivers; spine
7 must-have
8 self-assured

Exercise 6

1 modest
2 barrier
3 out of
4 goose
5 broken
6 impulsive
7 heart
8 in

Exercise 7

9 **Shop assistant** It leaves your hair shiny and healthy. It's good for your hair and the environment. I think everyone should take a bit more care of the environment.
5 **Shop assistant** OK, I'll be quick. Imagine using a product on your hair that doesn't damage the environment.
1 **Shop assistant** Excuse me. Can I introduce you to our new eco-friendly hair products?
3 **Shop assistant** I said, can I introduce you to our new eco-friendly hair products.
7 **Shop assistant** In that case, using a product like Green Hair means you won't need to think about it ever again.
10 **Freya** So do I. OK. I'll try it!
6 **Freya** I've never thought about the hair products I use like that.
2 **Freya** Sorry, I didn't catch what you said with all the noise.
8 **Freya** So, why should I buy this and not my usual brand?
4 **Freya** OK but be quick, I'm a bit short of time.

Exercise 8

1 Unprosperousness 2 Feedback 3 purple 4 bookkeeper 5 Uncopyrightable 6 rhythm 7 euouae 8 ough 9 pangram
Final fact: angry / hungry

Exercise 9

Students' own answers

UNIT 9 FAIRNESS MATTERS

GRAMMAR

Exercise 1

1 Never
2 Rarely
3 Not only
4 No sooner
5 Never
6 Not only
7 Rarely
8 Under no circumstances
9 On no account
10 Little

Exercise 2

1 had; seen
2 will; climb
3 had; struck
4 have; had/do; have
5 was
6 will; freeze
7 will; return
8 has; visited/does; visit

Exercise 3

1 Never have I been so shocked by a programme shown on TV.
2 Not only was it untrue, but wildly exaggerated, too.
3 Rarely do I complain about TV programmes.
4 No sooner had the programme finished than I phoned the TV company.
5 Not only was the person I spoke to rude, but he seemed to think my complaint was funny.
6 Little did I know the programme was meant to be a comedy.

Exercise 4

Not only did he work on the cars but he was also allowed to drive them on the test track.
The track was designed to test racing cars but the boss told Jeb that under no circumstances could he go faster than 100 kph.
Never had he enjoyed a job so much.
No sooner had he turned the last bend than the car slid off the track.
'Rarely have I seen such bad driving from my staff!'
Little did he know that there was oil on the track.

Exercise 5

1 To be honest
2 If you ask me
3 On the other hand
4 Mind you
5 However
6 Let's face it
7 The thing is
8 That said

Exercise 6

3 ~~Nevertheless~~ For example
5 ~~On the other hand~~ If you ask me / Let's face it
6 ~~As a result~~ Mind you. However / On the other hand
8 ~~While~~ Anyway / Personally
11 ~~For a start~~ By the way / Anyway

Exercise 7

Students' own answers

GET IT RIGHT!

1 ✓✓
2 I do believe Kate was treated unfairly. That said, she should have studied harder.
3 There seems to be a lot in the news about corrupt politicians at the moment. Mind you, there are lots of other corrupt people, too!
4 ✓✓
5 At the end of the day it isn't really justifiable to spend so much money on prisons when there are so many other important things. OR: It isn't really justifiable to spend so much money on prisons when, at the end of the day, there are so many other important things.

VOCABULARY

Exercise 1

A	K	U	F	[1]E	V	I	D	E	N	[2]C	E	I
B	F	[3]W	N	C	P	J	D	O	G	O	M	E
[4]G	U	I	L	T	Y	A	L	R	H	N	Q	C
T	K	T	H	C	I	H	P	O	K	F	J	M
D	U	H	V	F	S	[5]W	[6]I	T	N	E	S	S
V	R	H	A	F	[7]A	Y	N	W	B	S	E	S
I	D	O	W	Q	P	G	N	C	Z	S	Q	[8]R
X	M	L	Z	U	P	T	O	G	[9]L	I	F	E
Q	R	[10]D	E	F	E	N	C	E	K	O	G	T
B	E	X	H	O	A	P	E	F	D	N	Y	R
N	N	N	L	J	L	Q	N	T	I	S	M	A
H	W	O	M	U	B	R	T	V	S	L	G	C
J	E	S	M	B	C	X	K	A	U	I	O	T

Exercise 2
1 innocent
2 evidence
3 witness
4 defence
5 a confession
6 retract
7 withheld
8 found
9 imprisonment

Exercise 3
1 violent
2 obese
3 Social
4 evident
5 general
6 equal
7 political
8 unfair

Exercise 4
1 a – trial
2 d – way
3 e – basis
4 c – behalf
5 b – terms

VOCABULARY EXTRA

Exercise 1
1 e 2 f 3 a 4 b 5 c 6 d

Exercise 2
1 carry out an investigation
2 go on trial
3 appear in court
4 reach a verdict
5 face a (heavy) fine
6 have a fair trial

Exercise 3
Students' own answers

READING

Exercise 1
A

Exercise 2
1 Personal needs and the needs of other people.
2 Admit that they are not a fair person.
3 The writer tried to find out how fair people really are.
4 Situation 2
5 Situation 3
6 The real purpose was to show that there are different sides to arguments about what is fair.

Exercise 3
Students' own answers

Exercise 4
Students' own answers

DEVELOPING WRITING

Exercise 1
1 C 2 B

Exercise 2
1 However
2 Imagine
3 Now
4 In fact
5 Arguably
6 Consequently

Exercise 3
1 offence
2 first-time offender
3 convicted
4 community service
5 severe
6 to take into account
7 use their discretion
8 lenient

Exercise 4
Students' own answers

Exercise 5
Students' own answers

LISTENING

Exercise 1
b

Exercise 2
1 In the 1960s.
2 National Aeronautics and Space Administration.
3 They began in the era of segregation in America. They faced constant and unfair discrimination at home, at school and in their work.
4 African American women had to work in a separate building.
5 They are usually white and in higher positions than women in NASA.
6 That even today women face barriers in certain professions, particularly Science, Technology, Engineering and Maths jobs.

DIALOGUE

Exercise 1
Dialogue 1

5 **Mo** No, it doesn't. And more to the point, that's six years of his life that he'll never get back. He's in his mid-50s now.
1 **Mo** Did you hear about that man who got released from prison?
7 **Mo** I'm not sure, but I'd have thought it won't be easy for him to restart his life.
9 **Mo** Or even longer. It can be hard for people who've left prison to find a job.
3 **Mo** Something like six years, if I'm not mistaken. And for something he didn't do!
4 **Sam** Wow, that's a long time. It really doesn't seem fair, does it?
2 **Sam** Well, I heard something, yes. How long had he been in prison?
8 **Sam** You're right, it'll take some time – around a couple of months, I'd think.
6 **Sam** Well, when you put it like that, it sounds even worse. Poor guy. What do you think he'll do now?

Dialogue 2

5 **Alana** Really? So, how much is too much?
9 **Alana** OK, sorry. Well, it's a shame you can't come. Maybe next month?
1 **Alana** Do you want to come out tonight? I'm meeting up with Jack and the others.
3 **Alana** That doesn't seem fair. Why on earth have they done that?
7 **Alana** Well when you put it like that, I can see what your parents mean.
8 **Leah** Hey, you're supposed to be my best friend – don't take my parents' side!
2 **Leah** Well, I'd like to, but I can't. My parents have told me I can only go out twice a month.
6 **Leah** Well, one evening last month I spent in the region of £50, give or take. It was just under my whole allowance for the month.
4 **Leah** Oh, they say I've got to do more studying. And more to the point, they reckon I spend too much.

PHRASES FOR FLUENCY

Exercise 1
1 have
2 to the
3 news to
4 I'm; mistaken
5 when; put; like

Exercise 2
1 if I'm not mistaken
2 that's news to me
3 Apparently
4 I'd have thought
5 when you put it like that
6 more to the point

C1 ADVANCED

Exercise 1
1 shadowing
2 committed
3 commuters
4 deliveries
5 dull
6 (personal) judgement
7 human resources
8 complaints

Exercise 2
Students' own answers

UNIT 10 LEARNING FOR LIFE

GRAMMAR

Exercise 1
1 for
2 to
3 for
4 to
5 on
6 to

Exercise 2
1 studying
2 taking
3 not going
4 to apply
5 not passing
6 to speak

Exercise 3
1 Ms Gibbs warned me to work harder.
2 My parents insisted on me going straight to university.
3 Jasper admitted making a mistake.
4 My headteacher suggested applying for a job instead of applying for university.

Exercise 4
1 to change
2 for not featuring
3 to ask
4 including
5 to review
6 for not including
7 to review
8 not making

Exercise 5
1 My friends recommended telling the police.
2 The police warned me not to contact the thief.
3 The police accused the man of stealing my bike.
4 He confessed to stealing it.
5 He apologised for taking it.
6 And he promised never to steal anything again.

Exercise 6

1 are said to
2 is known to
3 are believed to
4 is thought that
5 is considered (to be)

Exercise 7

1 It has been found that 59 percent of UK graduates would choose a positive workplace over a good salary.

2 It has been reported that in the UK in 2020, 60 percent of 2018/2019 graduates were working in a job that didn't require a degree.

3 It has been established that in 2020, only 55 percent of 2018/2019 graduates were working in their chosen field.

4 Companies have been warned by a recruitment agency that if they failed to create career development programmes, they would miss the opportunity of attracting top talent.

5 It has been confirmed that by 2020, only 58 percent of 2018/2019 graduates had found secure full-time work.

Exercise 8

1 It is thought that eating pomegranates can strengthen your bones.

2 You probably won't catch a cold if you eat garlic.

3 Adding blueberries to your diet is said to improve your memory.

4 Drinking green tea seems to help you lose weight.

5 It is believed that eating oily fish two or three times a week will protect your eyesight in old age.

GET IT RIGHT!

1 The government is reported to have plans to make cuts to the education budget.

2 The world was thought to be flat at one time.

3 Having a gap year is known to be beneficial to character development.

4 The dissertation was found to have been plagiarised.

5 The family next door is said to have won the lottery last year.

6 The US president is reported to be going to visit the UK.

VOCABULARY

Exercise 1

1 dissertation
2 sailed
3 Master's
4 scholarship
5 fully qualified
6 full-time

Exercise 2

a 3 b 2 c 1 d 6 e 5 f 4

Exercise 3

1 do
2 went
3 go to
4 get
5 do
6 done
7 take

Students' own answers

Exercise 4

Suggested answers

1 went
2 took
3 did
4 did
5 to get
6 didn't go
7 did

Exercise 5

Students' own answers

VOCABULARY EXTRA

Exercise 1

1 d assignment
2 f coursework
3 a feedback
4 c module
5 b seminar
6 e overall mark

Exercise 2

1 module
2 seminar
3 feedback
4 coursework
5 assignment
6 overall mark

Exercise 3

Parts of a course: module, seminar

Pieces of work: assignment, coursework

Types of information: feedback, overall marks

READING

Exercise 1

B

Exercise 2

1 It's a good way to develop practical, professional, emotional and personal awareness and it's beneficial to character development.

2 It's a good time to think about what is missing in your life and what skills you want to develop.

3 It allows people to learn about local communities, develop empathy and give you a more global view of your place in the world.

4 You can learn new skills that you can't learn in your current situation. You can try a new line of work and see if you're doing the right job or choosing the right career path. It's a great way to experience work without committing to it for the rest of your life.

5 They can pursue their interests outside work and study things they may only have dreamed of.

6 There are no age limits – you are never too old to take time out of your current situation.

Exercise 3

Students' own answers

Exercise 4

Students' own answers

DEVELOPING WRITING

Exercise 1

Suggested answers

course fees; engineering; scholarships; the school education system

Exercise 2

Students' own answers

Exercise 3

1 para 2
2 para 4
3 para 1
4 para 3

Exercise 4

Students' own answers

Exercise 5

Students' own answers

LISTENING

Exercise 1

1 They're a huge distraction in class.

2 Cyber-bullying taking place on school grounds.

3 Pupils being attacked and having their phones stolen on the way to and from school.

4 Road traffic accidents caused by pupils being distracted by their phones.

Exercise 2

1 T 2 T 3 DS 4 T 5 F 6 T 7 DS 8 F

DIALOGUE

Exercise 1

1 What will they think of next
2 I'm glad to hear it
3 I think it's about time
4 That's the best news I've heard in ages
5 They've got to be joking
6 That's outrageous

C1 ADVANCED

Exercise 1

Task one

1 Speaker 1 – H
2 Speaker 2 – A
3 Speaker 3 – D
4 Speaker 4 – B
5 Speaker 5 – C

Task two

6 Speaker 1 – F
7 Speaker 2 – G
8 Speaker 3 – D
9 Speaker 4 – E
10 Speaker 5 – B

CONSOLIDATION UNITS 9 & 10

Exercise 1

People being allowed to pay to avoid queuing.

Exercise 2

1 Because the rides were so popular and it was the school holidays.

2 A family walked to the front of the queue and straight onto the rollercoaster.

3 It allows you to book a ride electronically and turn up at the appointed time.

4 Because everyone else has to wait.

5 A quick route through security that can be paid for.

6 It shouldn't be able to buy you everything.

5 My parents thought I would / I'd probably be late home, but not this late.
6 I didn't think I would / I'd pass the history exam, so I was surprised when I got such a good mark.
7 Ana was going to do a cooking course next week. Now she can't go because she's broken her arm.

Exercise 8
Students' own answers

GET IT RIGHT!

1 I won't be at the lecture tomorrow. Perhaps the day after tomorrow I can borrow your notes on what you will have done tomorrow.
2 All of next week we will be campaigning for the fight against child poverty.
3 By next Saturday the final candidates will have been shortlisted.
4 The moment Eve appears on stage tomorrow, her lifelong ambition will have been fulfilled.
5 Next Tuesday the whole country will be voting in the general election.
6 I will be lying on the beach and relaxing this time next month.

VOCABULARY

Exercise 1
1 put; forward for
2 campaigned for
3 vote for; wasn't elected
4 is in the running for; was shortlisted
5 nominate

Exercise 2
1 pull off
2 fulfilled my ambition of
3 failed spectacularly
4 his plans fell through
5 hasn't given up on her dream
6 is recognised as

Exercise 3
Students' own answers

Exercise 4
1 particular
2 eye
3 mind
4 spite
5 time

VOCABULARY EXTRA

Exercise 1
1 dedication
2 humility
3 courage
4 resourcefulness
5 compassion
6 persistence

Exercise 2
1 persistence
2 compassion
3 humility
4 dedication
5 courage
6 resourcefulness

Exercise 3
1 dedication
2 courage
3 resourcefulness
4 persistence
5 compassion
6 humility

READING

Exercise 1
1 Alice earned her BSc in Bacteriology.
2 Alice showed how drinking raw milk could cause brucellosis.
3 Alice contracted brucellosis.
4 Alice became the first female president of the Society of American Bacteriologists.
5 Alice was added to the National Women's Hall of Fame.

Exercise 2
1 American
2 Teacher
3 Scientist
4 Bachelor of Science and Master of Science in Bacteriology.
5 That drinking raw unpasteurised milk could cause brucellosis.
6 Contributions in the field of infectious illnesses, including meningitis and throat infections.
Summary: Students' own answers

Exercise 3
1 A 2 F 3 F 4 A

Exercise 4
Students' own answers

DEVELOPING WRITING

Exercise 1
1 The LifeStraw
2 It filters dirty water and so it allows people who don't have access to safe / clean water to drink.

Exercise 2
1 would change his life.
2 had not seen the problems and consequences of not having clean drinking water – death and illness.
3 he took over his grandfather's business – manufacturing uniforms.
4 save thousands of lives, as well as produce water filters for use in homes and a LifeStraw for hikers and walkers.

Exercise 3
Paragraph A 2; Paragraph B 4; Paragraphs C & D 1; Paragraph E 3

Exercise 4
Students' own answers

Exercise 5
Students' own answers

LISTENING

Exercise 1
1 wildlife
2 The Mayans
3 A Sam; B Joe

Exercise 2
1 T 2 DS 3 DS 4 F 5 T 6 DS 7 F 8 T

DIALOGUE

Exercise 1
1 He's dying to
2 I'm really looking forward to
3 This time tomorrow, I'll be
4 I'm so excited about
5 It's going to be amazing
6 it can't happen soon enough

Exercise 2
Students' own answers

PHRASES FOR FLUENCY

Exercise 1
1 like
2 fancy
3 ages
4 weird
5 know
6 question

Exercise 2
[3] **Cara** Of course! The 23rd of April. How weird is that?
[1] **Cara** Hi, Adele. I haven't seen you for ages.
[7] **Cara** Yes, there is. There's a new James Bond film on. Do you like Bond films?
[5] **Cara** I'd like that. What do you fancy doing?
[6] **Adele** We could go to the cinema. The question is, what's on? I don't think there's anything good on this week.
[4] **Adele** I know, it's really strange, isn't it? Listen. We should go out some time.
[2] **Adele** No, we haven't seen each other since Helen's last birthday. And guess what! It's Helen's birthday today.
[8] **Adele** Of course. What's not to like? Lots of action – lots of cool gadgets!

C1 ADVANCED

1 B 2 B 3 A 4 A 5 D 6 A 7 C 8 C 9 D 10 B

CONSOLIDATION UNITS 11 & 12

Exercise 1
He's unfriended Tina.

Exercise 2
1 C 2 C 3 A 4 A

Exercise 3
1 car got broken into
2 having a new kitchen installed
3 accidents must be reported
4 afternoon I will have finished my exams
5 will/'ll be watching
6 was going to phone you

Exercise 4
1 lose; bit
2 nominate; myself
3 for; for
4 let; go
5 off; failed
6 running; shortlist
7 calm; up
8 up; fulfilled

Exercise 5
1 pessimism
2 bite
3 Socialism
4 overcome
5 ageism
6 fallen
7 capitalism

Exercise 6

1 **Azra** Oh no!! My mouse has stopped working.

11 **Azra** Very funny. Just fix it will you?

7 **Azra** How should I know when? I just turned the computer on and it was broken.

3 **Azra** It just won't respond. How weird is that? It's just died on me.

9 **Azra** What? Can you fix it?

5 **Azra** OK, but you won't be able to fix it. You're just wasting your time.

8 **Omer** It isn't actually broken. I know what's happened.

10 **Omer** I can. The question is – should I?

2 **Omer** Calm down. What's the problem exactly?

6 **Omer** Maybe I am but I can try. Now let me see. When did it stop working exactly?

12 **Omer** OK, this button here on the side is switched off. You just need to switch it to on.

4 **Omer** Computer mice don't just die. Let me have a look.

Exercise 7

1 Because he is blind.

2 When his father taught him to play bird songs on the piano and took him to the natural history museum.

3 His guide dog Ronja, to allow him to navigate through the jungle.

4 To introduce people to the sounds of a day in the life of the Brazilian jungle.

5 He thought the birds with the most beautiful songs would have the brightest colours, but it was the plainest birds that had the most beautiful songs.

6 Because sighted people are distracted by sight and do not tap into their natural ability to truly appreciate sound.

Exercise 8

Students' own answers

WORKBOOK PRONUNCIATION KEY

UNIT 1

Intonation: showing emotions

Exercise 2

1 enthusiastic
2 disappointed
3 puzzled
4 sympathetic
5 cheerful

UNIT 2

Different ways of pronouncing *c* and *g*

Exercise 1

/k/ biscuit, occasionally, topic;
/s/ accident, cyberspace, decision;
/ʃ/ artificial, beneficial, sufficient;
/g/ guilty, disagree, regular;
/dʒ/ dangerous, generally, urgently.

UNIT 3

Unstressed words in connected speech

Exercise 1

1 If I had **money**, I would've gone out for **dinner**.

2 If she **hadn't** invited him, they wouldn't have **met**.

3 If he **hadn't** missed the **train**, we'd be having **coffee now**.

4 A **kinder** person would've **apologised** for making us **wait** so long.

5 We'd still be **friends** if she hadn't **said** those things.

UNIT 4

Telling jokes: pacing, pausing and punchlines

Exercise 1

The second version of the joke has been told well. In the first version, the actor has used pacing and pausing more suitable for reading a newspaper article.

Exercise 2

A man went to see the doctor (P) and sat down to explain his problem. (P)

'Doctor, doctor! I've got this problem,' he said. (P) 'I keep thinking that I'm a dog. (P) It's crazy. I don't know what to do!' (P)

'Interesting,' (S) said the doctor soothingly. 'Relax, come here and lie down on the sofa.' (S)

'Oh no, Doctor,' (P) the man said nervously, (P) 'I'm not allowed on the furniture.'

UNIT 5

Connected speech feature: elision

Exercise 1

The last consonant of the first word is lost when saying the underlined linking words quickly:

1 Millie and Frida came to the house for cake and tea.

2 Julie ran her fastest marathon last year.

3 I lost my ticket and missed the train.

4 She jumped from the building onto the cardboard boxes.

5 He travelled from France to England by boat.

Exercise 2

The consonants *t* and *d*.

UNIT 6

Modal stress and meaning

Exercise 1

1 Jack **might** like your help – even though he's very independent.

2 Are you going to Paris too? We could **go** together.

3 I **could** tell you the answer, although it wouldn't be fair on the other students.

4 Julie's lost her job; they may have to **sell** their house.

5 Tom **may** look young, but he's actually about to retire.

6 It **can** take two hours to get to that village by train.

Exercise 2

1 a 2 b 3 b 4 a 5 a 6 b

UNIT 7

Connected speech feature: assimilation

Exercise 1

/n/ changes to /m/: brown bird, green pencil, London Bridge, thin person;
/n/ changes to /ŋ/: common cold, foreign guest, green grass, London cab.

UNIT 8

Stress in multi-syllable words

Exercises 1 & 2

Three syllables: comfortable, extremely, recognised;
Four syllables: contribution, fundamental, undefeated;
Five syllables: anticipated, communicative, congratulated;
Six syllables: incomprehensible, materialistic, unrecognisable.

UNIT 9

Unstressed syllables and words: the /ɪ/ phoneme

Exercise 1

1 decided
2 justice
3 arrested
4 been
5 pocket
6 bullets
7 subsequent
8 prejudice
9 convicted

UNIT 10

Lexical and non-lexical fillers

Exercises 1 & 2

1 I mean
2 um
3 like
4 er
5 well
6 like
7 sort of
8 I mean
9 uh/er

Exercise 3

Lexical fillers: I mean, like, well, sort of
Non-lexical fillers: um, er, uh

UNIT 11

Intonation: mean what you say

Exercise 1

The sentences said in an appropriate way are:
1 a 2 a 3 b 4 b

UNIT 12

Shifting word stress

Exercise 1

1 conflict
2 contract
3 present
4 protest
5 record
6 suspect

Exercise 2

1 conduct (V)
2 suspect (V)
3 record (N)
4 conflict (N)
5 contract (N)
6 protest (V)